SECURITY IN NIGERIA

SECURITY IN NIGERIA

Contemporary Threats and Responses

Edited by Caroline Varin and Freedom Onuoha

I.B. TAURIS
LONDON • NEW YORK • OXFORD • NEW DELHI • SYDNEY

I.B. Tauris
Bloomsbury Publishing Plc
50 Bedford Square, London, WC1B 3DP, UK
1385 Broadway, New York, NY 10018, USA

BLOOMSBURY, I.B. TAURIS and the I.B. Tauris logo are trademarks
of Bloomsbury Publishing Plc

First published in Great Britain 2020

Copyright © Caroline Varin and Freedom Onuoha, 2020

Caroline Varin and Freedom Onuoha have asserted their right
under the Copyright, Designs and Patents Act, 1988, to be identified
as Author of this work.

For legal purposes the Acknowledgments on p. xv constitute
an extension of this copyright page.

Cover design by Catherine Wood
Cover image: © STEFAN HEUNIS/AFP via Getty Images

All rights reserved. No part of this publication may be reproduced
or transmitted in any form or by any means, electronic or
mechanical, including photocopying, recording, or any information
storage or retrieval system, without prior permission in writing
from the publishers.

Bloomsbury Publishing Plc does not have any control over, or responsibility
for, any third-party websites referred to or in this book. All internet
addresses given in this book were correct at the time of going to press.
The author and publisher regret any inconvenience caused if addresses
have changed or sites have ceased to exist, but can accept no
responsibility for any such changes.

A catalogue record for this book is available from the British Library.

A catalog record for this book is available from the Library of Congress.

ISBN:	HB:	978-1-8386-0429-5
	PB:	978-1-8386-0443-1
	ePDF:	978-1-8386-0761-6
	ePUB:	978-1-8386-0759-3

Typeset by Integra Software Services Pvt. Ltd.

To find out more about our authors and books visit www.bloomsbury.com
and sign up for our newsletters.

To those killed, injured, or displaced by violence and insecurity in Nigeria.

CONTENTS

List of Illustrations	ix
Author Biographies	x
Acknowledgments	xv
List of Acronyms	xvi

INTRODUCTION—Caroline Varin 1

Chapter 1
COLONIAL LEGACY AS FOUNDATION OF INSECURITY IN NIGERIA
  Michael I. Ugwueze 11

Chapter 2
CORRUPTION: A ROOT CAUSE OF INSECURITY IN NIGERIA
  Leah Wawro 29

Chapter 3
NOWHERE TO RUN: CLIMATE CHANGE AND SECURITY CHALLENGES IN NIGERIA
  Anthony Chukwuebuka Okoye 43

Chapter 4
SMALL ARMS PROLIFERATION
  Freedom Chukwudi Onuoha and Gerald Ekenedirichukwu Ezirim 65

Chapter 5
HUMAN TRAFFICKING
  Olusesan Ayodeji Makinde and Deborah Fry 83

Chapter 6
MARITIME PIRACY
  Dirk Siebels 103

Chapter 7
MILITANTS OF THE NIGER DELTA
  Jude Cocodia 119

Chapter 8
GUNS AND DEATHS—THE CONFLICT BETWEEN FARMERS AND HERDERS
   Chris M. A. Kwaja   135

Chapter 9
BOKO HARAM AND ISLAMIC EXTREMISTS
   Dauda Abubakar   147

Chapter 10
SECESSIONIST MOVEMENTS AND STRUCTURAL DETERMINISM IN NIGERIA
   Usman A. Tar and Bashir Bala   167

Chapter 11
INTERNALLY DISPLACED PERSONS AND SECURITY IN NIGERIA
   Olajumoke Yacob-Haliso and Michael Ihuoma Ogu   187

Chapter 12
INFORMAL SECURITY SECTOR AND SECURITY PROVISIONING IN NIGERIA: TRENDS, ISSUES, AND CHALLENGES
   Ufiem Maurice Ogbonnaya   203

CONCLUSION: THE NIGERIAN SECURITY DILEMMA
   Caroline Varin and Freedom Chukwudi Onuoha   225

Bibliography   231
Index   264

LIST OF ILLUSTRATIONS

Figures

3.1	Causative factors of climate change	45
4.1	SALWs proliferation and human (in)security dynamics in Nigeria	76
6.1	Incidents of piracy and armed robbery at sea as reported by IMB and Risk Intelligence in a commercial database between 2007 and 2017	105

Tables

1.1	The linkage of colonial legacies with governance and insecurity in Nigeria	16
3.1	The major greenhouse gases and their sources	45
3.2	NEMA zonal offices and the states under each zone	56
4.1	Some examples of Small Arms and Light Weapons trafficking dynamics in Nigeria	72
7.1	Ethnic distribution of Indigenously owned oil wells in Nigeria	124
8.1	Some farmer-herder-, cattle rustling-, and banditry-related peace enforcement operations in Nigeria	141
11.1	Displacement population in some West African state as of 2017	194
11.2	Internal displacement from conflict and disaster	194
12.1	Profile of non-state security providers in selected states of Nigeria	205
12.2	Security sector budgetary allocations: 2010–2017	217

AUTHOR BIOGRAPHIES

Dauda Abubakar received his PhD in political science from the University of Wisconsin-Madison, USA. He is Associate Professor of Political Science and African Studies at the University of Michigan-Flint, where he is also the Chair of Africana Studies Department. Prior to joining the Faculty at the University of Michigan, Professor Abubakar taught at the University of Maiduguri, Nigeria, where he was the Chair of Political Science Department and Coordinator of Graduate Program. He was also a Visiting Professor at Ohio University Athens, USA, where he taught numerous courses at undergraduate and graduate levels. His recent works include a co-edited volume (with Caroline Varin)—*Violent Non-State Actors in Africa: Terrorists, Rebels and Warlords*, Palgrave, 2017. His current research agenda interrogates the intersection of sectarian identity formation and violence in Sub-Saharan Africa, with Nigeria in particular.

Bashir Bala, Captain in the Nigerian Army, graduated from the Nigerian Defence Academy, commissioned at the Royal Military Academy Sandhurst, UK, and thereafter attended Shijiazhuang Mechanized Infantry Academy for Basic and Advanced Special Operations Courses, China. Capt. Bala is a Research Fellow, Centre for Defence Studies and Documentation, Nigerian Defence Academy. Formerly, a tactical commander in several critical Counter-Insurgency Operations in the northeast region of Nigeria. He is the co-author of "Insurgency, Terrorism and the Challenges of Peacebuilding in the Lake Chad Basin" in *Contemporary Peacebuilding in Africa* edited by Kennth Omeje (London/New York Routledge, 2019), author of *Insurgency and Counter-Insurgency in Nigeria* (Nigerian Defence Academy Publishers, 2019), and co-editor of *New Architecture for Regional Security in Africa: Perspectives on Counter-Terrorism and Counter-Insurgency in the Lake Chad Basin* (Lanham, MD, Lexington Books, USA, 2019). He has published widely on terrorism, insurgency, CT-COIN, security and development, cattle rustling, and armed banditry.

Jude Cocodia is Senior Lecturer with the Department of Political Science, Niger Delta University, Nigeria. He has an MSc in International Relations from the University of Benin, Nigeria (1999), an MA in Philosophy from Erasmus University Netherlands (2004), and a PhD from the University of Nottingham, UK (2016). He is a recipient of the International Peace Research Association Foundation research grant and an Associate Fellow of the Higher Education Academy, UK (2016). He is the Secretary to the Nigeria Political Science Association South-South Zone. His research interests are in the areas of peace, conflict, security, and democracy in Nigeria/Africa. His publications include *Peacekeeping in the African Union:*

Building Negative Peace (Routledge, 2018). His current project examines the relevance of the African Union to the continent's development. Outside academics, Jude worked with Everyone Counts International Charity, a London-based NGO as the Project Coordinator in Yenagoa, Nigeria (2011–2012) and London, UK (2013–2016).

Gerald Ekenedirichukwu Ezirim is Senior Lecturer in the Department of Political Science, University of Nigeria, Nsukka, from where he received his doctorate. A 2010 Research Fellow with Friedrich-Ebert-Stiftung West African Regional Office on Oil and Gas Governance in the Gulf of Guinea, he has written on terrorism and transnational organized crimes in West Africa; election security threats; small arms and light weapons; energy hegemony and maritime security in the Gulf of Guinea; oil crimes, and national security in Nigeria in high-impact journals and for various organizations. His areas of interest are international relations, security, conflict and peace, democratization, oil politics, and African politics. He is a member of the Nigerian Political Science Association (NPSA), Nigerian Institute of International Affairs (NIIA), and Society for Peace Studies and Practice (SPSP). He has been a member of the editorial board of many journals such as the *Journal of Liberal Studies, University of Nigeria Journal of Political Economy, Journal of International Relations and Diplomacy, Studies in Politics and Society*, among others. He was onetime Director of Research and Publications of NPSA, South East Zone, and elected Secretary-General of NPSA in March 2018. He has supervised over forty undergraduates, twenty-five post-graduates, and presently supervising ten doctoral candidates.

Deborah Fry is Senior Lecturer in Child Protection and leads the Preventing Violence in Childhood Research work at Moray House School of Education and Sport, University of Edinburgh. She is also a co-Director of the Safe Inclusive Schools Network, which is part of the UNESCO Platform for the Monitoring of School Violence and Bullying. She undertakes primary research in three main areas: (1) to understand and unpack the drivers of violence affecting children; (2) to measure and develop regional and global estimates on the burden of violence against children and case for investment in prevention; and (3) to develop, test, and evaluate interventions to prevent violence. She also undertakes postgraduate teaching on research methods and violence prevention and is the Deputy Director of Research and Knowledge Exchange (Impact) at the Moray House School of Education and Sport.

Chris M. A. Kwaja, PhD, is Senior Lecturer and Researcher at the Centre for Peace and Security, Modibbo Adama University of Technology, Yola, Adamawa State. His research interests cover issues around peace and security studies, the politics of identity in Africa, elections and governance, as well as security sector reform in transition societies.

Olusesan Ayodeji Makinde is Managing Partner at Viable Knowledge Masters, a research and consulting firm and a member of the board of trustees of Viable Helpers Development Organization, a non-governmental organization. He has a broad research interest, including in child abuse, gender, health information systems, health systems and in monitoring and evaluation. He has published extensively in reputable journals across these domains. Dr. Makinde has consulted for a wide range of organizations, including UNICEF and the World Health Organization. He holds a medical degree and a master of science in epidemiology and medical statistics from the University of Ibadan in Nigeria, a master of science in applied health sciences informatics from the Johns Hopkins University, USA, and a PhD in demography and population studies from the University of the Witwatersrand in South Africa. In addition, he is certified as a project management professional.

Michael Ihuoma Ogu is a faculty and researcher with the Department of Political Science and Public Administration at Babcock University in Nigeria. He has almost a decade of University teaching experience in Nigeria and the United States, and his areas of core research interest are in security studies and African International Relations. Michael has published over two dozen articles and book chapters with both local and international journals and publishers. He is also a recipient of the William J. Fulbright Scholarship and alumnus of the US Department of State-sponsored International Exchange Program.

Anthony Chukwuebuka Okoye, PhD, is Lecturer II in the Department of Political Science, Federal University Otuoke, Bayelsa State, Nigeria. He obtained his PhD degree in political science with specialization in political economy from the University of Nigeria, Nsukka. His current research focuses on peace and conflict studies, conflict analysis, conflict resolution, peace building, elections, development studies, crude oil and environmental politics in the Niger Delta, climate change and human security, democracy and good governance, security studies, ethnic and identity politics, politics, and economy. He has published on these themes in reputable journals and books. He can be contacted via okoyeac@fuotuoke.edu.ng; anthonybcokoye@gmail.com

Ufiem Maurice Ogbonnaya is Senior Research Fellow with the Department of Defence, Security and Strategic Studies, Directorate of Research, National Institute for Policy and Strategic Studies (NIPSS), Kuru. He had previously worked as Security and Policy Analyst at the National Institute for Legislative and Democratic Studies (NILDS), National Assembly, Abuja. A Laureate of the 7th South-South Institute jointly organized by the Council for the Development of Social Science Research in Africa (CODESRIA), International Development Economic Associates (IDEAs), and the Latin American Council of Social Sciences (CLACSO) in Bangkok, Thailand, Ogbonnaya holds a PhD in international relations from University of Uyo.

Freedom Chukwudi Onuoha is Senior Lecturer in the Department of Political Science, University of Nigeria, Nsukka. He is also the Coordinator of the Security, Violence and Conflict (SVC) Research Group at the University. Prior to joining the University, Dr. Onuoha worked for over a decade as a Research Fellow at the Centre for Strategic Research and Studies, National Defence College, Nigeria. Dr. Onuoha received his PhD from the University of Nigeria, Nsukka, with specialty in political economy. He also holds a certificate in higher defense and strategic studies, in addition to other professional certificates in peace support operations, lessons learned, disaster management, protection of civilians, defense and security management, and United Nations Framework, among others. His teaching and research interests focus on diverse aspects of peace, conflict, and security studies, with emphasis on political violence, terrorism, organized crime, state fragility, and maritime security. He was listed among the top 100 Global Thinkers of 2014 by the Lo Spazio della Politica for his groundbreaking studies on Boko Haram. Dr. Onuoha has several publications to his credit.

Dirk Siebels works as Senior Analyst at Risk Intelligence, a Denmark-based security intelligence company where he is mainly responsible for assessments and analysis on coastal countries in Sub-Saharan Africa. He holds a PhD from the University of Greenwich in London. His research largely concentrates on maritime security issues in Africa, including the role of ports and maritime trade, IUU (illegal, unreported, and unregulated) fishing, offshore energy production, and the evolution of private maritime security providers. Dirk has contributed to a number of research projects, including the annual State of Piracy report published by Oceans Beyond Piracy (now the Stable Seas project). He is an academic advisor for the Turkish Navy's Maritime Security Centre of Excellence in Istanbul and part of the expert network for CEMLAWS Africa, a think tank based in Accra, Ghana.

Usman A. Tar (PhD) is Professor and Director at the Centre for Defence Studies and Documentation, Nigerian Defence Academy. Formerly, he was an Associate Research Fellow at John and Elnora Ferguson Centre for Africa Studies, University of Bradford, UK. He is the author of *The Politics of Neoliberal Democracy in Africa* (London/New York: I.B. Tauris, 2009); editor of several books including: *Globalization in Africa: Perspectives on Development, Security, and the Environment* (Lanham, MD, Lexington Books, 2016), *Routledge Handbook of Counter-Terrorism and Counter-Insurgency in Africa* (London/New York, Routledge, forthcoming), *Palgrave Handbook of Small Arms and Conflict* (London: Palgrave Macmillan, forthcoming), *Defence Transformation and the Consolidation of Democracy in Nigeria* (Kaduna: Academy Publishers, 2017), and *New Architecture for Regional Security in Africa: Perspectives on Counter-Terrorism and Counter-Insurgency in the Lake Chad Basin* (Lanham, MD: Lexington Books, U.S., 2019). Prof Tar has provided consultancy services to the United Nations Development Programme (UNDP), Westminster Foundation for Democracy (WFD), and Konrad-adenauer-Stiftung, Nigeria. He is External Examiner and Resource Person to several institutions in Nigeria and overseas.

Michael I. Ugwueze holds a PhD in political science with specialization in international relations. He is both Lecturer in the Department of Political Science and Senior Research Fellow, Center for American Studies, University of Nigeria, Nsukka (UNN). Dr. Ugwueze was among the twelve Junior African Scholars sponsored by Goethe University in Frankfurt/Main, Germany, and the Stellenbosch Institute for Advanced Studies (STIAS), South Africa, to attend the 2017 Summer School in Bamako. Ugwueze has authored many publications both locally and internationally, and his research interest is in the areas of security, governance, gender, and development studies.

Caroline Varin is Senior Lecturer in International Relations at Regent's University London and Associate Fellows at LSEIdeas at the London School of Economics, where she received her doctorate in 2012. She has published extensively on security in Africa. Her recent books include *Boko Haram and the War on Terror* (ABC Clio Praeger, 2016), *Mercenaries and the State* (Routledge, 2014), and *Violent Non-State Actors in Africa* (Palgrave, 2017). Caroline is Co-Founder of Professors Without Borders, an education social enterprise.

Leah Wawro is the European Representative for Independent Diplomat, a non-profit diplomatic advisory organization that provides advice and assistance to democratic governments and political groups on political strategy, international law, and public diplomacy. Wawro is also a member of the board of the Independent Defence Anti-Corruption Committee of Ukraine (NAKO). Previously, she worked for Transparency International Defence and Security, where she was the Head of Conflict and Insecurity. From 2014 to 2015, Wawro was a Network Fellow at Harvard University's Edmund J. Safra Center for Ethics, where she worked on research into institutional corruption in the defense sectors of states transitioning to democracy. She holds an MA in international relations and Arabic from the University of St. Andrews.

Olajumoke Yacob-Haliso is Associate Professor of Political Science at Babcock University in Nigeria. Her research focuses on women in conflict and peace, gender and politics, and the comparative politics of African states. Olajumoke is co-editor of the *Journal of Contemporary African Studies*, co-editor of the new Rowman and Littlefield book series, "Africa: Past, Present and Prospects," and lead editor of the forthcoming *Palgrave Handbook of African Women's Studies*. She is the recipient of numerous research grants and several fellowships, including from the Harry Frank Guggenheim Foundation, American Council of Learned Societies (ACLS), the Graduate Institute of International and Development Studies, Geneva, Switzerland, Council for the Development of Social Science Research in Africa (CODESRIA), African Studies Association, African Association of Political Science (AAPS), University for Peace Africa Program, among others.

ACKNOWLEDGMENTS

This book on security in Nigeria would not have been possible without the expertise and hard work of all our contributing authors. Our sincere gratitude goes to everyone who shared their valuable time and knowledge with us.

Thanks also to the three students who assisted with research and editing of this book: Jeanette Bachelor, Njomeza Blakcori, and Samara Zauhy. Your diligence and timeliness are much appreciated!

To LSEIdeas for generously sharing their resources and work space.

Last but not least, to our families, Daniel, Alexia, and Adriana; and Amarachi, Nnaedozie, Ugonna, Uchenna, and Chimgozirim, for your patience and encouragement during all those hours we spent working on this volume. Thank you!

LIST OF ACRONYMS

ABSVG	Abia State Vigilante Group
AD	Alliance for Democracy
AG	Action Group
AMMATA	Aba Main Market Traders Association
APC	All Progressive Congress
AU	African Union
BH	Boko Haram
CAN	Action Congress of Nigeria
CDUs	Community Development Unions
CEMA	Community Emergency Management Agency
CJTF	Civilian Joint Task Force
CLEEN Foundation	Center for Law Enforcement Education Foundation
CSO	civil society organization
DDR	Disarmament, demobilization and reintegration
DFID	Department for International Development
DIA	Defence Intelligence Agency
DICON	Defence Industries Corporation of Nigeria
DRUs	Disaster response units
DSS	Department of State Services
DTM	Displacement Tracking Matrix
ECOWAS	Economic Community of West African States
EFCC	Economic and Financial Crimes Commission
EU	European Union
EWS	Early warning system
FAO	Food and Agricultural Organization
FCO	Federal Coordinating Officer
FFS	Federal Fire Service
FOWA	Federation of Ogoni Associations
GI	Government Defense Anti-Corruption Index
HNO	Humanitarian Needs Overview

HRW	Human Rights Watch
ICG	International Crisis Group
ICRC	International Committee of Red Cross
IDP	Internally displaced person
IOM	International Organization for Migration
IPCC	Intergovernmental Panel on Climate Change
IPCR	Institute for Peace and Conflict Resolution
IPOB	Indigenous Peoples of Biafra
IYC	Ijaw Youth Council's
JRC	Joint Revolutionary Council
JTF	Joint Task Force
KAROTA	Kano Road and Transport Authority
KSPC	Kaduna State Peace Commission
KVGN	Kano State Vigilante Group of Nigeria
LEMA	Local Government Emergency Management Agency
LFN	Laws of the Federation of Nigeria
LGAs	Local government areas
LNSC	Lagos Neighborhood Safety Corps
MACBAN	Miyetti Allah Cattle Breeders Association
MASSOB	Movement for the Actualization of the Sovereign State of Biafra
MDAs	Ministries, Departments and Agencies
MEND	Movement for the Emancipation of the Niger Delta
MNCs	Multi-National Corporations
MNJTF	Multinational Joint Task Force
MOSOP	Movement for the Survival of the Ogoni People
MoU	Memorandum of Understanding
MRRR	Ministry of Reconstruction, Rehabilitation and Resettlement
NA	Nigerian Army
NAF	Nigerian Air Force
NBS	Nigerian Bureau of Statistics
NCFRMI	National Commission for Refugees, Migrants and Internally Displaced Persons
NCNC	National Council of Nigerian Citizens
NCP	Niger Coast Protectorate

NCP	National Contingency Plan
NCS	Nigerian Customs Service
NDA	Niger Delta Avengers
NDDC	Niger Delta Development Commission
NDLEA	National Drug Law Enforcement Agency
NDMF	National Disaster Management Framework
NDPVF	Niger Delta People's Volunteer Force
NDR	Niger Delta region
NDRP	National Disaster Response Plan
NDV	Niger Delta Vigilante
NDWJ	Niger Delta Women for Justice
NEMA	National Emergency Management Agency
NHRC	National Human Rights Commission
NIA	National Intelligence Agency
NIMASA	Nigerian Maritime Administration and Safety Agency
NIMET	Nigeria Meteorological Agency
NIS	Nigerian Immigration Service
NN	Nigerian Navy
NOA	National Orientation Agency
NPF	Nigeria Police Force
NPS	Nigerian Prisons Service
NSCDC	Nigerian Security and Civil Defence Corps
NSYES	Nasarawa State Youth Empowerment Scheme
OHUN	Oodua Hunters Union
OLM	Oodua Liberation Movement
OMDG	Oodua Muslim-Christian Dialogue Group
OMPADEC	Oil Mineral Producing Areas Development Commission
OPC	O'odua People's Congress
OPEC	The Organization of the Petroleum Exporting Countries
OR	Operation Rainbow
ORC	Oodua Republic Coalition
ORP	Oil River Protectorate
OSH	Operation Safe Haven
PDP	Peoples Democratic Party
PGCs	Private Guard Companies
PPBA	Plateau State Peacebuilding Agency

PRESCOM	Presidential Committee on Small Arms and Light Weapons
PSOs	Private Security Organizations
PWAN	Partners West Africa-Nigeria
RNC	Royal Niger Company
RNCT	Royal Niger Company Territories
RPA	Recovery and Peacebuilding Assessment
SALWs	Small arms and light weapons
SARS	Special Anti-Robbery Squad
SAS	Senator Ali Modu Sheriff
SEMA	State Emergency Management Agency
SGBV	Sexual and Gender-Based Violence
SNC	Sovereign National Conference
SPDC	Shell Petroleum Development Corporation
SSAs	Support Service Areas
STF	Special Task Force
TI-DS	Transparency International Defence and Security
UN	United Nations
UNDP	United Nations Development Programme
UNHCR	United Nations High Commission for Refugees
UNN	University of Nigeria, Nnsuka
UNODC	United Nations Office for Drug and Crimes
UNREC	United Nations Regional Centre for Peace and Disarmament in Africa
VGN	Vigilante Group of Nigeria
WIFE	World Igbo Environmental Foundation
YORC	Yoruba Revolutionary Congress
YOSNF	Yoruba Students Nationalist Front

INTRODUCTION

Caroline Varin

Why Nigeria?

Since independence in 1960, Nigeria has prided itself as the "Giant of Africa" and a regional hegemonic power.[1] With a predicted population of over 400 million people by 2050[2]—surpassing the United States as the world's third most populous country—Nigeria accounts for a third of Africa's 1.3 billion people. Nigeria's role and significance on the world stage in the last four decades are undeniable. Its economy surpassed that of South Africa in 2014 as the continent's largest economy. A leading member of the Oganisation of Petroleum Exporting Countries (OPEC) with the largest population, Nigeria is Africa's biggest oil producer and one of the world's most prolific exporters.

Leveraging its human and material resources, Nigeria has on different occasions helped to influence positive change regionally and globally. In the not too distant past, Nigeria served as a bulwark of regional stability, with strong commitment to conflict resolution and promotion of regional integration, particularly in West Africa. Its role in the formation of the Economic Community of West African State Monitoring Group (ECOMOG) and eventual resolution of civil wars in Liberia and Sierra Leone in the 1990s are legendary testimonies to Nigeria's contributions to regional peace and stability.[3]

Nigeria has also become a trendsetter in English-speaking film, music, and literature. In 2009, it overtook Hollywood to become the world's second largest film industry after India's Bollywood, producing over 2,500 films a year. The global phenomenon of Afrobeats originates in Nigeria and represents the country's buzzing energy and powerful cultural strides in the music world. And Nigerian authors have received some of the most important awards in literature, claiming an influential voice that echoes beyond the continent. Nigeria's growing soft power, channeled via the creativity and resourcefulness of its citizens, is self-evident. Thus, a case can be made that Nigeria is the most important country in Africa, a leader of its continent and a world player in terms of its demographic and economic growth and its potential to influence events. Its recent attainment of two decades of uninterrupted democratic rule and a long-standing alliance with Beijing also place it in a unique position to be a diplomatic bridge between the East and the West.

All this potential, however, is tainted by Nigeria's internal security and governance deficits, which continue to mar it as a developing nation. As a result, analysts contend that Nigeria's ability to play to its leadership strength and aspiration in Africa is gradually declining since the last two decades.[4] The country is plagued by multiple security challenges such as terrorism, militancy, insurgency, ethno-religious conflict, corruption, poverty, banditry, farmer-herdsmen clashes, climate change, environmental degradation, food security, arms trafficking, organized crime, and forced population displacements, among others.[5] In addition, the ugly legacy of colonialism lingers on, affecting political, economic, and social relations between Nigerians, undermining the unity and viability of the country. Despite its affluence, Nigeria's spiraling afflictions have underpinned the poignant resonance that the country is becoming a strategic failure.[6]

Nigeria's fate should be of concern to everyone because its present and future challenges cannot be contained within its borders. In 2018, Nigeria had approximately 1.9 million internally displaced people (IDPs) and some 228,000 of her citizens living as refugees in neighboring Cameroon, Chad, and Niger.[7] Nigerians are already the most numerous African asylum seekers in the EU[8] with applicants claiming they are fleeing Boko Haram or being prosecuted for their sexual orientation.[9] Nigeria's internal security challenges are further compounded by broader regional security dynamics in the Sahara-Sahel region that is witnessing heightened proliferation of small arms and light weapons (SALWs) and cross-border movement of mercenaries, terrorist, and foreign fighters. The United Nations High Commissioner for Refugees (UNHCR) points to "a deteriorating security situation as well as socio-economic fragility, with communities in the Sahel region facing chronic poverty, a harsh climate, recurrent epidemics, poor infrastructure and limited access to basic services."[10] The predicted population growth will further compound these challenges, prompting a domino-effect in surrounding nations and possibly beyond.

This book on security focuses on Nigeria, but many of the problems explored and solutions suggested can also be exported to other countries. A shared legacy of post-colonial exploitation, endemic corruption, and environmental degradation connects many states around the world, big and small. Nigeria is particularly fascinating because of the role it plays on the world stage, but the lessons learned in this study are relevant beyond its borders. For example, the proliferation of SALWs in Nigeria has acted as a force multiplier to its problems, exacerbating existing tensions by weaponizing individuals. But it also transcends the nation's frontiers given the foreign origin of most of these weapons, fluidity of trafficking networks, and the knock-on effect of violence and migration.

Understanding the security dilemmas of Nigeria, how they emerged, prevailed, and, infrequently, were overcome, can also act as guidance for other governments on how to manage, mitigate—or what not to do—when faced with threats such as popular uprisings, the rise of extremist groups, and the aggressive onslaught of organized crime. Finally, Nigeria can be a warning to other states of the security threats ahead, and motivate national governments to take heed, anticipate the impact of environmental change and other probable occurrences typical of emerging nations, and implement policies to preserve the stability and security of their societies.

In this edited volume, the contributing authors not only engaged critically with the security dilemma the Nigerian state faces but also proffered relevant recommendations for addressing the problem. This means thrashing out a thorough review of the many sources of the threat in order to suggest potential working policies that address the origins and drivers of the issue at hand. As a result, the chapters below integrate a human security approach into a review of state building and nation building. This is an important contribution to the literature on post-colonial security, the security of developing countries, and more specifically African security. Furthermore, many of our authors have a personal and professional interest in the stability and future of Nigeria, leading to a complexity of original views and approaches with an authentic desire to improve security in the region by mitigating, if not removing, the many threats facing this hobbling giant.

Synopsis

The first four chapters of this book examine the underlining causes of insecurity in Nigeria. In colonialism, Ugwueze shows, lies the foundations of corruption. Wawro then explains that corruption undermines the capability of the state to respond to security threats. Furthermore, argues Chukwuebuka, climate change worsens existing problems while creating new problems for the state to manage. Finally, the possession and proliferation of SALWs, according to Onuoha and Ezirim, are particularly acute in Nigeria, exacerbating an already complicated security environment.

In Chapter 1, Michael Ugwueze argues that the foundation of insecurity in Nigeria lies in the legacy of colonialism. From ethno-religious clashes to corruption, social unrest, terrorism, and separatism, all find their root in the system of governance that the modern Nigerian state inherited from their colonial predecessor. The British divide and rule system made religion and ethnicity preeminent markers of identity and marginalized entire populations from the political and economic arenas. The colonial practice of replacing traditional rulers with puppet governments systematized corruption and poor leadership in both local and domestic politics and created a precedence for overthrowing political leaders. Ugwueze demonstrates that many of the security problems covered in this volume find their source in British colonial rule; the Nigeria government's failure to address these issues is the result of the post-colonial mentality of corruption, poor leadership, and a divide and rule philosophy that continues to transcend Nigerian politics today.

It naturally follows that Chapter 2 discusses corruption as a root cause of insecurity in Nigeria. Leah Wawro uses examples from the Nigerian defense sector and defense procurement in particular to argue that policy decisions are systematically made in the interests of a narrow and sectarian elite. This is further enabled by failures of institutional controls and chronic inadequate oversight both domestically and internationally—leaving Nigeria as one of the most corrupt nations in the world, according to the Corruption Perception Index. As resources are syphoned off from the security sectors, the police and military lack the capability to respond to the rising threats of violent extremism, secessionism, conflicts, and organized crime. Furthermore, unable to depend on the government, citizens tend to turn toward informal support systems based around ethnicity and religious identity. This has enabled Boko Haram's recruitment of disenchanted Muslims in the North and exacerbated ethno-religious clashes in the Middle Belt. With a corrupt security apparatus and alienated citizenry, the country remains ill-equipped to address the subsequent threats outlined in this volume.

The next two chapters continue with this exploration of root causes of insecurity in Nigeria. In Chapter 3, Okoye Anthony Chukwuebuka shows that many of the socio-economic problems in Nigeria today lie in the rapid environmental changes the country has been experiencing. Flood, droughts, desertification, and shrinking water sources have all threatened food security, prompting entire populations to flee their homes. In the Chad Basin, displaced populations are vulnerable to recruitment by the extremist group Boko Haram. In the Middle Belt, shrinking water supplies have put pressure on herdsmen to expand their movements, encroaching further on farming land and leading to violent clashes with farmers or host local communities. In the Niger Delta, pollution has led to more violence as communities of farmers and fishermen compete with multinational companies for the usufruct of their land and coast. Pollution as a result of oil exploitation has led to livelihood collapse, further exacerbating competition for food and land and inflaming existing social tensions. Finally, Chukwuebuka argues that climate change and environmental catastrophes have led to a health emergency, with a rise in malaria, influenza, cholera, malnutrition, and dengue, to name a few. This further adds pressure on the central government to address the source of the problems and assist its displaced and vulnerable populations. Failure to do so, exacerbated by prevalence of political corruption and especially in the National Emergency Management Agency, continues to alienate a citizenry forced to rely on informal support systems.

Chapter 4, written by Freedom Onuoha and Gerald Ezirim, demonstrates that Nigeria's worsening security environment is exacerbated by proliferation of SALWS. From the Islamist insurgency in the Northeast to militancy in the Niger Delta, to the escalation of clashes between farming communities and herders, rising incidents of violent crime including trafficking, banditry, cattle rustling, kidnapping, and piracy all profit from the easy availability of SALWs. In one report, 21 million arms and ammunition were smuggled into the country in 2017 alone[11] with no less than 350 million alleged to be circulating in Nigeria.[12] Onuoha and Ezirim trace this back to the high-stake political game where politicians have made it a practice to recruit and arm militias to help gain or retain political power. One consequence of the escalation of violence across the nation is the increase in displaced people, who are made vulnerable to recruitment by violent groups or become a burden on the state, as mentioned above.

The second part of this book focuses on specific violent threats to the state, with each chapter exploring a particular security angle. Chapter 5 shows that the prevalence of human trafficking and kidnapping has generated revenue for gangs, creating a chronic sense of terror and insecurity, particularly in some communities. Maritime hostage taking has also increased in recent years, buoying militant groups such as Movement for the Emancipation of the Niger Delta (MEND) and the Niger Delta Avengers (NDA). Chapter 6 describes the impact of maritime piracy on the security of the Gulf of Guinea and accuses the Nigerian government of failing to tackle the problem despite, Siebels argues, sufficient military capacity. In Chapter 7, Cocodia focuses on the problem of militancy in the Niger Delta region, arguing that the government's response has exacerbated the problem by using indiscriminate violence to squash the insurgency and throwing money at the militants to discourage them from using violence, thereby inspiring others to pick up arms. Government despondency is also blamed for the clashes between herders and farmers in Chapter 8. Kwaja argues that these rural populations are most vulnerable to climate change as their livelihoods depend on water supply. Encroaching desertification, water scarcity, and the ensuing climate refugees put pressure on the Middle Belt region that, if not managed properly, will continue to be the site of violent conflict. Chapter 9 on Boko Haram shows that security failures enabled the militants to rise into a credible threat to the state, occupying territory and terrorizing populations in the name of a twisted interpretation of "Islam." Abubakar delves into the religious, political, and social origins of the extremist group to assess the impact on the security of the Nigerian state. In a nod to Chapter 4, Abubakar highlights the role of small arms proliferation in the violent rise of Boko Haram.

Human trafficking, Olusesan Ayodeji Makinde and Deborah Fry explain, is the third most profitable illegal industry in the world, after arms and narcotics. Nigeria is both a source of and transit point for sex trafficking and a destination point for the trafficking of humans to serve as domestic servants. In one State, as many as 17 percent of respondents reported having been the victim of human trafficking.[13] And at least 15 million children are thought to work as slaves in Nigeria alone.[14] The authors outline the prevalence of baby factories throughout the country and the risks associated with this practice. Men, women, and children trafficked are often tricked into the situation, exploiting their vulnerability due to high level of poverty. The demand for cheap human labor (sex, domestics, baby vessels, and soldiering) and human organs has led to a rise in kidnapping. In fact, there is currently no part of the country where people have not been kidnapped for ransom.[15] This is particularly the case in the northeast where Boko Haram militants have kidnapped thousands of people who they have used as child soldiers and sex slaves. Those released from captivity have found reintegration into society particularly difficult as they are often treated as "radicals" or "criminals" and marginalized from their communities. The government, argue the authors, has yet to put in place or implement necessary legislation to curb the activities of human traffickers, and a corrupt judicial system further undermines existing efforts to address the problem. Such failure has enabled gangs of criminals to prosper and terrorize the population.

Continuing on the theme of criminality, Chapter 6 offers an analysis of the growing problem of maritime piracy in the Gulf of Guinea. Dirk Siebels highlights that incidents from illegal fishing, bunkering, armed robbery, and more recently hostage taking of crew have increased in recent years. While reliable data are difficult to find, at least eighty-four vessels were attacked in 2017 and fourteen seafarers kidnapped off Nigeria's coast between January and March 2018.[16] The problem is not perceived as a priority for the government, according to the author, despite it affecting oil companies' investment decisions and consequently the economy of Nigeria. However, it remains a major concern for international shipping and oil companies operating in the region. Maritime piracy also feeds the informal economy and supports the activities of some militant groups in the Niger Delta. The solution, Siebels suggests, lies in public-private partnerships where policing and military security is buffeted by private security companies, a model that may be useful to address some other security threats prevalent in the country and that is explored further in Chapter 12.

Chapter 7 zooms in on the Niger Delta to investigate the causes of prevalent militancy in the region. Jude Cocodia argues that decades of exploitation and neglect of the people of the Niger Delta are the source of the problem, leading to a failed secessionist attempt in the 1960s, civil militancy, and eventually a violent insurgency. As the interest of oil companies prevailed over the local fishing and farming communities, inhabitants vied with private companies for control over resources. This was exacerbated by the "ethnic dimension" as indigenes of the Niger Delta region believed there was a conspiracy of a northern cabal to hold their region to ransom. MEND saw itself as the chief advocator of the rights of the people of the region and promised to fight for a fair share of the dividends of oil resources. Attempts to financially redress the situation have been met with allegations of corruption, embezzlement, and lack of accountability, leaving the Delta region in a perpetual state of poverty and underdevelopment and eventually facilitating the rise of other militant groups, including the NDA. There is no long-term solution as militant groups have inspired the local youth, according to Cocodia, who have been integrated into cult groups and continue to be recruited into MEND and the NDA. Finally, the situation has been exacerbated by the government's failure to address the source of the problem, their use of indiscriminate violence against communities perceived to be colluding with militants, and their propensity to throw money at the gangs thereby inspiring a culture and economy of violence in the region.

The conflict between farmers and herders in the Middle Belt is the result of a complex security environment, the sources of which can be found in the previous chapters. In Chapter 8, Chris Kwaja argues that increasing water scarcity has forced many herders to move inward toward the Middle Belt area, which creates the basis competition between the herders and the sedentary farmers. In addition, easy access to guns has turned occasional clashes between communities into a deadly local conflict. The breakdown in law and order has led to a rise in banditry and organized crime characterized by cattle rustling in the region. In view of the government's inability to provide security to the population, the demand for weapons has continued to grow, creating a sinew that continues to feed the vicious cycle of violence.

Chapter 9 reviews the violent rise of Boko Haram in the northeast against the socio-political and historical backdrop of the region. According to Dauda Abubakar, the extremist group capitalizes on a history of Salafi movements, failures of the Nigerian government to fully implement Shari'a law as promised by political leaders, and general disillusionment with the political and judicial system to mobilize its following. In addition, a defective security response to the rising threat of Boko Haram further prompted the increased and arbitrary use of violence in retaliation to the extrajudicial killing of its leader Mohammed Yusuf and other members in 2009 and henceforth. The insurgency has led to a massive rise in IDPs fleeing the region and chronic food shortages as rural populations are kidnapped, killed, or forced to leave their crops by Boko Haram militants. It has also encouraged the proliferation of weapons across the community, especially as the extremists have been pushed out of the strongholds by the armed forces and sought refuge elsewhere. The situation has been exacerbated by the politicization of identities by politicians who have fueled the conflict in the northeast by arming thugs and mobilizing voters across ethno-religious lines.

Part 3 of this volume takes a more macro-approach, with Chapter 10 examining the crisis of governance on the legitimacy of the Nigerian state and the ensuing secessionist movements that have threatened to tear apart the country. Chapter 11 turns to the major consequence of all the above-mentioned threats: internally displaced populations that suffer first-hand from natural and man-made disasters and are then left to their own devices, or to poorly run refugee camps where they continue to be vulnerable to violence, exploitation, disease, and eventually radicalization. Our last chapter examines the canvas of formal and informal security providers in Nigeria, highlighting the challenges the state faces in providing its population with an effective military and policing force.

In Chapter 10, Usman Tar and Bashir Bala question the federal formation of the Nigerian state and blame the colonial political and economic legacy, corruption, terrorism, militancy, and insurgency for the secessionist movements. A diverse ethnic and cultural panorama comprising over 500 ethnic groups has been amalgamated into thirty-six states and a federal center that compete for resources without any sense of collective nationalism. Each region seems to suffer from some sort of secessionist movement: In the eastern part of Nigeria is the Movement for the Actualization of the Sovereign State of Biafra (MASSOB). O'odua People's Congress (OPC) remains a vibrant organization in the southwest of Nigeria and works to promote Yoruba culture and push for Yoruba autonomy. In Northern Nigeria, a coalition of socio-political groups called the Arewa Youth Forum Consultative Assembly (AYFCA) further excited the politics of secessionism. In Nigeria's oil-rich Niger Delta, groups have emerged that manifest mainly as ethnic militancy with a tinge of separatist undertone, as explained in Cocodia's Chapter 7. The ability of Boko Haram to occupy territory in the northeast and call itself the "Islamic State of West Africa" further underscores the violent promise of secessionist movements in the country. Contrary to Ugwueze's suggestion in Chapter 1, Tar and Bala advocate the Nigerian state should focus on its functionality and utility without breaking up the nation.

The many security threats studied above have led to a massive problem of IDPs in Nigeria. In Chapter 11, Olajumoke Yacob Haliso and Michael Ihuoma assess that internal displacement is the most significant consequence of insecurity in Nigeria, and in turn it has a disruptive and potentially explosive impact on the socio-economic makeup of the country. There is an estimated 2,155,618 IDPs across thirteen states in Nigeria.[17] Government-run IDP camps are notoriously bad, overcrowded with unsanitary conditions, prompting people to seek refuge in local communities wherever possible. In northeast Nigeria, many IDP camps remain under the control of the military and have been targeted by Boko Haram and infiltrated by militants. Displaced people, especially women, are at increased risk of violence and exploitation. Numerous outbreaks of cholera and other water-borne diseases continue to be reported in displacement-affected areas and severe malnutrition is prevalent. As a result, IDPs are allegedly more vulnerable to radicalization and recruitment by extremist/terrorist groups. The psychological needs of IDPs are largely ignored, leaving a generation of Nigerians traumatized and distrustful of the state. Return of IDPs to their homes is also often impossible, as insecurity continues to prevail and many crops and communities have been entirely destroyed by conflict or natural disasters. The authors conclude that "insecurity reinforces internal displacement, and displacement also deepens the level of insecurity."

In the final chapter, Ufiem Maurice Ogbonnaya examines the trends, issues, and challenges of formal and informal security providers in Nigeria. Core security-related functions that were once the exclusive preserve of formal security institutions—arrest and prosecution of suspected criminals, public safety, crime and violence prevention—now constitute key functions performed by the informal security institutions. This undermines the notion on which sovereignty is built: that the state is responsible for security provision toward its people. It also creates a crowded marketplace where private security providers protect the wealthy whereas poor communities are left to fend for themselves using vigilante groups and organized militias. The latter have also been used repeatedly by political candidates to rig the elections in favor of specific ethnic groups. Nigeria's formal security sector is chronically under-funded, infamously corrupt, and as a result, military and police personnel, especially in rural areas, are vulnerable to attacks by organized criminals, thugs, and terrorist groups like Boko Haram. The level of trust between the populace and security providers is notoriously low, undermining the legitimacy of the state and prompting people to revert to informal networks in search of security from the many threats listed above. This further entrenches Nigerians in their ethno-religious communities, deepening the divide between people and alienating the federal government from those it is meant to serve.

Issues bordering on security in Nigeria addressed in this volume are certainly not exhaustive. However, many of the security challenges and their consequences analyzed here contribute to Nigeria's gradual loss of strategic relevance. But its affluence and potentials hold great promise for its future rebound. How early it will do this and how successful it will be depend to a large extent on the ability of its political leadership to recognize the magnitude of the problem and work creatively to address the root causes of its security challenges. Huge as these challenges appear, they are not entirely insurmountable. This volume, much as other publications on Nigeria, has grappled with different aspects of security in Nigeria with valuable suggestions on the way forward.

Notes

1. Ogunnubi, O. 2017. "Effective Hegemonic Influence in Africa: An Analysis of Nigeria's 'Hegemonic' Position." *Journal of Asian and African Studies* 52, no. 7: 932–946; Seteolu, B. and Okunye, J. 2017. "The Struggle for Hegemony in Africa: Nigeria and South Africa Relations in Perspectives, 1999–2014." *African Journal of Political Science and International Relations* 11, no. 3: 57–67.
2. "Nigeria: United Nations Sustainable Development Partnership Frameworks (UNSDPF) 2018–2022." 2017. *United Nations System in Nigeria*. Available from: http://www.undp.org/content/dam/undp/library/corporate/Executive%20 Board/2017/Second-regular-session/DPDCPNGA3_Master%20Consolidated%20 UNSDPF%202018-2022%2023-May-2017.doc.
3. Ojakorotu, V., and Adeleke, A. A. 2018. "Nigeria and Conflict Resolution in the Sub-Regional West Africa: The Quest for a Regional Hegemon?" *Insight on Africa* 10, no. 1: 37–53.
4. Sule, S. A. et al. 2017. "The Influence of Leadership Personality on the Nigeria's Hegemonic Decline in West Africa." *The Social Sciences* 12, no. 2: 2293–2298; Odigbo, J., Udaw, J. E., and Igwe, A. F. 2014. "Regional Hegemony and Leadership Space in Africa: Assessing Nigeria's Prospects and Challenges." *Review of History and Political Science* 2, no. 1: 89–105.
5. Oshita, O. O., Alumona, I. M., and Onuoha, F. C., eds. 2019. *Internal Security Management in Nigeria: Perspectives, Challenges and Lessons*. Singapore: Palgrave Macmillan.
6. Lyman, P. 2019. "How Nigeria May Become a Strategic Failure to the World." *Thisday*, July 27.
7. Refugees, United. 2018. "Nigeria Emergency." *UNHCR*. Available from: http://www. unhcr.org/uk/nigeria-emergency.html.
8. "Migration to Europe in Charts." 2018. *BBC News*. Available from: https://www.bbc. co.uk/news/world-europe-44660699.
9. "Nigerian Minister Warns against Nigerian Citizens Seeking Asylum in Germany." 2018. *Council On Foreign Relations*. Available from: https://www.cfr.org/blog/ nigerian-minister-warns-against-nigerian-citizens-seeking-asylum-germany.
10. Refugees, United. "Nigeria Emergency."
11. Adenubi, T., Ebipade, A., Ovat, M., Agwaza, A. C., Ogunesan, T., and Michael, I. 2018. "21 Million Guns, Ammo Smuggled into Nigeria—Investigation." *Tribune*. Available from: http://www.tribuneonlineng.com/21-million-guns-ammo-smuggled-nigeria-investigation/.
12. Premium Times. 2016. "Nigeria Accounts for over 70% of 500 Million Illicit Weapons in West Africa." August 2.
13. Abdulraheem, S. and Oladipo, A. R. 2010. "Trafficking in Women and Children: A Hidden Health and Social Problem in Nigeria." *International Journal of Sociology and Anthropology* 2, no. 3: 34.

14. UNICEF Nigeria. 2007. "Child Labour." Available from: https://www.unicef.org/children_1935.html.
15. Osumah, O., and Aghedo, I. 2011. "Who Wants to Be a Millionaire? Nigerian Youths and the Commodification of Kidnapping." *Review of African Political Economy* 38, no. 128: 277–287. DOI: https://doi.org/10.1080/03056244.2011.582769.
16. IMB. 2018. "Pirate Attacks Worsen in Gulf of Guinea." Available from: https://www.icc-ccs.org/index.php/1244-pirate-attacks-worsen-in-gulf-of-guinea.
17. IOM Nigeria Situation Report 2016.

Chapter 1

COLONIAL LEGACY AS FOUNDATION OF INSECURITY IN NIGERIA

Michael I. Ugwueze

Introduction

African states have continually been blamed for heaping the fault-lines of their developmental challenges on colonial legacies. Specifically, when addressing the Ghanaian Parliament on July 11, 2009, President Barack Obama of the United States noted that African nations should blame their economic and social problems on their own mismanagement and lack of democracy, not on colonial legacies. As Obama argued in the speech:

> *Yes, a colonial map that made little sense bred conflict, and the West has often approached Africa as a patron, rather than a partner. But the West is not responsible for the destruction of the Zimbabwean economy over the last decade, or wars in which children are enlisted as combatants ... No person wants to live in a society where the rule of law gives way to the rule of brutality and bribery. That is not democracy; that is tyranny, and now is the time for it to end.*[1]

This argument is particularly rife given that African nations' counterparts in Asia, Eastern Europe, and South America have long moved on, making in-roads into the world of science and technology, as well as devising sophisticated indigenous methodologies that help tame the beast of political malfeasance. Aware of this scenario, it is important to note that it is very difficult to conclude a study in the social sciences without having to refer to its historical foundation. This foundation helps in understanding the root cause(s) of the social problem, and thereby positioning the researcher to offer a better solution. In this light, it is still very germane to talk about the colonial legacies that laid the foundation upon which the insecurity situation in Nigeria was built.

Nigeria, as a child of colonialism, continues to face social unrest that largely threatens its unity. These challenges range from prebendalism to ethnic politics and ethno-religious conflict, poor governance, military rule, militancy and terrorism, separatist agitations, and endemic corruption. Hardly could any study on social relations be completed in Nigeria without having to refer to any of these problems that combine to create a tense security environment that exacerbates the problems of poverty, unemployment, and social insecurity. These problems, which have their foundation in colonialism, have become monsters in their spheres of manifestation. As a result, proffering solutions to them is becoming increasingly difficult, especially as those who should lead the fight are themselves actors that benefit largely from the shaky foundations of the Nigerian state. Nevertheless, there is no social problem without a solution.

Extant literature has largely dealt with the security implications of military rule,[2] prebendalism,[3] corruption,[4] ethnic politics and ethno-religious conflict,[5] militancy, insurgency, and terrorism,[6] and electoral violence.[7] In most cases, studies often link conflicts to inter-ethnic animosities and competition over scarce resources, while ignoring historical root causes of conflict such as colonialism and now imperialism through the process of capitalist accumulation in Africa.[8] Although not foreclosing further studies in these areas, scholars have not sufficiently addressed how colonial legacies have laid down the foundations for these problems. As a result, this chapter situates the historical contributions of colonial legacies and forced governance, the divide and rule system and false consciousness to the emergence of insecurity in Nigeria, such as the military intervention in politics, endemic corruption, ethno-religious conflicts, electoral violence, and lack of a national cohesion that results in separatist agitations, militancy, insurgency, and terrorism, among others. To achieve this objective, the chapter has been divided into five sections beginning with this brief introduction. The next section explores the evolution of the Nigerian state from the colonial period. The third section explains the major colonial legacies that laid down the foundation for insecurity in Nigeria, and the fourth section suggests the way forward, while the fifth section concludes the study.

Evolution of the Nigerian State: 1849–1960

Before colonialism, there was no entity called Nigeria. However, there were kingdoms and hamlets scattered across the territories that later became Nigeria. These kingdoms and hamlets included the Oyo Empire, the Benin Empire, the Opobo Kingdom, the Sokoto Caliphate, Kanem Borno Empire, the Calabar Empire, the Onicha (Onitsha) province, Nri Kingdom, Igbo-Ukwu, Arochukwu, Nsukka, and Igala, among others. These, and more kingdoms and hamlets, existed independent of each other in a society that was later to be called Nigeria. They fought many international wars and cooperated (where necessary) with one another just like other empires and hamlets in world history. Supporting this argument, Okwudiba Nnoli noted that:

> *Historical records indicate that before the British came (to Nigeria), these various kingdoms fought disastrous interstate wars among themselves. On one occasion, the Ibadan people were opposed by an alliance of the Egba, Ijebu, Ekiti, Ijesha*

and Ilorin peoples over the control of trade in the area. Similarly, the Igbo were organized into separate and autonomous political societies conterminous with the village (system). International wars among these polities sometimes occurred.[9]

The journey of a country called Nigeria started in the middle of the nineteenth century when the British government made up its mind to suppress slave trade in the notorious slave route within the Bights of Benin and Biafra.[10] This began with the appointment of John Beecroft as the Consul for the Bights of Benin and Biafra in 1849. As a Consul, his jurisdiction extended from Dahomey to the Cameroons at a time when Oba Kosoko was the King of Lagos. Apart from being deeply involved in the slave trade, Kosoko was openly hostile to the British and their allies on account of the enormous profits they were making from the slave trade. Beecroft's effort to abolish slavery through negotiation of a treaty with Kosoko on the advice of the British Colonial Secretary proved abortive. As a result, in 1851 British forces attacked Lagos and Kosoko together with his men ran away.[11] Thereupon, Oba Akintoye, who was until then in asylum in Abiokuta, was invited and reinstated as the Oba of Lagos.[12] This invitation by Beecroft was on account of a petition prepared for Akintoye by a British missionary Reverend C.A. Gollmer detailing how Akintoye would support the government of England in taking over Lagos in return for British protection. In the prepared petition, Akintoye noted:

> *My humble prayer to you is that you would take Lagos under your protection, that you would plant the English flag there and that you would re-establish me on my rightful throne at Lagos and protect me under my flag; and with your help I promise to enter into a treaty with England to abolish the slave trade at Lagos and to establish and carry on lawful trade, especially with the English merchants.*[13]

Convinced that Akintoye would be more amenable to British interest, he was reinstated as the Oba of Lagos. On January 1, 1852, Akintoye signed a treaty with the British government for the abolition of slavery, the encouragement of legitimate trade, and the protection of missionaries. A year after the treaty, a special Consul was appointed for Lagos and the Bight of Benin. This marked the beginning of the separation of Lagos from the rest of the Oil Rivers and the journey toward having a country called Nigeria.

Following Akintoye's death in 1853, his son Dosumu inherited power as the new Oba of Lagos. Given his inability to effectively suppress the slave trade (as claimed by the British government), the British Secretary of State for the Colonies (British Colonial Secretary) instructed the Consul to negotiate a treaty with Dosumu aimed at bringing Lagos permanently under the control of Britain in order to suppress slavery and encourage legitimate trade. Although Dosumu and his chiefs declined signing this treaty for the cession of Lagos to Britain, allegedly, he together with four of his principal chiefs was kowtowed to either sign for the cession or risk being attacked by the British Forces.[14] The signing of the treaty on August 6, 1861,[15] heralded officially the beginning of colonialism in an entity later to become Nigeria that took off in 1862 with the creation of Lagos Colony.

The balkanization of Africa in the Berlin Conference of 1885 marked the next phase in the evolution of the Nigerian state. The territories that were in the coastal region that had come under British influence became known as the Oil River Protectorate (ORP) in 1885. The expansion of British influence further into the hinterland and Northern Hemisphere not only created a new administrative challenge, but also resulted in the renaming of ORP to Niger Coast Protectorate (NCP) in 1893. To fill the administrative gap, the Royal Niger Company (RNC)[16] was granted a permission not only to trade in the new territory but to administer it on behalf of the British government. This sphere of British influence added to the list of the RNC Territories (RNCT). The expanded protectorate included the Oil River (today called the Niger Delta), the valley of the Rivers Niger up to Lokoja and Benue.[17]

The name Nigeria, which literally translates to "Niger area," first appeared in an essay written by Flora Shaw[18] published in *The Times of London* on January 8, 1897. In the essay, Shaw made a case for the replacement of RNCT, which was too long a name for an entity she referred to as "*the agglomeration of pagan and Mohammedan states.*"[19] The phrase of "*pagan and Mohammedan states*" metaphorically translates to mean southern and northern Nigeria, respectively. She therefore coined Nigeria, in preference to such other names as "*Central Sudan*," a name that some geographers and travelers associated with the Nigerian territory, and "Sudan," a name associated with a territory in the Nile basin housing the current state of Sudan. According to her:

> *The name Nigeria applying to no other part of Africa may without offence to any neighbors be accepted as co-extensive with the territories over which the Royal Niger Company has extended British influence, and may serve to differentiate them equally from the colonies of Lagos and the Niger Protectorate on the coast and from the French territories of the Upper Niger.*[20]

Owing to the restrictions on trade caused by artificial boundaries and the virtual monopoly that the RNC exercised, it became necessary for the British government to assume a more direct control over the colonial territory called Nigeria. The inability of the Company's forces to restrain the slave-raiding propensities of the Fulani chiefs, as well as foreign aggression on the western frontiers, also contributed in the administrative takeover of the territory from the RNC by the British government. The RNC charter was therefore revoked on January 1, 1900.[21] Thereupon, the territory known as Nigeria, including those hitherto under the administration of the RNC, was divided into three distinct entities, namely, the colony of Lagos, the Protectorate of Southern Nigeria, and the Protectorate of Northern Nigeria. Consequently, a colonial administrator who was directly answerable to the Colonial Office in Britain independently administered each of these protectorates. In 1906, the colony of Lagos and the Protectorate of Southern Nigeria were joined together under one administrator and renamed the Colony and Protectorate of Southern Nigeria. Thenceforth, Nigeria became an entity of two protectorates—the Protectorate of Northern Nigeria and the Colony and Protectorate of Southern Nigeria.

The highest phase in the evolution of the Nigerian state was on January 1, 1914, when Lord Lugard amalgamated the Colony and Protectorate of Southern Nigeria with the Protectorate of Northern Nigeria. The two entities thereafter became the Colony and Protectorate of Nigeria under centralized administration of a British Governor-General. Meanwhile, Lord Lugard, who pioneered the amalgamation for administrative convenience, became the first Governor-General of Nigeria. Therefore, Nigeria as a unified state officially started on January 1, 1914, from where several colonial administrators ruled in the following order. Although Oliver Lyttleton was never recorded as a governor-general, his constitution introduced federalism in Nigeria in 1954. Subsequent governor-generals administered Nigeria more like military dictators. When on October 1, 1960, Nigeria won its independence from British rule, the Queen of England remained the governor-general (head of state) of the newly created country called Nigeria and was represented, no longer by a British administrator but a Nigerian by the name Dr. Nnamdi Azikiwe. On October 1, 1963, Nigeria became a republic and the Queen ceased being Nigeria's head of state. The full ceremonial power was handed over to Azikiwe who had hitherto acted on the Queen's behalf. Since then, Nigeria has continued to be ruled by Nigerians with intermittent military interventions in politics. The next section explains the colonial legacies and how they laid the foundation for insecurity in Nigeria.

Colonial Legacies and Insecurity in Nigeria

Colonialism brought with it several legacies into Nigeria. While some were benign, others were pernicious. Some of the pernicious ones that laid the foundation for insecurity in Nigeria include forced governance, implantation of false consciousness that birthed ethnic politics, and the divide and rule policy inherent to the British Indirect Rule system. From historical accounts of colonialism, as well as the ones briefly highlighted in the evolution of the Nigerian state, it is evident that the colonial annexation and control of Nigeria was done without recourse to the concern of the local people or even the rulers of the different kingdoms and hamlets that made up the entities that later became Nigeria. This underscored the *forced governance* that came to characterize the colonial administration in Nigeria. To worsen the situation, the colonial masters crafted and implanted *false consciousness* that sowed the seeds of antagonism among the different ethnic and religious groups in Nigeria. This also prevented Nigerians from advancing a common front on matters of national concern. The third pernicious fault-line that summarizes the colonial legacies that laid the foundation for insecurity in Nigeria is the British *divide and rule system*. Table 1.1 demonstrates the linkage of these colonial legacies with governance and insecurity in Nigeria.

Table 1.1 The linkage of colonial legacies with governance and insecurity in Nigeria

Colonial legacy	Implication for governance	Security risk
Forced governance	Military rule	Military intervention in politics
	Poor governance	Elite rivalry, corruption
	Electoral malpractice	Corruption
	Violent political culture	Political violence
False consciousness	Ethnic politics	Ethno-religious conflicts
	Prebendalism	Corruption
	Lack of a national cohesion and marginalization	Separatist agitations, militancy, insurgency, terrorism
	Heterogeneous ruling class	Suspicious government
Divide and rule system	Unity in diversity	Indigene-settler dichotomy
	Unclearly established sphere of influence	Boundary disputes and corruption
	Social atomization	Mutual distrust
	Structural imbalance	Minority agitations

Source: Developed by the author

Every colonial legacy has implication for governance and insecurity in Nigeria. Colonial patterns of administration that thrived on *forced governance* laid the foundation for military rule through military intervention in politics, poor governance through elite rivalry and corruption, as well as violent political culture through electoral malpractice. Implantation of *false consciousness* laid the foundation for ethno-religious conflicts through ethnic politics, corruption through prebendalism, separatist agitations, militancy, insurgency and terrorism through lack of a national cohesion and marginalization, and suspicious government through a heterogeneous ruling class. The British *divide and rule system* laid the foundation for indigene-settler dichotomy through unity in diversity, boundary disputes through the establishment of an unclearly defined sphere of influence, mutual distrust through social atomization, and minority agitation through structural imbalance. These legacies together with their governance and security implications were not mutually exclusive. Sometimes they collectively reinforced one another. Although effort was made to connect each colonial legacy with its related governance and security risk, the pairing was scrupulously crafted for ease of explanation. The next subsections illustrate how these pernicious fault-lines separately or collectively contributed to laying down the foundations for insecurity in Nigeria.

Forced Governance

The first pernicious legacy of colonialism in Nigeria was forced governance executed through gunboat diplomacy, direct attacks, and the forceful annexation and occupation of territories. The amalgamation of the northern and southern protectorates in 1914 into a unified country called Nigeria without the consent of the people forming such a union represents the height of colonial governance by force. Worst still, the amalgamation was not borne out of any genuine desire to integrate the two heterogeneous protectorates. Instead, it was a complete act of administrative convenience on the part of the colonial master, designed to ensure a contiguous colonial territory that stretches from the arid Sahel to the Atlantic Coast.[22] The amalgamation made little or no sense and has often been invoked by Nigerians as the foundation of the rancorous relationship between the two regions of Nigeria.[23] While the north (predominantly Muslims) had a completely different style of civilization fashioned along the tradition of the Middle East, the south (mostly Christians) were more amenable to a Western style of civilization, and the British colonialists made no attempt to integrate these two regions beyond cartographic mapping. If anything, they divided them more by using the principle of divide and rule. These differences have bred serious antagonisms between the two regions, which have been identified as a source of political disagreements and suspicions witnessed since the colonial times.[24] The antagonisms were "deliberately" created by the colonial masters to facilitate continued imperial rule and domination.[25]

The differences in religion and ethnic groupings were so deep that even prominent nationalists from both the northern and southern divides of Nigeria visibly expressed their doubt of a compatible one Nigeria. For instance, Chief Obafemi Awolowo (one of the leading nationalists from southern Nigeria) once argued that "Nigeria is only a geographical expression to which life was given by the diabolical amalgamation of 1914; that amalgamation will ever remain the most painful injury a British government inflicted on southern Nigeria." According to him, "if rapid political progress is to be made in Nigeria, it is high time we were realistic in tackling its constitutional problems. Nigeria is not a nation. It is a mere geographical expression. There are no Nigerians in the same sense as there are English, Welsh, or French."[26] Nigeria being a mere geographic expression implied that the three entities that were joined together had no cultural affinity, and as such, could not have harmoniously cohabited. Therefore, the East remained for the easterners, the North for the northerners, the West for the westerners and Nigeria for nobody.[27] Similarly, while addressing the Northern House of Assembly in 1952, Sir Abubakar Tafawa Balewa[28] publicly stated that:

> *The Southern people who are flocking into this region (northern region) daily in such large numbers are really intruders; we don't want them and they are not welcomed here in the North. Since 1914, the British government has been trying to make Nigeria into one country. But the people are different in every way, including religion, custom, language and aspirations. We in the north take it that Nigeria unity is only a British intention for the country they created. It is not for us.*[29]

The Sardauna of Sokoto Alhaji Ahmadu Bello (foremost nationalist of northern Nigeria extraction) confirmed these statements when he called the 1914 amalgamation of Nigeria, a "colonial mistake."[30] Bello in an interview granted to *Parrot Newspaper* on October 12, 1960, argued that "the new nation called Nigeria should be an estate from our great-grand father Othuman Dan Fodio. We must ruthlessly prevent a change of power. We must use the minorities of the North as willing tools, and the South as conquered territories and never allow them to have control of their future."[31] These comments coming from those that inherited power from the colonialists reflected the deep-seated conviction of the two regions that they were not meant for each other, and by implication, should not have been brought together into an irreconcilable marriage of colonial making. The animosity arising from this forceful amalgamation continues to create a tensed security environment in Nigeria, including the amplification of hate speeches. For instance, during the 2015 general elections in Nigeria, the Oba of Lagos Rilwan Akiolu threatened that any Igbo person living in Lagos who failed to vote his preferred governorship candidate of the All Progressive Congress (APC) Akinwumi Ambode would be drowned in a lagoon.

False Consciousness

False consciousness is a concept that is largely associated with Marxian literature, particularly the theory of social class analysis. This term refers to the systematic misrepresentation of dominant social relations in the consciousness of subordinate classes.[32] The cradle of ethnicity and ethnicism, ethnic politics and tribalism, prebendalism and favoritism has been traced to colonial urban settings.[33] What we refer to as ethnic groups such as the Igbo, Yoruba, and Hausa-Fulani, first acquired a common consciousness under colonialism. Thus, before colonialism there was no such collective ethnic naming as Yoruba, Igbo, or Hausa-Fulani.

It has been emphasized that many pre-colonial polities in Nigeria did not have the consciousness of a common ethnic groupings or descent as they have today. The Igbo pre-colonial polities, for instance, were self-consciously divided into the Olu and the Igbo peoples, and there was no war fought together by the Igbo as a collectivity.[34] Ethnicity is therefore a product of social constructivism that has no biological connection. However, the British creation of false consciousness made Nigerians assume ethnicity to be a biological phenomenon and have since treated it as such. Thus, indigene-settler divides that continue to confront many Nigerian states today, especially in Jos, Plateau State, are a colonial invention shaped by the creation of false consciousness. It was not by accident that Plateau has the highest record of ethnic violence arising from the indigene-settler dichotomy. This is because Jos in Plateau State represented the center of economic activities in northern Nigeria in particular, and Nigeria in general during the colonial time. This was the result of the large deposit of tin in Jos and the attendant tin mining. Importantly, tin was then to the colonial government what oil is to Nigeria today. Thus, Jos recorded the highest level of migration of both southerners and northerners in search of greener pasture. The increasing interethnic migration and settlement among the various groups in Nigeria became a source of concern to the colonial government. The government feared that such settlement had the potency to unite the ethnic groups against colonial administration. As a result, the colonial administrators began to craft the stratagem to dismantle such settlements. Some of the stratagems were the discouragement of contiguous settlements of the various ethnic groups through several divisive mechanisms, including the division of their spheres of settlement, which catalyzed false consciousness among them.

Having before now perfected the building of a cordial intraethnic consciousness among the various ethnic groups (particularly the Igbo, Hausa-Fulani, and the Yoruba) in Nigeria, it was time to implant a false consciousness that would set these groups against each other. Essentially, interethnic migration was gradually uniting these groups against colonial interests by building a cordial interethnic consciousness. The British government first started with an internal balkanization of Nigeria through the separation of these linguistic groups from one another, particularly in residential areas. In northern Nigeria, for instance, it was a colonial policy to separate the Hausa-Fulani from the southerners. Nnoli argued that "at first, southern and northern migrants to northern cities lived together in harmony with their hosts in the native city. This embarrassed the official view that only conflict characterized contact among African tribes."[35] When it became obvious to the colonialists that Africans can relate and live cordially instead of being hostile to one another given what was happening in several native and urban cities in Nigeria, they made a policy to prevent these ethnic groups from living together. As such, northern migrants who had lived in peace with southern migrants in *Sabon Gari*[36] were forced to live in another section of the city called *Tudun Wada*[37] and the indigenous northerners living in their place were made to settle in another section called the *Walled City*.[38] Thereupon, the colonialists began to recreate the existing consciousness that gave room for hatred among the ethnic groups. This situation paid off in the colonial state because interethnic contact was thenceforth characterized by animosity and rivalry. It was easy to understand which groups progressed better and faster. The Igbo migrants were dominating the commerce and making serious progress in their businesses more than the indigenous Hausa people. The situation bred envy and jealousy and division set in. With this division, it was easier for the colonial masters to allege that the southerners were responsible for the suffering in the North. During the general strike of 1945 in protest against the colonial administration in Nigeria, organized by the nationalists and led by Dr. Nnamdi Azikiwe (Zik for short), British district officials in Jos alleged that the suffering of the people, including the food shortage, was caused by the Igbo ethnic group. Nothing could have been more corrupt than this allegation, which was also an example of false news officially carried by the press. Nnoli rightly observed:

> *The 1945 general strike adversely affected food supplies to the town (of Jos) by rail, causing a general feeling of anxiety and severe shortage of food … since the strike was a nationalistic outburst against the colonial administration, the British colonial officials seized on the resultant hardship in the North to incite the Northerners against the strike and the Igbo. They blamed the strike and shortage on the Igbo led*

by Azikiwe and manipulated Igbo-Hausa animosity over competition on trading and residential area to incite the Hausa against the Igbo.[39]

Because of the manipulation of information by the British officials, the North virtually boycotted the general strikes so the masses could not have known the source of their food problems. This was responsible for the first outbreak of ethnic violence in Nigeria, which took place in 1945 in Jos, Plateau State.

Permeating the internal balkanization further south, the British colonial government, through the Richard's Constitution of 1946, divided southern Nigeria into the West and the East, while the North was allowed to remain together. This division together with the undue advantage given to the North by the colonialists in the Central Legislative House laid the foundation for the rancorous political conflicts and violence that have come to characterize north-south relations in Nigeria, including the notorious Kano Riot of 1953. In the East, there were further attempts to balkanize the people through the creation of the Warrant Chief System of Indirect Rule. Although the population vehemently rejected this move, it still gained in-road into the administration of the eastern province however unsuccessful. But it could not undermine the cordial intra-ethnic consciousness of the Igbo. Nonetheless, the balkanization of southern Nigeria into the East and West resulted in a division of the Igbo and Yoruba people. The height of the division was shown in the 1951 western Nigeria election. This election was won by Dr. Nnamdi Azikiwe (an Igbo easterner living in the west) but he was denied the opportunity to form a regional government in the West. This was because the Yoruba members of his party—the National Council of Nigerian Citizens (NCNC)—cross-carpeted overnight to the Action Group (AG) led by Azikiwe's rival Chief Obafemi Awolowo (a Yoruba westerner). What worked against Azikiwe was his ethnic background that Nigerians failed to appreciate as a product of social construction; instead elevated to the status of a biological phenomenon. This was exactly how the colonialists wanted Nigerians to view ethnicity, and what happened between Azikiwe and Awolowo did not fall short of colonial expectation.

Colonial implantation of false consciousness was a deliberate ploy to permeate the social atomization of the different ethnic groups in Nigeria while ensuring that the British divide and rule policy gained ground. It was this false consciousness that laid the foundation for ethnic violence and ethno-religious conflicts in Nigeria, which are consequences of ethnic rule. This is why ethnicity remains central to the security discourse of Nigeria. According to Ukiwo, "no work is deemed 'scholarly' that does not consider the salience or irrelevance of ethnicity to its analysis and conclusions."[40] As such, analysts who have interests in such issues as national integration, political violence, military intervention in politics, endemic corruption, nationalism, economic development, democratization, militancy, insurgency, terrorism, violent conflict, and many more have all considered the variable of ethnicity central to their analysis. Yet Nigerians continue to view ethnicity (the cradle of their problem) as a biological creation when indeed it was socially constructed. If ethnicity were to be a biological creation, why would the British government officially recognize only the Hausa-Fulani, Igbo, and Yoruba when we have more than 250 others? It was this creation that resulted in the minority and separatist agitations that have continued to plague Nigeria up till this moment. Therefore, there was no genuine intention by the colonial masters to build a united Nigeria, and the Nigerian elite that inherited power from them made no effort to rewrite the history of the country by underplaying ethnicity and religion, which are both products of social constructivism. To the contrary, they play it up at every local and national election.

Divide and Rule System

Divide and rule, otherwise called divide and conquer, is a political strategy employed by most dictatorial leaders to gain and maintain power by breaking up larger concentrations of power into smaller units such that, individually, the units cannot be powerful enough to subdue the sovereign. The strategy is aimed at breaking up existing power structures, while preventing smaller power blocs from linking up to the extent of causing rivalries and fomenting discord among the people.[41] Divide and rule (*divide et impera*) is one of the three political maxims employed by tyrants such as Phillip II of Macedon, Emperor Augustus Caesar, Emperor Napoleon Bonaparte, and political advisor Niccolo Machiavelli in dealing with subjects. Others being the *fac et excusa* (act now, and make excuses later) and *Si fecisti, nega* (when you a commit crime, deny it). Divide and rule is a strategy that exploits the negative contradictions among a people that aims to frustrate or weaken their resistance against a common enemy.[42] The strategy thrives on the following principles of:

- Encouraging divisions among the subjects to prevent alliances that could challenge the sovereign;
- Aiding and promoting those who are willing to cooperate with the sovereign;
- Creating and fostering mutual distrust and enmity among local rulers such as the traditional rulers; and
- Encouraging meaningless expenditures that undermine the capability for political and military spending.

The British government made use of this axiom of tyranny in the administration of its colonies, including Nigeria. In several instances, the colonial government encouraged the forcible removal of traditional rulers within the territories that later became Nigeria, particularly those who proved intransigent to British control. Some of these rulers included Oba Kosoko of Lagos, King Jaja of Opobo, Nana of Itsekiri, Sultan Attahiru XII of Sokoto, to mention but a few. Having deposed these rulers, the British government encouraged the emergence of their surrogates, including the Oba Akintoye who was mentioned in the evolution of the Nigerian state above. Essentially too, the balkanization of southern Nigeria into the East and West and the division of cities in the north into the *Walled City*, *Tudun Wada*, and *Sabon Gari* were done to prevent alliances that could challenge the colonial administration. The division of the south, for instance, was purposefully done to reduce the pressure being mounted by southern nationalists against colonialism. The implication of this division has been emphasized under the discussion of false consciousness.

The British divide and rule system that required sharp ethno-religious differentiation among Nigerians made religion and ethnicity the preeminent markers of identity and pushed exclusionary identity politics (marginalization) into the political arena.[43] As such, friendships were destroyed, families ruined, geography hacked, history misread, tradition denied, minds and hearts torn apart.[44] The case of Azikiwe and Awolowo in the infamous cross-carpeting saga comes to mind here. In northern Nigeria as well, minority ethnic groups, mostly Christians, defined and still define themselves against the Muslim Hausa-Fulani majority, under the political rubric of Middle Belt, which is usually a metaphorical expression for "non-Muslim."[45] Other countries that share a similar colonial history with Nigeria, such as India and Sudan, experienced or continue to experience comparable antagonism either on grounds of religion or ethnicity. For instance, the creation and perpetuation of Hindu-Muslim antagonism in India was identified as the most *significant accomplishment* of British imperial policy of divide and rule.[46] This also applied to the ethnic groups in India and Pakistan as well as in Northern and Southern Sudan. Notably, all these regions continue to witness serious security challenges that resulted in the separation of Pakistan from India and more recently South Sudan from Sudan. These four regions—India, Pakistan, Northern Sudan, and Southern Sudan—have since become four different countries. It is only Nigeria that is still managing its own sharp and fierce regional antagonisms without a considerable effort to form a strong coalescence.

Colonialism established the basis for using identity politics as a means of accessing political and economic powers, and religious differences have exacerbated political crises in Nigeria.[47] These have been implicated in major national conflicts, including the Nigerian Civil War (1967–1970). Although the Federal military government led by General Yakubu Gowon succeeded in suppressing the Biafran separatist movement initiated by the predominantly Christian Igbo people, the act of exacting victory using pogroms, blockades, and starvation has been condemned by many scholars and analysts.[48] Thus, the methods adopted by the Nigerian government in executing the war only ended up exacerbating the prevailing religious and ethnic animosities in the country. Meanwhile, having recognized the enormity of destruction done to the Nigerian state, the colonial masters at the point of exit began to advocate for *unity in diversity* among the different ethnic and religious groups. Conceivably, the degree of animosity that characterizes the social relations of the amalgamated entities also accounted for the prevalence of this slogan after independence.

Since independence, religious and ethnic rhetoric has leveraged claims to political representation and opportunities and often degenerates into fierce zero-sum conflicts. Corruption and incompetent leadership have added another wrinkle, preventing the equitable distribution of resources and opportunities and making the politics of religious and ethnic exclusivity more appealing.[49] This practice could also be attributed to colonial influence. For instance, the colonial masters instilled corruption and poor leadership in Nigeria by encouraging the installation of their surrogates as leaders. Evidently, Britain preferred a less qualified Tafawa Balewa as the prime minister to the more qualified Azikiwe or Awolowo. Added to the colonial policies that discouraged harmonious co-existence among the different ethnic groups especially in the urban centers, ethnicity and religion were elevated to a more worrisome level. Even the maxim of *unity in diversity* that would have helped in deconstructing ethnicity and religion among the different ethnic and religious groups in Nigeria has only ended as a political statement. This maxim is only exploited by the ruling class when the use of ethnicity and religion to gain state power seems not to be working perfectly.

The Way Forward

No solution to Nigeria's current security problems will yield significant results without addressing the colonial legacies of forced governance, false consciousness, and divide and rule systems; perchance, through the convocation of a Sovereign National Conference (SNC). It is therefore the belief of this study that, for the current social problems in Nigeria to be resolved, the foundational questions inherited through colonialism must be holistically addressed through the convocation of the SNC.

First, the SNC should address the issue of the general deconstruction of ethnicity and religion, in return for a social reconstruction of Nigeria. This reconstruction should exclude nothing, including discussing the need for division of the geographical entities. As such, the maxim of *no go areas* that have always characterized Nigeria's constitutional and political reform conferences right from the London to the Ibadan Constitutional Conferences of 1957 and 1958, respectively, should not apply. The conference should address three main areas of the foundational questions, beginning with the amalgamation of 1914. If all the entities chose to remain as Nigeria, then the conference should move to address constitutional arrangements under which the country should be united. The prevailing argument in some quarters that "Nigeria's unity is non-negotiable" is not only undemocratic and unethical but also illogical and detrimental to the survival of the Nigerian state. This statement is a product of forced governance, which has been identified as very perilous to Nigeria's continued unity. People should be convinced by why they should live together and not be forced to do so.

Second, the issue of false consciousness that erodes national identity should be seriously addressed in the SNC. It suffices to say that the current application of the state of origin instead of the state of residence in all that is done in Nigeria is a mission in falsehood. It is not only a colonial constitutional injection but also a constraining factor toward building national consciousness and integration. As such, the conference should leverage advanced practice and ensure that Nigerians are treated as Nigerians and not as Igbo, Hausa-Fulani, Yoruba, Ijaw, and so on.

This labeling creates animosity and antagonism among the different ethnic groups while limiting the opportunities inherent in their diversity.

Third, the divide and rule system should give room for the unity in diversity, assuming the entities that make up Nigeria chose to remain united. The conference should aim to build a common culture for all Nigerians that will soon condition the way of life of every Nigerian. As Raph Uwechue argued:

> *For our country (Nigeria), with its colonial stamp of "made in England," the three hundred odd ethnic and sub-ethnic units in this land have good cause to thank God for the astonishing abundance of human and material resources bestowed on us. We are still in the process of nation-building, struggling to blend together and harmonize our various traditions, customs and cultures. Although, this is by all account a herculean task, it is both achievable and supremely worthwhile, as a successful fusion of so many valuable elements is bound to bring forth a unique socio-economic product that could astound the world.*[50]

If Nigeria must be united, a common identity must be advanced. By so doing, it will be difficult to know who is an Igbo, Hausa, or Yoruba in the Nigerian project. A Nigerian name will simply be common to all entities. This is akin to the common identity approach France adopted in turning "peasants into Frenchmen" between 1870 and 1914.[51] Being a nation-building project, everybody must be carried along in the SNC.

Importantly, the conference should not be in a hurry to reach a consensus, especially because issues that touch on foundations are never resolved in a hurry. If every phase of the discussion should take between two and four years to reach a consensus, the conference delegates and Nigerians should be patient enough to receive its outcome. At worst, it is this author's opinion that will take twelve years to conclude the SNC in the event that Nigerians opt to be together and every phase takes four years for a consensus to be reached by the different entities.

Conclusion

The study started on a premise that, while it is necessary for African nations to stop blaming colonialism for their security challenges, they should not wish away the pernicious foundation laid by the colonial legacies of forced governance, false consciousness, and the divide and rule system. Regrettably, the ruling elite who inherited power from the colonial masters permeated these legacies through an unpatriotic discourse and actions. No doubt, colonialism created a cordial intra-ethnic consciousness that helped in building ethnic cohesion, but it failed to replicate the same for interethnic relations. Instead, it created a hostile interethnic consciousness that eroded national cohesion while breeding hatred and suspicion among the ethnic groups, including their political class. As a result, the absence of national integration in Nigeria is the result of a country that lacks a national consciousness. Both the leaders and the led suffer the same fate in this regard.

This accounts for the existence of two antagonistic classes of people. The first being a heterogeneous ruling class that is united only by their resolve to milk our commonwealth, and the second, a divided ruled class that takes delight at insulting each other.

Notes

1. *Huffington Post*. 2009. "Obama Ghana Speech: Full Text." Available from: http://huffpost.com/us/entry/230009.
2. Panter-Brick, S. K., ed. 1970. *Nigerian Politics and Military Rule: Prelude to the Civil War*. London: The Athlone Press.
3. Joseph, Richard A. 1987. *Democracy and Prebendal Politics in Nigeria: The Rise and Fall of the Second Republic*. Ibadan: Spectrum Books Limited; Joseph, Richard. 2013. "Prebendalism and Dysfunctionality in Nigeria." *Africaplus*, July 26. Available from: https://africaplus.wordpress.com/2013/07/26/prebendalism-and-dysfunctionality-in-nigeria/
4. Ugwu, Tagbo C. O., ed. 2002. *Corruption in Nigeria: Critical Perspectives*. Nsukka: Chuka Educational Publishers; Ogbeidi, Michael M. 2012. "Political Leadership and Corruption in Nigeria since 1960: A Socio-Economic Analysis." *Journal of Nigeria Studies* 1, no. 2: 1–25; Duruji, Moses M. and Azu, Dominic E. 2016. "The Challenges of Combating Corruption in Nigeria." In *The State in Contemporary Nigeria: Issues, Perspectives and Challenges*, edited by J. S. Omotola and I. M. Alumona. Ibadan: John Arches Publishers Ltd.
5. Nnoli, Okwudiba. 1978. *Ethnic Politics in Nigeria*. Enugu: Fourth Dimension Publishers; Suberu, Rotimi T. 1996. *Ethnic Minority Conflicts and Governance in Nigeria*. Ibadan: Spectrum Books Limited; Ukiwo, Ukoha. 2005. "The Study of Ethnicity in Nigeria." *Oxford Development Studies* 33, no. 1: 7–23, DOI: 10.1080/13600810500099592; Ugwueze, Michael I. 2016. "Ethno-Religious Conflicts and Nigeria's National Security." In *The State in Contemporary Nigeria: Issues, Perspectives and Challenges*, edited by J. S. Omotola and I. M. Alumona. Ibadan: John Arches Publishers Ltd.
6. Onuoha, Freedom. 2012. "The Audacity of the Boko Haram: Background, Analysis and Emerging Trend." *Security Journal* 25, no. 2: 134–151; Onuoha, Jonah and Ugwueze, Michael I. 2014. "United States Security Strategy and the Management of Boko Haram Crisis in Nigeria." *Global Journal of Arts Humanities and Social Sciences* 2, no. 2: 22–43; Duruji, Moses M. 2016. "Ethnic Militias in Post-Military Rule Nigeria." In *The State in Contemporary Nigeria: Issues, Perspectives and Challenges*, edited by J. S. Omotola and I. M. Alumona. Ibadan: John Arches Publishers Ltd; Ugwueze, Michael I., Onuoha, Jonah and J. Nwagwu, Ejikeme. 2016. "Electronic Governance and National Security in Nigeria." *Mediterranean Journal of Social Sciences* 7, no. 6: 363–374.
7. Kurfi, Amadu. 1989. *Election Context: Candidate's Companion*. Ibadan: Spectrum Books Limited; Ibeanu, Okey and Luckham, Robin. 2006. *Niger-Delta: Political Violence, Governance and Corporate Responsibility in a Petro-State*. Abuja: Centre for Democracy and Development; Transition Monitoring Group. 2007. *An Election Programmed to Fail: Final Report of the April 2007 General Elections in Nigeria*. Nigeria: Transition Monitoring Group; Ezirim, Gerry and Mbah, Peter. 2011.

"Electoral Process and Political Violence in Africa: Preview of 2011 General Elections in Nigeria." In *Social Dynamics of African States*, edited by O. U. Nnadozie. Nsukka: REK Books.

8. Ayers, A. J. 2010. "Sudan's Uncivil War: The Global-Historical Constitution of Political Violence." *Review of African Political Economy* 37, no. 124: 153–171; Mustapha, M. 2017. "The 2015 General Elections in Nigeria: New Media, Party Politics and the Political Economy of Voting." *Review of African Political Economy*. DOI: 10.1080/03056244.2017.1313731.
9. Nnoli, *Ethnic Politics in Nigeria*.
10. Adigwe, Francis. 1974. *Essentials of Government for West Africa*. Ibadan: Ibadan University Press Limited.
11. Nevertheless, Kosoko continued to launch attacks on Lagos until he was later reinstated as the King of Lekki—a neighboring Lagos city.
12. For more information on what led to Akintoye deposition, read Ajayi (1965); Adekoya (2016).
13. Ajayi, J. F. A. 1965. *Christian Missions in Nigeria 1841–1891*. Hong Kong: Commonwealth Printing Press.
14. Adigwe, *Essentials of Government for West Africa*; Adekoya, Preye. 2016. "The Succession Dispute to the Throne of Lagos and the British Conquest and Occupation of Lagos." *African Research Review* 10, no. 3: 207–226.
15. This was the day Dosumu and four of his principal chiefs signed a treaty with the British government that resulted in Lagos becoming a British crown colony.
16. RNC is an amalgam of various British companies trading along the Rivers of Niger and Benue. The amalgamation took place in 1879 and in 1887 a Charter was granted to the amalgamated companies, which became known as the Royal Niger Company, Chartered & Limited. By this Charter, the Company became responsible for the government of the River Basins and the whole of Hausaland and Bornu, but, in practice, their influence extended little beyond the banks of the rivers (Colonial Reports, 1923, 4).
17. Adigwe, *Essentials of Government for West Africa*.
18. Shaw was *The Times of London* correspondent who later became Friedch Lugard's (the first governor general of Nigeria's) wife.
19. Shaw, Flora. 1897. Letter. *The Times of London*, 8 January, 6.
20. Ibid.
21. Colonial Reports. 1923. *Nigeria: Annual General Report for 1923, No 1197*. London: His Majesty's Stationery office.
22. Ochonu, Moses. 2014. "The Roots of Nigeria's Religious and Ethnic Conflict." *Global Post*, 10 March. Available from: https://www.pri.org/stories/2014-03-10/roots-nigerias-religious-and-ethnic-conflict.
23. Ibid.
24. Ibid.; Ochonu, Moses. 2004. "1914 and Nigeria's Existential Crisis: A Historical Perspective (parts 1&2)." An NVS essay on Nigeria's centenary celebration May 29 and June 5, 2004.
25. Tharoor, Shashi. 2017. "The Partition: The British Game of 'Divide and Rule.'" *Al Jazeera*, August 10, 2017. Available from: http://www.aljazeera.com/indepth/opinion/2017/08/partition-british-game-divide-rule-170808101655163.html.
26. Awolowo, Obafemi. 1947. *Path to Nigerian Freedom*. London: Faber & Faber.
27. Ibid.

28. Nigeria's first prime minister and also one of the two most influential northern politicians at independence, and the other being the Sardauna of Sokoto, Alhaji Ahmadu Bello.
29. Nze, Chris. 2017. "Nigeria's Unity and the Conquest Mentality." *The Guardian*, October 6. Available from: https://guardian.ng/opinion/nigerias-unity-and-the-conquest-mentality/.
30. Bello, Ahmadu. 1962. *My Life*. Cambridge: Cambridge University Press.
31. Nze, "Nigeria's Unity and the Conquest Mentality."
32. Little, Daniel. n.d. "False Consciousness." Available from: http://www-personal.umd.umich.edu/~delittle/iess%20false%20consciousness%20V2.html.
33. Nnoli, *Ethnic Politics in Nigeria*.
34. Ibid.
35. Ibid.
36. Quarters reserved for southern migrants, mostly the Igbo, living in the northern part of Nigeria.
37. Quarters reserved for northern migrants, living in other parts of the North.
38. Quarters reserved for northerners living in their place. This section of the northern quarters has been immersed by the *Tudun Wada*.
39. Nnoli, *Ethnic Politics in Nigeria*.
40. Ukiwo, "The Study of Ethnicity in Nigeria."
41. Xypolia, Ilia. 2016. "Divide et impera: Vertical and Horizontal Dimensions of British Imperialism." *Critique: Journal of Socialist Theory* 44, no. 3: 221–231.
42. Igwe, Obasi. 2005. *Politics and Globe Dictionary*. Aba: Eagle Publishers.
43. Nnoli, *Ethnic Politics in Nigeria*; Ochonu, "The Roots of Nigeria's Religious and Ethnic Conflict."
44. Tharoor, "The Partition."
45. Ochonu, "The Roots of Nigeria's Religious and Ethnic Conflict."
46. Tharoor, "The Partition."
47. Ochonu, 'The Roots of Nigeria's Religious and Ethnic Conflict."
48. Achebe, Chinua. 2012. *There Was a Country: A Personal History of Biafra*. New York: Penguin Books Ltd.; Duru, A. 2012. "Dangerous Memory: The Nigerian Civil War, the Postwar Generation, and a Legacy of Frustration." In *The Nigeria-Biafra War*, edited by C. J. Korieh. Amherst, NY: Cambria Press; Ukiwo, Ukoha and Chukwuma, I. 2012. *Governance and Insecurity in South-East Nigeria*. Lagos: Cleen Foundation; Heerten, L. and Moses, D. 2014. "The Nigeria–Biafra War: Postcolonial Conflict and the Question of Genocide." *Journal of Genocide Research* 16, no. 2–3: 169–203.
49. Ochonu, "The Roots of Nigeria's Religious and Ethnic Conflict."
50. Uwechue, Raph. 2009. Ndigbo: Nigeria's Nation Builders. A speech delivered at the *Igbo Day 2009 Celebration*, held at Dan Anyaiam Stadium, Owerri, Imo State on September 29.
51. Weber, Eugen. 1976. *Peasants into Frenchmen: The Modernization of Rural France, 1870–1914*. Stanford: Stanford University Press.

Chapter 2

CORRUPTION: A ROOT CAUSE OF INSECURITY IN NIGERIA

Leah Wawro

Introduction

In 2012, seven decommissioned Norwegian naval vessels left Norway for the UK. As far as the Norwegian Ministry of Foreign Affairs knew, they were going to be used by European crews to protect fisheries in the ECOWAS region. But these vessels changed flags and hands and ended up in the Niger Delta, owned by a company controlled by Government Ekpemupolo, also known as Tompolo.[1] Tompolo is a former militant who had gone, in the space of a few years, from being wanted by the government for leading the militant group Movement for the Emancipation of the Niger Delta (MEND) to controlling a company that won a major ten-year contract with the state's Maritime Security Agency (MASECA).[2]

How could this happen? The case, described in more detail later in this chapter, paints a picture of defense policy decisions made in the interests of a narrow and sectarian elite, rather than the interests of the Nigerian people or stability for the country; corruption and inadequate oversight in Nigeria and its Western partners; and systematic bribery, cronyism, and a failure of institutional controls.

Corruption is increasingly understood as a threat to stability and peace, weakening public trust in the state, and fueling the narratives of violent non-state actors. Nigeria holds the dubious honor of being an exemplary case of this: corruption has formed a key part of the rhetoric of violent groups, reduced the state's ability to respond to conflict in a way that serves the average citizen, and diminished public trust in the government.

This chapter explores the nature of corruption in Nigeria, with a focus on the Nigerian defense sector and the impact it has on peace and security. It examines the role corruption has played in the rise of violent extremism—and how corruption in defense procurement and the armed forces has left a state that lacks the capability and incentives to respond effectively to crisis. Finally, it looks at the international dimension of corruption. Ultimately, it argues that if the country fails to address the endemic corruption, particularly in the defense and security sector, it will be unable to build a secure society.

General Patterns of Corruption in Nigeria

Nigeria scores badly across corruption indices and surveys. It is ranked 148th out of 180 (with a score of 27) in the 2017 Corruption Perceptions Index, a global index produced by Transparency International annually that measures the level of perception of corruption in the public sector.[3] In the 2015 Global Corruption Barometer, a survey-based index also produced by Transparency International, Nigeria's scores are similarly dismal. When asked how many of the following people within various state institutions are corrupt, 63 percent of those surveyed stated that most or all government officials are corrupt; 61 percent stated that most or all members of parliament are corrupt; and 72 percent reported that most or all police are corrupt. Forty-five percent of those surveyed reported that they had paid a bribe to the police.[4]

According to the Ibrahim Index of African Governance (IIAG) 2017, Nigeria's overall governance score is 48.1 (out of 100), and is measured to have "slowing improvement" in the past decade.[5] This is slightly lower than the West Africa regional average overall governance score (53.8). Its sub-score on Accountability is 32.7 (out of 100); on corruption in government and public officials, it scores 20; diversion of public funds, a score of 16.1.[6]

Beyond these numbers, corruption has been recognized as a fundamental feature of Nigerian political life. Wealth is extracted from the state by individuals or groups and redistributed through patronage networks.

In clientelistic systems like this with weak governance controls, a vicious cycle is established: citizens tend to turn toward informal support systems—those in common ethnic groups or communities—rather than the state. Those in power within government seek rents from natural resources and state budgets in order to sustain the patronage networks that elect them and offer contracts and positions to individuals from their own community or networks.[7] This further weakens the state and its ability to serve the broader public interest, reinforcing communities' requirement to rely on informal networks for security and support and sustaining divisions between communities.

Grand corruption and clientelism are inextricably linked to the country's vast oil resources. The "resource curse" or "paradox of plenty" is a well-known phenomenon—the tendency for the existence or discovery of natural resources to lead, counter-intuitively, to poor development outcomes, weak economic stability and growth, and higher rates of conflict and instability.[8] Inge Amundsen, writing in 2010, argues that the discovery of oil has led to "the development of pervasive patronage and rent-seeking cultures," heightening competition between politicians for control over oil revenues and the rents they provide. "The oil resources," Amundsen writes, "give the ruling elites both the incentives for controlling the state apparatus (and thus the income) and the means to retain control over the state."[9]

It has been argued that this rent-seeking political behavior can lead to greater political stability in some instances, by allowing for balance between different parties and preventing violent competition for these resources. For example, a report from the Anti-Corruption Evidence program in 2017 stated:

> *This achieves a measure of political stability through 'live and let live' arrangements, where different groups work out ways (not in the most transparent manner) on how to replace each other in and out of power, or how to continue having access to captured resources. Without such arrangements, including over the distribution of resources captured from the oil and gas sector, internal conflicts would pose existential threats to stability.*[10]

This may well be true in the short-term and power-sharing over rents might have a stabilizing effect among elites who would otherwise be in conflict, but in the long run, these forms of corruption are visible to the population—who cannot help but see that the elites who are supposed to represent their interests fail to do so. This diminishes public trust in the state and the legitimacy of government, creating the risk of greater instability and violence in the long run.

Corruption and the Rise of Extremism

There is growing evidence that corruption is linked to conflict. Research by the Institute for Economic Development and Peace found that "there is a statistically significant relationship between peace and security," when assessing corruption indicators against indicators of political terror, political instability, violent crime, violent demonstrations, organized conflict, access to small arms, homicides per 100,000 people, and the level of perceived criminality in society.[11] Transparency International has highlighted the role that corruption plays in enabling terrorist recruitment, citing examples from ISIS to the Taliban, Al Shabaab, and Boko Haram: "Systemic economic and political problems, including exploitative, exclusive governance arrangements, high-level corruption and abuse at the hands of state institutions bring humiliation, cause anger, and create a sense of injustice and powerlessness which can push individuals to seek alternative, even violent redress."[12]

The factors influencing individuals to join extremist groups are complex, and there is no one reason that these groups form or successfully recruit members. But corruption has certainly played a part in the rise of Boko Haram in Nigeria.

The founder of Boko Haram, Mohamed Yusuf, preached about the injustice and lack of accountability in the Nigerian government and security forces. His messages resonated with a population frustrated by the lack of public services, and the systemic, vertically integrated corruption in the security forces.[13] The name Boko Haram, which translates as "Western education is forbidden," is itself linked to corruption—government officials were seen to have been trained in Western schools, which Yusuf described as "corrupt and elitist."[14] The Nigerian police and army escalated its response to Boko Haram in the late 2000s, prompting allegations of disproportionate attacks and extra-judicial killings against Boko Haram members. These were arguably an expansion of the abuse of power that had fed the creation of the group.

A study by the CLEEN Foundation, a Nigerian NGO, conducted extensive interviews across the country to better understand the drivers of extremism. Their research cites corruption as one of the factors that drives young Nigerians toward joining Boko Haram today:

> The Nigerian government's high rate of corruption and neglect of citizen welfare also feeds the extremist narrative. In Sokoto state, 70 percent of participants cited this as an important factor, while in Kano state, 67 percent cited it as important. Widespread corruption in Nigeria has not only deprived communities of needed amenities and infrastructure but has created an environment conducive for recruitment and radicalization. Pervasive malfeasance, especially in the public sector, provides a key referent around which extremists can frame antisecular ideology and radicalization.[15]

What is often seen as a movement fueled by a radical ideology is not so simple in its roots—although radical fundamentalist ideology plays a part, undoubtedly, in the power of Boko Haram, its leaders have drawn on public frustration at corruption and tied it to religious immorality. Research by Sarah Chayes supports these findings. In an interview following a period in Maiduguri speaking to internally displaced persons and locals, she said, "It was clear that Boko Haram was very explicitly tying the corrupt behavior of the government officials to the secular constitution."[16]

The narrative about government corruption is not only used by Boko Haram, but also by insurgent groups in the Niger Delta. For example:

> One of the leaders of the leading militant group who were making waves in the region, Movement for the Emancipation of Niger Delta (MEND); General Godswill claimed that the militants were fighting against the system because of bad governance and corruption. (CNN, 2007)[17]

Where state officials abuse their power and act in their—or their patronage network's—interest, it drives vulnerable populations toward alternative sources of security. This is particularly true where populations are poor and the messages of extremist groups speak to an existing sense of marginalization—for example, Muslims in Nigeria's north. As discussed in more detail below, this diversion of allegiance from state to extremist group has also happened within state forces— and even at the highest level of government, where "senior players in the Nigerian security sector have also profited from the insurgency."[18]

Hindering the State's Response to Insecurity: Defense Sector Corruption

Corruption not only fuels terrorism and public mistrust in the state—on a practical level, it also makes it more difficult for the security services to respond to threats from violent groups. Corruption makes militaries less effective. It wastes defense funds, leaves troops without the equipment they need, and can mean that leaders with the greatest funds or connections rise to the top of the military hierarchy, while others languish at the lower ranks. One of the most striking examples of this, in Nigeria's recent history, is Sambo Dasuki, the former National Security Advisor, who is currently under trial for misappropriating $68 million worth of national security funds assigned toward fighting Boko Haram, but instead using the money to help fund the campaigns of the Peoples Democratic Party (PDP). The government's investigation found more than $2 billion were "missing."[19]

In any state, "national security" often provides a veil of seemingly legitimate secrecy that allows corruption to thrive. The complex technical issues around defense equipment that require specialist knowledge to scrutinize, an institutional culture of secrecy, and a sense that the armed forces should be above reproach create a recipe for corruption that is extremely difficult to root out.

This is no less true in Nigeria. The defense sector was assessed to be at a very high risk of corruption in the 2015 Government Defense Anti-Corruption Index (GI), produced by Transparency International Defence and Security (TI-DS).[20] The GI measures institutional vulnerability to corruption in defense establishments worldwide, based on seventy-seven indicators of defense corruption. The GI covers five risk areas—political risk, financial risk, personnel risk, risk on operations, and procurement risk.[21] Nigeria scored in Band E (on a scale from A, the best, to F, the worst).

Procurement is recognized as a major area of corruption risk in Nigeria. The GI highlights the lack of a clear national defense strategy that guides decisions about what equipment the state should acquire and found that defense purchases were often conducted off-budget. It also found that procurement is frequently conducted with too much political influence and too little input from the military personnel who use it.[22] It found that single-source (i.e., non-competitive) procurement is common and that financing packages for major deals are not made publicly available. The EFCC case against former National Security Advisor Colonel Sambo Dasuki, for example, shows how these weak systems and a lack of transparency enabled the leader to steal more than $2 billion—procurement funds were siphoned away from the security forces, through secretive "briefcase companies," and into electoral funds for the PDP.

The research identified a severe lack of oversight over the defense sector and excessive secrecy as key corruption vulnerabilities. Despite the National Assembly having formal power in the constitution to legislate on security matters and oversee spending on defense and security, this often fails to happen in practice, preventing the Nigerian parliamentarians from accessing vital information on the spurious grounds of "national security."[23]

Fundamentally, the extremely high levels of corruption in the Nigerian defense sector are not simply a question of weak institutions, but a political one. According to Transparency International:

> *Kleptocratic capture of the defense sector rests on three pillars: capture of defense budgets and income, capture of defense spending and procurement, and capture of senior military posts. Facilitating this capture are powerful senior figures—godfathers—who select and appoint personnel to defense sector positions, in order to operationalize systemic control overs security finances.*[24]

As oil prices have declined in recent years and security threats have become more acute, the defense sector has become a target for corrupt elites to extract resources from the state in order to enrich themselves and sustain patronage networks that keep them in power.

Waste of funds and equipment

This lack of corruption controls and accountability identified in the Government Defence Anti-Corruption Index has had dire real-world consequences. In 2013, then-president Goodluck Jonathan announced a state of emergency in Borno, Yobe, and Adamawa states, launching an offensive against Boko Haram. But the troops sent in to face Boko Haram lacked the equipment, capability, and motivation needed to do so effectively;[25] according to the Borno State Governor Kashim Shettima, the Boko Haram rebels were "clearly better armed and more willing to fight."[26] Citizens in the region reported of "soldiers who fail to show up, or flee during attacks, or aid the insurgents."[27] Former US Ambassador to Nigeria John Campbell stated that "there are hints that sympathizers in the Nigerian army will deliberately leave doors of armories unlocked for Boko Haram."[28]

Perhaps Campbell was right that these individuals were Boko Haram sympathizers and shared an ideology. But it is just as likely that the pervasive corruption in the Nigerian military left many troops with fewer options other than to sell their equipment or information, or to accept bribes. Soldiers reported that they were sent to battle with only a few bullets and were forced to buy their own uniforms and cover their own medical expenses.[29] They said in interviews that half of their field duty allowances were stolen by commanders and reported the existence of "ghost soldiers"—those who exist only on official registers so that commanders can pocket their salaries.[30] In this context—asked to sacrifice their safety even as those at the top were known to line their pockets—it is perhaps unsurprising that troops reportedly sold equipment to the enemy and colluded with organized crime.[31]

In addition, badly managed stockpiles and inventories have strengthened terrorist movements. The Director of the UN Regional Center for Peace and Disarmament in Africa stated in 2017 that "unsecured stocks and ineffectively managed stockpiles were a major contributing factor to the trafficking and diversion of arms into the illicit market and their subsequent flow to terrorists and other criminal groups as Boko Haram and Niger Delta militants."[32] As seen above, what simply looks like poor management is often a symptom of corruption, with badly paid troops more likely to turn a blind eye or accept bribes, or even to sell their equipment to the highest bidder.

Security votes

One particularly pernicious form of wasteful security spending is the use of so-called "security votes." These off-budget expenditures (the use of the term "vote" in this context is for a budget item) are in place, in theory, to provide flexible, responsive spending for security purposes, at both the federal and state level. In

May 2018, Transparency International estimated that the annual cost of security votes is more than N241.2 billion annually ($670 million). This spending is higher than the Nigerian Army's budget and Police's budget, and those of the Nigerian Air Force and Navy combined.[33] They have been in place in Nigeria since the late 1960s and successive governments have done little to reduce them; under the Buhari presidency, the number of these secretive expenditures has actually increased, despite an initial dip in 2016.[34]

Despite the size of these funds, security votes are spent with very little oversight by either legislators or the public, no audits conducted and are often transacted in cash—making them an ideal vehicle for corruption. Contracts for security vote expenditure are exempt from the Public Procurement Act[35] while the recipients of security votes have raised cause for concern. Ministries, Departments and Agencies (MDAs) that have received security votes include a national theater, an institute for hospitality and tourism development studies, and a federal school of dental technology and therapy.[36]

Beyond just being wasteful, security votes have fueled election violence and intimidation. According to research by Matthew Page, security votes are often used to pad out election funds or hire political thugs.[37] In Anambra State, security votes were used to fund the vigilante group the "Bakassi Boys," who committed human rights abuses and allegedly murdered a critic of then-Governor Chinwoke Mbadinuju. In Bayelsa State, security votes are likely to support the Bayelsa State Waterways Security Patrol Task Force, headed by a former militant and ostensibly in place to provide security in the Delta—as well as sustaining a patronage network.[38]

With Friends Like These: Western Enablers to Nigerian Corruption

This corruption has been possible with the support of Western enablers and facilitators, both those that have directly profited from corrupt arms sales with Nigerians and the systems that allow corrupt the Nigerian elite to move and store their money in the UK.

The Case of CAS-Global

In 2012, a UK-based company called CAS-Global bought six Hauk Missile Torpedo Boards (MTBs) and a naval vessel called the KNM *Horten* from the Norwegian Defence Logistics Organisation ("FLO"). Those seven decommissioned naval vessels later turned up in the Niger Delta in the hands of Global West Vessel Specialist (GWVS), a Nigerian company controlled by Government Ekpemupolo—nicknamed Tampolo—a warlord and ally of Goodluck Jonathan. This case exemplifies the way that weak systems of export control and poor enforcement in European states have empowered warlords, fuelled conflict, and often counteracted the support these states have provided for governance and development in the country.[39]

When CAS-Global bought the vessels from Norway, the firm was alleged to have paid more than $150,000 to Bjorn Stavrum, an FLO official who was overseeing the sale. He was indicted by Økokrim, the Norwegian anti-corruption organization, in 2015 for colluding with CAS-Global to disguise the final destination from the Norwegian Ministry of Foreign Affairs; in 2017, he was convicted in Oslo of gross corruption and embezzlement.[40] The application stated that the MTB Hauks would "be used for fisheries protection in the ECOWAS region; registered and operated under a UK flag; crewed by European crews; and that the ships would be bound by UK export law if sold." FLO received ample evidence of CAS-Global's links with Nigeria, including letters that stated the connection between CAS-Global and Global West, when the Nigerian press had already reported on the NIMASA-Global West contract.

Once the vessels were in the UK, they were then sold on to Nigerian firm Global West—and allowed to do so by the UK government. The research produced by Corruption Watch UK indicates that the approval of the export license for the Horton from the UK should have been blocked because it failed to adhere to three of the Consolidated Criteria on Arms Control—criterion three, which prevents exports that could provoke or aggravate conflict; criterion seven, which blocks exports that might be diverted, particularly to organized crime or terrorist groups; and criterion eight, which requires that the UK take into account the economic capacity and development needs of the recipient country.[41] In addition, Corruption Watch UK found that there was no proper due diligence on the contract to export these vessels conducted by the Foreign and Commonwealth Office, the Department for International Development, or the Export Control Organisation, despite the high level of corruption risk known to exist in defense contracting in Nigeria and the fact that Global West—which was listed as the end-user—could easily have been identified as having conflict of interest risks.[42]

On the Nigerian side, the contract between NIMASA and Global West signed in 2012 raised red flags amongst the media and opposition. This contract was described in a memo to the Jonathan presidency as an "Award of Contract for the Strategic Concessioning Partnership with NIMASA to Provide Platforms for Tracking Ships and Cargoes, Enforce Regulatory Compliance and Surveillance of the Entire Nigerian Maritime Domain." The fact that a known warlord was running maritime security for the entire maritime domain was controversial in the Nigerian press. For example, an article in Sahara Reporters described how Tompolo moved from militant and "most wanted man" to ally of the federal government:

> Today, Tompolo is not only a free man, he is a darling of the very federal government that only three years ago considered him an arch enemy deserving of extermination. [...] There is no doubt that he is very close to President Goodluck Jonathan. To cement the romance, government has invested in Global West Vessel Specialist Limited (GWVSL), a firm widely believed to be owned by Tompolo, with a contract worth $103.4 million (over N15 billion) to supply 20 vessels for the use of the nation's military authorities to secure the waterways.[43]

The contract had been personally signed off by President Goodluck Jonathan, and was not subject to normal procurement regulations. One of its main shareholders, Leke Oyewole, was also President Goodluck Jonathan's Senior Advisor on Maritime Affairs.[44] Nigerian media outlets noted the sectarian aspect of the deal, observing that Jonathan, Akpobolokemi, and Tompolo all hail from the Niger Delta;[45] Tompolo had "a long track record of threatening to engage in renewed violence should President Goodluck Jonathan fail to win the 2015 elections."[46]

This was not just the question of a single contract, but a major decision about Nigeria's maritime security policy. Former president Yar'Adua had put forward a memo to the national assembly calling for the creation of a coastal guard made up of all security agencies.[47] MASECA would have provided the same services set out in the contract with Global West.[48] In the year that the Global West contract was signed, Director General of NIMASA Patrick Akpobolokemi made the case that instead of coastal security being managed by the state, a public-private partnership was required due to federal budget restrictions.[49] But this decision was made without public consultation. Opposition party the Action Congress of Nigeria (CAN) released a statement saying that "it is unconscionable that a decision that will have far-reaching implications for trade, security, ports and shipping will be taken so lightly, without a rigorous national debate."[50]

When Buhari won the election in 2015, the contract between NIMASA and Global West was suspended and NIMASA took over more than fifty of the firm's vessels.[51] This happened soon after Akpobolokemi was fired as the director general of NIMASA; he was later charged by the EFCC with fourteen counts of "converting" $314 million from NIMASA for personal use; media has also suggested that he controlled Global West and was a signatory to its accounts, even as he was involved in selecting the company for the contract.[52] In 2016, the EFCC froze the assets of Tompolo, and in 2017 an appeal court ruled that his assets would be temporarily forfeited.[53] As of June 2018, he remained wanted by the EFCC for conspiracy and illegal diversion from NIMASA.[54]

Beyond direct involvement in the trade of defense equipment to Nigeria, European nations including the UK have also enabled corruption in Nigeria by providing a home for corrupt assets.

In London, for example, the property market is ripe for abuse by corrupt officials seeking a secure and stable home for their assets. For example, research from Transparency International identified £15 million worth of property owned by a company with links to the current Senate President, Bukola Saraki, via his wife and an aide. Despite many similar cases, UK enforcement agencies have only prosecuted three state governors.[55]

A report by NGO Global Witness showed the complicity of international banks in moving corrupt Nigerian assets outside the country. Their report *International Thief Thief* exposed how Nigerian state governors Diepreye Alamieyeseigha of Bayelsa State and Joshua Dariye of Plateau State held accounts with UK banks Barclays, HSBC, the Royal Bank of Scotland, NatWest, and UBS. Alamieyeseigha's government salary was no higher than £17,000,[56] but he was later found to have $3.2 million in cash and $15 million in real estate holdings in the UK alone.[57,58]

Nigerian media had raised questions about his integrity and an investigation started by the Nigerian Independent Corrupt Practices and Other Related Offences Commission (ICPC)—this would have been easy to discover had the banks done proper due diligence.

They did not, however; a case in point is UBS, which, despite being aware that he was a politically exposed person (PEP), allowed a contractor to pay millions into Alamieyeseigha's account.[59] The bank's branch in the Bahamas created a trust, which in turn owned a company called Falcon Flights Ltd; he later tried to use this to buy a house, at which point UBS's controls kicked in enough to prevent that—though not enough to close the account. Although the UBS case exemplifies a failure to adequately examine and verify the source of wealth for PEPs, it is not the sole facilitator of Alamieyeseigha's corrupt wealth in the UK—for example, HSBC processed a transaction for a contractor to buy him a £1.4 house in London, and an account with RBS was used to receive bribes of £1.54 million from a contractor.[60]

Later, Alamieyeseigha was convicted of thirty-three counts of corruption, money laundering, and failure to declare accurate assets in Nigeria, and he was impeached by the state legislature.[61] He served a single day in prison, and was pardoned by Goodluck Jonathan in 2013.[62] Charged with money laundering in London, he fled the country—allegedly dressed as a woman, a charge he denied (unlike the charge of failure to declare assets).[63]

Conclusions

Buhari's efforts to tackle corruption in Nigeria are the subject of near-constant debate: are they genuine, or politicized? Will he be able to push through genuine reform? These questions are not new. Reform efforts have formed a part of political dialogue during the times of Buhari's predecessors, including President Obasanjo—who set up the Economic and Financial Crimes Commission (EFCC), which has seen some important successes. There are important concerns, from both Nigerians and international donors, about Buhari's anti-corruption efforts being politicized.[64]

There are some signs of important institutional progress, including in the notoriously difficult defense sector. For example, in 2018, the Nigerian Army inaugurated an electronic payment system, which streamlines payment and is intended to reduce corruption in payment of Army personnel.[65] The Nigerian Air Force has taken some promising steps, with the creation of an integrity committee designed to implement an anti-corruption plan in collaboration with Transparency International, but it remains to be seen how successful the panel's implementation efforts will be. Finally, actions in terms of enforcement have been necessary, despite charges of politicization. For example, former National Security Advisor Colonel Sambo Dasuki is, at the time of writing, currently on trial for the alleged diversion of funds intended for arms to combat Boko Haram toward the 2015 election campaign of the PDP.[66] EFCC has seen some important successes with bringing mid-ranking officials to account for corruption, including securing a forfeiture of two Naval officer's homes in Lekki.[67]

But in the long-term, reducing corruption will require a combination of approaches: putting in place institutional reforms that create barriers to corrupt practices; building the technical capacities of those in anti-corruption functions of the state; a civil society, both NGOs and media, that remains vibrant and critical. Successful anti-corruption will also not occur without concerted efforts by the international community to address the problem, particularly states like the UK that have enabled the transfer of arms that support the corrupt, and whose banks and property markets provide a home for corrupt assets. Also key is increasing prosecutions and ensuring that they are fair and apolitical, which will not only bring the corrupt to justice but also serve as a warning to others. Finally, the most difficult challenge and the one most likely to bring about permanent change will be to create a real shift of incentives for Nigeria's leaders and dismantle the patronage networks that run political life today.

Notes

1. Gibbs, Margot. 2017. "Dereliction of Duty: How Weak Arms Export License Controls in the UK Facilitated Corruption and Exacerbated Instability in the Niger Delta." *Corruption Watch UK*. Available from: https://docs.wixstatic.com/ugd/54261c_3f990fe3175c48c5b90ed65a41192d59.pdf
2. Odunlami, Temitayo. 2012. "Tompolo: The Billionaire Militant." *Sahara Reporters*, August 16. Available from: http://saharareporters.com/2012/08/16/tompolo-billionaire-militant-thenews-africa.
3. Transparency International, Corruption Perceptions Index. 2017. Available from: https://www.transparency.org/news/feature/corruption_perceptions_index_2017 [accessed July 20, 2018].
4. Transparency International, Global Corruption Barometer 2015/16/17. "Supplementary Data, Global Results." Available from: https://www.transparency.org/news/feature/global_corruption_barometer_citizens_voices_from_around_the_world [accessed July 20, 2018].
5. Ibrahim Index of African Governance (IIAG), 2017. Available from: http://iiag.online/
6. Mo Ibrahim Foundation. 2017. "Ibrahim Index of African Governance: Index Report." Available from: http://s.mo.ibrahim.foundation/u/2017/11/21165610/2017-IIAG-Report.pdf
7. Martini, Maira. 2014. "U4 Expert Answer: Nigeria: Evidence of Corruption and the Influence of Social Norms." *Anti-Corruption Resource Centre*, September 26. Available from: https://www.transparency.org/files/content/corruptionqas/Nigeria_overview_of_corruption_and_influence_of_social_norms_2014.pdf.
8. NRGI Reader. 2015. "The Resource Curse: The Political and Economic Challenges of Natural Resource Wealth," March. Available from: https://resourcegovernance.org/sites/default/files/nrgi_Resource-Curse.pdf
9. Amundsen, Inge. 2014. "Good Governance in Nigeria: A Study in Political Economy and Donor Support." *Norad Report 17/2010 Discussion*, August 24. Available from: https://www.researchgate.net/profile/Inge_Amundsen/publication/256952861_Good_Governance_in_Nigeria/links/0c960524177e5c1d4b000000/Good-Governance-in-Nigeria.pdf

10. "Anti-Corruption in Nigeria: Accepting the Constraints, and Moving Forward." Anti-Corruption Evidence (ACE) Briefing Paper 002, 2017. Available from: https://ace.soas.ac.uk/wp-content/uploads/2017/07/ACE-BriefingPaper002-NG-AntiCorruption-171027-LowRes.pdf
11. Institute of Economics and Peace. 2015. "Peace and Corruption 2015: Lowering Corruption—A Transformative Factor for Peace." Available from: https://reliefweb.int/sites/reliefweb.int/files/resources/Peace%20and%20Corruption.pdf
12. MacLachlan, Karolina. 2017 "The Fifth Column: Understanding the Relationship between Corruption and Conflict." *Transparency International*, July, page 17. Available from: http://ti-defence.org/wp-content/uploads/2017/09/The_Fifth_Column_Web.pdf.
13. Allen, D., Cafferky, W., Hendawy, A., Horn, J., Maclachlan, K., Nijssen, S., and de la Blache, E. V. 2017. "The Big Spin: Corruption and the Growth of Violent Extremism." *Transparency International: Defense and Security*, February. Available from: http://ti-defence.org/wp-content/uploads/2017/02/The_Big_Spin_Web-1.pdf
14. Ibid.
15. Onuoha, Freedom C. 2014. "Why Do Youth Join Boko Haram?" *United States Institute of Peace (USIP) Special Report*, June. Available from: https://www.usip.org/sites/default/files/SR348-Why_do_Youth_Join_Boko_Haram.pdf
16. Chayes, Sarah. 2016. "Corruption and Extremism: From Recognition to Response." Interview in *World Policy Journal*, February 12. Available from: https://carnegieendowment.org/2016/02/12/corruption-and-extremism-from-recognition-to-response-pub-62760 [accessed July 20, 2018]
17. Ayodeji, Dr. Gafar. 2016. "The Role of Corruption in Festering Boko Haram Insurgency and Terrorism under Jonathan Administration." *SSRN*. Available from: https://ssrn.com/abstract=2881193 or http://dx.doi.org/10.2139/ssrn.2881193.
18. Anderson, Eva and Page, Matthew. 2017. "Weaponising Transparency: Defence Procurement Reform as a Counterterrorism Strategy in Nigeria." *Transparency International*, May. Available from: http://ti-defence.org/wp-content/uploads/2017/05/Weaponising_Transparency_Web.pdf (page 5).
19. BBC News. 2015. "Nigeria's Sambo Dasuki Charged "$68m Fraud," December 14. Available from: https://www.bbc.co.uk/news/world-africa-35093785
20. Transparency International Defence and Security, *Government Defence Anti-Corruption Index 2015, Nigeria Assessment*. Available from: http://government.defenceindex.org/countries/nigeria/
21. Ibid.
22. Ibid.
23. Ibid.
24. Anderson and Page, "Weaponising Transparency."
25. Baker, Aryn. 2015. "Nigeria's Military Quails When Faced with Boko Haram." *Time*, February 10. Available from: http://time.com/3702849/nigerias-army-boko-haram/ [accessed July 28, 2018].
26. Allen et al., "The Big Spin."
27. Okeowo, Alexis. 2014. "Missing." *The New Yorker*, May 26. Available from: https://www.newyorker.com/magazine/2014/05/26/missing-4
28. Baffour, Katherine. 2014. "Boko Haram's Source of Weapons Revealed." *NAIJ.com*. Available from: https://www.naija.ng/66368.html#59827.
29. Robertson, Nic. 2015. "Nigerian Soldiers Discuss Boko Haram Fight." *CNN*, January. Available from: http://edition.cnn.com/videos/world/2015/01/15/ctw

30. Allen et al., "The Big Spin."
31. Torbjornsson and Michael Jonsson, "Boko Haram: On the Verge of Defeat or a Long Term Threat?" FOI-R–4488—SE, November 2017.
32. Isah, Ahuraka. 2017. "Nigeria: UN Raises the Alarm over 350 Million Illicit Weapons in Nigeria." *All Africa*, December 13. Available from: http://allafrica.com/stories/201712130072.html.
33. Page, Matthew. 2018. "Camouflaged Cash: How 'Security Votes' Fuel Corruption in Nigeria." *Transparency International Defence and Security*, May. Available from: http://ti-defence.org/wp-content/uploads/2018/05/DSP_Nigeria_Camouflage_Cash_Web2.pdf page 3
34. Ibid., 8.
35. Ibid., 7.
36. Ibid.
37. Ibid., 4.
38. Ibid.
39. Gibbs, "Dereliction of Duty."
40. Junghae, Waithera. 2017. "Økokrim Secures Conviction as UK CAS-Global Probe Continues." *Global Investigations Review*, May 16. Available from: https://globalinvestigationsreview.com/article/1141762/%C3%98kokrim-secures-conviction-as-uk-cas-global-probe-continues.
41. UK Department for Business, Innovation & Skills, Guidance on Consolidated EU and National Arms Export Licensing Criteria, November 21, 2012. Available from: https://www.gov.uk/government/publications/consolidated-eu-and-national-arms-export-licensing-criteria. *These criteria were in place in 2012, and were withdrawn in 2015.*
42. Gibbs, "Dereliction of Duty," 6.
43. Odunlami, "Tompolo."
44. Gibbs, "Dereliction of Duty," 17.
45. Ibid.
46. Ibid.
47. Odunlami, "Tompolo."
48. PM News, 2018. "CAN Queries Plans to Privatize Nigeria's Maritime Security," July 3. Available from: https://www.pmnewsnigeria.com/2012/01/22/acn-queries-plans-to-privatize-nigerias-maritime-security/.
49. Odunlami, "Tompolo."
50. PM News, "CAN Queries Plans to Privatize Nigeria's Maritime Security."
51. Agha, Eugene. 2016. "NIMASA Takes Over 20 Vessels from Tompolo's Firm." *The Daily Trust*, March 16. Available from: https://www.dailytrust.com.ng/news/general/nimasa-takes-over-20-vessels-from-tompolo-s-firm/138104.html.
52. Gibbs, "Dereliction of Duty," 36.
53. Godwin, Comrade Ameh. 2017. "Court Affirms Forfeiture of Tompolo's Assets to Nigerian Government." *Daily Post*, October 28. Available from: http://dailypost.ng/2017/10/28/court-affirms-forfeiture-tompolos-assets-nigerian-government/.
54. Economic and Financial Crimes Commission website page for Government Ekpemupolo (AKA Tompolo). Available from: https://efccnigeria.org/efcc/wanted/1723-government-ekpemupolo-a-k-a-tompolo [accessed July 3, 2018].
55. Anderson and Page, "Weaponising Transparency."
56. Global Witness, 2010. "International Thief Thief." October 2020. Available from: https://www.globalwitness.org/en/campaigns/corruption-and-money-laundering/banks/international-thief-thief/page3

57. Roberts, Sam. 2015. "Diepreye Alamieyeseigha, Nigerian Notorious for Corruption, Dies at 62." *The New York Times*, October 14. Available from: https://www.nytimes.com/2015/10/15/world/diepreye-alamieyeseigha-nigerian-ex-governor-dies-at-62.html.
58. Global Witness, " International Thief Thief."
59. Ibid.
60. Ibid.
61. Roberts, "Diepreye Alamieyeseigha, Nigerian Notorious for Corruption, Dies at 62."
62. Ibid.
63. Ibid.
64. See, for example, Abubakar, Ahmed. 2018. "Elite's Brinkmanship and the Politicization of Anti-Corruption Project in Nigeria: An Overview of the Anti-Corruption War under the Buhari Administration." Available from: http://www.hrpub.org/download/20171230/SA7-19610545.pdf and 2016. "Buhari's Act of Politicizing His Anti-Corruption War: A Reinforcement of Hostility among Southerners—Tom Marino." *Naija Per minute*, September 4, 2016. Available from: http://www.naijaperminute.com.ng/2016/09/04/buharis-act-politicizing-anti-corruption-war-reinforcement-hostility-among-southerners-tom-marino/
65. The Eagle Online, 2018. "Army Inaugurates E-NAPS for Payment of Salaries." April 19. Available from: https://theeagleonline.com.ng/army-inaugurates-e-naps-for-payment-of-salaries/.
66. Ososanya, Tunde. 2018. "Dasukigate: Witness Testifies against Dasuki, Says ex-NSA Transferred N280.4m to Individuals' Accounts." *Naij.NG*. Available from: https://www.naija.ng/1178249-dasukigate-witness-testifies-dasuki-nsa-transferred-n2804m-individuals-accounts.html#1178249.
67. Premium Times. 2018. "Corruption: Two Naval Officers Forfeit Lekki Houses, N11 Million to Nigerian Government," May 3. Available from: https://www.premiumtimesng.com/news/top-news/267090-corruption-two-naval-officers-forfeit-lekki-houses-n11-million-to-nigerian-govt.html.

Chapter 3

NOWHERE TO RUN: CLIMATE CHANGE AND SECURITY CHALLENGES IN NIGERIA

Anthony Chukwuebuka Okoye

Introduction

The question of climate change is perhaps the most complex and controversial in the entire science of meteorology. Countless scholarly man-hours and drums of intellectual inks have been dedicated toward the explanation and understanding of the issues surrounding climate change and its deleterious effects. Despite the lack of consensus among climatologists and meteorologists on the issue of atmospheric warming, as well as arguments of those that outright deny either the existence of climate change or the degree of the change, climate change science is now unequivocal that global warming is taking place.[1] Reliable temperature records date back to 1850. Our world is now about 1 degree Celsius hotter than it was in the period between 1850 and 1900—commonly referred to as the "pre-industrial" average. Data on global surface temperature even indicate exponential growth—compared to average temperatures between 1961 and 1990, 2016 was 0.8 degrees warmer, while 2017 was 0.68 degrees warmer.[2] In reality, the global climate had changed in the past, is changing now, and will continue to change.[3] The point is not whether the climate changes; it is the rate with which it occurs since the time of industrial revolution, and its associated adverse effect that is at issue. At present, the phenomenon is accelerating more rapidly and dangerously than predicated by scientists.[4] These changes are likely to have significant environmental, social, and economic impacts on agriculture and fisheries, desertification, biodiversity, water resources, energy supply, heat- and cold-related mortality, coastal zones, and flooding.[5] Ironically, whereas the manifestations of ongoing climate change are global, findings have suggested that the impacts will be felt the most by less developed countries of Africa, Asia, the Caribbean, Oceania, Pacific, and Latin America of who have contributed toward it the least.[6] Consequently, a landmark 2007 UN report based on the work of around 200 scientists[7] revealed that Africa would suffer the most from drought, agricultural change, rising sea levels threatening coastal areas, and the spread of tropical pests and diseases. In Africa, Nigeria has been identified as one of those countries that are highly vulnerable to its negative impacts due to its low adaptive, mitigation, and resilient capacities.

Accordingly, from the North, through to the Middle Belt to South and coastal parts of the country, the story is the same as each of the climatic zones manifests various symptoms of climate change. However, the most worrisome of these adverse manifestations is by far the social dimension, which is evident in numerous conflicts and environmental disasters that undermine human security[8] in Nigeria. There is *nowhere one can run to*[9] in order to escape the phenomenon. The security threat posed to Nigerians by climate change is demonstrated by escalation in extreme climatic events and disasters such as the 2012 flood, droughts, desertification, and shrinking of water bodies to mention but a few. Incidentally, these events further led to other calamities and chain reactions that undermine people's ability to enjoy their fundamental rights. It can be argued that the country is, at the moment, undergoing subtle security challenges far greater than the insurgent and militant activities associated with the dreaded Boko Haram (BH) sect, Niger Delta Avengers (NDA), marauding herdsmen, and separatist movements. Unfortunately, this is yet to come to the front burner of national consciousness and attention. It is against this backdrop that this study critically examines the various ways climate change creates and escalates insecurities in Nigeria with a view to identifying the means of addressing them.

What Is Climate Change?

Climate change is seen as "a broad range of global phenomena created predominantly by burning fossil fuels, which add heat-trapping gases to earth's atmosphere. These phenomena include the increased temperature trends described as global warming, but also encompass changes such as sea level rise; ice mass loss in Greenland, Antarctica, the Arctic, and mountain glaciers worldwide; shifts in flower/plant blooming; extreme weather events";[10] a change in the state of the climate that can be identified (e.g., using statistical tests) by changes in the mean and/or the variability of its properties and that persists for an extended period, typically decades or longer.[11] It refers to any change in climate over time, whether due to natural variability or as a result of human activity. "A change of climate that is attributed directly or indirectly to human activity that alters the composition of the global atmosphere and that is in addition to natural climate variability observed over comparable time periods."[12]

With regard to its cause, climate change is attributed to the earth's natural processes and anthropogenic factors (human activities). In both the policy circle and scholarly discourse, the term "climate change" is currently used in an anthropogenic sense as opposed to changes in climate that result as part of the natural processes. There is at the moment scientific consensus that the rapid and irreversible changes in climate are, in large part, caused by human activities[13] that put greenhouse gases (such as carbon dioxide, methane, and nitrous oxide) in the atmosphere. Human activities that result in climate change include: the burning of fossil fuels (coal, oil, and gas), land use change, cement manufacturing, transportation, bush clearing, slash-and-burn agriculture, aerosol, the burning of forests, bush burning, and animal husbandry all add carbon dioxide to the atmosphere. The burning of fossil fuels has increased the number of aerosol particles in the atmosphere, especially over and around major urban and industrial areas.[14] The major greenhouse gases and their sources are presented at Table 3.1 below.[15]

Other human activities, such as deforestation, are responsible for 10 to 20 percent of the excess carbon dioxide emitted into the atmosphere each year; agriculture contributes nitrous oxide and methane. Changes in land use and land cover also modify the reflectivity of the earth's surface; the more reflective a surface, the more sunlight is sent back into space. Cropland is generally more reflective than an undisturbed forest, while urban areas often reflect less energy than undisturbed land.[16] Figure 3.1 shows the causative factors of climate change.

Table 3.1 The major greenhouse gases and their sources

Gas	Sources (natural and man-made)
Water vapor	Evaporation from the oceans, evapotranspiration from the land and vegetation
Carbon dioxide	Burning of fossil fuels (power house, industry, transport), burning rainforests, transpiration
Methane	Decaying vegetation (peat and in swamps), farming (fermenting animal dung and rice-growing), sewage disposal, and landfill sites
Nitrous oxide	Vehicle exhausts, fertilizer, nylon manufacture, power stations
Chlorofluorocarbons	Refrigerators, aerosols sprays, solvents, and foam

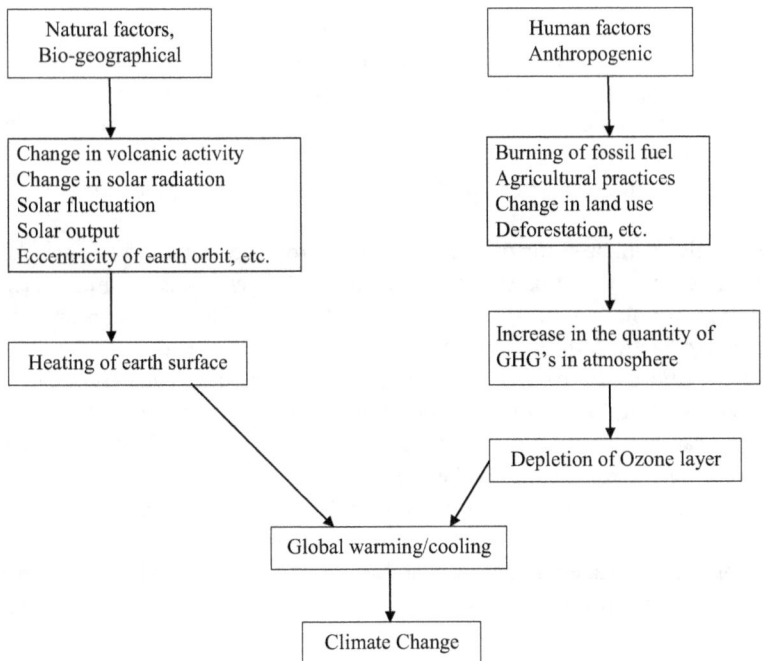

Figure 3.1 Causative factors of climate change.

Climate change effects manifest in various forms throughout different regions and countries around the world. It can take the form of frequent and severe droughts, rapid desert encroachment, shifts in rain patterns, a change in temperature, a change in precipitation, coral reef bleaching, receding glaciers, rising sea levels, the melting of snow and icecaps, and a change in planting season. Some of these effects are already happening while future predictions look even more worrisome and gloomy.

Perspective on Security and the Environment

Security is discussed in this paper from a human security perspective. This is because human security includes much more than security from violence and crime.[17] It primarily concerns itself with the analysis of a threat, or groups of threats, and how they affect particular groups of people. It offers a new dimension by considering various threats that people battle with on daily basis in the twenty-first century and how states in conjunction with international community respond to them. To this end, it enables government at all levels to analyze, establish, and implement coordinated responses aimed at enhancing human dignity and the quality of life for citizens. This suggests that human security broadens the scope of security analysis and policy from territorial security to the security of people.[18] The point is that anything that degrades their quality of life—demographic pressures, diminished access to or stock of resources, and so on—is a security threat.[19] It is for this reason that Hubert remarks:

> *In essence human security means safety for people from both violent and non-violent threats. It is a condition of being characterized by freedom from pervasive threat to people's rights, their safety or even their lives. It is an alternative way of seeing the world, taking people as its point of reference, rather than focusing exclusively on the security of territory or government. Like other security concepts— national security, economic security, food security—it is about protection.*[20]

Accordingly, human security deals with the protection of the vital core of all human lives from threat in ways that enhance their livelihoods and human rights, including economic security, food security, health security, economic security, personal security, community security, and political security.[21] It also denotes the reality and ability of every man and woman to live in a society where they can achieve their full environmental, political, social, and economic potential without fear or threat to their human rights and property.[22] Human security, therefore, starts from balancing the needs of the "stomach" through effective and positive focusing of the mental apparatus and psychic motor, and then manifests in developing a high sense of patriotism, affective orientation, and cooperative behavior with the state and people who live therein. It is driven by human-needs. At the macro perspective, human security encompasses general security of man as a member of a group. It is on account of this that it is often discussed in terms freedom from fear and freedom from want.

The concept of human security derives its compelling quality from four essential attributes. First, it is based on universal concerns because human beings, irrespective of the geographical location and socio-economic status, face similar threats that range from environmental threats, health threats, drugs, crimes, human rights violations, etc. Second, threats to human security are no longer isolated, since they engage the interests and intervention of other actors in the international system. Third, human security threats are easier to secure and cope with through the adoption of early warning preventative measures; however, where the measures are not adopted, the resultant costs in both human and non-human terms are usually devastating. Fourth, human security is centered on people and their existence.[23] Taking human security from its denominator of freedom from fear and freedom from want, this chapter therefore sees security as a human condition, characterized by the absence of fear, want, threat, anxieties, tensions, conflict, displacement, human rights violations, injury, loss of life, loss property, loss of cherished values, among others, that guarantee societal development and well-being. The adoption of the General Assembly resolution 66/290 on September 10, 2012, was a significant milestone for the application of human security. In paragraph 3 of the resolution, the General Assembly agreed by consensus that human security is an approach to assist member states in identifying and addressing widespread and cross-cutting challenges to the survival, livelihood, and dignity of their people.[24]

Nigeria is home to 195,875,237 million people (2018 estimate), making it the most populous country in Africa.[25] A significant portion of the country's labor force is employed in the agricultural sector,[26] which is estimated at about 70 percent of the population and contributes about 40 percent to the national economy. The country is ranked the third most vulnerable nation in the world with regard to climate change.[27] What this translates into is that climate change is likely to have strong negative observable effects on the country's economy and other sectors of development, such as agriculture, land use, energy, biodiversity, health, and water resources, among others, that will culminate in significant reduction in agricultural productivity and increase in illnesses, morbidity, and mortality rate.[28]

Nigeria is exposed to a range of climate conditions and extreme weather events that have significant implications for the country's food security. Climate change will significantly alter the dynamics of these events, possibly increasing their frequency and intensity in many parts of the country.[29] Rural households engaged in subsistence farming and smallholder farmers are most vulnerable to the impacts of climate change on agriculture. They may be affected in the following ways: increased likelihood of crop failure; increase in diseases and the mortality of livestock, forced sales of livestock at disadvantageous prices; increased livelihood insecurity, resulting in assets sale, indebtedness, outmigration, dependence on food aid; and a downward spiral in human development indicators, such as health and education.[30] Research findings, for example, have suggested that a sea level rise of 1 meter could result in the loss of 75 percent of the country's Niger Delta region.[31]

Climate Change and Insecurities in Nigeria: Interrogating the Linkages

Climate change has been identified as the greatest security threat of the century. In light of this, it constitutes a human right and security issue that presents a number of human security threats that undermine the well-being of Nigerians. It serves as a threat multiplier. Although the specifics of climate change are unclear and contested, Nigeria is one of the African countries vulnerable to its adverse environmental and security implications.[32] The manifestations of climate change undermine human security by escalating the environmental disasters that severely impact the ability of individuals, groups, and communities to survive. It does this by expanding the existing problems of resources scarcity, environmental refugees, competition (intra and inter group), poverty, malnutrition, spread of disease, conflict, increase in the number of internally displaced persons (IDPs), among others. These, by implication, create an environment that is filled with fear and want (fear of not knowing what the next day holds), uncertainty of one's life, the possibility of injury, losing cherished values, and want of basic life necessities (adequate supply of nutritious food, shelter, a stable society, family life, a secured environment, etc.).

Regrettably, there appears, at the moment, a grave lullaby in terms of citizen's consciousness about the dire consequences of climate change and its associated hazards in the country. In fact, President Buhari recently observed that climate change and environmental challenges are the major threats to the peace and prosperity of the nation and its citizens.[33] This suggests that even though the country had been experiencing a number of man-made and environmental challenges, the introduction of climate change into the matrix has unsettled the balance between these challenges and the coping capacities of the people by multiplying the security threats they pose to the quality of life and the survival of the people.

Drought/Desertification

The incidence of climate change is worsening the problem of drought and desertification in the northern fringes of the country. Currently, eleven states of the federation all in the northern part of the country, namely, Adamawa, Bauchi, Borno, Gombe, Kano, Katsina, Kebbi, Jigawa, Sokoto, Zamfara, and Yobe have been designated as desert frontline due to persistent droughts that result in desert encroachment. Statistically, about 35 percent of the country's landmass has been taken over by desert, which advances at the rate of 0.6 kilometers per annum.[34] Presently, about 105,000 sq km to 136,500 sq km landmass are lost to drought and desertification in the frontline states.[35] These desert frontline states, which cut across the northeast and northwest region of Nigeria, have a combined estimated population of 54 million. It engulfs about 2,168 sq km of rangeland and cropland each year, obliterates human settlements, induces forced migration, and exacerbates poverty and social conflicts.[36]

There are increasing reports of drought, a persisting dry atmosphere and increasing temperature.[37] Again, as the arid region becomes drier due to drought and desertification, active sand dunes that bury human settlement and farmlands are now common in such places like Yobe, Borno, Jigawa, and Sokoto states. These situations have serious implication for resource- and identity-based conflicts, as people will have to compete over fewer available resources, such as fertile land, fresh water, and arable land. Besides, by rendering land unproductive through harsh environmental conditions, it exposes people to poverty with its associated socio-economic consequences.

Reduction in Agricultural Production and Food Security

Shift and reduction in the amount of rainfall seriously affect the length of seasons in a country. Nigeria is experiencing a slow but steady decrease in the amount of rainfall, especially in the Sudan Sahel climatic belt, with many more places recording a late onset or early cessation of rain, a shortened rainy season, and reduced amounts of annual rainfall.[38] These climate change–induced events have severe effects on the planting and harvesting of crops. The late onset of rain often delays planting season, while its early cessation destroys late crops, resulting in poor crop yields, poor quality of crops, and so on,[39] all of which enhance the problem of food insecurity. Whereas food security depends on the ability of farmers to accurately predict when to plant their crops and when to harvest same, the unpredictable nature of rain onset in the past three to four decades results in the smothering of crops planted with early rains by the ensuing dry spell that often follows. The situation results in harvest failures for rain-fed agriculture, especially in the southern part of the country where irrigation agriculture is rarely practiced. Climate change–related events degrade yield from agriculture, cattle rearing, fisheries, and forestry as well as render many of the unemployed with fewer economic opportunities.[40] In a country like Nigeria where most individuals depend on agriculture as their means of subsistence, these events that undermine their sources of livelihood expose them to poverty and push them out of their ancestral homes. Conversely, most well-drained farmlands have been turned into marshy areas, thereby making them unsuitable for crop production. Such that water-loving crops like swamp rice experience stunted growth as a result of heavy rains which are concentrated within a specific period of the year, reducing photosynthesis due to reduction in sunlight duration and intensity.[41]

Similarly, climate-induced flood disasters destroy and wash away crops in farms, fish farms (ponds), poultry, domestic animals, and even the harvested crops in the barn. For instance, the 2012 flood disaster damaged an estimated $16.9 billion in the country's agricultural sector, affecting 1.5 million hectares of staple crops and over half a million households dependent on livestock farming.[42] The net effect of this is that it escalates food shortage/scarcity that in turn results in a hike in the prices of available food items. On a similar note, it should be noted that the eleven desert frontline states in northern region are the major producers of grains (guinea corn, millet, maize, groundnut, beans, and so on). Hence, the process of desert encroachment constitutes a threat to food security in Nigeria.

Water Scarcity/Health

For most Nigerians, especially those in the Northern region, accessibility to water (fresh/potable) constitutes a serious environmental threat. Different factors such as topography of the area, drought, and nearness to the Sahara Desert among others account for the situation, which climate change exacerbates. The shrinking of water bodies across the region as typified by the disappearing nature of Lake Chad underpins water crises among the people. Indeed, a considerable proportion of the country's population is at risk of water stress, with less than 40 percent having access to potable water.[43] This compels people to source and use all sorts of water for drinking, cooking, and other domestic needs, thereby increasing the threat of water-related diseases classified as waterborne, water impounding, water vector, water shortage, and water chemical diseases such as cholera, typhoid, among others. The phenomenon directly and indirectly contributes to health complications and challenges in the country. Climate change–related extreme weather conditions such as rises in temperature, changes in precipitation, heat waves, rises in sea level, and intense sunshine among others enhance the spread and migration of disease vectors to areas where they were non-existent before. For instance, tsetse flies that were initially restricted to southern parts now survive and thrive in the North, where they threaten livestock. The incidence of pests and diseases in Nigeria is now worrisome because the environment is becoming warmer, dryer, and more conducive for them.[44]

Again, increasing rainfall creates stagnant waters that serve as breeding grounds for mosquitoes, which infest people with malaria plasmodium that in turn result in illness, stroke, influenza, cholera, morbidity, respiratory problems, and mortality. Explaining the health implications of climate change in Nigeria and its neighbors, *The Guardian Newspaper* on October 3, 2010, stated:

> *Incidences of meningitis have been on the increase in Nigeria for the past one year as a result of excessive heat. This year has been unbearably hot in Nigeria and other countries of sub-Saharan Africa. In Nigeria, the eleven frontline states in the north that have suffered from desert encroachment have been suffering from heat related ailment. Early last year investigations revealed that over 200 people were killed by meningitis in Nigeria and Niger Republic in one week. There were outbreaks in 76 areas. There were 25,000 suspected cases and 1,500 deaths in the first quarter of 2009. Although meningitis is a disease caused by an infection of the meanings, which is the thin lining that surrounds the brain and the spinal cord, experts have found a correlation between the weather and this disease ... there were indications in the past one month that many people were treated for acute pneumonia in some hospitals as a result of the erratic and unpredictable weather.*[45]

Conversely, the incidence of flood that is occasioned by excessive rainfall and SLR (surface-to-liquid ratio), which contaminates water sources and points through the intrusion of sea water as well as dirty waters to fresh/drinking water, also creates health challenges in the southern region, especially in coastal communities in the Niger Delta.

Migration/Population Displacement/Conflict

Most people, especially farmers and herders, respond to drought, desertification, and the shrinking of water bodies that render the land they inhabit unproductive and inhospitable by migrating to new locations in search of arable land and water points for their agricultural activities. However, this *ecomigration*, especially at the face of marked religious, language, ethnic, and cultural differences between the migrants and the receiving communities, often generates conflict. Here, groups compete about access and the use rights over available scarce resources such as grazing land and water points. Until recently, herdsmen seasonally migrate from North to South during dry season and return to their base during the onset of rainy season. However, the rising incidence of drought, desertification, and the shrinking of Lake Chad, among others, have made migration an all-year affair, with many taking up residence on a more permanent basis. Specifically, the influx of nomadic herdsmen often results in violent conflict between these cowboys and farming communities across the country, especially in north central, where about 80 percent of Nigeria's food is produced.[46] A conflict has resulted in the loss of crops, cattle, property, population displacement, the destruction of farm and farm produce, the burning of communities, injury and the loss of thousands of human lives. The magnitude of fatalities, which accompany these conflicts, has resulted in the Global Terrorism Index (GTI, 2015) designating the Fulani herdsmen the fourth deadliest terrorist group in 2014, having caused the death of over 1,229 persons that year. Besides, the emergence, growth, and sustenance of the BH insurgent group that has been fighting the Nigerian state and its citizens for a decade now has equally been attributed to the multiplier effects of climate change. Although climate change does not have any direct cause-effect relationship with the insurgency, the more it exposes youth to unemployment, poverty, and redundancy by destroying their sources of livelihood, the more recruits it creates for BH insurgent sects. This is because in presence of poverty, unemployment, and lack of material wealth, BH recruits and radicalizes armies of unemployed youths and children through financial inducement and provision [or *promise*] of material reliefs.[47] These conflicts have led to countless injuries, destruction of property (both public and private), and destruction of crops and livestock. They have driven away investors; forced the closure of businesses and schools; prompted the loss of academic calendars, jobs, income; and caused millions of IDPs. In fact, the country presently houses over 10 million out-of-school children. A significant percentage of this number came from the BH-threatened and ravaged northeast.

Soil Erosion/Coastal Erosion

In the southeastern part of the country, namely, Abia, Anambra, Ebonyi, Enugu, and Imo states, most communities are ravaged by soil erosion on a daily basis. Out of the various types of erosion witnessed in the area, gully erosion and its associated threats are the most pervasive. There are over 960 active erosion sites in Anambra State, such that almost all the 177 communities in the state were affected by one form of erosion or other. Statistics of major gully erosions sites in the state, by local governments, demonstrates that Aguata/Orumba local government areas (LGAs) have about 78 gullies, Nnewi 60, Njikoka/Aniocha 50, Idemili 46, Ihiala 40, Awka 30, Onitsha 22, and Anambra/Oyi 16 gullies.[48] The state is famous with its Agulu-Nanka-Oko-Ekwulobia gullies that are about 120 meters deep and 2 kilometers wide.[49] For instance, in Oko, Orumba North Local Government Area of Anambra State, the community of the late first executive vice-president of the country, Dr. Alex Ekwueme, has had some regions cut-off from the rest by erosion, destroying about forty-nine buildings and displaced some ninety-one families. The threat was such that the Nigerian government had invested the sum of $500 million in the IDA-financed Nigeria Erosion and Watershed Management Project (NEWMAP) in order to tackle the challenge.[50] Other states in the southeast of Nigeria have had their fair share of the menace; in Imo, for example, there are about 300 erosion sites, and 500 each in Abia, Enugu, and Ebonyi.[51] On its part, the World Igbo Environmental Foundation (WIEF) noted that there are over 2,800 active erosion sites in the southeast of Nigeria.[52] These gully erosions threaten and in some cases have succeeded in sacking people [communities] from their ancestral lands. The impact of gully erosion to the survival of individuals and communities is such that many dwelling houses, school building, heath facilities, and power infrastructure have been swallowed: loss of ancestral homes, loss of property, loss of farmland and vegetation, separation/isolation of villages, collapse of roads, bridges, injuries and loss of human life.

Meanwhile, coastal erosion is the major environmental challenge that confronts Nigeria's coastal communities in the Niger Delta. Out of the country's 853-kilomter coastline, the Niger Delta accounts for about 450 kilometers of the coastal zone. The people are mainly fishers and farmers. Hence, the problem of coastal erosion constitutes a significant source of threat to life, property, livelihood, and infrastructure in the region,[53] undermining their rights to community and environmental security. The point is that these environmental challenges threaten the rights and lives of the members of these coastal communities through the destruction of cherished values, loss of lives, homelessness, population displacement, destruction of property, and loss of investments. It has been noted that a permanent sea level rise of only 7.8 inches (200 millimeters) might create 740,000 homeless people in Nigeria.[54]

Flood/Internal Displaced Persons

Climate change is gradually exacerbating and transforming the problem of flooding in Nigeria into an annual event as a result of high rainfall. Before now, flooding in the country was largely restricted to the Niger Delta region due to its environment. Recently, there has been an increase both in the frequency and perimeter of incidence of flooding in the country. The country experienced its worst flood in 2012, which affected about thirty out of the thirty-six in the federation while the six states of Anambra, Bayelsa, Benue, Delta, Kogi, and Rivers were the worst hit. The flood affected over 7 million persons, displaced 2.1 million, and resulted in about 363 deaths in addition to the 5,851 persons who suffered various degrees of injuries.[55] In 2018, heavy rainfall caused the Niger and Benue rivers to overflow their banks, displacing thousands across twelve states. The damage caused by the flood disaster compelled the National Emergency Management Agency (NEMA) to declare an emergency in Kogi, Niger, Delta, and Anambra states, while maintaining crisis level monitoring in eight other states in central and southern parts of the country. This climate change–induced environmental challenges created large crowds of IDPs. As of September 16, flooding across twelve states in central and southern Nigeria resulted in the displacement of more than 600,000 people with an estimated 100 deaths.[56] Worst still, the Niger River at Lokoja that was 10 meters on the 7th of September rose significantly reaching high levels of 11.06 meters on the 18th of September after days of heavy rainfall in Nigeria and neighboring countries.[57] The impacts of the flood threaten the sources of livelihood of farmers and fishers in these coastal communities, especially those in the Niger Delta region, bearing in mind that about 50 percent of the fishes consumed in the country come from this region, thus having severe implications on food insecurity. Aside from the Niger Delta, Lagos, which is one of the largest cities in the world with an exponential population growth that rose from 5.3 million in 1991 to 16 million people in 2006 to 21.3 million in 2015, is equally threatened due to its low-lying terrain that is in most cases slightly above the sea level. As the sea level rises, millions of inhabitants and millions of dollars in assets in the city are constantly threatened by flood.

Decrying the severe human insecurity challenges that are necessitated by flooding in Nigeria, Damilola Ojetunde observes:

Earlier this year heavy rains and thunderstorms caused havoc in Benue state. The aftermath of the torrential rainfalls in Makurdi left close to 3,000 houses submerged and thousands of residents were rendered homeless and had to flee. Also in Lagos, Nigeria's economic nerve center and one of Africa's most populous cities. Residents woke up in many parts of the city to find their streets and homes flooded and their property, including cars and other valuables, submerged. Lagos and Benue states were not alone. Suleja, a town near the capital city Abuja, suffered its own flooding challenge in early July. Heavy rains washed houses away and caused others to collapse, trapping occupants. Thirteen people were said to have died. Other states that affected by flooding this year include Ekiti, Osun, Akwa Ibom, Kebbi, Niger, Kwara, Ebonyi, Enugu, Abia, Oyo, Plateau, Sokoto, Edo and Bayelsa. Some of the worst flooding in recent memory happened five years ago in March 2012 when 32 of Nigeria's 36 states were affected, 24 severely. More than 360 people were killed and almost two million people were displaced.[58]

The point is that an upsurge in flooding across the country is not only washing off crops and farms (fish farm inclusive) and destructing property and social infrastructure, but is also causing huge population displacement. Consequently, it forces people to abandon their ancestral homes and migrate to other places. Displacements naturally result in loss of job, increases in unemployment, reduction in agricultural production, injury, exposure to diseases (infectious and communicable), rape, violation of human rights, loss of privacy, loss of independence, poverty, hunger and loss of family members, closure of schools, loss of qualified teachers, incompletion of academic curriculum, etc. It was at the face of these security threats from climate change that the USAID, in a January 2010 report, notes:

> *Changes in climate may alter Nigeria's major ecological zones. Agricultural ecosystems, freshwater and coastal resources, forests, and biodiversity are all susceptible to impacts from climate changes. Such impacts include increases in soil erosion, flooding, desertification, and salt-water intrusion. Additionally, the country's coastal zone and low-lying islands in the Gulf of Guinea are vulnerable to sea level rise. An estimated 27 to 53 million people in the country may need to be relocated with a 0.5 meter increase in sea level. Nigeria's coastal and marine areas are also home to the country's economically important petroleum and fisheries industries. The country's transportation infrastructure, which is inadequate for current needs, will be further degraded by extreme weather, negatively impacting industry and commerce and placing greater stress on the economy.*[59]

Environmental Disasters and the Nigerian Response System

As already indicated, the Nigerian environment is vulnerable to a number of environmental disasters, such as drought, desertification, flooding, coastal erosion, soil erosion, change in precipitation, SLR, shrinking of water bodies, among others. Meanwhile, climate change as a threat multiplier impacts and escalates these disasters in both frequency and magnitude. The Nigerian state had been responding to the situation through the formulation of policies, regulations, establishment of institutional mechanisms, and operational activities aimed at addressing the problem vide disaster management. Disaster management naturally involves many organizations that work together in order to prevent, prepare for, respond to, and promote recovery from the effects of a disaster.

The National Disaster Response Plan (NDRP) is the policy guideline for disaster management in Nigeria. It establishes a process and structure for the systematic, coordinated, and effective delivery of federal assistance, to any major disaster or emergency declared by the president of the Federal Republic of Nigeria. It prepared to set forth fundamental policies, planning assumptions, concepts of operation, response and recovery, and also a description of the responsibilities of agencies and private sector organizations. The NDRP provides a focus for inter-agency and inter-governmental emergency preparedness, planning, training, exercising, coordination, and information exchange. The plan also indicates the scope of federal government response assistance that a state is most likely to require under the thirteen Support Service Areas (SSAs), which include transport, communication, public works and engineering, firefighting, information and planning, mass care, resource support, health and medical services, search and rescue, hazardous materials, food and water, and military/police support, each of which has a designated Primary Agency that acts as lead in the SSA.

Meanwhile, NEMA under its Establishment Act of 1999, as amended, is the official coordinating and lead agency in disaster management in the country. To this end, it executes a wide range of administrative, programmatic, and specialized tasks. According to the NDRP, its tasks include notification, activation, mobilization, deployment, staffing, and facility setup when and wherever there is incidence of disaster in the country. In line with this mandate, NEMA processes a state governor's request for assistance, coordinates federal operations under a disaster declaration, and appoints a Federal Coordinating Officer (FCO) for each state where disaster emergency has been declared. NEMA also provides support for logistics management; communications and information technology; financial management; community relations, public information, and other outreach; information collection, analysis, and dissemination.[60]

Disaster response activities under the NDRP include direction and control, early warning, evacuation, and emergency services. These are designed to address immediate and short-term effects of the onset of any disaster. It aimed at reducing the number of casualties and damage as well as to speed up recovery programs. The recovery includes both short- and long-term activities. While short-term operations seek to restore critical services to the community and provide for the basic needs of the public, long-term recovery focuses on restoring the community to its normal or improved state of affairs. Examples of recovery actions could be temporary housing and feeding, restoration of non-vital government services, and the reconstruction of damaged areas. Ultimately, the NDRP also specified the roles of every stakeholder in emergency disaster management in such an explicit way that their activities can be performed with very little supervision and thus allows for a smooth operation of disaster management.[61] In order to enhance emergency response times, the country under the NDRP was divided into six disaster management zones (see Table 3.2).

These NEMA zonal offices serve as the eyes and ears of NEMA in their respective zones and coordinate NEMA's disaster operations therein.

Despite these elaborate plans, it is regrettable to note that the system of disaster management in Nigeria is a disaster in itself. Experience over time has demonstrated that the conduct of the nation's disaster management bodies is a far cry from the provisions of such documents like the NDRP, National Disaster Management Framework (NDMF), and National Contingency Plan (NCP), among others, that were developed to ensure the effective and efficient handling of incidences of disaster around the country most especially in relation to emergency response.

Table 3.2 NEMA zonal offices and the states under each zone

Zone	Headquarters	States under the zone
North Central Zone	Jos Zonal Office	FCT, Niger, Plateau, Kogi, Benue, Kwara, and Nasarawa states
Northeast	Maiduguri Zonal Office	Borno, Yobe, Adamawa, Bauchi, Taraba, and Gombe states
Northwest	Kaduna Zonal Office	Sokoto, Kebbi, Katsina, Zamfara, Kano, Jigawa, and Kaduna states
Southeast Zone	Enugu Zonal Office	Enugu, Abia, Anambra, Imo, and Ebonyi states
South-South Zone	Port Harcourt Zonal Office	Akwa Ibom, Cross River State, Delta, Bayelsa, Rivers, and Edo states
Southwest	Lagos Zonal Office	Oyo, Ogun, Ekiti, Osun, Ondo, and Lagos states

Source: As compiled by the author

In terms of disaster/emergency response, the country's disaster management bodies hardly carry out quick responses to disaster emergencies. It often takes days (and in some cases weeks) before one witnesses any meaningful intervention to disaster situations, during which the situation may have moved from bad to worse and thus escalating the problem of population of displacement, forced migration, loss of property, spread of infections and diseases, injury, and death. There is also the added problem of rape, abduction, recruitment by insurgent and militant groups, as well as conflict between the migrants and their host community over available scarce resources. This was witnessed during the 2012 flood as well as the 2018 flood disaster. In each of these cases, especially in the former, it took quite some time before NEMA, SEMA, and LEMA responded to the plights of affected communities across the country.

There is also a noticeable inadequacy concerning the early warning system (EWS). Disaster management bodies in the country are not in the habit of providing adequate early warning information about impending disasters. Even when carried out, it is usually restricted to urban centers at the expense of rural communities where the majority of the country's population resides. Not minding the fact that urban centers are more resilient than their rural counterpart, when it comes to mitigating and adapting to the effects of these natural disasters. This is made worse by the non-existence of SEMA, LEMA, and CEMA in most parts of the country, which could have provided the early warnings. It was on this account that most communities affected by the flood lamented that they were not alerted on time, stating that the information got them at a time when the flood waters had already taken over their communities.

Although the NDRP defined and allocated functions during disaster situation to various stakeholders under the coordination and supervision of NEMA, there is, however, a significant absence of proper coordination and control among stakeholders working in the field during such operations. The situation naturally results in the duplication of functions, wastages, and inefficiency. Also, the absence of memorandum of understanding (MoU) between NEMA and other stakeholders is used to hamper the smooth activation of the various disaster response units (DRUs) as stipulated in the NDRP. This not only causes a delay in response time but makes it difficult for the situation to be arrested on time with minimal damage to the victims of disaster situations in the country.

Ironically, NEMA, the lead agency in disaster management in the country, is grossly underfunded. This makes it difficult for the body to efficiently discharge its statutory responsibilities. Again, emergency response stakeholders and bodies in the country lack an adequate supply of modern operational facilities needed for the job; such as search and rescue operations.

Concluding Remarks

Climate change and its associated extreme weather events are currently at the center of global discourse as its effects transcend national and international boundaries such that no part of the universe is free from its tenterhooks. This chapter examined the interface between climate change and insecurities in Nigeria. In doing so, it approached security from a human security perspective. On this note, it focused on the various ways climate change–induced extreme events and environmental disasters threaten the security of Nigeria's citizens. Findings made in the study suggest that the security consequences arising from climate change in the country will continue to escalate under a business-as-usual attitude from various levels of government, especially in the areas of conflict, food security, health, population displacement, source of livelihood, and so forth. Again, because of its large size and location, various climatic zones in the country manifest different but related multiplier environmental extreme events associated with climate change, which exposes individuals and communities to the security problem of fear and want in their daily lives. Although climate change does not fit into the traditional security challenges of the Nigerian state, its effects on the nation's well-being and quest for development are nonetheless a grievous one, if left unattended to or mismanaged.

What Is to Be Done

Recognizing the many manifestations of extreme climatic events and their impacts in Nigeria, especially as it concerns human security of the people, this chapter suggests that:

1. The problem of climate change has induced food insecurity in the country due to shifts in rain patterns and reduction in rainfall while a decrease in the planting season can be tackled through the modernization of the country's agricultural sector in such a manner that our farmers will change from

rain-fed agriculture to irrigation-driven agriculture. This way our farmers will be able to produce year-round, both during rainy and dry season, as they no longer have to depend on rainfall before they can plant their crops.
2. The eco-conflict between herders and farmers in the country demonstrates the reality of the climate change and resource control interface and its embedded security challenges. To manage this, careful natural resource governance and management in the country, in addition to the amendment of the Land Use Act, have the capacity of de-escalating this crisis.
3. Greater emphasis should be placed on reforestation as a way of checkmating rising temperatures and desertification. Again, the Nigerian state should take seriously the Great Green Wall project.
4. State institutions particularly those that have to do with climate and environmental-related issues such as the Ministry of Environment, Department of Climate Change, Ministry of Agriculture, NEMA, and NIMET should adjust and improve on their actions to environmental stressors.
5. In order to contain and mitigate the harsh effects of climate change–induced events such as drought, SLR, coastal and soil erosions, unpredictability of planting seasons, reduction in rainfall, and changes in temperature and precipitation, among others, there should be a radical transformation in our policy toward climate change in addition to the technology used in detecting, mapping, and checkmating it. The point here is that although public administration is by nature a gradual process of change, climate change is non-incremental in nature and has to be treated as such.
6. Policy responses and interventions to the threats of climate change stressors in the country should be based on long-term planning. This is to afford the system enough time to critically understand the nuances involved in environmental changes to adequately plan against it rather than addressing the manifestations of a particular extreme weather event that characterize short-term planning.
7. Our disaster and emergency management departments should be proactive rather than reactive in their operations. They should follow up such predictions with positive actions aimed at either preventing the occurrence of the event or enhancing the resilience of communities in place of the current business-as-usual attitude of words without swords that hardly achieve any meaningful results.
8. Experts with cognate knowledge in the area of modern scientific and technological innovations should be actively involved by government and nongovernmental organizations alike in the formulation and implementations of climate change–related policies. This is to ensure that governmental interventions and resources are duly directed to the fundamental source of the problem, instead of addressing their symptoms. A situation that is akin to mopping the wet floor beneath a leaking roof rather than amending the source of the leakage. For instance, every rainy season NIMET and NEMA habitually jostle Nigerians, especially those living along the banks of rivers Niger and Benue, of impending flood without assisting with proper urban planning including drainages and the channelization of rivers that are capable of mitigating the impacts of the heavy rain and flood, if and wherever they occur.

9. The nature of climate change–induced environmental disasters in Nigeria demands that the government, civil society organizations (CSOs), individuals, and communities must collaborate toward building proactive resilience measures.

Notes

1. Hodson, M. and Marvin, S. 2010. *World Cities and Climate Change: Producing Urban Ecological Security*. Berkshire: Open University Press/McGraw-Hill House.
2. WIRED. 2018. "What Is Climate Change? The Definition, Causes and Effects." Available from: http://www.wired.co.uk/article/what-is-climate-change-definition-causes-effects.
3. Okoye, Anthony. C. 2017. "Political Economy of Climate Change and Human Security in Nigeria." PhD diss., the Department of Political Science, University of Nigeria Nsukka.
4. Agbu, O. 2010. "Global Warming: An Overview and Implications for Nigeria." In *Climate Change and Human Security in Nigeria*, edited by O. Eze and O. Oche. Lagos: Nigerian Institute of International Affairs, 47–66.
5. Hodson and Marvin, *World Cities and Climate Change*, 44.
6. The World Bank. 2010. "Development and Climate Change: World Development Report 2010." Available from: http://documents.worldbank.org/curated/en/201001468159913657/pdf/530770WDR02010101Official0Use0Only1.pdf [accessed August 13, 2018]; United States Environmental Protection Agency. 2017. "International Climate Impacts." Available from: https://19january2017snapshot.epa.gov/climate-impacts/international-climate-impacts_.html [accessed June 5, 2018]; Justin Worland. 2016. "How Climate Change Unfairly Burdens Poorer Countries." Available from: http://time.com/4209510/climate-change-poor-countries/ [accessed November 12, 2017]; and UNDP. 2011. "Climate Change in Least Developed Countries." Available from: http://www.undp.org/content/dam/undp/library/corporate/fast-facts/english/FF-Climate-Change-in-Least-Developed-Countries.pdf [accessed September 4, 2018].
7. Agbu, "Global Warming," 47–66.
8. Raimi, L. and Jack Jackson TCB. 2017. "How Does Climate Change Pose Human Security Threats in the Niger Delta? Implications for Policy Makers." *Maiduguri Journal of Arts and Social Sciences* 14: 80–90.
9. The idea was borrowed from a 2015 documentary by the Shehu Musa Yar'dua Foundation titled "Nowhere to Run: Nigeria's Climate and Environmental Crisis."
10. NASA. 2018. "What's in a Name? Weather, Global Warming and Climate Change, 2018." Available from: https://climate.nasa.gov/resources/global-warming/ [accessed May 21, 2018].
11. Intergovernmental Panel on Climate Change (IPCC) 2007.
12. United Nations Framework Convention on Climate Change (UNFCCC), Solomon, S., Qin, D., Manning, M., Chen, Z., Marquis, M., Averyt, K. B., Tingor, M. and Miller, H. L. Climate Change 2007: The Physical Science Basis. Contribution of Working Group I to the Fourth Assessment Report of the Intergovernmental Panel on Climate Change, 2007. Cambridge: Cambridge University Press. (IPCC Report)

13. America's Climate Choices: Panel on Advancing the Science of Climate Change; National Research Council. 2010. *Advancing the Science of Climate Change*. Washington, DC: The National Academies Press.
14. National Research Council. 2012. "Climate Change, Evidence, Impacts and Choices: Answers to Common Questions about the Science of Climate Change." Available from: http://nas-sites.org/americasclimatechoices/files/2012/06/19014_cvtx_R1.pdf [accessed May 21, 2018].
15. Waugh, 1999, 236. cited in Ajaero, C. K., Akukwe, T. I. and Asuoha, G. C. 2010. "Climate Change: Concepts and Issues." In Conference Proceedings on Climate Change and the Nigerian Environment, edited by R. N. C. Anyadike, I. A. Madu and C. K. Ajaero, 1–17, held in Princess Alexandra Auditorium, University of Nigeria, Nsukka, 29th June–2nd July, 2009.
16. National Research Council, "Climate Change, Evidence, Impacts and Choices."
17. Kofi, Annan. 2000. "Secretary-General Salutes International Workshop on Human Security in Mongolia." Two-Day Session in Ulaanbaatar, May 8–10. Press Release SG/SM/7382. Available from: http://www.org/News/Press/docs/20000508.sgsm7382.html [accessed August 27, 2001]; Gómez, Oscar A. and Gasper, Des. "Human Security: A Thematic Guidance Note for Regional and National Human Development Report Teams." Available from: http://hdr.undp.org/sites/default/files/human_security_guidance_note_r-nhdrs.pdf [accessed July 12, 2018].
18. Gómez and Gasper, "Human Security."
19. Thakur, Ramesh. 1997. "From National to Human Security." In *Asia-Pacific Security: The Economics-Politics Nexus*, edited by Stuart Harris and Andrew Mack. Sydney: Allen & Unwin, 53–54.
20. Hubert, D. 1999. "Human Security: Safety for People in a Changing World." Presented at a Regional Conference on The Management of African Security in the 21st Century. Lagos: Nigerian Institute of International Affairs. 23–24 June.
21. United Nations Development Programme (UNDP). *Human Development Report 1994*. New York: Oxford University Press, 23; Ogata and Sen. 2003. "Women Environment and Development Programme, Gender, Climate Change and Human Security: Lessons from Bangladesh, Ghana and Senegal."
22. Omoyemen, O. E. 2010. "Climate Change and Human Security: A Gender Perspective." In *Climate Change and Human Security in Nigeria*, edited by O. C. Eze and O. Oche. Lagos: Nigeria Institute of International Affairs.
23. Oche, O. 2010. "Security, Globalization and Climate Change: A Conceptual Analysis." In *Climate Change and Human Security in Nigeria*, edited by O. C. Eze and O. Oche. Lagos: Nigeria Institute of International Affairs.
24. United Nations. 2016. "Human Security Handbook: An Integrated Approach for the Realization of the Sustainable Development Goals and the Priority Areas of the International Community and the United Nations System." Available from: https://www.un.org/humansecurity/wp-content/uploads/2017/10/h2.pdf [accessed December 7, 2018].
25. Population of Nigeria. Available from: http://worldpopulationreview.com/countries/ [accessed December 7, 2018].
26. USAID. 2013. "Nigeria Climate Vulnerability Programme," January. Available from: https://www.climatelinks.org/sites/default/files/asset/document/nigeria_climate_vulnerability_profile_jan2013.pdf.
27. Nnodim, O. 2016. "Nigeria Highly Vulnerable to Climate Change—NIMET." *PUNCH*, December 12. Available from: http://punchng.com/nigeria-highly-vulnerable-climate-change-nimet/

28. Usman, Y. D. and Dije, B. I. 2013. "Potential Challenges of Climate Change to the Nigeria Economy." *Journal of Environmental Science, Toxicology and Food Technology* 6, no. 2: 7–12. Available from: www.Iosrjournals.org.
29. Oche, "Security, Globalization and Climate Change."
30. United Nations, "Human Security Handbook."
31. The World Bank n.d. "Climate Change Knowledge Portal for Development Practitioners and Policy Makers: Nigeria Dashboard Natural Hazards." Available from: http://sdwebx.worldbank.org/climateportal/countryprofile/home.cfm?page=country_profile&CCode=NGA&ThisTab=NaturalHazards [accessed August 12, 2018]; Oladipo, Emmanuel. 2010. "Towards Enhancing the Adaptive Capacity of Nigeria: A Review of the Country's State of Preparedness for Climate Change Adapatation [sic]" Report submitted to Heinrich Böll Foundation Nigeria; Federal Ministry of Environment Abuja, Nigeria (Special climate change unit). 2010. "National Environmental, Economic and Development Study (needs) for Climate Change in Nigeria." (Final Draft) September. Available from: http://unfccc.int/files/adaptation/application/pdf/nigerianeeds.pdf [accessed August 13, 2018]; and Emodi Nnaemeka Vincent. "Climate Change in the Nigerian Context" Presentation at the APEC Climate Center, 12, Centum 7-ro, Haeundae-gu Busan 48058, Republic of Korea. Available from: http://www.researchgate.net/profile/Nnaemeka_Emodi/publication/280774425_CLIMATE_CHANGE_IN_THE_NIGERIAN_CONTEXT/links/55c5b41908aeca747d6190fd/CLIMATE-CHANGE-IN-THE-NIGERIAN-CONTEXT [accessed June 11, 2018].
32. Ezirim, G. E. and Onuoha, F. C. 2008. "Climate Change and National Security: Exploring the Theoretical and Empirical Connections in Nigeria." *Journal of International Politics and Development Studies* 4, no. 1&2: 89–108.
33. Usigbe, Leon. 2018. "Buhari Decries Negative Effects of Climate Change." *Nigerian Tribune*. Available from: https://www.tribuneonlineng.com/169698/ [accessed December 14, 2018].
34. Rakiya, A. M. 2008. "Nigeria: Stemming the Impacts of Climate Change." *Daily Trust*, distributed by all Africa Global Media. Available from: http://allafrica.com.
35. Owete, F., Okakwu, E., Ugbede, L. and Iroanusi, Q. E. 2018. "Nigeria: Buhari's Ministers' Scorecard after Two Years (Concluding Part)." *Premium Times*, January 5. Available from: https://www.premiumtimesng.com/news/headlines/254503-analysis-buharis-ministers-scorecard-two-years-concluding-part.html [accessed August 15, 2018]; Okeke, C. 2017. "Frontline States: Concern over Deepening Desertification Despite Relocation." Available from: https://leadership.ng/2017/10/31/frontline-states-concern-deepening-desertification-despite-relocation/; Okeke, C. 2016. "Issues as Desert Encroachment Takes Toll on Nigerian Landmass." Latest Nigerian News. Available from: https://www.latestnigeriannews.com/news/3652017/issues-as-desert-encroachment-takes-toll-on-nigerian-landmass.html [accessedAugust 15, 2018].
36. Combating Desertification in Nigeria. 2016. Available from: http://ggwnigeria.gov.ng/tag/frontline-states/.
37. Rakiya, "Nigeria."
38. Odogwu, G. 2016. "Nimet's 2016 Seasonal Rainfall Prediction." *PUNCH*. Available from: https://punchng.com/nimets-2016-seasonal-rainfall-prediction/ [accessed September 21, 2017]; Adelekan, I. O. and Adegebo, B. O. 2014. "Variation in Onset and Cessation of the Rainy Season in Ibadan, Nigeria." *Journal of Science Research* 13: 13–21; Sawa, B. A., Adebayo, A. A. and Bwala, A. A. 2014. "Dynamics of Hydrological Growing Season at Kano as Evidence of Climate Change." *Asian*

Journal of Agricultural Sciences 6, no. 2: 75–78; Variation in Onset and Cessation of the Rainy Season in Ibadan, Nigeria; Muhammad, Rakiya A. 2008. "Nigeria: Stemming the Impact of Climate Change." Available from: https://allafrica.com/stories/200807211032.html [accessed August 15, 2018].

39. Audu, E. B., Audu, H. O., Binbol, N. L. and Gana J. N. 2013. "Climate Change and Its Implication on Agriculture in Nigeria, Abuja." *Journal of Geography and Development* 3, no. 2 (September): 8–19. https://pdfs.semanticscholar.org/edbf/7ea74362b2922dd8c753c35c1d1e02673306.pdf
40. Ojetunde, D. 2017. "How Climate Change Is Fueling Conflicts in Nigeria." *International Centre For Investigative Reporting.* Available from: https://www.icirnigeria.org/how-climate-change-is-fueling-conflicts-in-nigeria/.
41. Audu, et al., "Climate Change and Its Implication on Agriculture in Nigeria, Abuja."
42. Department of Climate Change, Climate Smart Agriculture, 2015. Available from: http://climatechange.gov.ng/climate-smart-agriculture/
43. Federal Ministry of Environment (Special Climate Change Unit). 2010. National environmental, economic and development study (NEEDS) for climate change in Nigeria, 24–25.
44. Audu, H. O., Balogun, R. B., Nwoga, R. C., Kalejaiye-Matti, R. B., Amadi, G. and Audu, E. B., 2010. "Climate Change: Causes, Implications and Mitigation Strategies." In national conference proceedings on *Climate Change Impact and Adaptation: Is Nigeria Ready?* Published by the Nigerian Meteorological Society.
45. Akingbade, T. 2010. "Climate Change Effects in Nigeria: Heat, Dust, Weather Raise Health Concerns." *The Guardian Newspaper*, October 3.
46. Oguamanam, C. 2016. "Nigeria Faces New Security Threat Fuelled by Climate Change and Ethnicity." *The Conversation.* Available from: http://theconversation.com/nigeria-faces-new-security-threat-fuelled-by-climate-change-and-ethnicity-58807
47. Okoye, Anthony C. "*Victims, Not Perpetrators: Boko Haram Insurgency and the Juvenisation of Suicide Bombing in Nigeria*" Paper presented at the 31th annual conference of the Nigeria Political Science Association (NPSA), held at the Ebonyi State University, Abakaliki, March 26–29, 2018.
48. Obi, N. I. and Okekeogbu, C. J. 2017. "Erosion Problems and Their Impacts in Anambra State of Nigeria: A Case of Nanka Community." *International Journal of Environment and Pollution Research* 5, no. 1: 24–37.
49. Ibid., 24–37.
50. World Bank, 2013. "Combating Erosion in Nigeria: New Project Spells Hope in Seven States." Available from: http://www.worldbank.org/en/news/feature/2013/11/26/combating-erosion-in-nigeria-new-project-spells-hope-in-seven-states.
51. Premium Times, 2018. "Over 2,800 Active Erosion Sites in South-East Nigeria—Group." Available from: https://www.premiumtimesng.com/regional/ssouth-east/274938-over-2800-active-erosion-sites-in-south-east-nigeria-group.html [accessed December 8, 2018].
52. Ibid.
53. Ezirim G. E. 2008. "Petropolitics and Environmental Criminality in the Niger Delta: Advocacy for Enforcement of Global Convention." *University of Nigeria Journal of Political Economy* 2, no. 1&2.
54. Ayodele, I. 2016. "Confronting Climate Change Doom in Lagos." *Guardian.* Available from: https://guardian.ng/features/science/confronting-climate-change-doom-in-lagos/ [accessed July 9, 2018].

55. Federal Government of Nigeria. 2013. "NIGERIA Post-Disaster Needs Assessment 2012 Floods." A report by The Federal Government of Nigeria with Technical Support from the World Bank, EU, UN, and Other Partners; Niyi (2013). 7 million Nigerians displaced by flood—NEMA. Available from: http://www.informationng.com/2013/09/7-million-nigerians-displaced-by-flood-nema.html [accessed July 30, 2018]; Atake, C. E. 2016. "Sea Level Rise in Coastal Areas of Nigeria?" Voices of Youth. Available from: http://m.voicesofyouth.org/en/posts/sea-level-rise-in-coastal-areas-of-nigeria.
56. Nigeria flood. 2018. Acaps, Briefing Note—21 September 2018. Available from: https://reliefweb.int/sites/reliefweb.int/files/resources/20180921_acaps_briefing_note_floods_in_nigeria_0.pdf [accessed November 12, 2018].
57. Ibid.
58. Niyi, 2013. Ibid.
59. USAID. 2013. "Nigeria Climate Vulnerability Profile." Available from: https://www.climatelinks.org/resources/nigeria-climate-vulnerability-profile.
60. NEMA. 2013. "The National Disaster Response Plan." [NDRP] p. 15. Available from: http://nema.gov.ng/the-national-disaster-response-plan/[accessed November 24, 2018].
61. Ibid.

Chapter 4

SMALL ARMS PROLIFERATION

Freedom Chukwudi Onuoha and Gerald Ekenedirichukwu Ezirim

Introduction

Nigeria in recent decades has witnessed an unprecedented increase in security challenges that undermine peace, stability, and development at community, state, and national levels. Violent conflicts such as the Boko Haram insurgency in the northeast, militancy in the Niger Delta, and escalating clashes between herders and farming communities across the country have seriously impacted governance, the economy, and the society at large. In addition, violent crimes like kidnapping, cultism, piracy, armed robbery, cattle rustling, and banditry, among others, have equally assumed a worrisome dimension. A common factor underlying the violent nature of multiple security challenges currently confronting Nigeria is the proliferation of small arms and light weapons (SALWs).

The media in Nigeria is awash with frightening reports of sophisticated SALWs seized by security operatives almost on a daily basis. It was reported that a total of 21,548,608 arms and ammunition were smuggled into Nigeria at the close of 2017.[1] Consequently, SALWs proliferation has become a pressing security concern in Nigeria for citizens and government alike. The concern is driven by three interrelated issues: the ease of penetration of these lethal weapons into the country through legal and illegal routes; the frequency of their use by non-state actors or parties to conflicts; and the level of deprivation, destruction, and death that are associated with their use.[2,3] Thus, Nigeria's *National Security Strategy* recognizes that "the threat posed by the proliferation of SALWs are of such significance that a security strategy that contemplates the herculean task of monitoring the manufacture, flow and use of the SALW is required."[4] However, what is often overlooked in the discourses on SALWs proliferation is how factors that are largely internal to Nigeria, particularly the crude nature of Nigeria politics, underpin this pressing national security threat.

This chapter, therefore, examines the phenomenon of SALWs proliferation, with a view to highlighting its attendant consequences for human security and proffering recommendations for checking the spread. It pursues this objective by interrogating the nature of arms trafficking in Nigeria and how it is implicated in the persistence and escalation in frequency and intensity of violence in Nigeria. The chapter is divided into seven parts. Following this introduction, section two contains a brief clarification of key concepts while section three presents an overview of arms proliferation in Nigeria. Section four takes a look at the nature of arms trafficking that feeds into SALWs proliferation, highlighting the dimensions, levels, and methods prevalent in Nigeria. Section five examines the varying factors contributing to SALWs proliferation in Nigeria, followed by a discussion on the effects of SALWs proliferation on human security in section six. The last section contains concluding reflections and recommendations.

Conceptual Clarification

Concern over "SALWs proliferation" is ubiquitous in media, academic, policy, and security circles given the impact of these instruments of death in different conflict scenes around the globe. For all the attention that the concept has received, there is the absence of a clear and universally accepted definition. To better comprehend what constitutes to SALWs proliferation, it is logical to explain what are SALWs. The term "SALW" has been defined in different ways by various authors, instruments, organizations, and states. While there is no universally accepted definition of a small arm or light weapon, portability is considered as an essential criterion.

An often-cited definition of SALWs is one provided by the UN Panel of Governmental Experts on Small Arms,[5] which includes, among others, small arms revolvers and self-loading pistols, rifles and carbines, sub-machine guns, assault rifles, and light machine guns. Light weapons include heavy machine guns, hand-held under-barrel and mounted grenade launchers, portable anti-aircraft guns, portable anti-tank guns, recoilless rifles (sometimes mounted), portable launchers of antiaircraft missile systems (sometimes mounted), and mortars of caliber less than 100 mm. Ammunition and explosives include cartridges (rounds) for small arms, shells and missiles for light weapons, mobile containers with missiles or shells for single-action antiaircraft and anti-tank systems, anti-personnel and anti-tank hand grenades, landmines, and explosives.

Given the above understanding of SALWs, Alex Ekemenah defines SALWs proliferation as the illegal acquisition and circulation of arms and ammunitions of different types (usually small, light, and medium) and from one degree to another (at the local, state, or national scale).[6] For the purposes of this chapter, SALWs proliferation is defined as a situation of rapid and excessive increase in the ease of illicit acquisition, transfer, circulation, storage, and use of arms and weapons by individuals and groups within a geographic space with destabilizing effects on peace, security, stability, and development. At the center of SALWs proliferation is the portability of these objects, making it possible for them to be easily acquired, transferred, concealed, maintained, stored, and deployed by users. For this reason, it can be transferred easily from one individual or group to another or transported from one location to the other with very little chances of being detected. These qualities have therefore made SALWs an instrument of choice by militants, insurgents, and other criminal groups that challenge the capacity of the state to govern.

As with the idea of SALWs proliferation, there is no universally agreed definition of the term "human security." Caroline Thomas, for instance, defines human security as a "condition of existence in which basic material needs are met and in which human dignity, including meaningful participation in the life of the community, can be realized."[7] In a similar vein, Don Hubert conceives of human security as the safety of people from both violent and non-violent threat.[8] It is a condition or state of being, characterized by freedom from pervasive threats to people's rights, their safety, or even their lives. A human security perspective, according to him, asserts that the security of the state is not an end in itself. Rather, it is a means of ensuring the security of people. In this sense, state security and human security are mutually reinforcing and supportive.

The specific term "human security" was first officially introduced by the United Nations Development Programme (UNDP) in its Human Development Report of 1994. The report identified two main aspects of human security: safety from chronic threats such as hunger, disease, and repression, and protection from sudden disruptions in the pattern of daily life, whether in homes, jobs, or communities. It captured seven dimensions of the human security concept: economic security, food security, health security, environmental security, personal security, community security, and political security.[9]

Human security is therefore defined here as freedom from actual and potential threats to human life that may arise either as a result of human actions or inactions, or from natural disaster such as flood, earthquake, famine, drought, disease, and other natural calamitous events resulting in death, human suffering, and material damage. The emphasis on human security derives essentially from three fundamental convictions, namely, the sanctity and inviolability of human life, the universality and dignity of human rights, and the existential imperatives of and value for individual safety in a world full of multifarious threats. Human security is therefore rooted in three core human values: self-preservation, self-extension, and self-fulfillment. The fact that SALWs proliferation denies people or communities of their entitlement to these core values is a major concern globally.

Overview of Small Arms and Light Weapons Proliferation in Nigeria

The exact period or genesis of SALWs proliferation in Nigeria is difficult to ascertain. However, most studies explain the growth in illicit possession and use of SALWs as an aftermath of the Nigerian Civil War (1967–1970) arising from the failure of the government to conduct a comprehensive arms collection program.[10] Over time, the dynamics of international politics such as Cold War rivalry, the outbreak of violent intra-state conflicts in West Africa typified by the Liberia and Sierra Leone civil wars in the 1990s, and the nature of domestic politics in Nigeria have contributed to heightened proliferation of SALWs. As a result, SALWs proliferation increasingly has become a subject of serious concern in any discussion on public safety and security in Nigeria.

There are laws regulating the possession of firearms in Nigeria such as the Nigerian Firearms Act 1999 as well as the Robbery and Firearms (Special Provisions) Act 2004. At the sub-regional, continental, and international levels, several instruments have been adopted to curb the proliferation of SALWs. Some of these instruments include the *ECOWAS Convention on Small Arms and Light Weapons: Their Ammunition and Other Related Materials (2006)*; the *Bamako Declaration on the Common African Position on the Proliferation, Circulation and Illicit Trade in Small Arms and Light Weapons (2000)*; and the *Arms and Trade Treaty (ATT)* that entered into force on December 24, 2014. Despite the existence of these instruments, Africa in general and Nigeria in particular figure prominently in the global map of places with high circulation of SALWs.

Experts estimate that the total number of small weapons held around the world is at least 875 million, of which about 650 million are in civilian hands.[11] There are more than 1,000 companies in about 100 countries involved in some aspect of small arms production, with significant producers in around thirty countries.[12] Conservative estimates mention 7.5 to 8 million small arms being produced per year.[13] Yet the trade of SALWs is the least transparent of all weapon systems. Indeed, according to the *Small Arms Survey*, "more is known about the number of nuclear warheads, stocks of chemical weapons and transfers of major conventional weapons than about small arms."[14]

It is estimated that out of approximately 500 million illicit weapons in circulation worldwide in 2004, about 100 million were in sub-Saharan Africa, with 8 to 10 million concentrated in the West African sub-region.[15] Nigeria features prominently in the three-spot continuum of transnational organized trafficking of SALWs in West Africa: origin, transit route, and destination. Weapons in circulation in Nigeria come from local fabricants, residue of guns used during the civil war, thefts from government armories, organized cross-border smuggling, dishonest government-accredited importers, militias, insurgents, and some multinational oil corporations operating in the Niger Delta.[16]

The high rate of SALWs proliferation in Nigeria is indexed by the intermittent seizure of various types, sizes, and calibers of arms by security and border control officers, the frequency of their deployment in conflict and crime scenes, and the level of human casualty and material damage recorded in the aftermath of their use in Nigeria. For instance, the large quantity of sophisticated arms and ammunition surrendered by Niger Delta militants in the amnesty program in 2009 shows the alarming level of loose weapons in the country and the grave implications for security and development in Nigeria. The Amnesty initiative saw over 15,000 militants surrender arms at the expiration of the disarmament and demobilization phase of the Amnesty. Weapons recovered during the disarmament process included 2,760 assorted guns, 287,445 ammunitions of different caliber, 18 gun-boats, 763 dynamites, 1,090 dynamite caps, 3,155 magazines, and several other military accessories, such as dynamite cables, bullet-proof jackets, and jack-knives.[17] It is widely believed that militants only surrendered a small fraction of their arms.

With the escalation of violent intra-state conflicts in some African countries, especially in Libya and Mali, observers believe that the level of SALWs proliferation has increased significantly in West Africa with destabilizing consequences for Nigeria. In 2016, the United Nations Regional Centre for Peace and Disarmament in Africa (UNREC) posited that out of an estimated 500 million SALWs circulating in West Africa, no less than 350 million or 70 percent of them are circulating in Nigeria.[18] Some observers dismissed it as sounding alarmist and lacking in accuracy, given that it is difficult to ascertain the number of weapons smuggled in or out of Nigeria, or even to determine the quantity being illicitly produced locally through artisanal fabrications.

Notwithstanding, there is hardly any state in Nigeria where security forces have not uncovered or seized huge cache of arms and weapons in recent times, underscoring the speed and scale with which the gravity of the threat has evolved. The regular interception of illegal arms trafficking by security agencies reveals the worrisome dimension arms proliferation has recently assumed in the country. Two recent revelations by security chiefs in Nigeria will suffice at this point. In May 2017, for instance, Nigeria's inspector general of police disclosed that some 4,000 illegal firearms were recovered by the police across the country in just three months.[19] Similarly, the Customs Service chief revealed that about 2,201 weapons of different sizes and caliber of weapons were seized by customs officials in Lagos port in the first nine months of 2017.[20] Hence, breaking the chain of influx and circulation of SALWs has remained a major challenge to the government.

Understanding Small Arms and Light Weapons Proliferation and Trafficking in Nigeria

SALWs proliferation in Nigeria is integrally related to the issue of arms trafficking. A closer scrutiny of cases of discovery and seizures of SALWs in recent years in Nigeria reveals that arms trafficking has assumed different dimensions, operates at multiple levels, and involves diverse methods. It is important to examine the nature and distinctions between these dimensions, levels, and methods of arms trafficking that underpin SALWs proliferation.

In terms of the dimension of arms trafficking, there are two broad forms, namely, transnational or international and national or domestic trafficking. Transnational or international trafficking refers to the movement of arms and weapons across borders of sovereign states. Investigations into illegal arms importation in Nigeria in the last few years point to China, India, Iran, Pakistan, and Russia as mainly the countries of provenance or origin of these arms, while Benin, Cameroon, Chad, Equatorial Guinea, Gabon, Greece, Niger, Spain, and Turkey, among others, have served as the transit or transshipment trade routes. Thus, the international component of arms trafficking—actors, networks, and trade routes—shows that the issue is a shared burden, not just a Nigerian responsibility. In contrast, national or domestic trafficking refers to the illicit movement or smuggling of arms from one location to another within the boundary or territory of sovereign states—in this case, Nigeria. While international or transnational trafficking involves the crossing of international borders, national or domestic transportation is confined to the territory of one country.

Regarding levels of trafficking, it could be divided into three broad practice categories: macro, meso, and micro. Macro-level trafficking is concealment and transfer operations carried out in a large scale, using large means of transportation such as ship, train, and aircraft to carry huge quantities of arms, weapons, and ammunitions from one location to another. Sophisticated cartels or arms brokers involved in the illicit global arms trade are mainly behind this category of trafficking. The cartels' weapons of choice are pump action rifles, high-caliber rifles, as well as AR-15 and AK-47-type semi-automatic rifles, which can be easily dismantled and reassembled. Most, but not all international or transnational trafficking takes place at the macro level. Meso-trafficking happens on an intermediate scale, involving concealment and transportation of significant quantities of arms, weapons, and ammunitions from one location to another using smaller means of transportation such as tankers, trucks, and speed boats. This form of trafficking often operates at the level of national or domestic trafficking, usually involving long-distance transportation. Organized arms dealers with access to corrupt state officials as well as militant and insurgent groups are usually behind the meso level of trafficking. Micro-trafficking is the lowest level in the trafficking chain. It involves the movement of small quantities of SALWs and ammunitions from one location to another by an individual or fewer individuals. It may or may not require the use of smaller conveyances such as cars, boats, tricycles, and motorcycles. Criminal gangs involved in kidnapping, sea piracy, armed robbery, cattle rustling, and cultism, among others, often engage in this level of trafficking.

Individuals or groups behind SALWs trafficking in Nigeria adopt various ways to move them from one location to another to avoid detection, using containerizing, compartmenting, loading, stuffing, tunneling, and lapping methods. In the *containerizing* method, traffickers conceal SALWs and/or ammunition in legitimate goods that will be packed in containers for transfer. This method derives from containerization, which is a system of standardized transport that uses a common size of steel container to transport goods.[21] These containers can easily be transferred between different modes of transport—aircraft or container ships to lorries and trains. The *compartmenting* method involves constructing a false base or hidden chambers (compartments) in a vehicle—trucks, lorries, buses, and cars—where SALWs or ammunitions could be concealed to evade detection by security agents. In the *loading* method, traffickers conceal the arms by wrapping them with materials (polythene bags) and stacked into empty fuel, water, or sewage tankers for long-distance transfer. It offers the advantage of easy handling and generates less suspicion during haulage. The distinction between compartmenting and loading lies in the fact that the hold where these arms are hidden is not part of the original design of the vehicle. The *tunneling* method involves the digging of passageways underground for the purposes of undetected transfer of SALWs and ammunition from one spot to another. The *tunneling* method, though tedious, allows for the trafficking of arms from one house, storage depot, and bunker to another.

Another method that remains pervasive in the trafficking of arms within Nigeria is the *stuffing* method, which involves the practice of planting SALWs or ammunitions in bags, cartons, or other forms of packaging products that are often loaded on private or commercial vehicles, boats, or canoes. There is equally the *lapping* method. Lapping entails the tactics of enfolding or concealing SALWs or ammunition on the body of the courier (humans or animals) using veils or other material attachments to minimize the risk of detection. Such weapons could be hidden on any part of the body, carried in a backpack or strapped at the back so that women appear to be carrying babies, to evade detection. Lapping is the easiest and least sophisticated method of concealing and transporting weapons within a short distance. Although data in Table 4.1 are not exhaustive, they reveal some examples of the dimensions, levels, and methods of trafficking in Nigeria.

The data reveal that Nigeria's sea ports have been used by cartels to traffic weapons by declaring containers as household goods or construction material to evade detection. Insurgents such as the Boko Haram have used tunneling to move weapons inside the city of Maiduguri. In addition, conveyances of different types and people of different gender have equally been employed to traffic arms within and across Nigeria. This brings to the fore the need to examine some of the factors that contribute to SALWs proliferation in Nigeria.

Factors Contributing to Small Arms and Light Weapons Proliferation in Nigeria

Several generic factors contribute to the circulation of SALWs around the world, particularly in Africa. First, SALWs are used in close range combat and irregular fighting; second, they are cheaper and can be easily bargained; third, SALWs can be easily dismantled and concealed while in transit; fourth, they require little logistical support, training, and maintenance; fifth, increase in intra-state conflicts and violent crimes, especially in developing countries, has fueled their demand; and sixth, they are miniaturized, thereby making it easy to use by individuals, including child soldiers.[22] In relation to Nigeria, however, the problem is associated with the interplay of varying factors. The proliferation of SALWs derives principally from factors that are largely internal to Nigeria but exacerbated by external forces like the outbreak of the Libyan uprising and globalization.

The crude nature of Nigerian politics, especially since the return to democratic politics in 1999, is the principal factor behind SALWs proliferation. The stake in Nigerian politics is incredibly high given the enormous benefits that go with occupying elective and appointive offices as well as the dangers of losing state power. This is evident in the highly corrupt and monetized nature of the electoral process in Nigeria due to the desperation of politicians to win elective positions,

Table 4.1 Some examples of Small Arms and Light Weapons trafficking dynamics in Nigeria

Date	Location	Incident	Dimension	Level	Method
January 30, 2017	Apapa Port (Lagos State)	Interception by custom officers of 40-foot container filled with 661 pump-action rifles. The manifest of the container shipped from China *enroute* Turkey falsely declared its contents as steel doors and other merchandise goods	Transnational	Macro	Containerizing
May 31, 2018	Igbogila-Ilara (Ogun State)	Interception by military officers of about 300,000 cartridges concealed in a false base of three heavy-duty trucks that were smuggled into Nigeria through Benin Republic border	International	Meso	Compartmenting
July 12, 2013	Kebbi State	Soldiers impounded a petrol tanker loaded with three AK-47 rifles, one rocket propelled grenade, nine AK-47 magazines, two bombs, three RPG chargers, and 790 rounds of 7.62 mm of special ammunitions	National	Meso	Loading
November 16, 2010	Dabar Masara (Borno State)	Interception by the police of a woman with ten AK-47 rifles and nine rounds of ammunition concealed in four bags of maize. They were ferried into Nigeria from Mederina in the Republic of Chad through Kofia in Cameroon Republic	Transnational	Micro	Stuffing
July 8, 2013	Maiduguri (Borno State)	Discovery by security forces of vast network of underground tunnels connecting houses and many bunkers used by Boko Haram for trafficking SALWs. Some of the tunnels can accommodate over 100 persons	National	Micro	Tunneling
December 18, 2017	Egbeda area (Lagos State)	Arrest by police of a disabled beggar in possession of a gun. More guns were later recovered from his house. He was suspected of trafficking or keeping arms for some armed robbers	National	Micro	Lapping

Source: Authors' compilation

an approach that leaves no room for fair political competition.[23] Hence, politics in Nigeria, especially electoral politics, are approached by politicians as warfare. This violent brand of politics finds its strongest expression in the assertion of President Olusegun Obasanjo. Prior to the 2007 general elections, the then president unabashedly told members of the Peoples Democratic Party (PDP): "This election is a do-or-die affair for me and the PDP. This coming election is a matter of life and death for the PDP and Nigeria."[24]

As a result, many politicians resort to the recruitment and arming of *specialists of violence*—militias, cultists, gangs, and thugs—to gain and retain political power.[25] Often, the youths or militias who were armed by politicians are abandoned by their sponsors after the election. The practice of arming youths, mainly unemployed, for electoral violence and subsequently dumping them after elections is a well-established electioneering habit of most Nigerian politicians.[26] With no visible means of legitimate livelihood and frustrated over their fate in the aftermath of the elections, some of these youths have evolved into sophisticated criminal gangs or have fallen prey to extremist ideology propagated by groups such as Boko Haram. During a deliberation at the parliament on the proliferation of SALWs and violence in Nigeria, Senator Shehu Sani blamed Nigerian politicians of being responsible for the terrible situation. As he puts it:

> *It is not possible for our security agencies to bring an end to the violence, killings, bloodshed, and proliferation of arms in this country as long as the political class includes violence as part of their political strategy to retain political power or to assume political power. We are becoming an AK-47 nation. People are killed every day and our country is becoming a failed state.*[27]

This situation goes a long way to explain the logic and attendant consequences of Nigeria's brand of politics: highly monetized politics begets SALWs proliferation, which in turn begets blood spilling in politics. The violent politics inevitably become a recipe for governance, if not state failure in Nigeria.

Governance failure in turn adds another dimension to SALWs proliferation. The term "governance" encompasses not only how state institutions and structures are managed but also the processes of decision-making and policy formulation, the capacity to execute these policies, resource allocation, information flow, and the efficiency of officials.[28] Governance failure therefore entails progressive decline in the capacity of state actors and institutions to use public resources to ensure the delivery of public goods necessary for the advancement of human security and development. It manifests in the inability of the Nigerian state to provide public goods, not the least security.

In recent years, the Nigerian state has failed to provide public safety and security. As a result, its monopoly over the use of violence is increasingly up for grabs by all sorts of armed non-state actors. The consequence of failure of public security is the intermittent outbreak of violent conflicts in recent times, forcing communities to indulge in different forms of "self-help" security measures, ranging from the formation of vigilante groups to community-owned arms stockpiling for offensive and reprisal attacks. Having lost confidence in the Nigerian state, parties to some of these conflicts have become entangled in a security dilemma. The quest to procure more arms to guarantee personal and community safety is fueling the "domestic arms race." The outbreak and persistence of the Boko Haram insurgency have further exacerbated the situation.

This unfortunate situation in turn stokes the demand for more arms by both the government and non-state actors (individuals, groups, communities, among others) to maintain security. While the government increases its stock through importation and local manufacturing at the Defence Industry Corporation of Nigeria (DICON), non-state actors patronize transnational traffickers and unregulated local or artisanal arms manufactures. Local factories producing SALWs and ammunition are therefore adding to the proliferation challenge. In September 2017, for instance, the police uncovered an arms fabrication outfit in Zuba, Abuja, and subsequently arrested three suspects behind the illicit business of fabricating and selling firearms to criminals.[29] Many such fabrication outfits have been discovered in most states in Nigeria, including Abia, Anambra, Ebonyi, Edo, Enugu, Delta, Benue, Kwara, Nasarawa, Niger, and Plateau. Hunters, armed robbers, cultists, cattle rustlers, and kidnappers, among other criminal gangs, patronize these local fabrication outfits. Despite the prevalence and contributions of artisanal arms fabricators to SALWs proliferation in Nigeria, very little attempt has been made to interface with them in order to better monitor and regulate their activities.[30]

Another relevant factor in SALWs proliferation in Nigeria is ineffective stockpile management, particularly due to widespread corruption. Poor accountability and weak audit mechanisms have ensured the pilfering and diversion of arms from military and police armories in Nigeria. For example, a major and five other soldiers of the Nigerian Army were convicted in November 2008 of selling over 7,000 arms (valued at over N100 million) to the Niger Delta militants. These arms were stolen from the depots of the Nigerian Army at the Command and Staff College, Jaji, and the One Base Ordnance, Kaduna.[31]

The influence of corruption is not only evident in weak stockpile management; it also manifests in the activities of some unscrupulous security and government officials who assist cross-border arms trafficking in Nigeria. The confession of Mamudu Hassan, one of the suspects being prosecuted for unlawful importation of 661 sophisticated pump action rifles into Nigeria in December 2017, is quite revealing:

> *I gave ₦1 million to facilitate the moving of the container out of port .... The examiners were given ₦200,000; C.I.O. ₦100,000; Enforcement ₦200,000; Police, SSS—between ₦20,000, ₦25,000, and ₦30,000; the two gates—₦200,000; Exit gate, ₦20,000, and final gate ₦50,000.*[32]

Criminals such as Hassan have been able to bribe unscrupulous security and law enforcement officials in order to smuggle arms and ammunition into Nigeria. For every successful illicit importation of weapons through official entry points in Nigeria, there are inevitably state officials involved, facilitating their operations or looking the other way. The connivance and complicity of state officials contribute to the success of weapon importation through recognized state borders.

Another factor remains significant in SALWs proliferation in Nigeria. It is the porosity of Nigeria's land, sea, and air borders. Nigeria shares international borders with Cameroon, Niger, Benin, and Chad. Parts of its southern borders adjoin the Atlantic Ocean. However, most of the land border areas are either mountainous or in the jungle. Irrespective of the geographic nature of the nation's borders, porosity is a common feature of them all. Nigeria's former Minister of Interior Abba Moro disclosed that there are over 1,499 illegal and 84 legal entry routes into Nigeria.[33] Traffickers and non-state armed groups take advantage of this porous land, air, and sea routes to smuggle SALWs into Nigeria.

At the northeastern border with Cameroon, illicit weapons meant for Boko Haram fighters are routinely seized by the military. Cross-border arms trafficking in the northeast has increased in the wake of the Libyan uprising. Libyan arms first obtained by AQIM have been transferred to non-state armed groups such as Boko Haram, emboldening and enabling them to mount more deadly and audacious attacks.[34] Trafficking through Nigeria's poorly patrolled maritime borders adds to the problem. In the Niger Delta region, for instance, criminal and militant groups traded crude oil for sophisticated arms and ammunition around sea edges.[35]

As well as overland routes, Nigeria's sea ports have been used by cartels to import weapons. A high-profile interdiction was recorded in October 2010 when security agents impounded thirteen containers loaded with various sizes of grenades, rocket launchers, explosives, assault rifles, heavy machine guns, and ammunition at Apapa port in Lagos. The containers were aboard a vessel, MV CMA-CGM *Everest*, from Iran and were destined for The Gambia.[36] In addition, there are genuine concerns that the proliferation of illegal airstrips in Nigeria may be conduits for the trafficking of arms. It is reported that Nigeria has about 400 airstrips, largely used by government officials, multinational (oil) companies, and highly placed individuals.[37] Although yet to be confirmed by any security agency, there is growing speculation that aircraft laden with arms could be delivering them into the country through these uncontrolled airstrips.[38] This situation calls for the installation of automatic dependence surveillance broadcasts (ADSB) and multilateration systems to better monitor movements of unauthorized flying aircrafts, arms smuggling, and the use of illegal airstrips that dot the nation's landscape.

Furthermore, the dynamics of globalization has enhanced the movement of goods and peoples across borders have equally facilitated the activities of criminal groups. In this regard, the ECOWAS region and Nigeria are suffering from the negative effects of the relaxation of national boundaries intended to enhance regional integration, but inadvertently facilitating transnational organized crimes such as trafficking in SALWs.

Effects of Small Arms and Light Weapons Proliferation on Human (In)Security in Nigeria

Although the problem of SALWs availability is not new, its proliferation in the last decade has helped stoke a wave of violent conflict and crimes in Nigeria. As depicted in Figure 4.1, violent conflicts and crimes could be both causes and consequences of SALWs proliferation. When SALWs are used in violent conflicts and crimes, human security will be compromised, resulting in death, deformation, destruction, and the displacement of persons.

SALWs proliferation has fueled violence in different parts of Nigeria, especially communal, political, ethno-religious, and resource conflicts.[39] SALWs are easy to obtain in many parts of Nigeria, making armed violence so prevalent and leading to the prolongation of conflicts, inducement of forced population displacement, disruption of peace, and devastation of livelihoods of individuals and communities.

Their easy availability and high circulation within Nigeria fuel the escalation, intensity, spread, and duration of violent conflict and criminality. Between 1999 and April 2010, Nigeria recorded at least 187 ethno-religious conflicts, leading to the death of several thousand people.[40] Since 2009, the Boko Haram insurgency has claimed at least 20,000 lives, displaced more than 2.6 million people, created over 75,000 orphans, and caused about $9 billion worth of damage in Nigeria.[41] Escalating conflicts between herders and farmers in Nigeria add to the level of death, destruction, and displacement. Nigeria had recorded an annual average of more than 2,000 fatalities from 2011 to 2016 in pastoralists' violence.[42]

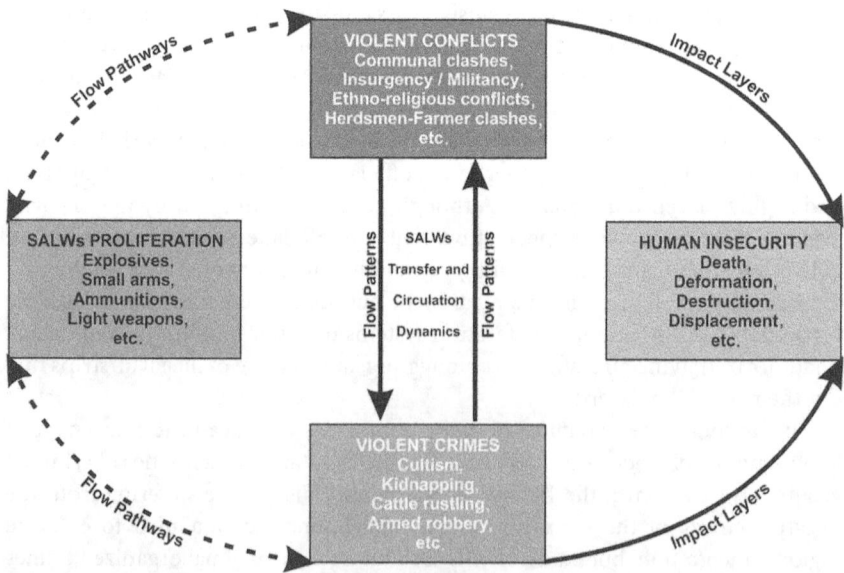

Figure 4.1 SALWs proliferation and human (in)security dynamics in Nigeria.
Source: Authors' illustration.[43]

As a result of insurgency and violent conflicts involving the use of SALWs, Nigeria is faced with the herculean task of responding to a fluctuating but always sizeable number of internally displaced persons (IDPs). As of December 2017, the total number of IDPs in Nigeria due to violent conflicts stood at 1,707,000.[44] The full scale and impact of internal displacement in Nigeria are unclear, due to, among other factors, poor methodologies of collecting and collating reliable data. Situations of forced displacement further undermine human security at individual and community levels. IDPs are usually vulnerable to violent crimes like rape and sexual exploitation, not to mention exposure to contracting contagious diseases due to poor sanitary conditions at the camps and (re-)settlement centers.

The impact of Nigeria's SALWs problem on human security is also evident in material and financial losses induced by conflicts. About ten major ethno-religious conflicts between 1999 and 2004 cost the Nigerian government over N400 million ($2.86 million).[45] Beyond the cost to government, there is equally loss of property by communities. In 2016 alone, recurrent herdsmen and farmers clashes in Benue, Kaduna, Nasarawa, and Plateau states resulted in the death of 2,500 persons, displacement of 62,000 people, loss of property worth $13.7, and 47 percent of the internally generated revenue in the affected states.[46] Violent conflicts involving the use of SALWs have further undermined food security in Nigeria, due to the killing of herds, destruction of farms, and overall devastation of livelihood assets. A report estimates that recurrent conflict between farmers and herdsmen across the North-Central is costing Nigeria at least $14 billion in potential revenues annually.[47] Consequently, the Food and Agricultural Organization in March 2018 listed Nigeria as one of the thirty-seven countries in need of external food assistance.[48] The loss of property compounds the problem of poverty, deprivation, and vulnerability of the affected population.

SALWs proliferation has equally led to an increase in the scale and frequency of violent crimes that undermine human security, such as cultism, armed robbery, piracy, and kidnapping in most parts of the country. The possession of sophisticated SALWs is behind the brazen audacity of several criminal gangs killing people in Nigeria, such as armed robbers, bandits, and kidnappers. For example, a raid by the police of a dreaded kidnapper's house yielded a large cache of arms:

> 27 AK-47 rifles, one K2 rifle, two type-06 rifles, one general purpose machine gun, one rocket launcher, 17 rockets, six pump action guns, three dane guns, one Barrett pistol and 13 rocket grenades, as well as 12,800 rounds of AK-47 live ammunition, 530 rounds of LAR ammunition, 95 rounds of GPMG live ammunition, 1,000 rounds of K2 live ammunition and 143 magazines.[49]

The use of SALWs in violent crimes and conflicts has resulted in the deep fracturing of kinship and family structures. On the one hand, this includes the direct physical harm often resulting in death. Many more are left injured, permanently disabled and traumatized. Many children have been left without parents, husbands without wives, and vice versa. That is why SALWs are often referred to as the true "weapons of mass destruction." Thus, for every person killed or injured in conflicts and crimes involving the use of SALWs, there are many more who must cope with the psychological, physical, and economic effects that endure in its aftermath.

Conclusion and Way Forward

The proliferation of SALWs has had a dramatic impact on peace, stability, and development in Nigeria. Proliferation of SALWs is a multi-dimensional problem that is deeply intertwined with other broader security challenges such as violent crimes and conflicts bedeviling Nigeria. Although SALWs do not in themselves cause the conflicts and criminal activities, the proliferation, easy access, and misuse of these weapons of death endanger the security of people, communities, and states. By contributing to the disruption of the pattern of daily life at individual, community, and societal levels, the proliferation of SALWs plays a key role in denying people entitlement to the three core human values that are central to the notion of human security. As the 2019 general elections drew closer, there was the need for the intensification of efforts at preventing the further proliferation of SALWs that could heighten insecurity before, during, and long after the elections. Past experiences have shown that politicians who are desperate to win elections equip youth gangs and political thugs with such dangerous weapons that the gangsters in turn deploy these weapons into criminal ventures after every election cycle, with tragic consequence for the country.

These arms should be mopped up if Nigeria is to achieve a measurable degree of security of life and property. In order to curb SALWs proliferation and to promote human security, the government should undertake broad political reform, especially targeting the electoral process, to address the crude and "monetized" nature of politics in Nigeria. There is need to initiate robust interventions at national, state, and local levels to promote peaceful coexistence amongst the diverse ethno-religious and political groups in Nigeria. This would help to minimize the outbreak and persistence of violent conflicts that stoke arms proliferation. Government agencies such as the National Orientation Agency should partner with credible civil society organizations and the media to mount enlightenment and orientation programs on the destabilizing effects of small arms proliferations. The proposed establishment of a National Commission on the Control of Small Arms and Light Weapons should be fast-tracked to lead in this effort, based on the sound blueprint or national arms control strategy to guide the mop-up and destruction of SALWs circulation through community-driven disarmament initiatives.

Furthermore, implementation of effective collaborative mechanisms between and among security agencies as well as between them and border communities to enhance information-sharing on cross-border trafficking is crucial. The Nigerian government should equally invest in the installation of advanced scanning machines at airports, seaports, and border points. In addition, relevant security agencies should be supported with the necessary logistics and equipment, including adapting mobile scanning machines to enhance the interception of arms trafficking along the highways, roads, and waterways. Security and military authorities need to conduct unscheduled but regular, comprehensive verification exercises to ensure the effective stockpile management of their armories. Finally, government should constantly and meticulously audit importers as well as licensed gun holders. The Nigerian government must deepen its partnership with other states at regional, continental, and international levels to set up a robust framework for effective implementation of the provisions of the ATT.

Notes

1. Adenubi, Tola, Ebipade, Austin, Ovat, Micheal, Agwaza, A. Callistus, Ogunesan, Tunde, and Michael, Ishola. 2018. "21 Million Guns, Ammo Smuggled into Nigeria—Investigation." *Tribune*. Available from: http://www.tribuneonlineng.com/21-million-guns-ammo-smuggled-nigeria-investigation/.
2. Olayiwola, S. S. 2017. "Proliferation of Arms and Security Challenges in Nigeria." *International Journal of History and Cultural Studies* 3, no. 3: 33–38.
3. Onuoha, Freedom Chukwudi. 2010. "Youth Unemployment and Poverty: Connections and Concerns for National Development in Nigeria." *International Journal of Modern Political Economy* 1, no. 1: 115–136.
4. Federal Republic of Nigeria. 2014. *National Security Strategy*.
5. UN Panel of Governmental Experts on Small Arms. 1997. Available from: https://www.sipri.org/sites/default/files/research/disarmament/dualuse/pdf-archive-att/pdfs/un-report-of-the-panel-of-governmental-experts-on-small-arms.pdf.
6. Ekemenah, Alex. 2013. "National Security and the Menace of Weapon Proliferation in Nigeria." *Business World*, 25. Available from: http://businessworldng.com/web/articles/2847/1/National-Security-and-the-Menace-of-Weapon-Proliferation-in-Nigeria/Page1.htm.
7. Thomas, Caroline. 1999. "Introduction." In *Globalisation, Human Security and the African Experience*, edited by Caroline Thomas and Peter Wilkin, 1–22. London: Lynne Rienner.
8. Hubert, Don. 2001. "Human Security: Safety for People in a Changing World." In *Beyond Conflict Resolution: Managing African Security in the 21-st Century*, edited by Richard A. Akindele and Bassey E. Ate, 87–102. Ibadan: Vantage Publishers.
9. United Nations Development Programme. 1994. *Human Development Report*. New York: Oxford University Press.
10. Jekada, Kabirat Emmanuel. 2005. "Proliferation of Small Arms and Ethnic Conflicts in Nigeria: Implication for National Security." Dissertation, Clement University, September. Available from: http://www.stclements.edu/grad/gradjeka.pdf.
11. Small Arms Survey. 2007: *Guns in the City*. Cambridge: Cambridge University Press.
12. Chelule, Esther. 2014. "Proliferation of Small Arms and Light Weapons: Challenge to Development, Peace and Security in Africa." *Journal of Humanities and Social Science* 19, no. 5: 81.
13. Jazeera, A. L. 2013. "Fact and Figures: Global Trade in Small Arms." Available from: https://www.aljazeera.com/news/americas/2013/03/201331885519413442.html.
14. Small Arms Survey. 2001. *Profiling the Problem*. Oxford: Oxford University Press.
15. Bah, Alhaji. 2004. "Micro-Disarmament in West Africa: The ECOWAS Moratorium on Small Arms and Light Weapons." *African Security Review* 13, no. 3: 33–46.

16. Ifijeh, Godwin. 2006. "SSS Raises Alarm over Arms Proliferation." *Thisday*, May 28.
17. Onuoha, Freedom Chukwudi. 2011. "Small Arms and Light Weapons Proliferation and Human Security in Nigeria." *Conflict Trends* 1: 50–56.
18. Premium Times. 2016. "Nigeria Accounts for over 70% of 500 Million Illicit Weapons in West Africa." August 2.
19. Abubakar, Aminu. 2018. "Banned Weapons Stoke Deadly Violence in Nigeria." *AFP*. Available from: http://www.digitaljournal.com/news/world/banned-weapons-stoke-deadly-violence-in-nigeria/article/524233.
20. Agha, Eugene. 2017. "How Illegal Arms Find Their Way into the Country." *Daily Trust*. Available from: https://www.dailytrust.com.ng/how-illegal-arms-find-their-way-into-the-country.html.
21. Pettinger, Tejvan. 2013. "Containerisation." *Economics Help*. Available from: https://www.economicshelp.org/blog/7637/trade/containerisation/.
22. Eze, Chinedu. 2012. "Nigeria Risks Influx of Illegal Arms through Airstrips." *Thisday*. Available from: http://www.thisdaylive.com/articles/nigeria-risks-influx-of-illegal-arms-through-airstrips/130767/.
23. Omotola, S. J. 2008. "Engendering the Legislature in Nigeria: Faltering Prospects and New Hopes." In *Nigeria beyond 2007: Issues, Perspectives and Challenges*, edited by Hassan A. Saliu, I. O. Taiwo, R. A. Seniyi, B. Salawu, and A. Usman. Ilorin: Faculty of Business and Social Sciences, University of Ilorin.
24. Bello, Emmanuel. 2007. "Nigeria: Politicians Fault Obasanjo over Utterances." *Daily Trust*. Available from: http://allafrica.com/stories/200702121248.html.
25. Onuoha, Freedom Chukwudi. 2010. "Youth Unemployment and Poverty: Connections and Concerns for National Development in Nigeria." *International Journal of Modern Political Economy* 1, no. 1: 115–136.
26. Ojo, Jide. 2013. "Arming Jobless Youths to Win Elections." *Punch*, May 15.
27. Omonobi, Kingsley, and Umoru, Henry. 2018. "Killings: Senate Summons Security, Service Chiefs, Customs Boss, Others." *Vanguard*.
28. Moulaye, Zeine. 2006. *Democratic Governance of Security in Mali: A Sustainable Development Challenge*. Nigeria: ADPROMO Ltd.
29. NAN. 2017. "Abuja Police Uncover Illegal Firearm Factory, Arrest Three Suspects." *Premium Times*. Available from: https://www.premiumtimesng.com/news/top-news/243919-abuja-police-uncover-illegal-firearm-factory-arrest-three-suspects.html.
30. Ikelegbe, Augustine. 2013. "Special Report: Proliferation of Illegal Weapons Blamed on Our Porous Borders." *Frontier News*. Available from: http://frontiersnews.com/index.php/news/5726–special-report-proliferation-of-illegal-weapons-blamed-on-our-porous-borders.
31. Onuoha, Freedom Chukwudi. 2009. "Corruption and National Security: The Three Gap-Thesis and the Nigerian Experience." *Nigerian Journal of Economic & Financial Crimes* 1, no. 2: 1–13.
32. Anaba, Innocent, and Dania, Onozure. 2018. "I Paid DSS Men, Others N1m to Bring In 661 Rifles." *Vanguard*. Available from: https://www.vanguardngr.com/2018/02/paid-dss-men-others-n1m-bring-661-rifles/.
33. Ojeme, Victoria, and Odiniya, Ruth. 2013. "Nigeria Has over 1,499 Illegal Entry Routes—Interior Minister." *Vanguard*. Available from: http://www.vanguardngr.com/2013/06/nigeria-has-over-1499-illegal-entry-routes-interior-minister/.
34. Onuoha, Freedom Chukwudi. 2013. "Porous Borders and Boko Haram's Arms Smuggling Operations in Nigeria." *Report*. Doha: Al Jazeera Centre for Studies.
35. Okeke-Uzodike, Ufo, and Ojakorotu, Victor. 2006. "Oil, Arms Proliferation and

Conflict in the Niger Delta of Nigeria." *African Journal of Conflict Resolution* 6, no. 2: 85–106.

36. Ohia, Paul. 2010. "Gambia Cuts Ties with Iran over Nigeria's Arm Seizure." *Thisday*, November 23.
37. Eze, "Nigeria Risks Influx of Illegal Arms through Airstrips."
38. Ibid.
39. Jekada, "Proliferation of Small Arms and Ethnic Conflicts in Nigeria."
40. Anza, Philips. 2010. "Jos Crisis Is More than Religious." *Newswatch*.
41. Ibuku, Yinka. 2016. "Nigeria's Boko Haram Caused $9 Billion in Damage since 2011." *Bloomberg*. Available from: https://www.bloomberg.com/news/articles/2016-04-04/nigeria-s-boko-haram-caused-9-billion-in-damage-since-2011.
42. ECOWAS, "ECOWAS Promotes Peaceful Cross-Border Transhumance."
43. ECOWAS. 2018. "ECOWAS Promotes Peaceful Cross-Border Transhumance." *ECOWAS Press Release*. Available from: http://www.west-africa-brief.org/content/en/ecowas-promotes-peaceful-cross-border-transhumance.
44. Internal Displacement Monitoring Centre. 2018. "Fragmented Response to Internal Displacement amid Boko Haram Attacks and Flood Season." July 23.
45. Xinhua. 2004. "Nigeria Worried about Cost of Lingering Ethno-Religious Crisis." *Xinhua News Agency*. Available from: http://www.encyclopedia.com/doc/1P2-16579278.html.
46. Agbese, Dan. 2017. "Fulani Herdsmen? Here Are the Grim Statistics." *The Guardian*. Available from: https://guardian.ng/opinion/fulani-herdsmen-here-are-the-grim-statistics/.
47. Mercy Corps. 2016. "The Economic Costs of Conflict and the Benefits of Peace: Effects of Farmer-Pastoralist Conflict in Nigeria's Middle Belt on State, Sector, and National Economies." Portland; USA: Mercy Corps.
48. Muanya, Chukwuma. 2018. "Nigeria, 36 Others Need Help on Food Security, Says FAO." *Guardian*. Available from: https://guardian.ng/news/nigeria-36-others-need-help-on-food-security-says-fao/.
49. Ujumadu, Vincent. 2014. "Anambra and Defiant Abductors: 200 Kidnappings and the N1 Billion Ransom." *Vanguard*, July 27.

Chapter 5

HUMAN TRAFFICKING

Olusesan Ayodeji Makinde and Deborah Fry

Introduction

According to the UN's definition, trafficking in persons is

> the recruitment, transportation, transfer, harboring or receipt of persons, by means of the threat or use of force or other forms of coercion, of abduction, of fraud, of deception, of the abuse of power or of a position of vulnerability or of the giving or receiving of payments or benefits to achieve the consent of a person having control over another person, for the purpose of exploitation.[1]

It is a modern form of slavery, which has been overlooked and handled with less importance than it deserves by the international community and national governments. Human trafficking is almost a universal problem across the world, as many countries have either served as an origin, transit point, or destination for trafficked people. While globalization to boost trade has been encouraged, human trafficking has been identified as the "underside of globalization."[2] The significant growth in transnational business opportunities and relationships in the last four decades has also led to the increase of human trafficking alongside legitimate business expansion. The trafficking of people can occur within a country, across the regions, or over large distances (e.g., transatlantic trafficking).

Human trafficking is the third most profitable illegal industry in the world only behind arms dealing and narcotics trading.[3] It has seen a rise with increasing globalization that facilitates business dealings across borders and the increasing use of modern telecommunication techniques.[4] Modern telecommunication systems provide an opportunity for easy business transactions by international trafficking rings along trafficking routes and they also use these means for intelligence gathering on the location and movement of law enforcement agents. Trafficking is increasingly favored as the preferred business for transnational organized crime because of the low risks for retribution and the high profit margins. In cases concerning arms and narcotics, when detected by law enforcement agents, the commodities are seized and destroyed. However, in cases of human trafficking, the commodities are released into society and can be reengaged by the human traffickers. Proceeds from human trafficking are estimated to be worth between $7 and 10 billion in annual profits, although there is widespread belief that the method used in determining the amounts might have underestimated its true value.[5,6,7] About 800,000 people are estimated to be trafficked annually across borders and there are an estimated 2.4 million people in trafficking situations across the world at any point in time.[8]

Women and children are the most trafficked individuals with women trafficked for sex and children for exploitation including labor.[9] About 20 percent of those trafficked across the world are children, although these statistics may vary considerably across geographic regions.[10] Emphasis by governments, law enforcement agents, and human rights advocates has been on sex trafficking with less attention devoted to child trafficking and labor, which may result in the latter being underestimated.

While efforts have been ongoing to increase awareness and action on human trafficking, there is still much to do. Convictions of human traffickers are not proportional to the estimated magnitude of the problem, which has been well documented in countries worst affected by this crime.[11] In 2016, the US Department of State reported that there were 66,520 victims of human trafficking identified across the world, 14,897 prosecutions, and 9,071 convictions.[12] The paltry number of prosecutions suggests that trafficking is underreported. This impunity indirectly allows this crime to continue to grow because of the low-associated risks.

Trafficking is fostered by both push and pull factors. The push factors include bad governance, corruption, societal crisis, and other forms of conflict, poverty, diseases, and unemployment.[13] The pull/external factors include economic imbalance between low-, middle- and the highest-income countries. Better policing in high-income countries and awareness of human trafficking make their citizens less vulnerable to becoming victims of trafficking. The search for cheaper labor as a result of globalization has favored migration across borders. While legal migration in search of jobs is accepted, most would-be migrants are unable to legally migrate, thereby turning to human traffickers who often promise them a better life in the destination country, only to find themselves trapped in the trafficking rings. Many migrants are, to some extent, aware of the illegalities associated with trafficking, but most engage in the migration for labor under false promises and lies presented by the traffickers who turn the migration process into an exploitative relationship.

Human trafficking has been denounced as a crime against humanity, which makes it applicable for prosecution at the International Criminal Court.[14] Yet to date, researchers are concerned about the few cases that have been successfully concluded. For the successful prosecution of a human trafficking case, the victim needs to act in support of the state. However, absence of victim protection in countries affected by the crisis provides the opportunity for the intimidation of would-be state witnesses and their families. Criminal gangs who perpetuate human trafficking are usually well-connected networks, thereby facilitating such threats and intimidation and if necessary extermination of witnesses. They also use *juju* and traditional beliefs of witchcraft or sorcery to intimidate their victims.[15]

Efforts at addressing human trafficking have focused on the development of cross-country legal instruments that facilitate collaboration among law enforcement agencies. Some of the legal instruments that are active today include the Convention on the Rights of the Child (CRC), the United Nations Convention against Transnational Organized Crime (UNTOC), and the Protocol to Prevent, Suppress and Punish Trafficking in Persons, Especially Women and Children, supplementing the UNTOC. The last document is popularly known as the Palermo Protocol.[16,17,18]

Despite the availability of these legal instruments, combatting human trafficking has been a challenge. The CRC addresses human trafficking by calling out the governments in Article 11 on preventing children from being taken out of their countries illegally.[19,20] The Protocol to Prevent, Suppress and Punish Trafficking in Persons has been in existence since December 2003. By 2016, 158 (88 percent) countries have passed laws that criminalize most forms of human trafficking.[21] Yet trafficking across countries has persisted. The Palermo Protocol addresses human trafficking through the 3Ps: prevention, victim protection, and prosecution. A review ten years after the enactment of this global treaty showed that these strategies are still not adequately achieved.[22]

Just as it was a hub for the slave trade, Nigeria has again earned a poor reputation as a source, transit point, and destination for trafficked people.[23] This chapter describes the current trends of human trafficking and efforts at addressing human trafficking in Nigeria. It further attempts to break down the different types of trafficking that have been described by various authors across the country.

Types of Trafficking in Nigeria

There are many types of human trafficking taking place in Nigeria or with Nigeria used as a source or transit destination for trafficked victims. This section highlights the different types of trafficking across the country.

Trafficking by Region

As noted earlier, Nigeria is a source, transit point, and destination for human trafficking. Nigerian women are the most trafficked for sex slavery in Italy and the Netherlands.[24] The country is also a transit point for young girls from surrounding countries who are being taken to Europe for commercial sex work.[25,26] The strategic location of Nigeria, with a popular airport, seaports, and poorly policed land borders, makes it an easy transit route for human traffickers in the region. Furthermore, the country has also served as the destination point for victims from Benin, the Togo Republic, and other surrounding countries who come to serve as domestic servants in Nigeria.

In a study conducted in Kwara State, about 17 percent of the respondents claimed to have been victims, at one time or another, of human traffickers. In these situations, they were mostly being trafficked for sex and labor.[27] Edo State has also been repeatedly mentioned as a source for sex trafficking while the southeast of Nigeria is now known as the hub for baby factories.[28,29,30] Baby factories are places where young women have been willingly or coerced into carrying pregnancies who are subsequently sold into trafficking rings.[31]

The media has been recently awash with news of African immigrants attempting to cross into Europe through Libya and other North African countries. Many of the West Africans attempting this journey have identified as Nigerians. While they have made the illegal trips out of their own free will, paying significant amounts to smuggling gangs, many have become trapped and forced into servitude in the process. The smuggling groups have also been known to rob and abandon their clients in the Sahara Desert in the process. Reports emerged in 2017 of slave markets in Libya where sub-Saharan Africans were being auctioned as slaves to farmers.[32] The report further notes the consistent trading of migrants across the migration routes and killing off the slaves when they were of no more use. The outcry that followed the release of the report by CNN has provided additional impetus for the government of Nigeria and the international community to make efforts to address this problem. As a result, the Nigerian government, in collaboration with the International Organization for Migration, has recently repatriated some victims from Libya who showed an interest in returning voluntarily to the country. Notwithstanding, illegal migrants are still attempting to make the daredevil crossing from sub-Saharan Africa through the Sahara Desert to North Africa and subsequently into Europe, through the Mediterranean Sea, despite the very high risks.

Child Labor

An estimated 15 million children were in child labor in Nigeria according to a 2003 study, a rate that has probably increased since then.[33] Children are trafficked for various reasons, including to work on farms, homes, or industries.[34] The international nature of child trafficking and labor has resulted in a series of conventions such as the CRC and the Protocol on the Sale of Children, Child Prostitution and Child Pornography and Convention (C182) by the International Labour Organization (ILO).[35] Children are predominantly trafficked from poorer countries to wealthier ones, as has been reported from neighboring less prosperous countries of Togo and Benin Republic to Nigeria.[36] Children are also trafficked within Nigeria from rural to urban areas to serve as domestic servants in homes.[37] There are also children who are exploited in street begging as has been seen in the *Almajiris* in northern Nigeria, discussed later in this chapter.[38]

Various socioeconomic factors have been identified as promoting child trafficking. Children of parents who are well educated have lower chances of being engaged in child labor than their peers. However, a few studies have shown there is no significant effect amongst these relationships.[39] Such observation could have been by chance or the low sample size of the studies, which could not detect slight variations. Similarly, parental income and parental employment status have reported mixed findings. Children in families where the mother works were found to have a higher chance of being in employment than their peers. In Nigeria, similar observations were made by Dimeji Togunde and Arielle Carter in their study in Abeokuta, Ogun State, which aligned with both the poverty and social learning theories of child labor.[40] Two types of child labor are described below.

Domestic Servitude

The National Agency for the Prohibition of Trafficking in Persons (NAPTIP) has over the years published cases of children who were taken from their parents in rural Nigeria by relatives with the promise of educating them in the cities only to turn them into domestic servants. There are also reports of children who are placed in various homes to become servants while payments go to the middlemen.[41]

Children who are trafficked have also been forced into generating income through acts such as hawking. A recent report highlighted a thirteen-year-old Nigerian child who was trafficked to Gabon and poorly treated by his "master." His supposed master had taken custody of him from his parents with a promise to provide him with better education than he could get in the village. The young child was allegedly burnt using an iron rod when he did not make as much money as expected by his "master."[42] The act of engaging young children in street trading exposes them to various dangers. Young girls who are made to hawk are also exposed to sexual harassment and rape by their potential clients.[43]

Child Begging

The use of Almajiri children in northern Nigeria for street begging has been on the rise, among other security risks associated with the children in the North. The Almajiris are young male children, from primary school age to their early twenties, who are placed with Islamic clerics (*Mallams*) in northern Nigeria within the informal Qur'anic educational systems.[44] In Kano alone, there were an estimated 300,000 Almajiri children in the state, 12.5 percent of all children between six and twenty-one years in the state. While the Almajiri system has been described as a noble system that was used to train children and permit Muslims to fulfill their religious beliefs of providing alms to the less privileged in the society several centuries ago, the evolution of the Almajiris has become more of a social reprieve for poor families who send off their children to live with clerics who receive no compensation in exchange for their care or upkeep. These clerics, in order to make ends meet, send the children out to the streets to beg for alms. The resulting evolution of Almajiris (from religious practice to destitutes) has been rejected by the elites, and children from middle- and high-class families in these societies are hardly found in Almajiri schools.[45] Because of the lack of supervision, about two-thirds of these children are reported to engage in substance misuse and other social vices.[46] The Boko Haram insurgency in northeast Nigeria has also been linked to the recruitment of Almajiri children as foot soldiers, further fueling the reduced acceptance of Almajiri practice by elite Muslims.[47]

There have also been reports of begging on the streets in southern Nigeria by mothers who carry their young or borrowed children in open spaces or on roads with the aim of drawing compassion and receiving alms from passersby.[48] This practice is often explained by traditional beliefs and religion, as some parents claim that they are only responding to the calls of their god.[49] However, parallel studies disagree with this practice and suggest that rather it is poverty that drives alms begging with children.[50,51,52]

Trafficking for Sexual Exploitation

Trafficking for sexual exploitation is the most common reason for the trafficking of women and girls across the world. Nigerian women have been trafficked to various European countries, including Italy, Spain, the Netherlands, Germany, Belgium, UK, and France.[53] Amongst sex trafficking victims across Europe, there is a very high representation from Nigeria. About 60 percent of foreign prostitutes in Italy are from Nigeria with an estimated 80 percent of them from Edo and Delta states.[54] In a study among 1,456 young women of ages between fifteen and twenty-five years in Edo State, about 32 percent of them stated that they had been approached with an offer to travel abroad in order to better their economic standing. While many of the women had been told they would work as hairdressers, baby sitters, and cleaners in the countries where they were being invited, 32 percent of the women were not told what they would do in the countries after migration.[55]

This study also found that many young women in Edo State have been influenced by the quick wealth that has been acquired by neighbors who have traveled abroad and within relatively short periods returned to build houses for their families. Thus, when approached to be trafficked for prostitution, many willingly agree based on the economic benefits they have observed from friends who have worked in the business. Seventeen married women, among the respondents in the study, reported that they had been pressured by their husbands to migrate to Europe for prostitution as a means of supporting their families.[56] Unlike many crimes that are mainly committed by men, women play a central role as the recruiters and facilitators of trafficking for sexual exploitation. In an article that analyzed a police investigation of a sexual trafficking gang in Italy, it was discovered that the madams often played a central role in the recruitment and the perpetration of the crime.[57] Many of the madams were once prostitutes held in bondage and had to pay for their release through prostitution. The madams do not operate in isolation and usually work with men in relatively organized criminal gangs. Many members of the gangs are Nigerian, although other nationals including Europeans have also been discovered in the gangs.[58,59]

The engagement of male trafficking and smuggling male victims for survival sex has also recently been reported. Many of those who make an attempt to travel to Europe for a better life across the Sahara Desert have reported engaging in homosexual prostitution as a means of survival.

Child Marriage

Over 40 percent of young girls in sub-Saharan Africa are married off before their eighteenth birthday.[60] Within Nigeria, 22.5 percent of fifteen- to nineteen-year olds had begun childbearing during the 2013 Demographic and Health Survey.[61] The practice of betrothing young girls to adult men is still well practiced among the Hausa-Fulani ethnic groups of northern Nigeria.[62] About 48 percent of young girls from these groups are married by the age of fifteen, and 78 percent are married by their eighteenth birthday.[63] The recent "domestication" of the United Nations Convention on the Rights of the Child in the Child Rights Act of 2003 has provided a national framework for the protection of children from early marriage.[64] However, the legislative structure of Nigeria does not provide the federal government with absolute legislative powers over states. The Nigerian constitution requires that states adopt such national laws before they can be locally enforced within their territories.[65] Many northern states, where Sharia law is practiced, have opposed the eighteen-year age limit stated by the Marriage Act and openly voiced their discontent with the Act. Reasons stated were based on religious and cultural beliefs, which permit girls to be married off once they attain puberty. While some states have now integrated the Child Rights Act into local law, they made significant modifications to the document including reducing the age of marriage prior to adopting it.

Children who are forced into marriage often experience physical, sexual and/or psychological violence as a result.[66] A recent case of a thirteen-year-old child bride who poisoned her husband and three of his friends with rat poison only days after getting married to him has made headlines.[67] She stated her lack of preparation to get married and that she did not love him. She further confided in her lawyer that she had been tied to the bed and raped by her husband on the wedding night.[68] While she was discharged following a public outcry and support by female activists and lawyers, a case of another thirteen-year-old who poisoned her husband under similar circumstances resulted in a death sentence for the young woman. She subsequently spent three years on death row before the judgment was overturned following a protracted legal battle.[69] While not as common as has been seen in northern Nigeria, child marriage has also been reported among some ethnic groups of southern Nigeria.[70] Low levels of education and low socioeconomic status are the main predisposing factors.[71]

Infant Trafficking through Baby Factories

Trafficking of infants in Nigeria, in what have been widely described as "baby factories," was first reported in 2006.[72] Since then, published studies have found it to be unusually high in some parts of the country, with the increasing discovery of baby factory centers over the years.[73] Most cases have been concentrated in the southeastern part of the country, although reports in the southwest have also been made. In April 2018, the Lagos State government shut three orphanages and rescued 162 children from these homes because they were suspected to be involved in the baby factory business.[74] Cultural beliefs and practices are believed to be part of the promoting factors for baby factories in Nigeria. The stigmatization of infertility and the undue placement of priority on male children, especially among the Igbos, put couples under intense pressure to satisfy societal acceptance.[75] Human trafficking that is associated with baby factories is two-fold: first, there are the young girls who are held against their will, forcefully impregnated, and taken undue advantage of in the baby factories. Secondly, the infants who are born in the baby factories are sold in undocumented transactions, thereby violating their rights.[76] To many infertile couples, baby factories might be seen as a reprieve for their childlessness. However, there are several reasons why women should desist from getting children from these sources.[77] This includes the lack of information on the health of the mothers, including the possibility of sexually transmitted infections that can be passed on to the children, knowledge of the trafficked girls who are forcefully groomed for the pregnancies, the potential for birth injury to the neonates during delivery and as a result on the birth mothers who may change their mind at a later date.[78]

The profits of the infant trafficking business were identified as an important reason to quickly address infant trafficking as inattention will embolden others to begin to engage in such practice.[79] Male children could sell for as high as $4,400, while females sell for a little less.[80] In these situations, most of the money goes to the baby factory proprietor who gives the young indigent mothers a paltry fraction of the money. The risk of more jobless indigent women turning to baby factories is particularly true as there has been a consistent rise in the number of baby factories discovered over the years. Between 2013 and 2014, the number of baby factories discovered by the police rose by 60 percent.[81] With increasing focus on baby factories arising from the attention drawn by the media, the human traffickers have taken precautionary measures. In a case in Enugu State, mothers are guarded and prevented from leaving high-walled compounds.[82]

Besides the children bred in baby factories for sale, there have also been cases of children who are stolen from their mothers and sold to infertile couples, as reported by NAPTIP.[83] In these cases, the traffickers abducted the children without the cooperation of the parents. They often watched the parents and struck when their attention was drawn away. In the instances reported by NAPTIP, the children were taken from their homes while their mothers were distracted.

Organ Trafficking

With the changing epidemiological landscape, non-communicable diseases (NCDs) are beginning to feature significantly in the disease burden in different parts of the world, including sub-Saharan Africa.[84,85] In some cases such as in chronic hypertension, end organs (kidneys, eyes, brain, and the heart) may be damaged due to poor blood pressure control. The number of cases of end organ damage arising as a result of these NCDs is on the rise.[86] The treatment for end organ damage is organ replacement. One of the end organs frequently damaged in poorly treated hypertension is the kidney.[87] Fatiu Arogundade demonstrated a consistent increase in the proportion of cases of end-stage renal disease among medical admissions at the Obafemi Awolowo University Teaching Hospital in Ile Ife between 1989 and 2007 by examining admission records.[88] Demand for kidneys for transplantation far exceeds its availability and this has provided an opportunity for traffickers to make money from the illicit trade in kidneys and other human body parts.[89] About 5–10 percent of organs transplanted annually are from the organ market.[90]

Undocumented immigrants are becoming a source of organs for the wealthy in some of the destination countries for migrants.[91] While the victims have not been absolutely identified to be Nigerians, migrants have been reportedly kidnaped, and ransoms demanded from their families, among those who have attempted to cross into Europe through North Africa. Those who are unable to pay have been reportedly killed and had their organs harvested for sale.[92] In July 2016, the Italian government arrested thirty-eight members of a criminal gang that specialized in this practice.[93]

Aside from being victims of the organ trafficking market, Nigerian patients have also been identified as patrons of the organ market. A study in the southeastern part of the country found that a majority of the 126 post-transplant patients reviewed had their renal transplant surgeries in India, where the operation is more affordable, and the kidney received was from a commercial organ donor.[94]

Kidnapping

While kidnapping is different from human trafficking, the number of reported kidnapping cases in Nigeria has been on the rise.[95] Kidnapping in Nigeria has predominantly been for ransom.[96] Starting within the oil-rich Niger Delta, with the kidnapping of oil workers for ransom, the practice has spread across the country. There is currently no part of the country where people have not been kidnapped for ransom.[97] The rise of the Boko Haram insurgency in the northeastern part of Nigeria has however changed the narrative and provided lawlessness within that part of the country, which allow for the perpetuation and impunity of such criminal acts.

Since the insurgency began over ten years ago, there have been repeated cases of the kidnapping of women and children, some of whom are forced to become child soldiers and sex slaves.[98] Several suicide bombing incidents carried out were noted to have been executed by children who were kidnapped and coerced into carrying out such dastardly acts.[99] Two large instances have been recorded where young school girls were taken from their schools in droves and kept as sex slaves and domestic servants for the Boko Haram fighters. The first instance was the kidnapping of the 276 girls from the Chibok Government Girls Secondary School in Borno State in April 2014.[100] In February 2018, Boko Haram terrorists struck again, kidnapping another 110 school girls from the Government Girls Science

Technical College, Dapchi in Yobe State.[101,102] While some of the girls from Chibok managed to escape, many were held in captivity for over three years before the government was able to secure their release, and a significant number have never been found. The released girls provided information on how they were physically, sexually, and psychologically violated while kept captive by the Boko Haram insurgents.

Legislation and Human Trafficking

West Africa and indeed Nigeria are a hotspot for different types of human trafficking.[103] Sex trafficking is the most frequently occurring crime and has been reported widely in the literature as discussed throughout this chapter. As part of the governments' effort toward addressing the challenge of human trafficking, the National Agency for the Prohibition of Trafficking in Persons (NAPTIP) was established in 2003 by the Trafficking in Persons (Prohibition) Enforcement and Administration Act. This was in line with the provisions of the Palermo Protocol. NAPTIP's role was to enforce the provisions of the Act and to coordinate and enforce all other laws on trafficking in persons and related offences.[104]

Trafficking is a secretive business and traffickers make an extra effort to hide the true nature of their businesses, usually doing this under the shadow of legal businesses. For example, such secrecy made the investigation of a case in Italy last for two years before the gang was successfully rounded up.[105] Identifying cross-country traffickers requires collaboration between several government agencies within countries and across countries if transnational. This makes investigation and prosecution a complex situation where gaps and loopholes in the system and lack of interagency coordination and communication have been exploited to foster the trading in humans across the world. The establishment of NAPTIP provides a central coordination point, although it is noteworthy that addressing the types of trafficking taking place in Nigeria still requires different security and government agencies.

Victims of transnational human trafficking are at risk of being tagged as criminals who have violated the entry rules of the destination countries. Human traffickers have been reported to seize the travel documents of their victims using this to put additional fear in them and also to prevent them from approaching authorities about their condition or from running away.[106] The health and social consequences on victims of sex trafficking can also be significant, including polyvictimization, beatings, forced abortions, lack of access to contraceptives, and exposure to sexually transmitted infections.[107,108]

The unusually large numbers of sex trafficking victims from Edo and Delta states have not gone unnoticed. Efforts to address sex trafficking in Edo State have resulted in the enactment of the Prostitution Law.[109] The Law was targeted at prosecuting the victims, middlemen, and the businesses of the traffickers. While this is a step in the right direction, prosecution of the victims of human trafficking might violate the Palermo Protocol as many victims are coerced into trafficking and prosecuting them can result in double punishment. An alternate approach might be to challenge the social acceptance of prostitution which has been accepted as a means of livelihood in this part of the country.[110] Also the sex trafficking rings and gangs have been known to recruit people from within their own kith and kin.[111] As such, the identification of these trafficking rings, their barons, and prosecution of those caught will be a major step toward addressing sex trafficking in this part of the country.

As has been reported across the globe, the number of convictions in comparison to the magnitude of human trafficking in Nigeria is unduly low, peaking at only fifty-one convictions in 2011 based on a ten-year analysis from 2004 to 2013.[112] In 2016, there were 654 investigations, 24 prosecutions, and 23 convictions.[113] This was an improvement over the previous year during which there were 507 investigations.[114] More collaborative efforts are needed to address the problem of human trafficking in Nigeria.

Despite the availability of laws against trafficking in Nigeria, these have not adequately addressed the emerging baby factory phenomenon. Baby factories are being used as child breeding centers to provide babies to unfertile couples through illegal and shadowy means. This is similar to surrogacy, which is a legally arranged process where a woman can be engaged by an infertile couple on a contract for gestational or traditional surrogacy. As such, concerted efforts are required to establish laws against baby factories, which must include differentiating baby factory, surrogacy, and adoption. In addition, destigmatizing infertility and challenging the normative views against adoption and surrogacy, which have forced many people to patronize the secretive baby factories, might be a step toward addressing the baby factory proliferation in the country.

Patriarchy and gender inequality in Nigeria have also been pointed out as contributory factors explaining the delay in enacting several legislations, including those against the trafficking of women and children.[115] In many Nigerian communities, male children are favored over girls. In such situations, the young girls are sent to cities to work and make money for the families back in rural villages.[116] Male children also sell for a higher fee in the illegal baby factories ($4400 for a boy vs. $4000 for a girl).[117] The continued perceived superiority of males has recently resulted in the failure to pass the Gender and Equal Opportunities Bill by a male-dominated Nigerian Senate.[118] The Bill was voted out based on its perceived opposition to the cultural and religious beliefs of most Nigerians. A member of a civic group opposed to the Bill stated that "the provisions promoted abrasive western liberation of women, gay practices, legalization of abortion and gender stereotyping, adding that all these were contrary to the Nigerian laws, religious, cultural and philosophical convictions of the Nigerian people."[119]

The consequences of child labor are diverse and include both immediate and long-term consequences. These include motor accidents while hawking, kidnapping, rape and sexual molestation, invitation to join gangs as well as other antisocial activities.[120] The lack of adequate supervision has also resulted in an increase in substance abuse.[121]

While the Nigerian government continues to make efforts to address human trafficking in its entirety, the multiple types of human trafficking in Nigeria continue to be a concern. The US Department of State ranks the performance of countries according to their efforts toward addressing human trafficking based on a series of criteria. The performance of Nigeria as ranked by the US Department of State has been on the decline, resulting in a downgrading of status. Nigeria is now ranked as a Tier 2 Watch List country (previously Tier 2) and the 2017 report notes that the country does not fully meet the standards for the elimination of trafficking.[122]

Human Trafficking and Insecurity

Human trafficking has a wide range of consequences on the security of a nation. In cases where trafficking gangs are involved, they are often involved in more than one line of crime, for example, trafficking in drugs alongside human trafficking.[123] Likewise, the trafficking of young girls for breeding of children in baby factories has been reported to result in rape of some of them and the murder of uncooperative victims.[124] Stifling their means of livelihood of these gangs and prosecution whenever caught (for human trafficking) will go a long way in ridding the country of criminal elements. Trafficking gangs are also increasingly carrying arms along trafficking routes (see chapter on SALWs). In situations where they do not make enough money from this criminal means of livelihood, traffickers could easily turn into armed robbers and kidnappers in the countries where they operate. The Almajiris in northern Nigeria have also been linked to the Boko Haram insurgency in the northeast (see chapter on Boko Haram). Some of them are believed to have been recruited as fighters in the insurgency, which has already severely stretched the security apparatus of the country.[125] Thus, addressing human trafficking has the potential of making the country safer on many different levels.

Challenges to Human Trafficking Control

The challenges to bringing human trafficking in Nigeria under control are numerous and continue to hamper progress. High rates of poverty in Nigeria make vulnerable people easy targets for human traffickers.[126] In addition, the different types of human trafficking happening in Nigeria require different institutions that often poorly coordinate activities with one another.[127] For instance, addressing the movement of people across land borders requires engagement with the Nigeria Immigration Service, investigating transnational and economic crimes will involve the Economic and Financial Crimes Commission and possibly the police, addressing baby factories will involve the police and social services, etc. Each of these needs to be coordinated by the NAPTIP. The important role of the judiciary in the prosecution of cases also cannot be underestimated. However, the delay in the delivery of justice across Nigeria makes pursuing these routes a challenge.

Inadequate and unclear legislation is another major issue affecting the successful prosecution of cases. Corruption and delay in conclusion of cases remain another challenge to the success of combating human trafficking in Nigeria (see chapter on corruption). NAPTIP, which is responsible for addressing human trafficking, is predominantly present in the state capitals and not well established across rural areas where a significant proportion of the recruitment and trafficking takes place. Poor funding of NAPTIP activities with the reduction in allocation from N2.5 billion in 2015 to N1.69 billion in 2016, a 32 percent decline, further hampers their services.[128] In addition to this decline, a significant amount was yet to be allocated to NAPTIP by the government of Nigeria for the implementation of projects in December of 2016.[129]

Conclusion

Combating human trafficking requires a multifaceted approach and the transnational cases cannot be addressed in one country alone. Many efforts at addressing trafficking have failed because emphasis has been on victim identification and the prosecution of traffickers. Poverty, which predisposes many in West Africa to trafficking, requires a long-term economic approach that remains elusive. In Nigeria, the proportion of people who live below the poverty line has been on the rise.[130] Thus, efforts at reversing this trend, including addressing corruption that continues to hamper development in Nigeria, must be fostered.

Programs targeted at women empowerment and liberation will provide them with more power and economic strength in society. In addition, addressing structural drivers such as the enforcement of the different legislations enacted for the different types of human trafficking that have been described is necessary. In some situations, such as the absence of reproductive health/surrogacy laws, efforts should be made to enact laws that will protect young children and their mothers from baby factory exploitation. Furthermore, efforts must include challenging the normative views that support sex trafficking as a means of livelihood, the stigmatization of infertility which makes infertile women patronize baby factories as an alternative means to get desired children, and the practice of sending off children to Islamic schools without the necessary financial support for their upkeep. Finally, there is the need for increased awareness on the modus operandi of the human trafficking rings so that fewer people will fall victims.

Notes

1. UN General Assembly, 2002. "Protocol to Prevent, Suppress and Punish Trafficking in Persons, Especially Women and Children, Supplementing the United Nations Convention against Transnational Organized Crime."
2. Fitzgibbon, K. 2003. "Modern-Day Slavery? The Scope of Trafficking in Persons in Africa." *African Security Studies* 12, no. 1: 81–89.

3. Hyland, K. 2001. "The Impact of the Protocol to Prevent, Suppress and Punish Trafficking in Persons, Especially Women and Children." *Human Rights Brief* 8, no. 2: 12.
4. Ollus, N. 2002. "The United Nations Protocol to Prevent, Suppress and Punish Trafficking in Persons, Especially Women and Children: A Tool for Criminal Justice Personnel." *Resource Material Series*, no. 62. Available from: http://www.ungift.org/docs/ungift/pdf/knowledge/unafei_analysis.pdf.
5. Hyland, "The Impact of the Protocol to Prevent, Suppress and Punish Trafficking in Persons, Especially Women and Children," 12.
6. UNESCO, 2006. "Human Trafficking in Nigeria: Root Causes and Recommendations." *Policy Paper Series*. Available from: http://unesdoc.unesco.org/images/0014/001478/147844e.pdf.
7. UNODC, 2015. "Human Trafficking." *Transnational Organized Crime*. Available from: http://www.unodc.org/toc/en/crimes/human-trafficking.html.
8. Ibid.
9. Rao, S. and Presenti, C. 2012. "Understanding Human Trafficking Origin: A Cross-Country Empirical Analysis." *Feminist Economics* 18, no. 2: 231–263. DOI: https://doi.org/10.1080/13545701.2012.680978.
10. Beyrer, C. 2004. "Global Child Trafficking." *The Lancet* 364: 16–17.
11. Heinrich, K. 2010. "Ten Years after the Palermo Protocol: Where Are Protections for Human Trafficking Victims?" *Human Rights Brief* 18: 2–5.
12. US Department of State, 2017. "Trafficking in Persons Report 2017." Available from: https://www.state.gov/j/tip/rls/tiprpt/2017/.
13. Onuoha, B. 2011. "The State Human Trafficking and Human Rights Issues in Africa." *Contemporary Justice Review* 14. no. 2: 149–166, DOI: https://doi.org/10.1080/10282580.2011.565973.
14. Obokata, T. 2005. "Trafficking of Human Beings as a Crime against Humanity: Some Implications for the International Legal System." *International and Comparative Law Quarterly* 54, no. 2: 445–458.
15. Mancuso, M. 2014. "Not All Madams Have a Central Role: Analysis of a Nigerian Sex Trafficking Network." *Trends in Organized Crime* 17, no. 1–2: 66–88.
16. UNICEF, 1989. "Convention on the Rights of the Child." Available from: http://digitalcommons.ilr.cornell.edu/cgi/viewcontent.cgi?article=1007&context=child.
17. UN General Assembly, 2002. "Protocol to Prevent, Suppress and Punish Trafficking in Persons, Especially Women and Children, Supplementing the United Nations Convention against Transnational Organized Crime."
18. UN General Assembly, 2000. "United Nations Convention against Transnational Organized Crime and the Protocols Thereto."
19. Makinde, O. 2016. "Infant Trafficking and Baby Factories: A New Tale of Child Abuse in Nigeria." *Child Abuse Review* 25, no. 6: 433–443. DOI: https://doi.org/10.1002/car.2420.
20. UNICEF, "Convention on the Rights of the Child."
21. UNODC, 2016. *Global Report on Trafficking in Persons 2016*. Vienna, Austria: United Nations.
22. Heinrich, "Ten Years after the Palermo Protocol," 2–5.
23. Onuoha, F. 2014. "The Evolving Menace of Baby Factories and Trafficking in Nigeria." *African Security Review* 23, no. 4: 405–411. DOI: https://doi.org/10.1080/10246029.2014.941886.
24. Mancuso, "Not All Madams Have a Central Role," 66–88.

25. Huntley, S. 2013. "The Phenomenon of Baby Factory in Nigeria as a New Trend of Human Trafficking." *International Crimes Database*. Available from: http://www.internationalcrimesdatabase.org/upload/documents/20131030T045906-ICD%20Brief%203%20-%20Huntley.pdf.
26. Mancuso, "Not All Madams Have a Central Role," 66–88.
27. Abdulraheem, S. and Oladipo, A. R. 2010. "Trafficking in Women and Children: A Hidden Health and Social Problem in Nigeria." *International Journal of Sociology and Anthropology* 2, no. 3: 34.
28. Makinde, A. et al. "Baby Factories in Nigeria: Starting the Discussion toward a National Prevention Policy." *Trauma, Violence & Abuse* 18, no. 1: 98–105. DOI: https://doi.org/10.1177/1524838015591588.
29. Huntley, "The Phenomenon of Baby Factory in Nigeria as a New Trend of Human Trafficking."
30. UNESCO. "Human Trafficking in Nigeria."
31. Makinde, et al., "Baby Factories in Nigeria," 98–105.
32. Elbagir, N. et al. 2017. "People for Sale: Where Lives Are Auctioned for $400." *CNN*. Available from: https://www.cnn.com/2017/11/14/africa/libya-migrant-auctions/index.html.
33. UNICEF Nigeria. "Child Trafficking."
34. Todres, J. 2010. "Taking Prevention Seriously: Developing a Comprehensive Response to Child Trafficking and Sexual Exploitation." *Vanderbilt Journal of Transnational Law* 43, no. 1. Available from: http://heinonlinebackup.com/hol-cgi-bin/get_pdf.cgi?handle=hein.journals/vantl43&section=4.
35. Dessy, S. and Mbiekop, F., and Pallage, S. 2005. "The Economics of Child Trafficking (Part II)." *Cahier de Recherche/Working Paper* 5, no. 9. Available online: https://s3.amazonaws.com/academia.edu.documents/38636657/CIRPEE05-09.pdf?response-content-disposition=inline%3B%20filename%3DThe_Economics_of_Child_Trafficking_Part.pdf&X-Amz-Algorithm=AWS4-HMAC-SHA256&X-Amz-Credential=AKIAIWOWYYGZ2Y53UL3A%2F20191211%2Fus-east-1%2Fs3%2Faws4_request&X-Amz-Date=20191211T121854Z&X-Amz-Expires=3600&X-Amz-SignedHeaders=host&X-Amz-Signature=40a021b3a11189f608523ba5b3f8ed8a738266f5f994f4ca9bfbdb6544887dd1.
36. Huntley, "The Phenomenon of Baby Factory in Nigeria as a New Trend of Human Trafficking."
37. Ibid.
38. Aghedo, I. and James, S. 2013. "From Alms to Arms: The Almajiri Phenomenon and Internal Security in Northern Nigeria." *The Korean Journal of Policy Studies* 28, no. 3: 97–123.
39. Togunde, D. and Carter, A. 2006. "Socioeconomic Causes of Child Labor in Urban Nigeria." *Journal of Children and Poverty* 12, no. 1: 73–89. DOI: https://doi.org/10.1080/10796120500502201.
40. Ibid.
41. Aibangbe, M. 2015. "Child Trafficking: A Hindrance to the Girl-Child Education." *Planning and Changing; Normal* 46, no. 3/4: 311–323.
42. Fitzgibbon, "Modern-Day Slavery? The Scope of Trafficking in Persons in Africa," 81–89.
43. Fawole, O. et al. "Prevalence and Nature of Violence among Young Female Hawkers in Motor-Parks in South-Western Nigeria." *Health Education* 102, no. 5: 230–238.
44. Hoechner, H. 2011. "Striving for Knowledge and Dignity: How Qur'anic Students

in Kano, Nigeria, Learn to Live with Rejection and Educational Disadvantage." *The European Journal of Development Research* 23, no. 5: 712–728.
45. Abdulmalik, J. et al. 2009. "Psychoactive Substance Use among Children in Informal Religious Schools (Almajiris) in Northern Nigeria." *Mental Health, Religion and Culture* 12, no. 6: 527–542.
46. Ibid.
47. Aghedo and James, "From Alms to Arms," 97–123.
48. Aibangbe, "Child Trafficking," 311–323.
49. Igbinovia, P. 1991. "Begging in Nigeria." *International Journal of Offender Therapy and Comparative Criminology* 35, no. 1: 21–33. DOI: https://doi.org/10.1177/0306624X9103500103.
50. Bukoye, R. 2015. "Case Study: Prevalence and Consequences of Streets Begging among Adults and Children in Nigeria, Suleja Metropolis." *Procedia—Social and Behavioral Sciences*. 5th ICEEPSY International Conference on Education & Educational Psychology, no. 171: 323–333. DOI: https://doi.org/10.1016/j.sbspro.2015.01.129.
51. Ogunkan, D. and Fawole, O. 2009. "Incidence and Socio-Economic Dimensions of Begging in Nigerian Cities: The Case of Ogbomoso." *International NGO Journal* 4, no. 12: 498–503.
52. Ikọtun, R. and Balogun, T. 2016. "Alms-Begging and Human Rights in Yorùbá Land." *Ihafa: A Journal of African Studies* 8, no. 1: 176–198.
53. UNESCO, "Human Trafficking in Nigeria."
54. Okonofua, F. et al. 2004. "Knowledge, Attitudes and Experiences of Sex Trafficking by Young Women in Benin City, South-South Nigeria." *Social Science & Medicine* 59, no. 6: 1315–1327.
55. Ibid.
56. Ibid.
57. Mancuso, "Not All Madams Have a Central Role," 66–88.
58. UNODC, 2009. "Transnational Trafficking and Rule of Law in West Africa: A Threat Assessment." Vienna, Austria.
59. Mancuso, "Not All Madams Have a Central Role," 66–88.
60. UNICEF, 2014. "25 Years of the Convention on the Rights of the Child: Is the World a Better Place for Children?" *UNICEF*. Available from: http://www.unicef.org/publications/index_76027.html.
61. National Population Commission, 2013. Federal Republic of Nigeria and ICF International. Maryland USA. "Nigeria Demographic and Health Survey 2013."
62. Braimah, T. 2014. "Child Marriage in Northern Nigeria: Section 61 of Part I of the 1999 Constitution and the Protection of Children against Child Marriage." *African Human Rights Law Journal* 14, no. 2: 474–488.
63. Ibid.
64. Federal Government of Nigeria, 2003. "An Act to Provide and Protect the Right of the Nigerian Child and Other Related Matters, 2003." *UNICEF*. Available from: http://www.unicef.org/nigeria/ng_publications_Childs_Right_Act_2003.pdf.
65. Braimah, "Child Marriage in Northern Nigeria," 474–488.
66. Ibid.
67. Rahman, S. 2014. "Child Bride Poisons Husband." *Mirror*. Available from: https://www.mirror.co.uk/news/world-news/child-bride-aged-14-killed-4867292.
68. Fayokun, K. 2015. "Legality of Child Marriage in Nigeria and Inhibitions against Realisation of Education Rights." *US-China L. Rev.* 12: 812.

69. Igbanoi, J. 2016. "Maimuma the Child Bride in Katsina Finally Released from Death Row." Available from: https://www.pressreader.com/nigeria/this day/20160913/281981787045628.
70. Akpan, E. 2003. "Early Marriage in Eastern Nigeria and the Health Consequences of Vesicovaginal Fistulae (VVF) among Young Mothers." *Gender & Development* 11, no. 2: 70–76. DOI: https://doi.org/10.1080/741954319.
71. National Population Commission, Federal Republic of Nigeria and ICF International, Maryland USA, "Nigeria Demographic and Health Survey 2013."
72. UNESCO, "Human Trafficking in Nigeria."
73. Makinde, et al., "Baby Factories in Nigeria," 98–105.
74. Olowoopejo, Monsuru. 2018. "Lagos Seals Three Baby Factory, Rescues 162 Abandon Babies." *Vanguard News* (blog), April 25, 2018. Available from: https://www.vanguardngr.com/2018/04/lagos-seals-three-baby-factory-rescues-162-abandon-babies/.
75. Makinde, O., Odimegwu, C., and Stella O. Babalola. 2017. "Reasons for Infertile Couples not to Patronize Baby Factories." *Health & Social Work* 42, no. 1: 57–59. DOI: https://doi.org/10.1093/hsw/hlw054.
76. Makinde, "Infant Trafficking and Baby Factories," 433–443.
77. Makinde, et al., "Reasons for Infertile Couples Not to Patronize Baby Factories," 57–59.
78. Makinde, O. et al. 2016. "Baby Factories Taint Surrogacy in Nigeria." *Reproductive Biomedicine Online* 32, no. 1: 6–8.
79. Onuoha, "The Evolving Menace of Baby Factories and Trafficking in Nigeria," 405–411.
80. Ibid.
81. Makinde, et al., "Baby Factories in Nigeria," 98–105.
82. Sahara Reporters, 2015. "Nigeria Army Busts Baby Factory in Enugu." *News, Sahara Reporters*. Available from: http://saharareporters.com/2015/08/26/nigeria-army-busts-baby-factory-enugu.
83. Adekoye, V. 2018. "NAPTIP Arrests 11 Child Traffickers in Anambra State … Rescues 3 Children—NAPTIP." Available from: https://www.naptip.gov.ng/?p=1679.
84. Jedy-Agba, E. et al. 2015. "Developing National Cancer Registration in Developing Countries—Case Study of the Nigerian National System of Cancer Registries." *Epidemiology*, no.186. Available from: https://doi.org/10.3389/fpubh.2015.00186.
85. Murray, C. et al. 2010. "Disability-Adjusted Life Years (DALYs) for 291 Diseases and Injuries in 21 Regions, 1990–2010: A Systematic Analysis for the Global Burden of Disease Study 2010." *The Lancet* 380, no. 9859: 2197–2223. DOI: https://doi.org/10.1016/S0140-6736(12)61689-4.
86. Arogundade, F. 2013. "Kidney Transplantation in a Low-Resource Setting: Nigeria Experience." *Kidney International Supplements*, Disparities in Renal Disease-Moving towards Solutions: Proceedings from the WCN 2011 Satellite Symposium 3, no. 2: 241–245. DOI: https://doi.org/10.1038/kisup.2013.23.
87. Ibid.
88. Ibid.
89. Capron, A. and Delmonico, F. 2015. "Preventing Trafficking in Organs for Transplantation: An Important Facet of the Fight against Human Trafficking." *Journal of Human Trafficking* 1, no. 1: 56–64. DOI: https://doi.org/10.1080/23322705.2015.1011491.

90. Budiani-Saberi, D. and Delmonico, F. 2008. "Organ Trafficking and Transplant Tourism: A Commentary on the Global Realities." *American Journal of Transplantation* 8, no. 5: 925–929. DOI: https://doi.org/10.1111/j.1600-6143.2008.02200.x.
91. UNODC, "Global Report on Trafficking in Persons 2016."
92. Ibid.
93. Ibid.
94. Okafor, U. 2017. "Transplant Tourism among Kidney Transplant Patients in Eastern Nigeria." *BMC Nephrology* 18: 215. DOI: https://doi.org/10.1186/s12882-017-0635-1.
95. Akpan, N. 2010. "Kidnapping in Nigeria's Niger Delta: An Exploratory Study." *Journal of Social Sciences* 24, no. 1: 33–42.
96. Ibid.
97. Osumah, O. and Aghedo, I. 2011. "Who Wants to Be a Millionaire? Nigerian Youths and the Commodification of Kidnapping." *Review of African Political Economy* 38, no. 128: 277–287. DOI: https://doi.org/10.1080/03056244.2011.582769.
98. Chiaramonte, P. 2014. "Girls Held by Boko Haram Face Auction, Life as Sex Slaves if Rescue Fails." *FoxNews*. Available from: http://www.foxnews.com/world/2014/05/08/girls-held-by-boko-haram-face-auction-life-as-sex-slaves-if-rescue-fails/.
99. Abubakr, A. and Almasy, S. 2015. "Girl, 13: Boko Haram Tried to Force Me to Become a Suicide Bomber—CNN.Com." *CNN*. Available from: http://edition.cnn.com/2014/12/26/world/africa/nigeria-teenage-girl-suicide-bombing/index.html.
100. Peters, M. 2014. "'Western Education Is Sinful': Boko Haram and the Abduction of Chibok Schoolgirls." *Policy Futures in Education* 12, no. 2. DOI: https://doi.org/dx.doi.org/10.2304/pfie.2014.12.2.186.
101. Ibid.
102. Martin, M. 2018. "In Dapchi, Mourning after Mass Kidnapping of Schoolgirls: NPR." Available from: https://www.npr.org/templates/transcript/transcript.php?storyId=592766452.
103. UNODC, "Transnational Trafficking and Rule of Law in West Africa."
104. *Trafficking in Persons (Prohibition) Law Enforcement and Administration Act 2003* (Nigeria, 2003).
105. Mancuso, "Not All Madams Have a Central Role," 66–88.
106. Obokata, "Trafficking of Human Beings as a Crime against Humanity," 445–458.
107. Silverman, J. et al. 2007. "HIV Prevalence and Predictors of Infection in Sex-Trafficked Nepalese Girls and Women." *Jama* 298, no. 5: 536–542.
108. Okonofua, et al., "Knowledge, Attitudes and Experiences of Sex Trafficking by Young Women in Benin City, South-South Nigeria," 1315–1327.
109. Omorodion, F. 2009. "Vulnerability of Nigerian Secondary School to Human Sex Trafficking in Nigeria." *African Journal of Reproductive Health* 13, no. 2: 33–48.
110. Abubakar, S. and Egunyanga, V., and Monday Osayande. 2010. "In Edo, Delta, Women Trafficking to Europe for Sex Is a Pride." Available from: https://www.dailytrust.com.ng/news/others/in-edo-delta-women-trafficking-to-europe-for-sex-is-a-pride/4505.html.
111. Mancuso, "Not All Madams Have a Central Role," 66–88.
112. Onuoha, "The Evolving Menace of Baby Factories and Trafficking in Nigeria," 405–411.
113. US Department of State, "Trafficking in Persons Report 2017."

114. Ibid.
115. Para-Mallam, F. 2017. "Gender Equality in Nigeria." In *Gender Equality in a Global Perspective*, First, Routledge Advances in Management and Business Studies 68, 23–53. https://www.routledge.com/Gender-Equality-in-a-Global-Perspective/Ortenblad-Marling-Vasiljevic/p/book/9781138193246.
116. Aibangbe, "Child Trafficking," 311–323.
117. Cristiansson, T. 2013. "Expressen Reveals Baby Factories." *Expressen*. Available from: http://www.expressen.se/nyheter/exclusive-expressen-reveals-baby-factories/.
118. Makinde, O. et al. 2017. "Rejection of the Gender and Equal Opportunities Bill in Nigeria: A Setback for Sustainable Development Goal Five." *Gender in Management: An International Journal* 32, no. 3: 234–240. DOI: https://doi.org/10.1108/GM-02-2017-0023.
119. Premium Times. 2016. "Nigerian Civic Groups Reject Gender Equality Bill." *Premium Times Nigeria* (blog). Available from: http://www.premiumtimesng.com/news/top-news/201201-nigerian-civic-groups-reject-gender-equality-bill.html.
120. Togunde, D. and Carter, A. 2008. "In Their Own Words: Consequences of Child Labor in Urban Nigeria." *Journal of Social Sciences* 16, no. 2: 173–181.
121. Abdulmalik et al., "Psychoactive Substance Use among Children in Informal Religious Schools (Almajiris) in Northern Nigeria," 527–542.
122. US Department of State, "Trafficking in Persons Report 2017."
123. UNODC, "Global Report on Trafficking in Persons 2016."
124. Onuoha, "The Evolving Menace of Baby Factories and Trafficking in Nigeria," 405–411.
125. Osumah, O. 2013. "Boko Haram Insurgency in Northern Nigeria and the Vicious Cycle of Internal Insecurity." *Small Wars & Insurgencies* 24, no. 3: 536–560. DOI: https://doi.org/10.1080/09592318.2013.802605.
126. UNESCO, "Human Trafficking in Nigeria"; UNICEF Nigeria, "Child Trafficking."
127. Maki'de, et al., "Baby Factories in Nigeria," 98–105.
128. US Department of State, "Trafficking in Persons Report 2017."
129. Ibid.
130. The World Bank, 2016. "Nigeria Data." Available from: http://data.worldbank.org/country/nigeria.

Chapter 6

MARITIME PIRACY

Dirk Siebels

Introduction

The lack of maritime security off Nigeria has been a long-standing concern for the shipping industry as well as for companies involved in offshore oil and gas production. While numbers and types of security incidents at sea have fluctuated over the past decade, the underlying threat of attacks has not changed significantly. Purely domestic maritime traffic, such as passenger boats in the Niger Delta or small trawlers fishing close to the coastline, is also affected and potentially even more at risk, yet it is impossible to provide a thorough analysis due to the lack of detailed and comprehensive reporting.[1] It should nevertheless be mentioned that insecurity at sea is a problem for international and domestic stakeholders.

For the Nigerian government, however, it has not been a priority to address maritime security issues such as piracy and armed robbery at sea with the necessary resources. Politicians, the Nigerian Navy, the Nigerian Maritime and Safety Administration (NIMASA), and other agencies have often pledged to tackle the problem,[2] yet words have not been translated into action. Because of the number and severity of security challenges on land, the government has to prioritize resources and it is understandable that offshore attacks do not receive the same attention as, for example, the fight against Boko Haram, counter-insurgency activities in the Niger Delta, or conflicts between farmers and nomadic herdsmen throughout central Nigeria. Nevertheless, insecurity at sea is a critical issue, mainly because of the importance of offshore oil and gas production and the economic reliance on maritime routes for imports and exports.

This chapter provides a deeper view into some of the problems created by piracy and, more generally, a lack of maritime security in Nigerian waters. It draws partly on extensive personal interviews with a broad range of interlocutors, conducted in the context of the author's PhD research between 2013 and 2017 on a non-attributable basis under the rule of confidentiality.

The first part of the chapter contains a look at statistics about piracy and armed robbery at sea, arguably the most noteworthy maritime security threats, particularly for international stakeholders. Most importantly, this part shows that even seemingly simple background data are not easy to gather, complicating further analyses.

The second part offers an overview of security concerns for private companies, from both the shipping industry and the offshore oil and gas sector. Finally, the chapter presents challenges and opportunities of public-private partnerships that have been established in recent years to address some of the most pressing concerns faced by the private sector.

The common thread throughout this chapter is a focus on the unique response to specific maritime security issues in Nigeria rather than a description of Nigerian piracy, which has been conducted by many authors.[3] Most importantly, arrangements that have been made in recent years will be scrutinized. These are based on a unique situation, characterized by a military with sufficient manpower but a limited number of operational assets and a thriving private sector that includes many companies willing to provide additional security measures. Moreover, the situation is unlikely to change in the near future and therefore deserves attention. Successes and setbacks of public-private partnerships to combat maritime security issues may also provide valuable lessons to address other security problems throughout Nigeria.

Crunching the Numbers

Reports compiled by the International Maritime Bureau (IMB) are often considered to be the most important documents providing figures about piracy and armed robbery at sea. Not all incidents that take place, however, are reported to the IMB and therefore included in the organization's official statistics. In the Gulf of Guinea, the problem of under-reporting is particularly noteworthy, underlined by IMB Director Pottengal Mukundan himself. In 2015, Mukundan estimated that up to 70 percent of all attacks against ships in the region are not reported to the IMB.[4]

There are three main reasons for the lack of reporting. First and foremost, ship operators are worried about their own reputation—any reported attack against one of their ships could have commercial repercussions. Furthermore, operators and masters generally do not have a lot of trust in regional law enforcement agencies, particularly in Nigeria where security forces are widely perceived to be corrupt and inefficient. In a personal conversation, a former captain on a container ship summarized the general feeling among crews on ships calling at Nigerian ports:

> *When we report a theft in port or at the anchorage, we end up with three or four agencies on the ship and are not allowed to leave for a day or two. When something more serious happens, the last thing you want is police or military on your ship because the crew has already gone through a lot and agencies are not exactly subtle.*[5]

Even anonymous reports are not a perfect solution because it is relatively easy to identify ships based on incident positions or other information. In short, the shipping industry has much to lose and little to gain from reporting attacks against merchant vessels at sea.

Finally, it is very likely that at least some of the ships that are attacked off Nigeria are involved in illegal operations, ranging from fuel smuggling to illegal fishing.[6] For obvious reasons, masters or owners of these vessels will only report attacks to the relevant authorities in exceptional circumstances.

Despite these limitations, IMB statistics are among the most widely quoted figures on piracy and armed robbery at sea, particularly in academic articles,[7] although they were never meant to be used for academic analysis. Other sources, however, show a somewhat different picture of the situation, notably databases compiled by commercial companies such as Risk Intelligence, a Denmark-based security intelligence company, or providers like Oceanus Live and Dryad Maritime. These providers take official reports into account but can also use other sources, for example, media articles and confidential reports from their own clients or local contacts. Moreover, any credible commercial database is based on independent verification of incidents by at least two independent sources. Figure 6.1 shows a comparison of reports about piracy and armed robbery at sea off Nigeria as compiled by Risk Intelligence in a commercial database and by the IMB.

Commercial providers are sometimes criticized for exaggerated reporting,[8] yet this criticism does not apply to credible databases operated by companies offering independent security advice to clients from the maritime industry with operational experience in specific regions. Even providers of commercial databases, however, cannot gather information about every attack at sea. The numbers shown in Figure 6.1 therefore provide a better picture of the maritime security situation off Nigeria than the IMB database yet at least some under-reporting is still very likely.

While that is important to keep in mind, different short-term and medium-term trends in both databases are more significant as "the interpretation of maritime security in the Gulf of Guinea can differ significantly."[9] Increasing or decreasing numbers of piracy incidents as shown in Figure 6.1 are linked to different factors, ranging from weather conditions or the activity of militant groups throughout the Niger Delta to electoral cycles in Nigeria or the temporary presence of security forces in areas from where offshore attacks are frequently launched.

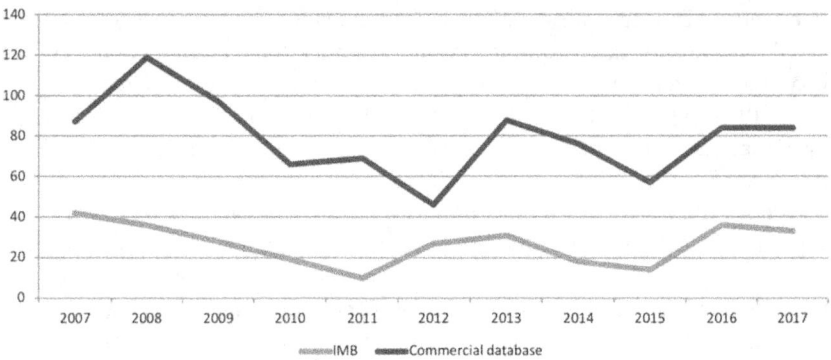

Figure 6.1 Incidents of piracy and armed robbery at sea as reported by IMB and Risk Intelligence in a commercial database between 2007 and 2017.

Moreover, a comprehensive analysis of incident types shows that maritime operators have to take precautions against different threats depending on the area. For example, hijackings for the purpose of cargo theft are often highlighted in media articles,[10] but these attacks are only directed against product tankers carrying refined petroleum products, not crude oil tankers or other types of ships. Since 2016, the situation has changed somewhat as attackers are even more likely to target vessels with the objective of taking crew members as hostages, a threat that has existed for many years but has developed into an increasingly lucrative industry, potentially affecting all types of ships, including supply vessels for Nigeria's offshore industry. The decrease in tanker hijackings from relatively high numbers of incidents between 2010 and 2013 is largely based on better law enforcement on land in Nigeria (where most of the stolen cargo was later sold) and an increasing responsiveness by the Nigerian Navy, underlined by the boarding of the hijacked product tanker *Maximus* in 2016.[11] The perceived shift has also been explained by a fall in oil prices that started at roughly the same time, yet there is no proven correlation. Lower prices for crude oil do not translate into lower prices for kerosene, premium motor sprit, or other refined products in Nigeria and elsewhere in West Africa. Based on a lack of supplies, prices for petroleum products may even rise despite lower crude oil prices.[12] Kidnap-for-ransom attacks generally take place no more than 150 kilometers from the coastline, particularly off Bayelsa and Rivers states where kidnappings on land have been a major security threat for years.[13]

Detailed analyses of specific types and locations of incidents are not only relevant for the maritime industry, they are also a valuable tool for strategic planning and policy decisions. When it comes to maritime security off Nigeria, however, perspectives of different stakeholders vary significantly. The maritime industry, particularly international shipping and insurance companies, points at numbers similar to those from the commercial database shown in Figure 6.1. Nigerian government agencies refer to statistics akin to those provided by the IMB, emphasizing that the problem is in fact much smaller than highlighted by international industry organizations. NIMASA and the Nigerian Navy, the two most important agencies in the context of maritime security, even have their own set of figures. During a presentation at Chatham House in January 2018, statistics for 2017 were shown, indicating that the Nigerian Navy or NIMASA recorded forty attacks against merchant vessels over the course of the year.[14] That is slightly higher than the thirty-three attacks reported by the IMB, but still considerably lower than the eighty-four incidents recorded in the commercial database quoted in Figure 6.1.

Overall, the lack of consensus on reliable figures on attacks against merchant ships enables various stakeholders to base their arguments on a different set of assumptions. While the exact number of incidents is just one aspect in any discussion about maritime security, it is a perfect example to highlight the challenges regarding maritime security. International shipping organizations are constantly pointing out that the Gulf of Guinea, particularly the area off the Niger Delta, is the most dangerous area for seafarers worldwide.[15] In Nigeria, the problem has been recognized but is by and large regarded as an extension of land-based security problems in the Niger Delta, which are more important for the Nigerian government, analyzed in other chapters throughout this book. Moreover, security agencies have to deal with a number of other security threats throughout the country, such as the Boko Haram insurgency, farmer-herdsmen clashes, and the Biafran independence movement. Compared with attacks at sea, those other threats often have an immediate impact on ordinary Nigerians, meaning that resources are more likely to be allocated to security agencies tasked with addressing them.

At the same time, problems with maritime security off Nigeria, exemplified by but not limited to piracy, are a constantly evolving threat, creating challenges for the Nigerian Navy and other security agencies. Groups that are linked to other forms of criminal activities such as oil theft, smuggling, and kidnapping, conduct many attacks, even militant attacks against the oil and gas industry.[16] From a Nigerian point of view, piracy is therefore just another symptom of security challenges in the Niger Delta, recognized by several operations conducted by the Nigerian Navy and the Joint Task Force in the Niger Delta in recent years.[17] It is therefore extremely unlikely that maritime security in general or piracy in particular can be addressed in isolation. Nevertheless, it would be important for the Nigerian government to recognize the scale of the problem as perceived from the outside and the implications on the Nigerian economy, especially the "blue economy,"[18] to allocate resources to security agencies accordingly.

Security Concerns for the Private Sector

Limited capacities to provide security in the maritime environment may be a low priority for the Nigerian government. In the private sector, however, the situation is a much more immediate concern. Insecurity at sea is a problem for shipping companies as well as oil majors operating offshore platforms and their subcontractors. Companies have to protect their operational assets and have a duty of care toward their own employees, creating the motivation to pay for additional security figures.

Overall numbers of piracy incidents off Nigeria have been shown in Figure 6.1. For shipping companies, the kidnapping of crewmembers has been the main problem in recent years. According to figures published by the IMB, sixty-five seafarers were kidnapped from merchant vessels off Nigeria in 2017.[19] In the first quarter of 2018, the number of attacks increased compared with the same period in the previous year, although relatively few of these attacks were successful. Between January and March 2018, fourteen seafarers were kidnapped off Nigeria.[20]

For the offshore industry, security has long been a challenge, even for platforms relatively far away from the coastline. Between 2006 and 2010, the Movement for the Emancipation of the Niger Delta (MEND) and affiliated groups successfully attacked several installations, notably in the Pennington, Okwori, and Bonga fields.[21] The attack against the Bonga field in 2008 was particularly noteworthy as the field is located about 120 kilometers off the coast and produces more than 10 percent of Nigeria's crude output. Furthermore, MEND attacks came after international oil companies had increased their investments in offshore projects "to offset the risk to onshore operations in the Niger Delta."[22] Such attacks continue to inspire militant groups, underlined by a statement issued by the Niger Delta Avengers in January 2018 that threatened attacks against several large offshore installations.[23]

Public-Private Security Partnerships

In a bid to protect their investments during the MEND insurgency, international oil companies wanted to increase security around offshore installations but Nigerian security forces did not have the necessary capacity. Between 2008 and 2010, this led to a hybrid model in which oil companies charter specific vessels, which are partly manned by security forces personnel, usually from the Nigerian Navy. Naval personnel are responsible for weapons and ammunition as well as the response to attacks, but the vessels are almost solely used for the protection of specific offshore oil fields or export terminals on the Nigerian coastline. Exceptions are made in cases of emergencies in the vicinity of the operational area, for example, to provide assistance to ships that are under attack and have sent a distress signal to call for help, but not for other more general purposes in the broader context of maritime security.

This type of collaboration between the Nigerian Navy and international oil companies has worked well, partly because the military and oil majors have a long history of cooperation, including under highly controversial circumstances.[24] In the maritime environment, this cooperation also led to the increasing role of private companies that were hired to protect merchant ships. Supply of security services finally began to match demand since piracy had been a problem for maritime operators in the country for a long time,[25] even though types and locations of attacks have constantly shifted over the years. At the same time, many shipping companies have grown increasingly comfortable with the employment of privately contracted armed security personnel after their experiences related to Somali piracy. In 2016, an estimated 34 percent of all transits through the high-risk area in the Indian Ocean—roughly including the southern Red Sea and the Gulf of Aden—were conducted with armed guards onboard.[26] For West Africa, Oceans beyond Piracy estimated the total costs of contracted maritime security services in 2016 at more than $300 million, indicating the widespread use of such services.[27]

Shipping companies often fail to recognize that the provision of additional security measures is completely different from the business model created by the private maritime security industry in the Indian Ocean, yet the willingness to pay for better protection of ships, crews, and cargoes increased dramatically within just a few years, starting around 2008.[28] Armed guards on merchant ships were quickly recognized as an effective deterrent against attacks by Somali pirates and shipping companies wanted to simply transfer the same model to the other side of the African continent.

From a security point of view, additional protection for merchant ships calling at Nigerian ports makes perfect sense. The country's territorial waters and large parts of the Exclusive Economic Zone are so-called "listed areas," effectively defined as a high-risk area by the Joint War Committee.[29] The committee's recommendations have enormous influence on the marine insurance market, making port calls in Nigeria more expensive.[30] In combination with low freight rates, this has led large shipping companies such as MOL or NYK to stop sending ships to Nigeria altogether.[31] Moreover, a lot of imports and exports are conducted via Cotonou in neighboring Benin instead.[32]

From a commercial point of view, added security measures are an expensive band-aid for the shipping industry. For oil companies operating offshore fields, the costs for several chartered patrol boats are almost negligible compared with the overall costs for offshore oil production. Shipping companies have to calculate on a much tighter budget, especially considering that the shipping industry has been in an almost constant financial crisis between 2009 and 2017.[33] Chartering an escort vessel is therefore a significant financial outlay, compared with the operating costs of a merchant ship.

Widespread demand from the shipping industry for "security on the cheap," combined with lax enforcement of existing regulations by Nigerian authorities, has led to opaque arrangements between private security companies and security forces. In theory, cooperation between the Nigerian Navy and security companies registered in the country is based on a memorandum of understanding (MoU), signed by the Chief of Naval Staff. The MoU was originally introduced as a framework for the Navy's collaboration with private companies that agreed to certain terms. The first version was issued in April 2013 to eventually more than forty companies[34] before a revised MoU came into force in January 2016, limiting the number of security providers with this type of official endorsement to twenty in a bid to curtail operational deficiencies.

The MoU is solely concerned with the provision of patrol boats that are owned and maintained by security companies but have to be certified by the Nigerian Navy. All boats then come under operational command by the navy and are partly manned by naval personnel when they are contracted to provide security for export terminals, offshore installations, or merchant vessels in Nigerian waters.[35]

Unfortunately, the Nigerian Navy has never made the MoU or the signatory companies publicly available, allowing security companies such as the Daimon Group[36] to claim that their services have been officially authorized. Even established companies with a track record of security provision in the Indian Ocean, therefore, have established Nigerian subsidiaries or relationships with local partners before adjusting their business model slightly and employing government security forces as armed guards on merchant ships. Despite the fact that there is no legal background for such arrangements, security companies and even ship agents have been able to provide these services for years, often facilitated by corrupt officers in the Nigerian Navy, the marine police, and other security agencies.[37]

It should also be noted that the shipping industry as a whole is not satisfied with the current situation. Although many shipping companies may be using additional security services, industry organizations have repeatedly criticized these arrangements. They have stressed that it is the Nigerian government's responsibility to provide adequate security without any direct financial contributions from ship operators.[38] It is an argument that goes back to the Westphalian model of the modern nation-state, which prescribes that states retain the monopoly on the use of force within their own borders, including in territorial waters.[39]

Overall, the provision of security in Nigeria's maritime environment is, at least in theory, governed by strict rules and regulations. For example, the Nigerian Navy is the only agency that has jurisdiction in territorial waters and the Exclusive Economic Zone. However, very little documentation and guidelines are publicly available. In practice, even marine police personnel are often employed as armed guards on merchant ships, despite the fact that no legal background for the employment of armed guards exists and marine police personnel would not be allowed to operate outside of the immediate vicinity of ports and harbors in the first place.[40] In short, a general lack of transparency in extant maritime security frameworks in Nigeria leads to opaque arrangements and, more importantly, the establishment or continuation of corrupt practices as detailed in Chapter 2 of this book. While these problems related to the maritime security sector are hardly unique in Nigeria, the involvement of international actors, namely, foreign shipping companies, offers the potential to introduce unique solutions, fitting the requirements of both the private sector and Nigerian security agencies.

Challenges and Opportunities

The growing involvement of private companies in the provision of maritime security in Nigeria has led to a range of political and legal questions. Increased involvement of the private sector may be beneficial because it will take a long time to remedy deficiencies in the Nigerian Navy and other security agencies that have developed over years, largely caused by inadequate funding. At the same time, it is highly controversial to assign security-related tasks to private companies or other actors outside traditional security agencies because it is one of the core functions of any state.

Another example from Nigeria underlines the reluctance to discuss the services of private security companies in a different context. Prior to the presidential election in 2015, then-president Goodluck Jonathan was desperate to achieve military success against Boko Haram after the group had wreaked havoc in the northeastern part of the country, diminishing Jonathan's chances of electoral success. The military then "brought in hundreds of mercenaries from South Africa and the former Soviet Union to give its offensive against Boko Haram a shot in the arm."[41] However, the involvement of private contractors was never officially confirmed.[42]

The situation in the maritime environment is similar. Private companies have been involved in the provision of security services for years, yet public information about their role is largely non-existent. In certain areas, that may be justified due to operational security or similar reasons. Overall, however, such a lack of transparency is the foundation for backroom deals between current and former politicians, ex-militants, senior military officers, and private investors. The controversy over a contract between NIMASA and a company linked to former militant leader Government Ekpemukpolo ("Tompolo") is arguably the most prominent example of such practices. In 2012, the company received a government contract over the provision of twenty patrol boats to Nigerian security agencies,[43] which was later canceled under the new government led by President Muhammadu Buhari. Tompolo also became subject of a corruption investigation in Nigeria[44] while the purchase of some patrol vessels was also linked to corruption among civil servants in Norway and the UK.[45]

Furthermore, it may be impossible to judge the quality of services provided by companies involved in any type of public-private partnership when no details about the actual partnership are available. That is problematic for two reasons: it complicates the due diligence process for private companies looking to employ security services in the maritime environment and it is almost impossible to assess the long-term success or otherwise of such public-private partnerships. From a political point of view, it will be difficult to say with certainty whether these partnerships are actually beneficial to Nigeria as a whole.

While it is tempting to look at the maritime sector in isolation, similar arrangements have led to a slow erosion of authority for Nigerian security agencies. Another example from the fight against Boko Haram is the Civilian Joint Task Force (CJTF), a vigilante group with more than 20,000 members.[46] The CJTF is not under the direct command of the military or the police, but it has been encouraged by the authorities and described as "the eyes and ears of the counter-insurgency campaign."[47] Other vigilante groups have been established in states throughout Nigeria to counter, often-local, security threats because official security agencies often lack capacities and resources. In most cases, vigilantes offer a short-term remedy for immediate problems but the repercussions of such arrangements in the longer term are rarely addressed.[48]

In the maritime environment, the difference is that the Nigerian Navy is cooperating with private companies rather than vigilante groups organized by the civilian population. On the one hand, that seems to complicate the cooperation because private companies have a commercial focus. They want to provide security specifically for their own clients while the Nigerian Navy has an overarching task to provide security in the country's maritime domain. On the other hand, it makes cooperation easier than between security agencies and vigilante groups because the commercial focus of private companies will remain independent of ongoing developments in the security sector.

Some examples show that private companies can indeed help to improve maritime security by addressing long-standing capacity constraints. That includes the use of patrol boats to protect offshore platforms and other facilities used by the oil and gas industry as explained above. Another example is a secure anchorage area that was established off Lagos, the country's largest port, in December 2013 because of shortcomings in port infrastructure, leading to problems with congestion. Ships often had to wait for several days to enter port, leaving them vulnerable to attacks in the area, yet the Nigerian Navy did not have enough patrol vessels to provide protection around the clock.

Ocean Marine Solutions (OMS) in cooperation with the Nigerian Navy developed the concept for the secure anchorage. OMS is a Nigerian company that operates a fleet of more than forty patrol boats based on the MoU explained above. All patrol boats are inspected by the navy and partly manned by naval personnel. OMS personnel make up the other half of the crew, consisting of fourteen to sixteen people overall. Naval personnel exclusively handle weapons and ammunition, while the management of all patrol boats is handled by OMS. The company is remunerated by clients looking for additional protection. Ship operators therefore have the choice between the general anchorage area, which they can use free of charge or for a daily rate, a designated anchorage area that is protected around the clock by patrol vessels.[49]

Representatives from the shipping industry are skeptical about this model because ship operators have to pay for additional protection, which, as they see it, should be provided by the Nigerian Navy.[50] However, the model was authorized by NIMASA, coordinates for the area are included in official charts. From the Nigerian Navy's point of view, naval capacities have increased without any budgetary commitments due to additional patrol boats that are owned and managed by OMS. The cooperation has therefore served its purpose, namely, to provide better security in the vicinity of the port without having to go through a long process of budget allocation and procurement. Despite objections from the shipping industry, this example therefore shows the potential of private-sector involvement to solve maritime security problems.

Conclusion

Employing private companies to provide services specified by relevant authorities could help the Nigerian government to address short-term capacity gaps, allowing the Nigerian Navy and other security agencies with a maritime remit to develop capabilities in the longer term. After all, even an unlimited budget would not enable the Nigerian Navy to instantly protect ports and harbors throughout the country, combat oil theft and fuel smuggling, supervise fishing activities, and conduct a diverse range of other duties. However, these issues have direct impacts on foreign and domestic companies involved in Nigeria's "blue economy," and more importantly, on the daily lives of millions of Nigerians. Maritime security, therefore, has to be an integral part of any discussion about security issues in Nigeria as a whole.

Sustainable development of naval capabilities should be based on a strategic framework that involves various stakeholders, ranging from government agencies to shipping companies, port operators, and local fishing communities. Long-term procurement decisions and the development of human resources can then be derived from such a framework, enabling the government to address capacity and capability gaps.

Some problems, such as piracy and armed robbery at sea, have to be addressed as soon as possible. Another issue is comprehensive surveillance of the maritime domain, which requires adequate and functional infrastructure to combat activities such as smuggling or illegal fishing.[51] Based on transparent contracts and routinely, scrutinized by government agencies, private companies could help to address such issues.

As outlined above, some public-private partnerships have already been created to enhance security at sea, yet these are neither transparent nor regularly scrutinized. That complicates responses to long-standing problems with piracy and armed robbery at sea, but also the introduction of public-private partnerships in other areas. It is, after all, largely a philosophical question for the government whether to privatize specific tasks as security continues to be regarded as one of the core areas of sovereignty for any modern nation-state.

Notes

1. For further details about the impact of piracy and armed robbery at sea on the Nigerian fishing industry see Uche, Usim. 2016. "Nigeria: Sea Pirates Killing Nigeria's Fishing Industry." *Fishery Committee for the West Central Gulf of Guinea*. Available from:https://fcwc-fish.org/publications/news-from-the-region/780-nigeria-sea-pirates-killing-nigeria"s-fishing-industry; Adongoi, Toakodi, Brown, Aniekan and Udensi, Lawrence. 2017. "The Impact of Sea Robbery on Artisanal Fishing in Rural Settlements in Niger Delta Region of Nigeria." *International Journal of Innovation and Sustainability* 1: 32–43.
2. Ejoh, Ediri. 2012. "Nigeria Navy Seeks Collaboration to Fight Piracy." *Vanguard*. Available from: https://www.vanguardngr.com/2012/12/nigeria-navy-seeks-collaboration-to-fight-piracy/; Una, Emma. 2014. "Navy Assures on Sustained Fight against Piracy, Others." *Vanguard*. Available from: https://www.vanguardngr.com/2014/06/navy-assures-sustained-fight-piracy-others/; Olawoyin, Oladeinde. 2017. "Buhari Pledges to Rid Nigerian Waters of Pirates." *Premium Times*. Available from: https://www.premiumtimesng.com/news/more-news/229534-%E2%80%8Ebuhari-pledges-rid-nigerian-waters-pirates.html; Abiodun, Eromosele. 2018. "Nigeria Strategic to Tackling Maritime Crimes in GoG, Says NIMASA." *This Day*. Available from: https://www.thisdaylive.com/index.php/2018/02/02/nigeria-strategic-to-tackling-maritime-crimes-in-gog-says-nimasa/.
3. Onuoha, Freedom. *Piracy and Maritime Security in the Gulf of Guinea: Nigeria as a Microcosm*; Steffen, Dirk. 2012. Maritime Security in the Gulf of Guinea in 2016. Maritime Executive. Al Jazeera Centre for Studies. Available at: https://www.maritime-executive.com/editorials/maritime-security-in-the-gulf-of-guinea-in-2016#gs.LassusE; Brume-Eruagbere, Omovigho Cynthia, "Maritime Law Enforcement in Nigeria: The Challenges of Combating Piracy and Armed Robbery at Sea." MSc diss., World Maritime University, Malmö, 2017, World Maritime University Dissertations (555).

4. Oceans beyond Piracy. *The State of Maritime Piracy Report 2014*. Denver, CO: One Earth Future Foundation, 2015. 37 Available from: http://oceansbeyondpiracy.org/reports/sop/east-africa.
5. Personal interview with representative from a West African shipping company, May 2015.
6. Onuoha, Freedom C. 2013. "Piracy and Maritime Security in the Gulf of Guinea: Trends, Concerns, and Propositions." *The Journal of Middle East and Africa* 4, no. 3: 276.
7. Nincic, Donna. 2009. "Maritime Piracy in Africa: The Humanitarian Dimension." *African Security Review* 18, no. 3: 2–16. & Anyimadu, Adjoa. 2013. *Maritime Security in the Gulf of Guinea: Lessons Learned from the Indian Ocean*. London: Chatham House; Forster, Bruce. "Modern Maritime Piracy: An Overview of Somali Piracy, Gulf of Guinea Piracy and South East Asian Piracy." *British Journal of Economics, Management & Trade* 4, no. 8: 1251–1272 ; Otto, Lisa. "Maritime Crime in Nigeria and Waters beyond Analysing the Period 2009 to 2013." *Africa Insight* 45, no. 1: 15–29.
8. The former Director General of NIMASA, Patrick Akpobolokemi, even made headlines when he accused foreign insurance companies of exaggerating the number of piracy attacks off Nigeria to hike their premiums. Dauda, Oluwakemi. 2014. "NIMASA Raises the Alarm over 'False' Pirates' Reports." *The Nation*. Available from: http://thenationonlineng.net/nimasa-raises-alarm-false-pirates-reports/.
9. Steffen, Dirk. 2015. Essay: Quantifying Piracy Trends in the Gulf of Guinea—Who's Right and Who's Wrong?. USNI News. *Nigeria's Booming Borders: The Drivers and Consequences of Unrecorded Trade*. London: Chatham House, 2015.
10. Ben-Ari, Nirit. 2013. "Piracy in West Africa. Africa Renewal." *African Renewal, UN*. Available from: http://www.un.org/africarenewal/magazine/december-2013/piracy-west-africa; Starr, Stephen. "Maritime Piracy on the Rise in West Africa." *CTC Sentinel* 7, no. 4: 23–25; Harper, Mary. 2014. "Danger Zone: Chasing West Africa's Pirates." *BBC*. Available from: http://www.bbc.co.uk/news/world-africa-30024009.
11. Busari, Stephanie. 2016. "Nigerian Navy Recovers Hijacked Oil Tanker After Gun Battle." *CNN*. Available from: https://edition.cnn.com/2016/02/23/africa/nigeria-navy-rescues-oil-tanker/index.html.
12. Despite evidence to the contrary, many academics and industry experts have stated that the threat of kidnap-for-ransom attacks off Nigeria has increased because hijackings of product tankers are less lucrative than in previous years due to lower oil prices; examples include: Mungai, Christine. 2016. "Another Twist from the Oil Price Crash—Pirates off West Africa Don't Want to Steal It, and They Are More Violent than Somalia's. Mail & Guardian Africa." Available from: http://mgafrica.com/article/2016-05-03-trends-in-piracy-2015-report; Thompson, Andrew. 2018. "West African Pirates Taking Hostages for Ransom as Oil Prices Tank." *ABC News*. Available from: http://www.abc.net.au/news/2018-02-20/struggling-west-african-pirates-taking-hostages-to-survive/9462082.
13. Aghedo, Iro. 2015. "Sowing Peace, Reaping Violence: Understanding the Resurgence of Kidnapping in Post-amnesty Niger Delta, Nigeria." *Insight on Africa* 7, no. 2: 137–153.
14. Private roundtable discussion "Nigeria's Role in Responding to Maritime Insecurity in the Gulf of Guinea" held at Chatham House, London on January 23, 2018.
15. World Maritime News, 2017. "Gulf of Guinea Piracy Raises Concerns among EU Shipowners." Available from: https://worldmaritimenews.com/archives/224076/gulf-

of-guinea-piracy-raises-concerns-among-eu-shipowners/; Hellenic Shipping News, 2018. "Piracy in West Africa—a Persistent and Serious Threat." Available from: http://www.hellenicshippingnews.com/piracy-in-west-africa-a-persistent-and-serious-threat/.
16. Onuoha, Freedom. 2016. *The Resurgence of Militancy in Nigeria's Oil-Rich Niger Delta and the Dangers of Militarisation*. Al Jazeera Centre for Studies.
17. Maritime security has been bolstered by several naval operations in 2016 and 2017, notably "Operation Tsare Teku," launched in April 2016 to suppress offshore piracy. The Nigerian military has also conducted "Operation Delta Safe" and "Operation Crocodile Smile" over the same timeframe to reduce the threat of insurgency in the Niger Delta, reduce oil theft in the region, and limit the number of attacks on inshore waterways. The military, however, has been stretched because forces are also engaged in the provision of security in other parts of the country where high-profile operations have been carried out in the same period.
18. The "blue economy" describes a concept that combines all economic activities linked to the maritime environment. For more information on the blue economy in Africa, see United Nations Economic Commission for Africa. 2016. *Africa's Blue Economy: A Policy Handbook*. Addis Ababa: Economic Commission for Africa.
19. IMB, 2018. "Maritime Piracy and Armed Robbery Reaches 22-year Low." Available from: https://www.icc-ccs.org/index.php/1240-maritime-piracy-and-armed-robbery-reaches-22-year-low-says-imb-report.
20. IMB, 2018. "Pirate Attacks Worsen in Gulf of Guinea." Available from: https://www.icc-ccs.org/index.php/1244-pirate-attacks-worsen-in-gulf-of-guinea.
21. Tattersall, Nick. 2008. "Nigeria Attack Stops Shell's Bonga Offshore Oil." *Reuters*. Available from: https://uk.reuters.com/article/uk-nigeria-shell-attack/nigeria-attack-stops-shells-bonga-offshore-oil-idUKL1961289220080620.
22. Ibid.
23. Agbinibo, Murdoch. 2018. "Happy Doomed Year Nigeria; Get Ready for Operation Bringing Down FPSO. Niger Delta Avengers." Available from: http://www.nigerdeltaavengers.org/2018/01/happy-doomed-year-nigeria-get-ready-for.html.
24. In 2011, court documents revealed that Shell had routinely worked with Nigerian security forces in the 1990s to suppress opposition to the company's activities in the Niger Delta: Visal, John. 2011. "Shell Oil Paid Nigerian Military to Put Down Protests, Court Documents Show." *Guardian*. Available from: https://www.theguardian.com/world/2011/oct/03/shell-oil-paid-nigerian-military; Similar accusations about the complicity of international oil companies active in Nigeria and the Nigerian military had been made as early as 1999 by Human Rights Watch: Human Rights Watch. *The Price of Oil: Corporate Responsibility and Human Rights Violations in Nigeria's Oil Producing Communities*. Human Rights Watch, 1999.
25. International Maritime Organization. 1983. *Circular 367: Piracy and Armed Robbery (incl. Add. 1 and Add. 2)*. London: IMO.
26. Oceans beyond Piracy, *The State of Maritime Piracy Report 2016*.
27. Ibid.
28. For a discussion about the background of the increasing role of private maritime security companies and attempts to regulate the industry see Siebels, Dirk. 2014. "International Standards for the Private Security Industry." *The RUSI Journal*, 159:5. 76–83.
29. The Joint War Committee comprises representatives from the maritime insurance industry in London, traditionally the biggest market for maritime insurance

services worldwide, see also No Author. 2018. Joint War Committee. Lloyds Market Association. Available from: http://www.lmalloyds.com/lma/jointwar. At the time of writing in May 2018, the most recent changes to the "Listed Areas" had been made in December 2015 but the most recent relevant change for Nigeria was made in August 2011 when the area covered was changed from territorial waters and offshore installations to "Gulf of Guinea, but only the waters of the Beninese and Nigerian Exclusive Economic Zones north of Latitude 3° N," a much larger area outside of Nigeria's territorial waters which has not been changed since. The most recent document detailing the Listed Areas is available on the Lloyd's Market Association website listed above.

30. "Ship owners must gain their underwriter's permission before their vessels can enter an area listed by the JWC. Underwriters may then amend cover terms before granting permission for vessels to enter the Listed Area, usually with an additional premium, or refuse to grant cover altogether." Page, Gray. 2013. "What Are the Impacts of an Expanded JWC Listed Area in the Gulf of Guinea." Available from: https://www.graypage.com/think-tank/what-are-the-impacts-of-an-expanded-jwc-listed-area-in-the-gulf-of-guinea/.

31. Wackett, Mike. 2015. "NYK Quits as Asia-West Africa Trade Goes 'from Bad to Worse' with Rates and Volumes Falling." *The Loadstar*. Available from: https://theloadstar.co.uk/nyk-quits-asia-west-africa-trade-goes-bad-worse-rates-volumes-plunging/.

32. The use of Cotonou as a hub for Nigeria is not only based on security-related issues. Other reasons include port and hinterland infrastructure as well as easier bureaucratic procedures. See also Hoffmann, Leena Koni, and Melly, Paul. 2015. *Nigeria's Booming Borders: The Drivers and Consequences of Unrecorded Trade*. London: Chatham House.

33. Barua, Akrur, and Mittal, Anshu. 2017. "Shipping: Sailing in Troubled Waters." Deloitte Insights, February 14. Available from: https://www2.deloitte.com/insights/us/en/economy/global-economic-outlook/2017/shipping-industry-crisis.html.

34. Steffen, Dirk. 2014. "Troubled Waters? The Use of the Nigerian Navy and Police in Private Maritime Security Roles." *CIMSEC*. Available from: http://cimsec.org/troubled-waters-use-nigerian-navy-police-private-maritime-security-roles/11918.

35. Personal interview with West Africa expert from a maritime security consultancy, November 2017.

36. The Whistler. 2016. "Group Alleges Fraudulent Practices by UK Shipping Provider." Available from: https://thewhistler.ng/story/group-alleges-fraudulent-practices-by-uk-shipping-provider/.

37. Ibid.

38. Personal interview with representative from the Baltic International and Marine Council (BIMCO), February 2015.

39. According to the United Nations Convention on the Law of the Sea (UNCLOS), territorial waters extend at most 12 nautical miles from the coastal state's so-called baseline into the ocean. All laws that apply on land also apply in territorial waters, making it essentially a maritime extension of a country's territory. The Exclusive Economic Zone is an area between 12 and 200 nautical miles from the coastline. Legal instruments that apply on land or in territorial waters cannot be applied here but the coastal state has the right to regulate economic activities such as fishing or oil production.

40. Steffen, "Troubled Waters? The Use of the Nigerian Navy and Police in Private Maritime Security Roles."
41. Cropley, Ed and Lewis, David. 2015. "Nigeria Drafts in Foreign Mercenaries to Take on Boko Haram." *Reuters*. Available from: https://uk.reuters.com/article/uk-nigeria-violence-mercenaries/nigeria-drafts-in-foreign-mercenaries-to-take-on-boko-haram-idUKKBN0M80VT20150312.
42. Freeman, Colin. 2015. "South African Mercenaries' Secret War on Boko Haram." *The Telegraph*. Available from: https://www.telegraph.co.uk/news/worldnews/africaandindianocean/nigeria/11596210/South-African-mercenaries-secret-war-on-Boko-Haram.html.
43. Sahara Reporters. 2012. "Jonathan Gives 'Tompolo' Contract to Supply 20 Marine Patrol Vessels to Navy." Available from: http://saharareporters.com/2012/07/24/jonathan-gives-"tompolo"-contract-supply-20-marine-patrol-vessels-navy.
44. Amaize, Emma. 2017. "Underground for 2 Yrs, Tompolo Still Looms Large in Ljaw Nation." *Vanguard*. Available from: https://www.vanguardngr.com/2017/12/underground-2-yrs-tompolo-still-looms-large-ijaw-nation/.
45. Gibbs, Margot, Holden, Paul, and Hawley, Susan. 2017. "Dereliction of Duty: How Weak Arms Export Licence Controls in the UK Facilitated Corruption and Exacerbated Instability in the Niger Delta." *Corruption Watch*. Available from: https://docs.wixstatic.com/ugd/54261c_3f990fe3175c48c5b90ed65a41192d59.pdf.
46. Matfess, Hilary. 2017. "Nigeria Wakes Up to Its Growing Vigilante Problem." *IRIN*. Available from: https://www.irinnews.org/analysis/2017/05/09/nigeria-wakes-its-growing-vigilante-problem.
47. Ibid.
48. Bamidele, Oluwaseun. 2016. "Civilian Joint Task Force (CJTF)—A Community Security Option: A Comprehensive and Proactive Approach of Reducing Terrorism." *Journal for Deradicalization* 7: 124–144. & Adamu, Ladi S. 2016. "The Media's Role in Quelling Violent Conflict Involving Youths as Foot Soldiers: A Content Analysis of News Report on Boko Haram Suicide Bombers and Civilian Joint Task Force-CJTF." *International Journal of Innovative Research & Development* 5, no. 9: 257–266.
49. Personal interview with West Africa expert from a maritime security consultance, November 2017.
50. Personal interview with representative from the Baltic International and Marine Council (BIMCO), February 2015.
51. NIMASA is supposed to operate a satellite surveillance system for territorial waters and the Exclusive Economic Zone, codenamed *Falcon Eye*. There are, however, frequent rumors that the system is still not fully operational, despite NIMASA representatives repeatedly stating the value of the system. Ogbuokiri, Paul. 2018. "NIMASA's Satellite Surveillance System Down in 2017-Sources." *New Telegraph*. Available from: https://newtelegraphonline.com/2018/01/nimasas-satellite-surveillance-system-2017-sources/.

Chapter 7

MILITANTS OF THE NIGER DELTA

Jude Cocodia

Introduction

Violent agitations may be a twenty-first century phenomenon of Nigeria's Niger Delta, but its seeds were sown and nurtured from the 1960s. Different theories meld to explain the increasing insecurity in the Niger Delta. The frustration-aggression, human needs, and resource curse theories provide justification for the violent response of Niger Deltans to decades of exploitation and neglect. While the militants of the Niger Delta region (NDR) allude to the frustration-aggression and human needs theories of conflict as the basis for their agitations, scholars present a more complex web of factors as responsible for the violence in the region. Scholars such as Bøås, Ikelegbe, Keen, Okumagba, Sayne, and Watts contend that economic opportunism such as criminality is masked underneath the hood of social liberation and economic emancipation,[1] but little attention has been paid to who these militants really are? How have they impacted society? What were the driving ideologies? This chapter undertakes the task of identifying the ideology of the militants of the pre- and post-amnesty program (PAP) era, their impact on security in the region, and the changing perception of the people of the NDR from accommodation and support to contempt and disassociation.

In contributing to this debate, this chapter examines the phases of agitations in the region and how each phase was the outcome of the previous one. It categorizes the rebellion in the NDR into three phases: civil agitations, pre-amnesty, and post-amnesty violent agitation. This chapter notes that there is no love lost between the pre-amnesty militants and their post-amnesty successors (whose emergence they were responsible for) and captures the changing perceptions of indigenes to these groups. While the justification for armed rebellion by the pre-amnesty militants may be strong and yielded some dividends for the region, their actions opened a Pandora's box of insecurity that will pervade the region for a long time to come.

The perspective to militancy in the NDR presented in this chapter corroborates as well as refutes some of the arguments put forward by eminent authors in the field. Paul Collier (2007), for instance, argues that where prospects of a good life are bleak, joining a rebel movement gives young men a small chance of riches.[2]

Although there is evidence that some children of western middle-class families are known to have joined the ranks of Islamic State in Iraq and Syria (ISIS), Collier's claim largely holds true for militants of the NDR. However, his contention, shared by Benjamin Okonofua (2013), that being young, uneducated, and without dependents are characteristics common to these groups of people, is inaccurate[3] as a lot of the members of these militant groups are educated having either completed their university degree or dropped out at some point and possess strong family ties. Hence this chapter captures the other side of the story beyond the theorizing, speculations, and analysis that make up much of NDR literature.

The Problem

Nigeria's Delta Region is today one of the world's hot spots of militancy. Violent militant activities such as kidnapping, oil pipeline vandalism, oil rig attacks, armed robbery, and sea piracy, among others, are steadily on the increase. To be sure, the NDR's responses to government neglect and worsening environmental conditions were not violent at the onset. In fact, as noted by Olusegun Adeyeri, apart from the Isaac Adaka Boro botched secession attempt at the start of the country's civil war in 1967, protest against deprivation, worsening living conditions, and destruction of livelihoods by NDR communities and leaders of thought were civil.[4] In more recent times, the NDR has become less governable with foreign and local workers detained or held hostage, spectacular attacks on onshore and offshore facilities are not uncommon, and militants are now able and willing to directly confront federal and state security services. How did this all begin? How safe is the NDR? What are the security implications for today and the future?

Making use of process tracing, this chapter's discourse takes us back to the first series of agitations when protests were civil, and examines its evolution to today's violent insurgency. So much has been written about the negative effects of NDR militancy—its contribution to the destruction of livelihoods and suffering in the region,[5] the growth of oil theft (bunkering) and further degradation of the environment,[6] and worsening insecurity in the region as kidnapping and cultism are on the rise. Although this text aligns with Temitope Oriola's work, which examines the benefits and disadvantages of militancy in the Niger Delta,[7] it goes beyond the confines of Oriola's research and examines the militant issue from the perspectives of the militants themselves, inhabitants of the region, and the implications for security in the region.

Civil Militancy

Civil militancy gained popularity through the works and struggles of activists such as Mahatma Gandhi and Martin Luther King Jr. King, who was influenced by Gandhi-advocated civil militancy, which is the strategy of protesting for ones rights without using violence.[8] Gandhi saw this as an alternative to armed uprising and encouraged it as the primary response to unjust laws and practices. This injustice, he said, was inflicted on the minority by the majority, and the minority had no part in enacting or creating codes of conduct because they have no rights.[9] This protest strategy against injustice aptly captures the early phase of militancy in the NDR, and it was largely ineffective because nothing changed.[10]

Issues that led to the first form of militancy were presented by Ken Saro-Wiwa when he contended, "Twenty years after the civil war, the system of revenue allocation, the development policies of successive federal administrators and the insensitivity of the Nigerian elite have turned the delta and environs into an ecological disaster and dehumanized its inhabitants."[11] For Adeyeri, this neglect existed even before Nigeria's independence, hence the Willinks Commission of 1957/1958 recommended a developmental board to address the peculiar developmental needs of the region.[12] Jędrzej Frynas ties the neglect of the NDR to the surge in oil revenue and marked decline in agriculture, which made oil companies more important than the farming and fishing communities of the NDR where they operated.[13] It was therefore not surprising that the development of the oil industry took precedence over the interest of the inhabitants of the region.

In response to this neglect and lack of development, and in view of the fact that oil companies were held responsible (being closer to the people in terms of proximity), protests against oil companies became rife across the NDR and these protests involved men, women, and youths. Of these protests, Oluwatoyin Oluwaniyi writes:

> *Urhobo women challenged oil companies in Ogharefe in 1984 and Ekpan in 1986. In the 1990s, the protests became better organized. Thus, the Federation of Ogoni Associations (FOWA) organized protests against Shell in Ogoni land between 1993 and 1995, while the Niger Delta Women for Justice (NDWJ) mobilized women to protest in 1999 in support of the Ijaw Youth Council's Kaiama Declaration, which sought among other things for control of oil by Ijaw people. In 2002, Gbaramatu and Kenyagbene women ... protested the activities of oil MNC operations ... for over thirty years, and the resultant oil spills, gas flares and unfair treatment resulting from oil exploration and production activities.*[14]

Two devastating confrontations that questioned the efficacy of civil militancy and arguably set the stage for the transition to the violent stage were the Umuechelem massacre in 1990 and the execution of Ken Saro-Wiwa in 1995.

The people of Umuechelem on October 30 and 31, 1990, organized a non-violent protest at Shell's facility in Umuchelem, east of Port Harcourt, Rivers State, that led to the death of more than fifty unarmed demonstrators and the destruction of 495 houses by the police.[15] This was the first major protest staged by a community against an oil multinational (Shell Petroleum Development Company of Nigeria—SPDC) and the outcome was tragic. The most significant effort to target oil production in an attempt to highlight minority grievances was spearheaded by the Movement for the Survival of the Ogoni People (MOSOP), which had Saro-Wiwa as its spokesperson. MOSOP had mobilized the Ogoni people to protest the activities of oil multinationals and called for the payment of royalties by these MNCs or cease oil exploration in the area. The result was the execution of Saro-Wiwa and his associates from a murder trial considered wrong, illogical, and perverse.[16] Hassan Ejibunu notes that:

> *The spirit and the consciousness to bring to the international level, the suffering of the Niger Delta was championed by Ken Saro-Wiwa in the 90s. He applied peaceful, non-violent means reminiscent of Mahatma Ghandi. ... The government and the oil companies were not comfortable with his activities, so in no time, Saro-Wiwa was accused of inciting members of MOSOP to kill four Ogoni elders. He and eight other fellow compatriots were arranged for trial, in a military tribunal, convicted and hanged. His more likely crime was his effort to organize the Ogoni ethnic minority to stop destruction of their homeland caused by operations of SPDC and Chevron. A decade after the hanging, the potential consequences of the Niger Delta conflict have escalated in both human and economic terms.*[17]

The death of Saro-Wiwa was the break point of the civil militant approach, and it marked a turning point in the relationship between inhabitants of the NDR on the one hand and MNCs and the Nigerian federal government on the other.[18] With poverty and underdevelopment still rife in the region, it was just a matter of time before this civil form of militancy transformed into the violent stage. Unfortunately, the oil minorities realized that they could not receive fair treatment from the Nigerian state without violent agitations.[19] These intense agitations came as predicted by Saro-Wiwa in 1990 when he affirmed that "the people must be joined in the lucrative sale of oil to avoid the cataclysm that is building up."[20] The control of oil has been a major demand of the violent insurgency phase.

Pre-Amnesty Violent Insurgency

There is an old axiom in the region that says if you will be mocked for eating a frog, then eat one that is big. The message here is if a heavy price will be paid for an act, then ensure maximum satisfaction is derived from committing that act. So, if Saro-Wiwa was put to death for demanding that the MNCs live up to their responsibilities, by the time the violent insurgency began, asking accountability of the MNCs was not enough because the stakes had increased. Resource control was now the ultimate goal. There was also an ethnic dimension to the agitation for resource control, and this was woven into the structure of the Nigerian state.

Although the failure of civil militancy had set the stage for the violent phase, other conceptions or misconceptions helped propel the insurgency. Environmental degradation, destruction of livelihoods, poverty, and underdevelopment were rife in the NDR, but beyond the obstinacy of the Nigerian government and MNCs to address these issues, one largely overlooked factor that contributed to the violent phase was the selective information provided by the media and thought-leaders in the region. These reports fueled resentment among indigenes of the NDR over what they believed to be the conspiracy of a northern cabal to hold the Delta region to ransom.

A great deal of the dissatisfaction within the NDR derives from the knowledge that money from the region's oil had built Nigeria since the mid-'70s, while the region itself remained squalid. Incensing these grievances were carefully crafted reports, disseminated by sections of the media and thought-leaders that oil blocs in the region were the privy of northern oligarchs.[21] These reports aggravated an already bad situation and incensed the need to fight for what they considered their share of the spoils. Sensational reporting and news headlines heightened grievances within the region.[22] It was just a matter of time before the protests would turn violent.

From the start of violent agitation in the NDR at the turn of the twenty-first century, much of militant rhetoric resonated this belief. What these reports carefully left out was the geographical spread of oil bloc ownership in Nigeria. The statement below by Toyin Akinosho explains this problem:

> *Senator ItaEnang's spirited claim at the National Assembly that 83% of the oil block is in the hands of northerners appears to be inspired from assertions contained in an old article by a newspaper commentator, Mr Ross Alabo-George .... Alabo-George's article plays up so well the sentiments of a good number of Nigerians ... largely because it plays to the ethnic schism; the suspicions that each of us harbors, in our different silos, about the other.*[23]

There have been efforts to counter these reports such as Akinosho's and Temi Banjo's articles,[24] but these efforts were too little, too late and were often presented to audiences at international conferences and seminars outside the country rather than locally, where such information was most needed. These reports argued that while indigenous ownership of Nigeria's oil blocks accounts for just 12 percent (the MNCs control 88 percent), indigenous ownership of these oil wells cuts across elites of the North, West, and East of Nigeria. Noticeably, these reports either deliberately omitted or erroneously failed to note that too few indigenes from the NDR were prominent actors in this sector. While government allocation of these wells may not be on merit, it is also difficult to argue that allocation is done along ethnic lines. Allocation has never been a transparent process due to the clientelism factor, but it is also part determined by who has more to pay. Table 7.1 shows the regional/ethnic distribution of indigenous ownership of oil blocks.

This table was put together from Banjo's (2015) data in the Nigerian Monitor, indicating the owners of indigenous oil wells in Nigeria. Majority of owners are in joint partnership, which crisscross ethnic lines. This table also captures the level of ethnic participation in the sector.

The table above shows that contrary to the popular perception in the NDR, actors from the western part of the country dominate indigenous oil well ownership, followed by those from the East. These same groups also dominate employment in the oil industry. So, rather than concede to being part of the problem of the NDR, it is expedient to construct a narrative that plays to the North-South divide

Table 7.1 Ethnic distribution of Indigenously owned oil wells in Nigeria

Capacity of oil blocks	Number of Indigenous oil blocks	East	North	West	South South/NDR
Major	49	16 (32.7%)	12 (24.5%)	21 (42.9%)	7 (14.3%)
Marginal	28	11 (39.3%)	11 (39.3%)	16 (57.1%)	17 (60.7%)
Total	77	27 (35.1%)	23 (29.9%)	37 (48.1%)	24 (31.2%)

Source: Author's compilation

of the country. This narrative blames the North alongside Nigeria's leaders for the woes of the NDR. The success of this blame avoidance strategy is evident from the regular blame ascribed to the North over issues of monopolizing the sector and the consistency at which northern control of oil blocs appears on the list of grievances of the NDR militants.[25]

It is argued that Nigeria's wealth distribution is skewed in favor of the North to the detriment of the South, especially the NDR. Part of the justification for violent agitation in the NDR is Nigeria's revenue sharing formula, which is partly based on the population and number of local government areas (LGAs) within each federating state. With this arrangement, the North holds an undue advantage where contentious census figures give it an overwhelming majority over the South, and the number of local governments in a single northern state is sometimes commensurate to the number of local governments in several states of the South-South combined. A good example is Kano State with 44 LGAs and the southern states of Bayelsa (8), Cross-Rivers (17), and Rivers (23) with a total of 48 LGAs.

Going by this yardstick, Nigeria's major ethnic groups of the North, East, and West, the regions with the larger populations, have a huge advantage over ethnic groups from the NDR (South-South), where oil is sourced, because they control the country's major institutions and have greater access to the country's wealth. This accounts for why too few oil wells are in the hands of indigenes from the NDR. It also explains why one of the regular demands of militants is a larger share of oil wells for the indigenes.[26] The demands and agitations of the militants have yielded some dividends in terms of increased recognition of their grievances and increased allocations to the region, but have these efforts brought about change?

A Militant's Perspective: Don Jacob Kurobo was an integral part of the Movement for the Emancipation of the Niger Delta (MEND) and he provides good insight into the perceptions, justifications, and ideologies of the major/umbrella guerrilla group of the NDR during the pre-amnesty era. MEND saw itself as the chief advocator of the rights of the people of the NDR. At the onset, the group painted itself as liberators. MEND emerged at the height of the resource control debate and had this concept as one of its key goals. The mission was to reawaken indigenes of the NDR into the struggle for what (they believed) rightfully belonged to the region—a fair share of the dividends of oil resources.

While the ideology spurring violent agitations in the NDR war was justified and clearly understood, the debate becomes complex when the outcomes are weighed against the goals of the struggle. On this, Kurobo contends:

Politically we have achieved, but in terms of physical output, we have not. Now, the world has come to identify with the Niger Delta Struggle and acknowledge the sufferings of the people in this region. The struggle allowed, for the first time in the history of Nigeria, for the president to come from this region. Such recognition indicates a way forward and caps the little we have achieved. With such recognition within the Nigerian system, I can say we had 30% of our goals achieved. In terms of output, while our struggle yielded the 13 percent derivation policy, politicians of the NDR have squandered this opportunity. Till date, we do not know where all the money has gone to as development is still greatly lacking in the region.[27]

This observation is captured in the work of Samuel Ibaba and Augustine Ikelegbe who contend that "in the Niger Delta, the political leaders who championed the grievance thesis have also often embezzled development funds through misuse of public offices."[28] The rate of wastage, the lack of accountability, and the level of corruption of governance in the NDR leave too little to be optimistic that more money flowing into the region or a larger allocation of oil wells to indigenes of the Delta would lead to the much-desired development of the region. This fact nullifies the justifications for militancy given that the basis for violent agitation is the development of the region.

There was a four-year lull occasioned by the amnesty deal offered by Nigeria's federal government to insurgents. This period of stability is affirmed by Iyabobola Ajibola and Aaron Sanye who contend that the amnesty program succeeded at establishing some security and stability in the Niger Delta because it was targeted at youths who were at the heart of the destabilization enterprise. The disarmament, demobilization, and reintegration (DDR) component of the amnesty program enabled the reorientation and empowerment of these youth and consolidated peace in communities affected by militant activities.[29]

However, the amnesty program has been criticized for attending to the needs of the militants while neglecting the core developmental issues that affect the daily existence of the people.[30] The period of quiet and the resurgence of militancy and crime in the region indicate the short-term success of the amnesty program and its long-term failure. Given that these struggles did not yield the desired outcome, especially as underdevelopment still pervades the region after twenty years of violence, what then is the reason for this new wave of insurgency and what does it have to prove?

Post Amnesty (PAP) and the Resurgence of Militarized Insurgency

One of the effects of the NDR's first wave of insurgents is the emergence of a new crop of violent agitators under a new umbrella body with the name Niger Delta Avengers (NDA). Even though it is almost certain that their actions will not lead to a developed NDR, their emergence can be explained in the light of the benefits and recognition that accrued to their predecessors and the issues that still plague the Delta.

The amnesty could not address the root causes of the conflict; it only provided conditions for the cessation of hostilities. Ideally, "amnesty" is nothing more than an early term in a negotiated peace settlement, but the Nigerian officials billed the program as a comprehensive DDR exercise.[31] Therefore, there remained a gulf between what it could achieve and what it was meant to achieve. Some actors used the amnesty program to enrich themselves, some of whom ironically were the militant commanders who were supposed to protect the interest of their "troops" and stay true to the development of the Niger Delta and its people.[32] The amnesty deal was meant to last for five years and stipulated a monthly stipend of $420 to be paid to the repented militants through their commanders. Some commanders pocketed part of the money outside the significant transfers of cash, goods, and contracts that they received directly from the government.[33] Sadly too, the majority of genuine militants estimated at 80 percent were left out of the scheme as politicians and other influential elites of the region enrolled their kin who became the frontline beneficiaries of the PAP.[34]

It was only a matter of time before these short-changed and aggrieved militants would return to the creeks and join forces with locals who command some community followership, possess local and international networks, and nurse the same ambitions of earning for themselves the fortunes that erstwhile militant commanders enjoyed post amnesty. Although the amnesty recorded successes in some areas, it provided national recognition for the commanders of the insurgency and was an avenue of self-enrichment for these commanders and other political opportunists. Ironically, these former militant commanders are now officially assigned police escorts. The corruption that engulfed the amnesty program, its dysfunctional implementation and the affluence of past militant leaders, prompted their aggrieved comrades to return to the creeks and become part of the new wave. This fear was amply expressed by Ajibola when he states: "If the PAP fails, there will be more than enough manpower to prosecute violence in the region. If these 80 percent go back to the creeks, or if they are employed by powerful third-party stakeholders under the guise of continuing the struggle, then there is no hope for peace in the region."[35]

Against this backdrop, the current breed of militants is perceived as being spurred by financial gains even though the issues of deprivation, squalor, poverty, underdevelopment, and destruction of the environment are still unsolved. The demands and justification of these new groups are still the same, but the feeling that pervades the region is that these issues are used to extract some level of recognition from the government, including enjoying the benefits that accrue from it. Surprisingly, ex-militant commanders feel the same way and there have been personality and ideological clashes between the old brigade and the new.[36] Kurobo states:

> I must tell you without mincing words that MEND was not misguided, they were a professional body, but the present crop of militants are sea pirates, they are kidnappers.

They do not have aims and objectives. Their agitations do not go anywhere because they work without guidelines. This is no way of survival because when they kidnap their kin, money is paid and it is not used judiciously. So we deny them.[37]

This statement coming from an ex-militant commander may seem ironic and weak especially when viewed from a rational choice perspective, but Kurobo makes a valid point in contrasting the insurgents of both periods. Without the benefit of hindsight, the pre-amnesty insurgents had greater justification for their actions. They had no inkling of what awaited them at the end of the tunnel. They can argue the suffering of their people and the need for a fairer deal drove their agitations for the NDR. For the militants of the post-amnesty period, the benefit of hindsight makes it difficult to accept their claims for "sustainability of the region" as their motivation for violent agitation. The wealth and recognition of erstwhile commanders are there for all to see. The belief of the majority of Niger Deltans is that this new crop of militants was driven by desire for wealth and influence, hence it is difficult differentiating them from criminals. This analysis is supported by Ben Bassey when, in reference to the major militant group in the Niger Delta, he asks: "What are the Avengers fighting for? Are they fighting for their people and their lands, or are they fighting for their own selfish interests? It is a legitimate question when you consider that past militant leaders … are very rich."[38] Whatever it is, these actions have consequences that are viewed from different perspectives.

Perceptions of Militancy

The nature and dynamics of militancy have impacted several communities across the NDR. Overall, the perception of militancy from the perspectives of communities can be qualified in terms of the good, the bad, and the ugly.

The Good

Insurgents of the NDR have been given different names. The term "militant" is expressly used by academics and the media, and this suits the Nigerian government considering the negative connotation it conveys. While MNCs in the region would rather have them branded as criminals, indigenes of the region see them (especially the pre-amnesty group) as freedom fighters, liberators, or heroes who fought a good cause. Not all indigenes of the NDR see them in this light however. Too little of the contributions of Niger Delta insurgents have been captured in texts and academic debates. To compensate for this shortfall, this section provides the perspective of locals who have seen and experienced first-hand the impact of NDR insurgents.

One of the major militant commanders of the pre-amnesty era, Government Ekpemupolo (aka Tompolo), who hails from Gbaramatu Kingdom in Warri South Local Government of Delta State, is credited as the founder of MEND. The impressive level of infrastructural development within the Kingdom has been attributed to his influence. Towns within the Kingdom, especially those close to his birthplace of Okerenkoko, have a steady supply of electricity, which most cities in Nigeria lack. In addition, standard road networks that a majority of villages in the NDR lack are equally visible in his area. Also, the rehabilitation of houses, destroyed by the military during prior invasions to arrest Okerenkoko, has been undertaken by the Nigerian government, apparently as a measure to placate the militant leader. Although residents of these communities are often at times victims of the brutality of the Nigerian Armed Forces during such raids,[39] they display unalloyed loyalty to their leader largely because of his contribution to the human and infrastructural development of his place. The people's support is captured in this report:

> *Niger Delta students comprising of the students of the National Association of Gbaramatu Students (NAGS) and Law Students Association of Nigerian Students, Delta State University chapter, have asked the Federal Government to drop charges against the former militant, Mr. Government Ekpemupolo, popularly known as Tompolo. The students ... have benefitted immensely from the scholarship program of the ex-militant .... and urged the federal government to encourage Tompolo to invest more rather than prosecute him. One of the beneficiaries of the United Kingdom Master's programs sponsored by Tompolo urged the government to allow and support developers of the Niger Delta region instead of persecuting them.*[40]

Stephen Kpodo who recounts his experience from visiting Okerenkoko corroborates this report: "You dare not speak evil of Tompolo in Gbaramatu, because he is seen as a liberator and a hero. The people there feel that because of him there is federal government presence in Okerenkoko, a presence that is lacking in most Niger Delta towns."[41] In a similar vein, Kurobo remarks of his contributions to his own community:

> *I went back to the creeks and protested against Nigerian Agip Oil Company in October 2003. The issue was eventually addressed when the government waded into the matter because of the extent to which we made the area unstable for Agip. The government advised the company to take care of me and develop my community (Apoi) whose support I had received .... We raised a Memorandum of Understanding and as we speak, Agip has completed more than ten of its development projects in Apoi.*[42]

Oriola makes a similar observation and asserts that the effects of the insurgency have been sweet and sour for members of oil-producing communities. First, kidnapping and other insurgent acts have become a convenient excuse for government failure in providing security and basic social infrastructure "but these actions" also help neglected communities to garner the attention of the Nigerian state.[43]

The Bad

Not all host communities of militants get lucky enough to win government attention. On many occasions, harboring militants have seen many communities reap huge losses. In 1999, militants killed twelve police officers close to Odi and took shelter in the town afterwards. The army razed the town to the ground and hundreds of civilians were killed.[44] In December 2010, the Nigerian Military invaded the Federated Ayakromo Communities in search of a militant and rendered hundreds homeless in the process.[45] No fewer than fifteen houses were destroyed when soldiers raided Ajakurama community in Edo State in October 2017.[46] In May 2016, Soldiers laid siege to Gbaramatu community, thereby disrupting trade in the area and the free movement of people.[47] These few examples show that communities pay a heavy price for association with militants. For a region deeply mired in poverty, the financial and sociological impact of these dislocations is immense and rehabilitation is extremely difficult despite community support.

It is easy to contend that militancy in the NDR "looks more like a protection racket than outrage provoked by environmental damage. ... There is a huge amount of money directed by the Nigerian federal government to the NDR and the oil companies are desperately paying protection money."[48] The other side of the story that is often untold is while the militant rebel-lords may be the financial beneficiaries, they have tried to ensure that their comrades and communities have received some of these benefits as well. This is in line with the local parlance in Nigeria which says *work small, chop small*. The broader interpretation is if given the opportunity to control resources, it is proper to appropriate some funds to oneself while carrying out the functions of the office. Unfortunately, many communities lacking agitators (especially of the violent kind) have had no one take up the responsibility of drawing attention to their plight of underdevelopment and deprivation.

Oloibiri town, where Nigeria's first oil well was drilled, had no such luck because there was no one to agitate violently on its behalf. From 1956 to 1978 when oil was drilled, the town had nothing to show for all the wealth that was generated and the degradation suffered. With this clear example of brazen exploitation, many inhabitants of the NDR sanctioned the actions of the pre-amnesty militant groups since they served to redress this neglect, no matter how small. Their actions were believed to fill the yawning gap created by the inertia of political elites and government agencies in developing the NDR. The two federal government agencies saddled with the responsibilities of developing the Niger Delta: the defunct Oil Mineral Producing Areas Development Commission (OMPADEC) and the Niger Delta Development Commission (NDDC), which were allocated huge funds, regularly had their various heads embroiled in huge misappropriation scandals. These political appointees enriched themselves at the expense of the region they were expected to serve, just like the state governors of the region have been known to do.[49] Thus, in the final analysis, and paradoxically too, despite the increasing security risks posed by the operations of militants, they were accommodated by much of the rural communities because of the global recognition it accorded to their plight and the benefits that accrued to the people in general. This goodwill is fast eroding for the post-amnesty militant groups as they are increasingly grouped alongside local politicians, who are seen as a major part of the problem of under development of the region.

The Ugly

The political implications of this conundrum are endless, and there is a latent, yet budding problem that has dire implications for the near and distant future of the NDR. While the pioneer violent insurgents may be justified, their actions have inadvertently destroyed the socio-cultural fabric of the region. The vast multitude of poor children in the NDR now look up to these militants as heroes.[50] They are fascinated by the sound of AK-47s and relish handling grenades. Nigeria's former President Goodluck Jonathan, who comes from the NDR and is the only southern minority indigene to have become president, conceives militancy as a self-destructive device in the NDR. He contends that in a region rife with poverty where the only ones who are rich are the militants/ex-militants, the message passed to the younger generation is that this is the way to go. This, he notes, is what happens in a majority of the villages in the Niger Delta as a lot of children aspire to become militants someday.[51]

Apparently, a Pandora's box is now open as events of the pre- and post-amnesty era have triggered a steady stream of militants and kingpins. Much of this is to avoid the poverty trap, but unfortunately the strategy adopted to escape the poverty trap diminishes the hope of durable peace and security in the region in the near and distant future. This pushes security issues to the fore at the expense of development issues, which have become consigned to the backseat of the Niger Delta discourse.

The personal rewards of militancy are exemplified in the 2012 Nigerian Maritime Administration and Safety Agency (NIMASA) award of a $103 million contract to a company owned by prominent ex-militant leader Government Ekpemupolo. This was to procure twenty vessels and gather intelligence for fighting maritime crime.[52] The long-term impact on the NDR is aptly captured by Ayodeji Aduloju and Omowunmi Pratt who they contend that, for adolescents, the moral compass of right and wrong has been distorted, leading to exposure to cultism and gangsterism, all aimed at making money.[53]

There is a strong link between cultism and militancy in the NDR, which is why the emergence and spread of cultism strengthen the view that militancy has come to stay in NDR for the long-term. The origin of the militant groups in the delta today can partially be explained by the evolution of Nigeria's cult groups. These cult groups began in the country's universities where their monopoly of violence on campuses and rituals of brotherhood and secrecy made them alluring to street gangs. This allure eventually spread to the creeks of the NDR and it is common place to have confraternity members in militant groups like MEND.[54] So, whether as a means to make money or to draw Nigerian government's attention to the plight of a people, since the exercise of violence is an effective means to achieve these objectives, cultism holds a strong appeal.[55] Even if the Nigerian government turns around to address the needs of the Delta, there is reason to be skeptical that it can reverse this trend as more and more youths aspire to be tomorrow's kingpins. The many years of neglect and the benefits that accrue to militants from violent agitations ensure that insecurity in the NDR has come to stay.

Conclusion

No matter how much the pre-amnesty insurgents may justify their actions, one thing is certain that they made later groups realize that violence pays. However, it would be wrong to direct all blame to this group because with the inglorious end of Saro-Wiwa the Nigerian government and the MNCs operating in the NDR have made it explicitly clear that civil protests yield no results. This researcher agrees with the majority of authors on the Niger Delta that the violent insurgency in the region is the creation of the Nigerian state and the MNCs through its years of neglect and oppression of the region's people.

As the Nigerian government and the MNCs continue on the course they have charted for the past sixty years, the Niger Delta puzzle gets more complex and finding solutions to the myriad of problems becomes ever more difficult. Added to this mix of complexities is the rise of violent insurgency, and for good measure this phase has shown the gains that accrue from violent agitations. The agitations of insurgent groups in the region, once spurred by human needs, frustration, and the preservation of livelihoods, seem to have morphed into the quest for wealth. Just as the actions of the militants compelled the federal government and MNCs to respond to the needs of the region, the rise of this group also opened a Pandora's box of insecurity as criminality and cultism have infested the NDR. Worse still, these militants who flaunt their wealth, by courtesy of their involvement in armed or violent agitations, are the heroes of youths in the region. This prevailing situation implies that there is no end in sight to this cycle of violence. This is the stark reality of the NDR militant's saga, and security in the region is a long way away.

Notes

1. Bøås, Morten. 2011. "'Mend Me': The Movement for the Emancipation of the Niger Delta and the Empowerment of Violence." In *Oil and Insurgency in the Niger Delta: Managing the Complex Politics of Petro Violence*, edited by Cyril Obi and Siri AasRustad. London: Zed Books; Ikelegbe, Morten. 2011. "Popular and Criminal Violence as Instruments of Struggle in the Niger Delta Region." In *Oil and Insurgency in the Niger Delta: Managing the Complex Politics of Petro Violence*, edited by Cyril Obi and Siri AasRustad. London: Zed Books; Keen, David. 2000. "Incentives and Disincentives for Violence." In *Greed and Grievance: Economic Agendas in Civil Wars*, edited by Mats Berdal and David Malone. Boulder, CO: Lynne Rienner; Okumagba, Paul. 2009. "Ethnic Militias and Criminality in the Niger Delta." *African Research Review* 3, no. 3: 315–330; Sayne, Aaron. 2013. "What's Next for Security in the Niger Delta?" *United States Institute for Peace*, Special Report 333: 4–5. Available from: https://reliefweb.int/sites/reliefweb.int/files/resources/SR333-What%E2%80%99s-Next-for-Security-in-the-Niger-Delta.pdf; Watts, Michael. 2008. "Petro-Insurgency or Criminal Syndicate? Conflict and Violence in the Niger Delta." *Review of African Political Economy* 34, no. 114: 640.
2. Collier, Paul. 2007. *The Bottom Billion*. Oxford: Oxford University Press.
3. Ibid.; Okonofua, Benjamin. 2013. "Triangulation, Emotional Reactivity, and

Violence in the Niger Delta." *SAGE*. Available from: http://sgo.sagepub.com/content/3/2/2158244013483758.
4. Adeyeri, Olusegun. 2012. "Nigerian State and the Management of Oil Minority Conflicts in the Niger Delta: A Retrospective View." *African Journal of Political Science and International Relations* 6, no. 5: 97.
5. Ibaba, Ibaba S. 2009. "Violent Conflicts and Sustainable Development in Bayelsa State." *Review of Political Economy* 36, no. 122: 556.
6. Nwogwugwu, Ngozi, Alao, Olatunji, and Egwuonwu, Clara. 2012. "Militancy and Insecurity in the Niger Delta: Impact on the Inflow of Foreign Direct Investment to Nigeria." *Kuwait Chapter of Arabian Journal of Business and Management Review* 2, no. 1: 29.
7. Oriola, Temitope. 2013. *Criminal Resistance? The Politics of Kidnapping Oil Workers*. Surrey, England: Ashgate.
8. Simkins, Chris. 2014. "Non-Violence Was Key to Civil Rights Movement." Available from: https://www.voanews.com/a/nonviolencekey-to-civil-rights-movement/1737280.html.
9. Powell, Jim. 2000. "Militant Nonviolence: A Biography of Martin Luther King, Jr." *libertarianism.org* Available from: https://www.libertarianism.org/publications/essays/militant-nonviolence-biography-martin-luther-king-jr.
10. Ibid.; Simkins, "Non-Violence Was Key to Civil Rights Movement."
11. Bassey, Celestine O. 2012. "Oil and Conflict in the Niger Delta: A Reflection on the Politics of State Responses to Armed Militancy in Nigeria." *Mediterranean Journal of Social Sciences* 3, no. 11: 77.
12. Adeyeri, "Nigerian State and the Management of Oil Minority Conflicts in the Niger Delta," 97.
13. Frynas, Jędrzej George. 2001. "Corporate and State Responses to Anti-Oil Protests in the Niger Delta." *African Affairs* 100: 29–30.
14. Oluwaniyi, Oluwatoyin. 2011. "Women's Protests in the Niger Delta Region." In *Oil and Insurgency in the Niger Delta: Managing the Complex Politics of Petro-violence*, edited by Cyril Obi and Siri AasRustad. New York: Zed Books.
15. Ibaba, "Violent Conflicts and Sustainable Development in Bayelsa State," 556.
16. Human Rights Watch. 1999. "Protest and Repression in the Niger Delta." Available from: https://www.hrw.org/reports/1999/nigeria/Nigew991-08.htm.
17. Ejibunu, Hassan Tai. 2007. "Nigeria's Niger Delta Crisis: Root Causes of Peacelessness." *EPU Research Papers*.
18. Bassey, "Oil and Conflict in the Niger Delta," 77.
19. Adeyeri, "Nigerian State and the Management of Oil Minority Conflicts in the Niger Delta," 97.
20. Watts, "Petro-Insurgency or Criminal Syndicate? Conflict and Violence in the Niger Delta," 640.
21. Bassey, Ben. 2016. "The Niger Delta Avengers: Heroes or Terrorists?" *Pulse*. Available from: http://www.pulse.ng/news/local/the-niger-delta-avengers-heroes-or-terrorists-id5114167.html.
22. Ikeke, Nkem. 2016. "List of 17 Oil Blocs Owned by Atiku, Danjuma and Other Northerners and South-Westerners." *Naija.ng*. Available from: https://www.naija.ng/827931-list-17-oil-blocs-owned-by-atiku-danjuma-northerners-south-westerners.html#827931; Akukwe, Obinna. 2017. "20 Owners of Richest Oil Blocks in Nigeria—

23. Akinosho, Tosin. 2013. "The North Does Not Control Nigeria's Oil Blocs." *Premium Times*. Available from: https://www.premiumtimesng.com/opinion/123588-the-north-does-not-control-nigerias-oil-blocks-by-toyin-akinosho.html.
24. Ibid.; Banjo, Temi. 2015. "Revealed: Check Out the Full List of Owners of Nigerian Oil Blocks." *Nigerian Monitor*. Available from: http://www.nigerianmonitor.com/revealed-check-out-the-full-list-of-owners-of-nigerian-oil-blocks/.
25. The News, 2016. "Niger Delta Avengers: Why We Are Crippling the Oil Sector." Available from: http://thenewsnigeria.com.ng/2016/05/niger-delta-avengers-why-we-are-crippling-oil-sector/.
26. Odunsi, Wale. 2017. "Niger Delta Warlords List Demands: Vow to Declare Republic September 1." *Daily Post*. Available from: http://dailypost.ng/2017/07/17/niger-delta-warlords-list-demands-vow-declare-republic-september-1/. & Ibid.
27. Interview with Don Jacob Kurobo, Ex-militant with MEND, Yenagoa, Nigeria, October 15, 2017.
28. Ibaba, Samuel and Ikelegbe, Augustine. 2010. "Militias, Pirates and Oil in the Niger Delta." *In Militias, Rebels and Islamic Militants: Human Insecurity and State Crises in South Africa*, edited by Wafula Okumu and Augustine Ikelegbe. Pretoria: Institute for Security Studies.
29. Ajibola, Iyabobola O. 2015. "Nigeria's Amnesty Program: The Role of Empowerment in Achieving Peace and Development in Post-Conflict Niger Delta." *Sage Open*: 8. Available from: http://journals.sagepub.com/doi/full/10.1177/2158244015589996; Sayne, "What's Next for Security in the Niger Delta?"
30. Ajibola, "Nigeria's Amnesty Program."
31. Sayne, "What's Next for Security in the Niger Delta?"
32. Ajibola, "Nigeria's Amnesty Program."
33. Ibid.; Golden-Timsar, Rebecca. 2018. "Amnesty and New Violence in the Niger Delta." *Forbes*. Available from: https://www.forbes.com/sites/uhenergy/2018/03/20/amnesty-and-new-violence-in-the-niger-delta/#6f7d44df263f.
34. Ajibola, "Nigeria's Amnesty Program."
35. Ibid.
36. Adetayo, Olalekan and Onojeghen, Theophilus. 2017. "Tompolo, Militants Clash over Avengers Threats to Attack Oil Facilities." *Punch*. Available from: http://punchng.com/tompolo-militants-clash-over-avengers-threats-to-attack-oil-facilities/.
37. Interview with Kurobo.
38. Bassey, "The Niger Delta Avengers."
39. Idowu, Sylvester and Addeh, Emmanuel. 2016. "Again, Soldiers Invade Tompolo's Community in Search of Militants." *This Day*. Available from: https://www.thisdaylive.com/index.php/2016/11/13/again-soldiers-invade-tompolos-community-in-search-of-militants/.
40. Vanguard, 2017. "Tompolo: Niger-Delta Students Fume, Ask FG to Drop Charges against Ex-militant," Available from: https://www.vanguardngr.com/2017/12/tompolo-niger-delta-students-fume-ask-fg-drop-charges-ex-militant/.
41. Interview with Stephen Kpodo, local government staff, January 3, 2018.
42. Interview with Kurobo.
43. Oriola, *"Criminal Resistance? The Politics of Kidnapping Oil Workers."*

44. The Punch, 2017. "Odi Massacre: Anyone with Tribal Marks on Their Chest Was Slaughtered, Corpses Littered Everywhere—Bolou, Former Bayelsa Commissioner," December 16. Available from: http://punchng.com/odi-massacre-anyone-with-tribal-marks-on-their-chest-was-slaughtered-corpses-littered-everywhere-bolou-former-bayelsa-commissioner/.
45. Ayakromo. 2010. "Nigerian Military Admits Genocide, Rape. Looting and Other War-Crimes against Ayakromo Communities," *CNN*, December. Available from: http://ireport.cnn.com/docs/DOC-534305; Omon-Julius Onabu. 2010. "Nigeria: FG Assures on Speedy Resettlement." *This Day*, December 22. Available from: https://allafrica.com/stories/201012230562.html
46. Ebegbulem, Simon. 2017. "15 Houses Were Razed as Operation Crocodile Smile II Operatives Raid Edo Community," *Vanguard*, October 18. Available from: https://www.vanguardngr.com/2017/10/15-houses-razed-operation-crocodile-smile-ii-operatives-raid-edo-community/.
47. Odunsi, Wale. 2016. "Soldiers Carry Out Midnight Raid in Gbaramatu, Search for Tompolo, Niger Delta Avengers," *Daily Post*, May 28. Available from: http://dailypost.ng/2016/05/28/soldiers-carry-out-midnight-raid-in-gbaramatu-search-for-tompolo-niger-delta-avengers/.
48. Collier, *The Bottom Billion*.
49. Adeyeri, "Nigerian State and the Management of Oil Minority Conflicts in the Niger Delta," 97.
50. Aduloju, Ayodeji and Pratt, Omowunmi. 2015. "Oil and Adolescents in the Contemporary Niger Delta, Nigeria." *Journal of Child and Adolescent Behaviour* 3, no. 3: 2.
51. Interview with Goodluck Jonathan, former president of Nigeria, Yenagoa, Nigeria, February 8, 2018; ibid.
52. International Crisis Group, 2015. "Curbing Violence in Nigeria (III): Revisiting the Niger Delta." *Africa Report* no. 231. Available from: https://www.crisisgroup.org/africa/west-africa/nigeria/curbing-violence-nigeria-iii-revisiting-niger-delta.
53. Aduloju and Pratt, "Oil and Adolescents in the Contemporary Niger Delta, Nigeria."
54. Wellington, Bestman. 2007. "Nigeria's Cults and Their Role in Niger Delta Insurgency." *Terrorism Monitor* 5, no. 3, July 6, 2007. Available from: https://jamestown.org/program/nigerias-cults-and-their-role-in-the-niger-delta-insurgency/.
55. Kpae, Gbenemene. 2016. "Cultism and Violent Crime: An Appraisal of the Security Challenges in the Niger Delta of Nigeria." *International Research Journal of Social Sciences* 5, no. 12: 38.

Chapter 8

GUNS AND DEATHS—THE CONFLICT BETWEEN FARMERS AND HERDERS

Chris M. A. Kwaja

Poor control of weapons has caused untold suffering to our people in the region. We see its manifestation in the high intensity of communal crises and violent insurgencies, conflicts as well as civil wars. Nigeria is not spared from these challenges.[1]

Introduction

For decades, relations between farmers and herders have been characterized by cordiality and interdependency. As herders move seasonally in search for arable land for grazing, they were often accommodated and given land by the sedentary farming communities for use.[2,3] In recent times, trends in the relations between farmers and herders are defined by violent confrontations, which are fueled and sustained through access to and use of guns.[4] Some of the triggers to the current conflict have to do with climate change and desertification, population expansion and urbanization, and shrinking natural resources, among others.[5] One defining feature of the current conflicts between farmers and herders is the use of guns,[6] which appears to be widespread and easily available to criminals. The long and unmanned borders of the country are major enablers that fuel conflicts and deaths. This is further compounded by factors such as weak national framework and laws on guns, activities of local manufacturers, as well as the weak capacity of security agencies to check the spread of weapons.

One major transformation that has taken place with respect to the current conflicts between farmers and herders is the phenomenon of banditry by organized criminal groups. This phenomenon also underscores the close link between banditry and the proliferation of arms in the country. In a recent statement by the Department of State Services (DDS) on the arrest of the leader of a criminal gang in Plateau State, the DSS argued that such an arrest would degrade and disrupt the booming illicit arms supply business that has sustained the crisis in Benue, Nasarawa, Plateau, and Taraba states[7]. There are concerns within the affected states too that since most of the insurgents in the northeast were chased away without being captured, they might mix with people outside the region and transform into organized criminal groups. As pointed out by a respondent:

> *Some of the attacks in Plateau state can be attributed to the failure of government to go beyond merely chasing Boko Haram out of the Sambisa forest in the North East. Most of the insurgents have mixed with the population and are involved in other forms of criminal activities such as deadly attacks on community and kidnapping.*[8]

Beyond the insurgency in the northeast region, states such as Benue, Kaduna, Plateau, and Zamfara have become the epicenter of organized crime, particularly banditry and kidnapping for ransom. The deadly attacks by persons suspected to be "herdsmen" introduce the dimension of organized crime or acts of criminality into what has been "mere" conflicts between farmers and herders in these states. In justifying the linkage between guns and deaths across Nigeria, a former secretary of the Miyetti Allah Cattle Breeders Association (MACBAN), Sale Bayeri, observed:

> *Because of the crisis in Libya, the crisis in Niger, the crisis in Mali we believe that a lot of arms, we know, got their way into Nigeria. More weapons mean more casualties in battles. More casualties mean more revenge attacks.*[9]

Across the country, conflicts between farmers and herders are generally linked to encroachment on farmlands, cultivation of crops on grazing routes, struggle over access to and control of natural resources such as land and water, and cattle rustling, among others.[10] In most cases, the actors resort to violence involving the use of guns as the primary and most potent strategy for settling such disputes. The weakness associated with state capacity to play a decisive role in the management of key natural resources such as water and land has been responsible for the recurring clashes between farmers and herders. With access to guns, such clashes became deadly. Another area of focus should be the facilitating role of governments at all levels, in ensuring that farming and herding communities work together in working out transhumance paths that are mutually agreeable.

The breakdown in inter-communal harmony as well as the weak capacity of the state to provide security across communities has led to heightened insecurity, thereby creating the conditions for rural banditry and social conflict to thrive. This occurs within a regime of waning citizens' trust in the state, in terms of its capacity to protect them. Hence, people are forced to rely on self-help measures as a means for protecting themselves and their livelihood. Under these conditions, the proliferation of guns that come from diverse sources has made efforts toward management or resolution difficult. These guns have become both causes and consequences of violent conflicts and insecurity arising from deep-seated frictions between and among the farming and herding communities.

There are four fundamental aspects that define the linkage between guns, deaths, and the current conflicts between farmers and herders. First, current trends show that the Nigerian state is losing its traditional power and monopoly over the control of the instruments of force, coupled with a lack of trust in the security agencies to protect them. Second, the transitional character of the current conflict between farmers and herders is one that has made the issue a complex one, from the standpoint of both analysis and response. Third, there has been a transformation of the conflicts between farmers and herders into generalized banditry in the rural areas.[11] Fourth, the notion of mercenaries, foreign volunteer fighters, and unknown gunmen has been used to describe the alleged involvement of persons, other than Nigerians, as perpetrators of the conflict, which has become more endemic and pervasive.

The Economic Community of West African States (ECOWAS) Protocol on Free-movement of Persons, Goods, Service and Capital provides for the movement of people within the West African region[12]. Also, the ECOWAS Action Plan on Cross-Border Transhumance provides for the movement of transhumance within the region too.[13] The adoption of the ECOWAS National Biometric Identity Card represents an attempt to manage the identity of migrants and strengthen the security architecture of the region. Unfortunately, the weakness associated with the implementation of these protocols contributes to the current conflict between farmers and herders, which has a transnational character.

From Conflict to Criminality—Understanding the Dynamics of the Relations between Farmer and Herder

There has been a major transformation in the relations between farmers and herders in Nigeria.[14] This relationship is defined largely by the transition from conflict in terms of violent confrontations between these two peasant communities to that of criminality. Although criminality and conflicts are different in their manifestations, guns continue to serve as the core linkage between the two. While conflicts are often linked to clashes between farmers and herders, criminality is linked to deliberate acts, which constitute crime, such as theft and banditry, among others. Increasingly, as criminal groups become more visible in this transition from conflict to criminality, banditry becomes the defining element. Many acts of banditry occur in remote villages that suffer from inadequate or weak security presence. In the words of Ibrahim, "in Nigeria, the level of violence has spiked dramatically over the past few years and we are witnessing a transformation of 'normal' conflicts between pastoralists and farmers into generalized rural banditry."[15]

Although most research on farmers and herders in Nigeria identifies conflict as a major factor responsible for the breakdown in their relations, the changing nature of this conflict poses a fundamental question about the extent to which armed groups have been able to entrench themselves as both principle actors and triggers. A key dimension here is the role of mercenaries whose criminal agendas are still not known.[16] This manifests under a climate of uncertainty and confusion among citizens about how governments at all levels are responding to this transformation from conflict to organized crime. In fact, there is a sense in which the failure of the government to define a clear and coherent response to the crises further heightens the citizens' risk.[17]

As a major security threat, environmental factors linked to climate change have become a phenomenon of global concern, which threatens the sustainability of the livelihoods of the majority of the population in Nigeria.[18] Vulnerability arises from a combination of factors such as poverty, population growth, urbanization, as well as the practice of agricultural systems (both farming and pastoralism) that are almost solely dependent on rainfall. The intensification of patterns of migration as a consequence of conflicts and shrinking livelihoods in the Lake Chad Area that had lost 90 percent of its water mass between 1963 and 2013 has forced many herders to move inwards toward the middle belt area, which creates the basis for competition between the herders and the sedentary farmers.[19] In a recent memo relating to the pressure faced by both farmers and herders, which sustains the current conflict, the Nigerian Working Group on Peacebuilding and Governance observed:

> Nigeria's population has grown from 33 million in 1950 to about 192.3 million today. The United Nations recently projected more growth in terms of population in the coming years, 364 million in 2030 and 480 million in 2050 respectively. This phenomenal increase of the population has put enormous pressure on land and water resources used by farmers and pastoralists.[20]

The activities of armed groups that are usually described as "suspected herdsmen" have further complicated the current state and spate of conflict between farmers and herders. Several communities have been sacked through guerilla-styled attacks, with little or no trace of the criminals' identities. Although there have been cases of arrest of some of the criminals, there has not been any prosecution of such persons. The weak criminal justice system of the country, as it relates to the prosecution of arrested persons, has contributed to the climate of impunity that characterizes their actions against the Nigerian state and its citizens. As the gatekeepers of Nigeria's criminal justice system,[21] there has been a significant decline in the level of citizens' trust in the police, largely due to how corruption and the slow process associated with prosecution negatively impact on the quest for justice. While there has been public display of arrested criminals, the citizens are not duly informed about the prosecution of such criminals. A former inspector general of police, Mohammed Abubakar observed that citizens' trust in the police for protection has waned due to the fact that:

> Police duties have become commercialized. … Our men are deployed to rich individuals and corporate entities such that we lack manpower to provide security for the common man. Our investigations departments cannot equitably handle matters unless those involved have money to part with. Complainants suddenly become suspects at different investigation levels following spurious petitions filed with the connivance of police officers. Our police stations, State [Criminal

> *Investigations Divisions] and operations offices have become business centers and collection points for rendering returns from all kinds of squads and teams set up for the benefit of superior officers. Our special anti-robbery squads (SARS) have become killer teams engaging in deals for land speculators and debt collectors. Toll stations in the name of checkpoints adorn our highways with policemen shamefully collecting money from motorists in the full glare of the public.*[22]

The ugly situation regarding the state of the Nigerian police as painted above draws attention to a security dilemma. The existence of security agencies that citizens cannot trust for protection and increased rate of insecurity exacerbated and sustained by criminal groups across the country. The principal incentive for criminality in the context of the transformation of the current conflict between farmers and herders is access to guns. Weak control mechanisms, the porosity of state borders, and armed conflict on the continent as witnessed in Libya particularly have been major catalysts for the spread of guns.[23] This situation has been further heightened by the activities of local gun manufactures and poor record-keeping of weapons stockpiles by the security agencies, which are often stolen. The Nigerian Immigration Service (NIS) is charged with the mandate of border management in line with the provisions of the 1963 Immigration Act, 1999 Constitution, and the 1979 ECOWAS Protocol relating to the movement of people and goods, respectively. In spite of efforts to regulate proliferation through the ECOWAS Moratorium and other national-level mechanisms, the spread of all categories of guns has been alarming in the West African region and beyond.[24] With borders that are poorly managed, there are about 1,499 irregular and 84 regular routes that account for the influx of criminals and guns into Nigeria.[25] As rightly observed by Freedom Onuoha:

> *Nigerian borders are known for the limited presence of security and law enforcement officials. The few that are deployed are poorly trained, work with inadequate and obsolete equipment, and sometimes poorly remunerated. In addition, the government has for long neglected most border communities, making it difficult for government to leverage on their position to curtail illicit cross-border activities.*[26]

The emergence of a criminal economy that is weaved around and sustained by cattle rustling has become a dominant phenomenon that fuels and sustains the current conflict between farmers and herders. In recent times, the rustling of cattle by criminals has become a dominant feature of an already soured relationship between farming communities and the herding communities. There have been accusations and counter-accusations between the two groups, in relation to the rustling of cattle. In most cases, the rustled cattle end up in the market where they are sold. It underscores the fact that there is well-established criminal network of cattle rustlers who are responsive to the market demand for rustled cattle.[27] It was reported that between 2013 and 2017, bandits rustled and killed an estimated 135,200 cattle across Nigeria.[28]

This is a transformation in the conflict that is characterized by the emergence of well-coordinated and well-funded banditry in virtually every part of the country.[29], [30] In establishing the complex relationship that exists between cattle rustling and criminality, it was observed that:

> There is a wave of collaborations at various levels of cattle rustling and there is an obvious inability of the police and other security outfits to deal with the problem because firstly they are insufficiently equipped to be able to handle the challenge. Second, there is a form of collaboration between criminal elements and security agents and thirdly there is outright corruption.[31]

The resistance associated with the fight between cattle owners and criminals involves the use of guns, which in turn accounts for injuries and deaths. While guns serve as an incentive for criminals carrying out violent attacks, the cattle owners often use them for self-defense. In this light, guns become available to both criminals and law-abiding citizens who require and use them for perpetration of crimes on one hand, or for self-defense and protection of their livelihoods on another hand.

Responses and Pathways

Deployment of Security Agencies Not Enough to Address Conflict

A defining feature of state response to the current conflicts between farmers and herders across the country is the deployment of the military. The military is currently the most active actor involved in the management of internal security. In the aftermath of the 2001 ethno-religious conflicts in Plateau State, the federal government deployed the Special Task Force-Operation Safe Haven (STF-OSH) to take over the internal security of the state. The mandate of the STF-OSH was expanded to cover Kaduna State because of the nature of the situation in Southern Kaduna, which was similar to that of Plateau State. In response to the heightened state of insecurity due to the conflicts between farmers and herders, as well as acts of criminality in Benue State, the Operation *Ayem Akpatuma* (Cat Race) was introduced by the army's high command to check the farmer-herder conflict and other criminal activities in the North Central region of the country.[32] The creation of operation *sharan daji* was designed to contain cattle rustling, banditry, and kidnapping in the northwest region of the country.[33] While the presence of the security agencies may help in the cessation or suppression of conflicts, a relapse is possible unless an integrated response is adopted.

While the deployment of security forces contributes to the cessation of violence, it cannot address the underlying causes of farmer and herder conflict in Nigeria. This would require a more robust strategy that is more comprehensive in terms of its ability to address the core issues of livelihood and access to natural resources within the broader context of natural resource management, which is central to the survival of farmers and herders.

Table 8.1 Some farmer-herder-, cattle rustling-, and banditry-related peace enforcement operations in Nigeria.

Location	Code Name	Mandate
Plateau State	Operation Safe Haven	It enforces peace as a result of communal conflict and the current farmer-herder conflict, as well as other criminal activities in the state. Its mandate was extended to Kaduna State due to similarity in the nature of threats between the two states.
Northwest region covering Kaduna, Kano, Katsina, Kebbi, Sokoto, and Zamfara states	Operation Sharan Daji (I)	It was established to battle the criminal activities of armed bandits, cattle rustlers, and robbers operating particularly in Zamfara, Kaduna and fringes of Sokoto, Kebbi, Katsina, and Kano states
Bauchi and Gombe states	Operation Shirin Harbi	It was launched in 2015 to combat restiveness in Bauchi and Gombe states
Zamfara State	Operation Harbin Kunama	This was the military's answer to cattle rustling and armed banditry in the Dansadau Forest of Zamfara State and environs. Harbin Kunama translates to "sting of a Scorpion"
Northwest and North Central states	Operation Harbin Kunama (II)	Its brief was similar to Harbin Kunama I—deal with cattle rustling, armed banditry, and clashes between pastoralists and farmers.
National	Operation Mesa	It is a Joint Task Force (JTF) operation against all forms of criminal activities in all the states of the federation.

Source: Author's compilation

Disarmament

Disarmament is also one approach adopted by the state in mopping up guns away from unauthorized persons and groups. The Inspector General of Police Idris Abubakar issued a directive that all persons and groups in possession of guns should surrender them to the police. As a consequence of this directive, categories of guns such as sixty-five rounds of ammunition and six cartridges were recovered in Jigawa State: 325 firearms in Cross River State; 120 firearms and thousands of ammunition in Ebonyi State; 70 firearms and ammunition in Kano State; 61 arms, 906 rounds of AK47 ammunition, 42 double barrel and single barrel guns, as well as 1,200 cartridges in Sokoto State, respectively.[34] Such an approach does not in any way address the root causes of the conflict as communities are increasingly relying on such arms for self-defense, in the face of increased insecurity that is associated with the ineffective response by security agencies.

For the Nigerian state, projecting itself as an entity with a sole and legitimate monopoly over the instrument of coercion is proving problematic. This is largely due to the sophisticated nature of the threats of armed attacks against communities by criminals, in terms of frequency, intensity, and consequences of their actions. A key explanation for this has to do with the fact that the pervasiveness of farmer-herder conflicts coupled with heightened criminality is linked to the state's inability to extend its authority (governance and security) to the rural areas that are marginalized. Under circumstances where suspects were arrested by security agencies, they are not prosecuted.

Despite its experience with high-intensity conflicts, insurgency, and the current acts of criminality that manifest within the broader discourse of farmer and herder conflicts, the Nigerian state has not been able to institutionalize its efforts around disarmament. This has often been pursued as an ad hoc arrangement that is episodic. Each situation gives rise to a specific response. Such uncoordinated responses toward tackling the menace posed by the availability of guns in the hands of unauthorized persons and groups have further incentivized the use of such guns by criminal elements within and outside the country. In fact, the easy movement of mercenaries and their involvement in varied forms of criminal acts are linked the hollowness of gun-related policies.[35]

Institutionalized Mechanisms for Peacebuilding

The adoption of soft approaches in responding to conflicts has not really been institutionalized in Nigeria. The establishment of the Institute for Peace and Conflict Resolution (IPCR) in 2001 represented the first attempt by the Nigerian state to institutionalize mechanisms for conflict management and peacebuilding. Unfortunately, the IPCR has been incapacitated due to lack of funds to carry out its mandate. Recently, the Plateau and Kaduna State Governments established the Plateau State Peace Peacebuilding Agency and the Kaduna State Peace Commission, respectively.[36, 37] With the exception of these two states, there is no state with an institutionalized structure and mechanism for conflict management and peacebuilding in Nigeria.[38]

The absence of an institutionalized mechanism for conflict management and peacebuilding across the states that make up the Nigerian federation is a major obstacle to sustainable peace and stability. This has given rise to the use of ad hoc and reactive approaches by the states and their institutions. In most cases, temporary respites are provided, while relapses occur at more devastating rates. The federal and state governments should adopt proactive measures in addressing security challenges in the country, through the establishment of sustainable mechanisms for conflict management across the country. So far, the IPCR and peace structures in Plateau and Kaduna are important examples that should be modeled. They represent efforts by the federal and state governments to institutionalize mechanisms for responding to conflicts in a proactive manner.

Border Security Management

Although the ECOWAS protocol on transhumance provides for the documentation of persons and livestock, the non-implementation of this policy through the issuance of a certificate is one of the exacerbating factors to the current conflict between farmers and herders. The transnational character of the conflict between farmers and herders that is linked to weak border security management would require better surveillance by the NIS. Within West Africa, there are about thirty-five international boundaries that are characterized by high levels of porosity, which makes them easy routes for criminal activities, particularly banditry and gun running.[39] The fact that immigration and other border security agencies—that have mandates for border surveillance—are ill-equipped, ill-trained, and poorly resourced has made it difficult to effectively contain these security challenges.

The NIS should ensure that all herds entering Nigeria possess the international transhumance certificate as a precondition for entry, in line with the ECOWAS protocol on transhumance, as well as the free movement of people and goods. For the federal government of Nigeria, the design of a border management strategy would be an important pathway toward a comprehensive and integrated framework for border control and security,[40] in light of the increased pressure on the country's border by criminals. Related to this is the fact that Nigeria has not given border communities the desired attention. Afua Lamptey "observed that most border management efforts do not take advantage of border communities."[41] The border communities refer to geographical boundaries that separate Nigeria from other countries. Some of the criminals even marry local women within the border communities in order to enjoy the social protection associated with being part of a community. This situation requires that the Nigerian government include border communities as part of its border management.

Conclusion

There is a sense in which the failure of governance is the fundamental factor that has given rise to the security dilemma the country faces. Be it conflict or criminality, its perpetrators merely exploited the vacuum created by state failure to protect its citizens. The consequence of the state of insecurity in Nigeria is underscored by the failure or inability of the Nigerian state to carry out its core responsibility of protecting its citizens. The 1999 Constitution of Nigeria makes it clear that "the primary purpose of government is the safety, security and welfare of all who live within its territory."[42]

One key lesson from the Nigerian experience as it relates to the relationship between guns and deaths in the context of the current farmer and herder conflict is that guns in themselves are not the sources of conflicts. They exacerbate tensions and mistrust, which account for violent confrontations between the farmers and herders. Across the country, increases in the level of mutual suspicion and mistrusts relating to access to guns by unauthorized persons and groups account for the increased level of coordinated and targeted attacks along religious and ethnic lines, under the guise of farmer and herder conflict.

Resource-based competition and climate change are inescapable realities that the world must come to terms with and confront. For the farmers and herders, they are the worst hit, in the light of the fact that their livelihoods are dependent on them. Since relations between farmers and herders would create conditions for violent clashes, if not managed properly, access to guns is a key factor that would exacerbate the conflict.

Notes

1. The ECOWAS Commissioner for Political Affairs, Peace and Security, Mrs. Halima Ahmed made this statement in her address during the symbolic arms destruction in commemoration of the 2017 United Nations Arms Destruction Day in collaboration with the Presidential Committee on Small arms and light weapons (PRESCOM) held at the cenotaph of the 35 Battalion, Nigerian Army, Katsina, Katsina State. Available from: https://leadership.ng/2017/07/11/nigeria-faces-illicit-arms-proliferation-risks-civil-war-ecowas-2/.
2. Bagu, C. and Smith, K. 2017. *Past Is Prologue: Criminality and Reprisal Attacks in Nigeria's Middle Belt*. Washington, DC: Search for Common Ground.
3. International Crisis Group, 2017. "Herders against Farmers: Nigeria's Expanding Deadly Conflict." Report No. 252.
4. Kwaja, A. and Adelehin, A. 2018. "Responses to Conflicts between Farmers and Herders in the Middle Belt Region of Nigeria: Mapping Past Efforts and Opportunities for Violence Prevention." Policy Brief, January.
5. Ibid.
6. In several research and policy discourses, Small Arms and Light Weapons (SALWs) are used in reference to guns, which connotes the same.
7. Odunsi, W. 2018. "DSS Finally Nab Wanted Gunrunner." *Daily Post*, March 18. Available from: www.dailypost.ng/2018/03/18/dss-finally-nab-wanted-gunrunner-jonah-abbey-others.photos/.
8. Interview with a Journalist in Jos, Plateau State, March 15, 2018.
9. Murdock, Heather. 2014. "Arms Fuel Sectarian, Insurgent Violence in Nigeria." *VOA News*, February 19. Available from: https://www.voanews.com/a/imported-arms-fuel-sectarian-insurgent-violence-in-nigeria/1854610.html.
10. Kwaja and Adelehin, "Responses to Conflicts between Farmers and Herders in the Middle Belt Region of Nigeria."
11. Kyari, M. and Chinyere, A. 2015. "Social Impact of Rural Banditry." In *Rural Banditry and Conflicts in Northern Nigeria*, edited by Kuna Mohammed and Ibrahim Jibrin. Abuja: Centre for Democracy and Development.
12. Ecowas, Protocol A/P.1/5/79 Relating to Free Movement of Persons, Residence and Establishment. Available from: http://documentation.ecowas.int/download/en/legal_documents/protocols/PROTOCOL%20RELATING%20TO%20%20FREE%20MOVEMENT%20OF%20PERSONS.pdf
13. Food and Agricultural Organization of the United Nations in collaboration with ECO WAS, 2012. "The Cross-Border Transhumance in West Africa Proposal for

14. Blench, R. 2010. "Conflict between Pastoralists and Cultivators in Nigeria," review paper prepared for the British government's Department for International Development (DFID). Nigeria.
15. Jibrin, I. 2014. "Pastoralist Transhumance and Rural Banditry." *Premium Times*. Available from: https://www.premiumtimesng.com/opinion/157305-pastoralist-transhumance-rural-banditry-jibrin-ibrahim.html.
16. Kwaja, C. 2017. "Towards Re-Energising the Nigerian military and Other Security Agencies to Meet Urgent National Demand." Presentation at the House of Representatives Hearing of the House Committee on Army, House of Representatives. National Assembly, Abuja, Nigeria.
17. International Crisis Group, 2017. "Herders against Farmers."
18. Olabode, A. and Ajibade, L. 2010. "Environment Induced Conflict and Sustainable Development: A Case of Fulani-Farmers' Conflict in Oke-Ero LGAs, Kwara State, Nigeria." *Journal of Sustainable Development in Africa* 12, no. 5: 259–2743.
19. Sow, M. 2017. "Figure of the Week: The Shrinking Lake Chad." *Brooking*. Available from: https://www.brookings.edu/blog/africa-in-focus/2017/02/09/figure-of-the-week-the-shrinking-lake-chad/.
20. Premimum Times, 2018. "How to Resolve Herdsmen Crisis—Nigerian Working Group." Available from: https://www.premiumtimesng.com/news/top-news/255364-resolve-herdsmen-crisis-nigerian-working-group.html.
21. Alemika, E. 2014. *Crime and Public Safety in Nigeria*. Abuja: CLEEN Foundation.
22. Daily Trust, 2012. "Corruption Is Endemic in Police—IGP Abubakar." Available from: https://www.dailytrust.com.ng/news/general/corruption-is-endemic-in-police-igp-abubakar/92106.html.
23. Alusala, N. 2016. "Lessons from Small Arms and Weapons Control Initiatives in Africa." Bonn International Centre for Conversion (BICC). Working Paper.
24. "The Flows: Firearms Trafficking in West Africa." UNODC, Report. Available from: https://www.unodc.org/documents/toc/Reports/TOCTAWestAfrica/West_Africa_TOC_FIREARMS.pdf.
25. The former Minister of Interior, Abba Moro, provided these figures. See https://www.vanguardngr.com/2013/06/nigeria-has-over-1499-illegal-entry-routes-interior-minister/.
26. Onuoha, F. 2013. "Porous Borders and Boko Haram's Arms Smuggling Operation in Nigeria." Aljazeera Centre for Studies, Report.
27. Kwaja, C. 2014. "Blood, Cattle, and Cash: Cattle Rustling and Nigeria's Bourgeoning Underground Economy." *West African Insight* 4, no. 3: 1–4.
28. Rexson, E. 2018. "Between Manslaughter and Cattle Rustling: The Tale of Fulani Herdsmen and Rural Banditry in Nigeria." Available from: https://www.calabarreporters.com/31436/manslaugtering-cattle-rustling.
29. Kwaja, "Blood, Cattle, and Cash," 1–4.
30. Olaniyan, A. and Yahaya, A. 2016. "Cows, Bandits and Violent Conflicts: Understanding Cattle Rustling in Northern Nigeria." *Africa Spectrum* 51, no. 3: 93–105.
31. Adamu, Muhammed. 2015. "Cattle Rustling Could Be More Dangerous than Boko Haram—Ya'u." *Blueprint.ng*. Available from: https://www.blueprint.ng/cattle-rustling-could-be-more-dangerous-than-boko-haram-yau/.
32. The key states targeted for the operation were Benue, Taraba, Kogi, Nasarawa, Kaduna, and Niger.

33. Lequte. 2016. "List of Ongoing Police, Military Operations in Nigeria." *Nigerian Bulletin*. Available from: https://www.nigerianbulletin.com/threads/list-of-ongoing-police-military-operations-in-nigeria.219510/
34. See "Police Recovers 692 Arms in Cross River, Ebonyi, Jigawa, Kano and Sokoto," *Daily Trust*, Thursday, April 5, 2018.
35. Recently, President Muhammadu Buhari was of the view that the current conflict between farmers and herders is linked to criminals who were part of the regime of the Late Muammar al-Gaddafi of Libya. See http://www.pulse.ng/news/local/buhari-blames-dead-gaddafi-for-herdsmen-farmers-crisis-id8242800.html.
36. See the Plateau State Peace Building Agency Law, 2015
37. See the Kaduna State Peace Commission Law, 2017.
38. The United States Institute for Peace (USIP) has been agitating for state-level mechanisms for peacebuilding and conflict management in Nigeria, in response to reactive approaches that have been counterproductive.
39. Lamptey, A. 2013. "Rethinking Border Management Strategies in West Africa: Experiences from the Sahel." Kofi Annan International Peacekeeping Training Centre, Policy Brief 12.
40. Senegal is the first country within West Africa to design such a strategy, with the goal of ensuring better management of the country's land, sea, and air borders, as well as strengthening its internal security.
41. Lamptey, A. 2013. "Rethinking Border Management Strategies in West Africa."
42. See 1999 Constitution of the Federal Republic of Nigeria (as amended).

Chapter 9

BOKO HARAM AND ISLAMIC EXTREMISTS

Dauda Abubakar

Introduction

Since the attainment of political independence from British colonial rule in 1960, Nigeria has encountered checkered experiences in nation-building. From 1967 to 1970, Nigeria plunged into a catastrophic ethnic-driven civil war that culminated in the death of approximately 1 million people,[1] thereby entrenching ethno-religious suspicions amongst its diverse population. After the civil war, the availability of oil resources increased national revenue and foreign exchange earnings that enhanced infrastructural development, including the expansion of seaports, airports, and road construction linking different regions of the federation; establishment of additional national universities; an experiment with free Universal Primary Education (UPE);[2] and building a new national capital in Abuja. However, by the mid-1980s the collapse in international oil prices, imposition of a harsh Structural Adjustment Program,[3] decades of military autocracy, kleptocracy and elite predation,[4] and the rising tide of ethno-religious conflicts deepened the frustrations of the citizenry toward the Nigerian post-colonial state project.[5] More specifically, in northern Nigeria, which is predominantly Islamic and relatively underdeveloped compared to the southern parts of the country, the endemic corruption of governments at national and local levels, rapid population expansion and urbanization, declining agricultural productivity, bulging youth unemployment, inter-religious violence, and rural and urban insecurity cumulatively exacerbated cynicism, uncertainty, and frustration with modernity and the democratic model of governance in Nigeria. It is pertinent to indicate at the onset that the most important processes of social and cultural transformation in northern Nigeria's religious landscape, which provided the context for the rise of violent extremism are: first, the emergence of Salafist doctrines, starting especially in the 1970s, with the teachings of Sheikh Abubakar Gumi who positioned his doctrinal treatise and exegesis primarily as a critique of the dominant Sufi orders—*Qadiriyya* and *Tijaniyya*—which have hitherto dominated the Islamic religious market place and palaces of traditional rulers in northern Nigeria.[6] Second, Gumi's teachings led to the establishment of a formidable Salafi-oriented movement called *Izala* or *Jama'atu Izalatil Bid'a wa Iqamat al-Sunna* (The Community for the Eradication of Innovations and Establishment of the Sunna) in 1978 by one of his *protégés* Sheikh Ismaila Idris.[7] Third, the return of Nigerian graduates from Saudi Arabia's Medina Islamic University who are well trained not only in the Arabic language but have been exposed to Salafi theology, doctrinal discourses, and its relation to Muslim faith and practice. The Medina graduates such as Sheikh Mahmoud Ja'afar Adam attracted a substantial followership especially during the Ramadan *tafsir* (Qur'an recitation and teaching) at Indimi mosque in Maiduguri as well as his own mosque at Dorayi quarters in Kano. Mohammed Yusuf, the founder of Boko Haram, was a protégé of Ja'afar Adam at the Indimi mosque in Maiduguri. Although Sheikh Ja'afar Adam along with other Medina returnees such as Sheikh Muhammad Awwal Albani Zaria and Dr. Ahmed Gumi remained as members of the *Izala* movement, they gradually developed their network of mosques where they taught their teeming followers on a regular basis about core Salafi-jihadi doctrines of Islamic religion, its interpretations and implications for Muslim practice. An important aspect of the teachings of these Medina University returnees is that they emphasized the decadence of Islam in northern Nigeria, the failure of the corrupt Nigerian elites and postcolonial state to implement *Shari'a* law as the national legal system, alleged attack on Islam in Nigeria,[8] and the seeming indolence of Muslims to openly condemn such practices in the public sphere. This group came to be known as *Ahls al-Sunna* (People of the Sunna), to which Mohammed Yusuf (the founder of Boko Haram) belonged. To coherently understand the rise of Boko Haram as an extremist terror group, this chapter briefly sketches its ideological discourses, tenets, and polemics against the Nigerian state and society. It also outlines the socio-religious and political context that provided an enabling environment for the group to mobilize the youth and radicalize them into its extremist jihadi agenda. Through its targeted attacks on the army, police, security agencies, Christians and their churches, traditional rulers, and educational institutions, especially in northeastern Nigeria, Boko Haram has devastated communities by displacing over 2.8 million people, and approximately 7 million are facing food insecurity.[9]

Background

After the political transition to democratic rule in 1999 and the subsequent declaration of *Shari'a* law in Zamfara state, several civilian governors in northern Nigeria increasingly came under pressure from *Izala* movement, Sufi clerics, *Ahls al-Sunna* Salafis, and their teaming followers for the implementation of *Shari'a* as the legal system within their states.[10] During the 2003 election cycle, debates about the implementation of *Shari'a* became the litmus test for governorship campaigns in Muslim majority states of northern Nigeria, specifically in the case of Borno State where the incumbent Governor Alhaji Malla Kachalla was criticized by the challenger candidate Senator Ali Modu Sheriff (hereafter SAS) for failing to fully implement *Shari'a*. SAS capitalized on the *Shari'a* implementation controversy accusing Malla Kachalla for failing to fulfill his promises to the Muslim majority electorate that demanded the introduction of *Shari'a* as a panacea for eradicating immorality, corruption, and social vices that were polluting Islam and the community. SAS also had a gang of thugs known as "ECOMOG" who intimidated his opponents (Malla Kachalla and Ibrahim Kashim) and their supporters. SAS assured Mohammed Yusuf, the leader of Boko Haram, also known as *Jama'at Ahl al-Sunna Lidda'awat wa-l-Jihad*, that if he were elected as governor, he would ensure that *Shari'a* was fully implemented. Report has it that the support of Yusuf's followers within the sprawling city of Maiduguri and surrounding local government areas was decisive for the victory of SAS at the polls.[11] Upon taking office, SAS created the Ministry of Religious Affairs and appointed Alhaji Buji Foi (a major patron and financier of Yusuf) as the commissioner for the newly created ministry in Borno State. A *Shari'a* Implementation Committee was also constituted with Professor Abubakar Mustapha—the vice chancellor of the University of Maiduguri as the chairman. Other members of the Committee included Mohammed Yusuf, Sheikh Ibrahim Ali, Sheikh Abubakar El-Miskin, *Uztaz* Abba Aji (the Imam of Mairi Mosque), and Sheikh Gabchiya of the Maiduguri Central Mosque. Most of the members of the Shari'a Implementation Committee in Borno, as well as other states in northern Nigeria, were Sufi clerics—perceived by the *Izala* movement and members of *Ahls—Sunna* as part of the religious establishment that may not be trusted to fully implement *Shari'a* in accordance with the precepts of the *Qur'an* and *Sunna*.[12] Although Yusuf was a member of the *Shari'a* Implementation Committee at both the state and national levels, he grew increasingly frustrated not only by the slow pace of the religious reform; but even more fundamentally, his supporters were involved in intermittent altercations with security agencies, specifically members of "Operation Flush," that were set up to tackle urban insecurity and lawlessness in Maiduguri. In one such encounter, Yusuf's supporters were wounded by gun shots from security personnel of Operation Flush. Thus, the stage was set for the onset of violent confrontation that was to follow between Boko Haram and the Nigerian state.

The foregoing narrative provides us with the social, political, and religious context for understanding the ferocious rise of Boko Haram and its violent ideological campaign not only against the state, police, and security agencies but also against Christians, Muslims, and Western modernity including education and the democratic model of governance. The following key questions are relevant for the analysis that follows in the rest of this chapter: what factors led to the entrenchment of Salafi-jihadist ideology, in the form of Boko Haram extremism, in northeastern Nigeria? What are Boko Haram's key doctrinal claims, methods of operation; and why does it utilize collective violence against innocent women and children across the regional landscape of Borno, Yobe and Adamawa states? What has been the response of Nigeria and other states in the Lake Chad Basin area toward the security threat from Boko Haram? What are the security implications of this complex crisis for the Nigerian state, local communities, and the region in general? To what extent does factionalization within Boko Haram exacerbate the violent insurgency in northeastern Nigeria?

Drawing on Eli Alshech's notion of Neo-Takfirism and Terje Ostebo's conceptual category of "politicization of purity," I argue that Boko Haram ideologically appropriated Salafi-jihadi doctrines of *al-wala w-al-bara* (loyalty and disavowal), *Takfir* (accusing other Muslims of apostasy with no legal basis), and *tawhid* (Oneness and Sovereignty of Allah) as religio-political tools for the pursuit of a sectarian agenda and the propagation of terrorist violence against innocent civilians. Furthermore, I argue that Boko Haram draws on the historical legacy of Usman dan Fodio's nineteenth-century jihad as a discursive framework for the legitimation of its agenda amongst the Muslim majority populace in northern Nigeria's religious market place. Although dan Fodio's Caliphate was primarily based on the Sufi *Qadriyya* order, Salafi-jihadis in northern Nigeria, nevertheless, draw on this powerful narrative and the symbol of Islamic political order for three important reasons. First, dan Fodio's jihad represents a relatively successful Islamic revolt against corrupt Hausa rulers, thereby indicating a concrete historical model for not only Islamic reform, but also a theocracy where *Shari'a* was the basis of the social, political, and religious organization of a pre-colonial society. Second, for Nigerian Salafi-jihadis, the Sokoto Caliphate remains a powerful symbol of resistance to British colonial conquest that resonates with Muslims seeking an alternative institutional framework of governance based on *Shari'a*, rather than Western democracy that has not delivered meaningful change in their socio-economic livelihood since independence from colonial rule. Finally, in a post-September 11 world and the global war on terror,[13] dan Fodio and his Caliphate are presented to Muslim northern Nigeria as powerful symbols of piety and a guiding path for the inevitable prosecution of jihad against local and global "enemies" of Islam. As is demonstrated later in the chapter, Mohammed Yusuf capitalized on this enabling socio-cultural and political environment to propagate his ideology of extremism and total war for the purification of Islam in the tradition of *salaf-al-salih* (The Pious Predecessors). The remaining part of the chapter proceeds in three inter-related sections. The next section attempts to situate Mohammed Yusuf and Boko Haram within the broader context of northern Nigeria's Salafi-jihadi movement, and more specifically, Salafi-jihadi ideology of *takfir*. According to Alshech, Neo-Takfiri thinking is anchored on impulsiveness, claims of doctrinal purity, theological ignorance, and violent extremism against state and society in the prosecution of jihad. The next section describes the 2009 uprising, the extra-judicial killing of Mohammed Yusuf and his close patrons, the ascendance of Abu Shekau as the new leader of Boko Haram, and the expansion of Boko Haram's violent campaign beyond the northeast theater into other parts of Nigeria. This chapter then examines the response of the Nigerian state including President Goodluck Jonathan's declaration of the state of emergency, the rise of the Civilian Joint Task Force (CJTF) that successfully facilitated the expulsion of Boko Haram and its foot soldiers from the city of Maiduguri into Sambisa forest, and the deepening of the insurgency in rural communities of Borno, Yobe, and Adamawa states. The conclusion summarizes the key arguments of the chapter, discusses the security implications of the Boko Haram insurgency, and provides specific policy prescriptions for addressing the dilemmas of extremism within the context of Nigeria's experiences. It discusses the future trajectory of the Boko Haram insurgency and suggests that in the context of a fragmented religious market place, such as northern Nigeria, it is imperative for the government, at all levels, to ensure effective policy coordination, especially in matters of religious proselytization.

Salafi-Jihadi Ideology and the Path to Boko Haram's Violent Extremism

Tracing the historical genealogy of Salafism, its connections to jihad and the notion of *takfir* (i.e., declaring a Muslim an unbeliever) will require a more extensive analysis of different theological and doctrinal orientations and creeds in the practice of Islam, which is beyond the remit of this chapter.[14] According to Alex Thurston,[15] the conceptual category of Salafi-jihadism "refers to the combination of Salafi theology with jihadist ideology, a hybridization that solidified in the 1990s" and for groups such as Boko Haram, the fusion of theology and ideology provides religious legitimation to commit violence not only against those who are regarded as *kufr* or infidels (non-Muslims including Christians and Jews) but also against nominal Muslims who are categorized as apostates who fail to adhere to the true path of Islam enunciated by the Prophet and *Salaf-al-Salih* (The Pious Predecessors).[16] For Alshech, the emergence of Salafism as a socio-political movement can be traced to the eighteenth-century sacred alliance of between Muhammad Ibn 'Abd al-Wahhab (1703–1792) *Ikhwan* fighters and Muhammad Ibn Saud (d. 1765) to form the present Saudi Arabian Kingdom through the power of the sword and territorial expansion of the Saudi realm.[17] Salafis believe that over the centuries, "religious innovations" (*bid'a*) have crept into Islam through corrupted interpretations of the *Qur'an* and extra-textual exegesis, thereby polluting the "purity" of the religion. Furthermore, Salafi-jihadis believe that "jihad should not just be waged against non-Muslim invaders of the *dar al-Islam* (The land/abode of Islam), but … also within the Muslim world against so-called apostate leaders for their alleged unwillingness to apply the *Shari'a'a* in full." Thus, following the tradition of the radical Egyptian Islamist ideologue Sayyid Qutb (1906–1966) most Salafis see themselves as the vanguard for prosecution of jihad as well as the renewal of Islam, not only through the process of *da'wa* (proselytizing) nominal and non-Muslims, but also through teaching the *Qur'an* and *Hadith* to their faithful followers.

Some important doctrinal concepts in Salafism that are crucial for understanding Boko Haram's violent extremism in Muslim majority societies like northern Nigeria are the principle of *al-wala wa-l-bara* (loyalty and disavowal) and *takfir*. As Wagemakers explains,[18] taken together with the notion of *tawhid* (Oneness and Sovereignty of *Allah* over all), Salafis insist on absolute loyalty and dedication toward *Allah*, "Islam and fellow Muslims and the disavowal and rejection they must simultaneously show towards all things that cause Muslims to deviate from [the right path of piety]." Thus, the conceptual category of *al-wala wa-l-bara* in Salafi doctrine "epitomizes Salafis' tendency to remain closely attached to religious 'purity' and, as such, can be used to ward off everything Salafis see as a threat to Islam," including democracy, Western education, constitutionalism, and the electoral process. For certain strands of Salafism, Western modernity is a corruptive influence that may divert Muslim's piety from absolute loyalty to *Allah* to worldly non-Islamic practices. As Umar rightly argues, "Salafi puritanism regards all the interpretations by the vast majority of Muslim scholars who came after the first three generations as lacking Islamic authoritativeness ... that contaminate the pristine tenets of Islam."[19] Salafis' insistence on rigorous scriptural literalism, puritanism, and exclusivism constitutes some of the "major radicalizing beliefs that set the Salafis apart from the vast majority of other Muslims." The doctrine of *al-wala wa-l-bara* in Salafi theology not only leads to sectarianism, but most importantly it is a recipe for extremism and violence against all those who are labeled infidels, apostates, and nominal Muslims who support the secular nation-state and Western modernity. Boko Haram's violent challenge to Nigeria's security, national cohesion, democratic rule, and constitutionalism is derived from its twisted interpretation of the doctrine of *al-wala-wal-bara* along with *tawhid* (Oneness and Sovereignty of Allah) to assert that the adaption of Western democracy in Nigeria violates an important tenet of Islam, because it appropriates divine legislative authority (an exclusive power that belongs to *Allah* and him alone) and arrogates it to human beings in the form of Parliament. Boko Haram and Nigerian Salafi-jihadis further argue that the failure of Nigerian governments to fully implement *Shari'a* as the legal system leads to polytheism (*shirk*), apostasy, and unbelief by the rulers, and that all those who participate in it have violated *Allah*'s law and must therefore be killed. Herein, therefore, lies the roots of Boko Haram's ideology that drives its violent extremism. Boko Haram's weaponization of selected Salafi theology as a jihadi tool for radicalization into violent extremism constitutes a major security threat to the Nigerian post-colonial state and neighboring countries including Cameroun, Chad, and Niger.

The 2009 Uprising and Its Aftermath

Although the major conflagration that brought Boko Haram's violent extremism to broader public attention is traced to the clashes with security forces in 2003–2004 in Yobe State and the confrontation of 2009, its formation can be located back from the 1990s when Muhammad Ali—a young Nigerian who was studying in Khartoum, Sudan, met with Osama bin Laden. Reports indicate that bin Laden provided Muhammed Ali with the sum of $3 million to establish a jihadist cell in Nigeria. This fund may have provided the seed money for the founding group (composed of about 200 youths) that organized themselves into what came to be known as the "Nigerian Taliban" and engaged in *hijra* (withdrawal) from Maiduguri and Damaturu into the rural community of Kanamma in northern Yobe State.[20] Following in the footsteps of the Prophet Mohammad who performed the *hijra* from Mecca to Medina, as well as Uthman dan Fodio from Degel to Gudu, prior to launching their jihad against perceived infidels and apostates, the "Nigerian Taliban" established itself as a puritanical Islamic community that was fed up with the immorality, corruption, and failure of the Nigerian state, as well as Muslim leaders, to establish *Shari'a* law. Within a short time, the group was involved in altercations with the local community over fishing rights in the river Komadugu-Yobe. In spite of interventions by local police authorities, the disputes only escalated into recalcitrance of the "Nigerian Taliban" toward security agencies, especially the police. In January 2004, the self-styled "Nigerian Taliban" attacked police stations in Kanamma and later in Damaturu, the Yobe State capital. Although the police and other security agencies crushed this incipient jihadi rebellion, the commitment of this Salafist group was never broken. As one of the participants in the Kanamma uprising, Aminu Tashen-Ilimi, put it:

> *Allah*, the almighty ... has authorized every Muslim to fight to establish an Islamic government over the world. One day it will happen in Nigeria and everywhere .... I'm ready to take up arms. I don't know who gave us the name Taliban, I prefer '*mujahideen*'; the fighters. I only know the Taliban in Afghanistan, and I respect them and what they did very much .... Those who fought in Kanamma and Gwoza are only Muslims who performed their holy duty.[21]

Most of the members of the Kanamma group were killed during this first open confrontation with security agencies in Yobe State. Some of them fled into the Gwoza hills where they clashed with security agencies again in September 2004, while others were imprisoned in Damaturu and later died in a failed prison break. Mohammad Ali, the leader of the Kanamma uprising, was also killed during these confrontations.

Although Mohammed Yusuf was not physically involved in the Kanamma rebellion, he nevertheless knew what the "Nigerian Taliban" were doing. In 2006, Yusuf told journalists about the Kanamma debacle:

> These youths studied the *Qur'an* with me and with others. Afterwards they wanted to leave the town, which they thought impure, and head for the bush, believing that Muslims who do not share their ideology are infidels .... I think that an Islamic system of government should be established in Nigeria, and if possible all over the world, but through dialogue.[22]

As stated earlier, after the victory of SAS in the 2003 governorship elections in Borno State, he established a Ministry of Religious Affairs and appointed one of Yusuf's financiers, Alhaji Buji Foi, as the commissioner. Buji Foi used his privileged government position to channel not only financial resources to Yusuf and his expanding followership, but also other incentives, including air tickets for going to Saudi Arabia for the hajj with his supporters. Yusuf utilized the resources he was getting from the Borno State government to finance a lavish lifestyle, and also set up a micro-finance entity that provided short-term loans for his followers to engage in small businesses. This strategy has three vital goals. First, by providing the youth with a secure source of livelihood, Yusuf raised his profile as a pious empathetic cleric who was fervently interested not just in the spiritual development of his followers but also in their physical welfare and existential survival in a corrupt system where government doesn't seem to take care of the poor. Second, the small businesses that his followers established enabled some of them to get married and establish families, thereby enhancing their social status and dignity in society. Third, as Yusuf's community expanded around his mosque (*Marqaz* Ibn Taymiyya) and the income generated from micro-finance expanded, he began to use some of the resources to procure armaments.

In early 2009, insecurity within the city of Maiduguri led to the establishment of "Operation Flush" by the state government. A law requiring all motor cycle users to wear helmet was also put in place. Members of Yusuf's sect clashed with security agencies for failure to comply with this new law and in the process some of them were wounded. Yusuf swore to revenge this action. Turning to the doctrines of *al-wala wa-l-bara* (exclusive loyalty and disavowal) and the notion of *tawhid* (Oneness and Sovereignty of Allah, above all else), Yusuf began to radicalize his followers against the Nigerian state, its laws, and security forces. In one of his sermons, Yusuf told his followers:

> What will make you a soldier of Allah first and foremost, you make a complete disavowal of every form of unbelief: Constitution, the legislature … worshiping tombs, idols, whatever. You come to reject it in your speech and your body and your heart. Moreover, Allah and His Messenger and the believers, you love them in your speech and your body and your heart.[23]

In July 2009, Yusuf's sect launched an attack on police stations and barracks in Borno, Bauchi, Yobe, Gombe, Kano, and Katsina states. It is estimated that about 1,000 people were killed during this round of violence, including forty Christians and twenty-two policemen. About twenty-five churches were burnt and over 200 houses destroyed. Yusuf's mosque, *Markaz* Ibn Taymiyya, was also razed to the ground by the army. Mohammed Yusuf was later arrested and handed over to the police who, in an extra-judicial manner, killed him. Furthermore, his financier Alhaji Buji Foi and Baba Fugu, Yusuf's father-in-law and close supporter, were all arrested and summarily executed in the Maiduguri police Headquarters along Kano road.[24] However, neither the death of Mohammed Yusuf nor the destruction of his mosque ended the violent extremism of the sect against the Nigerian state and innocent civilians. The emergence of a more boisterous and zealous Abu Shekau as the new leader of Boko Haram only accelerated the level of attacks and carnage against the police, army, and all state security agencies. From Salafi proselytization, Boko Haram transformed into a full-blown terrorist group threatening the peace and security of lives and property in northeastern Nigeria and the Lake Chad Basin area. Yusuf had three core lieutenants, including Mohammad Lawan, Maman Nur, and Shekau. Lawan who is from Potiskum, Yobe State, was reported to have criticized Yusuf over the issues of Boko Haram's ideology and interpretation of the *Qur'an*. Furthermore, Lawan accused Yusuf of grotesque insincerity. He later abandoned the group and joined the *Izala* movement; Boko Haram unsuccessfully targeted Lawan by attacking his house in Potiskum during the 2009 uprising.

The rise of Shekau marks the beginning of Boko Haram's terrorist insurgency against the Nigerian state, non-Muslims, nominal Muslims, traditional rulers, and all those who are opposed to their ideology. This second phase of the group's mutation witnessed not only the intensification of youth recruitment and radicalization by Boko Haram, but also open confrontation against the Nigerian state and its democratic institutions. Shekau escalated the level of violence by targeting police and security forces not just in the northeast region, but also in other parts of Nigeria. Boko Haram operatives began to use vehicle-borne improvised explosive devices (VBIEDs), especially during the run-up to the 2011 presidential elections, thereby causing massive civilian casualties. In August 2011, Boko Haram launched an attack in Abuja, the federal capital, targeting the National Headquarters of the Nigerian Police Force as well as the United Nations offices in the city. The campaign of violence against Christians and their Churches was also escalated. For example, on the eve of Christmas Day in 2011, a Boko Haram operative Kabiru Sokoto detonated a VBIED at St. Theresa Catholic Church in Madalla near Abuja killing over forty worshippers and wounding dozens more.[25] On January 20, 2012, in a series of coordinated bombings and targeted shootings against security agencies in Kano (a predominantly core Muslim city in the North), Boko Haram killed about 185 people (mostly innocent civilians), as a strategy to coerce the Kano State government to stop arresting some of its fighters who were fleeing Maiduguri to Kano.[26] Within Borno State and parts of Adamawa, Boko Haram unleashed ferocious violence targeting major towns, including Bama, Gwoza, Marte, Monguno, Dikwa, Baga, Madagali, and Mubi, to mention a few. In these towns and villages, Boko Haram killed hundreds of innocent civilians and destroyed their homes and livelihoods thereby reducing thousands of the citizenry in northeastern Nigeria into refugees as internally displaced persons (IDPs), an issue developed later in this book.

As of 2018, it is estimated that the terrorist violence unleashed by Boko Haram in northern Nigeria had killed over 20,000 people and displaced approximately 2.5 million civilians who are mostly living in IDP camps in Maiduguri, Mubi, Yola, and Damaturu. In its Vulnerability Report of 2017 on northeastern Nigeria, the United Nations High Commission for Refugees (UNHCR) observed that the violence perpetrated by Boko Haram and security agencies has undermined the safety and livelihoods of households, especially women and girls:

> Women and girls have been significantly affected by the crisis, with the number of female-headed households ... and widows increasing; with large numbers of men missing, including for reasons of engagement of men in the insurgency as active combatants and/or as a consequence of massive incarceration of alleged members of armed groups for national security reasons. Violence against women and girls is widespread but grossly under reported due to fear of retaliation by the perpetrator, stigmatization and subsequent ostracization by communities/family members .... Rape and sexual abuse has been perpetrated with impunity during all stages of the crisis ... including by members of security forces and non-state armed groups.[27]

Apart from violence against civilians, Boko Haram was also involved in kidnappings for ransom, bank robberies to fund its operations, and targeting traditional and religious leaders as well as political elites.[28] In 2014, Boko Haram ambushed and killed the Emir of Gwoza, Alhaji Ibrahim Timta. They also attempted to assassinate Emirs of Kano, Fika, as well as the Shehu of Borno.[29] In December 2013, Boko Haram attacked the military barracks in Bama town killing several soldiers along with their wives and children.[30] An audacious act of kidnapping by Boko Haram that drew local and international attention is the case of the 276 Chibok girls in April 2014.[31] Although some of Chibok girls have been rescued, many of them still remain in captivity, with some of them married off to Boko Haram commanders.[32] Furthermore, in 2015, Boko Haram insurgents abducted about 300 primary school children as well as 100 women and children from the town of Damasak in northern Borno. Most of the residents were killed; at least seventy bodies were later found in a river bank near the village.[33] Also in 2013, Boko Haram attacked Government Secondary School Mamudo in Yobe State killing thirty-two students sleeping in their dormitories and one teacher.[34] At Yobe State College of Agriculture, Gujba, Boko Haram insurgents killed another forty-two students and one lecturer; while in Federal Government College Buni Yadi, they killed twenty-nine male students during a night attack on the school.[35] Why did Boko Haram target educational institutions and traditional rulers? Boko Haram's attack on schools represents their agitation against Westernization and modernity that, for them, may delude Muslims from the right path of Islam. For Boko Haram, attacks on schools will deter parents from sending their children to such institutions. Targeting traditional rulers, on the other hand, is to demonstrate Boko Haram's war not only against Sufi Islam in northern Nigeria, but also to instill fear, uncertainty, and anxiety amongst the populace and instigate them to succumb to Salafi ideology.

In a national broadcast about the 2011 bombings at St. Theresa Church, President Jonathan described Boko Haram as a "cancer" in Nigeria's society. Shekau immediately responded by condemning the Nigerian state and society, asserting that:

> We are not a cancer .... The disease is unbelief, and Allah says, 'Disorder is worse than killing' (*Qur'an* 2: 191) ... Everyone knows democracy is unbelief, and everyone knows the Constitution is unbelief, and everyone knows that there are things Allah has forbidden in the Qur'an, and that are forbidden in countless *hadiths* of the Prophet, that are going on in Western schools ... We ourselves haven't forbidden anything, we haven't told the Muslim community to abandon anything, we simply stand on the path of truth.[36]

In his polemics against the Nigerian state, democracy, and Western education, Shekau is certainly drawing on the doctrine of *al-wala wa-l-bara* (loyalty and disavowal) and urges his vanguard of insurgents along with other Nigerian Muslims to acknowledge the supremacy of *Allah* as the only source of law. Shekau and his followers believe that anyone who fails to accept this interpretation of the Sovereignty and Oneness of *Allah* (*tawhid*), as stated in the *Qur'an*, commits apostasy and cannot, therefore, be part of the Islamic faith and community (*Ummah*). Salafi-jihadis such as Shekau base their claim on the passage from *Qur'an* 5: 44, which declares: "Whoever does not rule by what Allah has revealed, they are unbelievers …. O you who believe, do not take Jews and Christians as allies (*awliya*). They are allies of one another. And whoever is an ally to them among you, then indeed, he is one of them." Thus, for Shekau, the failure of Nigerian governments at federal and state levels to fully implement *Shari'a* in accordance with the *Qur'an's* injunction above makes them unbelievers, and that the citizenry who follow such regimes are also unbelievers who have deviated from *Allah's* path into unbelief (*kufr*) and should be killed. Wagemakers states that Salafis' twisted ideological interpretation of the *Qur'an* and selective use of creed and doctrines to support their actions are a recipe for destructive extremism, greater bloodshed, and violence against society.[37] By 2014 Boko Haram had captured a large swathe of territory in northern Borno and declared a Caliphate with its headquarters in Gwoza. Furthermore, on March 7, 2015, Shekau declared the allegiance of Boko Haram to the Islamic State of Iraq and al-Sham (ISIS) led by Abu al-Baghdadi.[38] As criticisms increased against the Jonathan administration for failing to contain Boko Haram, the government increased its active counter-insurgency initiative against the terror group.

Response of the Nigerian State and Security Implications

After the attacks on the National Headquarters of the Nigerian Police and UN offices in Abuja, the federal government began to take Boko Haram more seriously as a threat to national security. The defense budget was increased from $625 million in 2010 to $6 billion in 2011.[39] Further increases were recorded in national defense with the allocation of $6.25 billion between 2012 and 2014. A Terrorism Prevention Act was passed by the National Assembly and signed into law by President Jonathan in 2011. In addition to these legislative steps, the federal government designated Boko Haram and Ansaru, an offshoot of Boko Haram, as terrorist organizations. Between 2011 and 2012, the federal government deployed 3,600 additional ground troops to fight Boko Haram. In 2013, an additional 2,000 troops with military fighter jets and heavy equipment were deployed to Maiduguri, and a state of emergency was declared in northeastern Nigeria.[40] In a national broadcast, Jonathan directed the military and all security forces to "take all necessary action … to end the impunity of insurgents and terrorists" in Nigeria.[41] Boko Haram camps in northern Borno, especially the stronghold of Sambisa Camp, were bombed by jet fighters as porous borders with Chad, Niger, and Cameroun were sealed. The government also created a new army division known as the 7th Division to effectively prosecute counter-terrorism operations against Boko Haram. It is also important to note that civilian population within Maiduguri who bore the brunt of Boko Haram's deadly attacks became enraged and embarked on a coordinated self-help initiative, with security personnel to flush out Boko

Haram foot soldiers from the city.[42] The youth vigilante group that worked with security agencies came to be known as the Civilian Joint Task Force (CJTF). Since the youth are embedded within the society, they know some of the Boko Haram operatives. Thus, they stormed homes and hideouts of known and suspected Boko Haram fighters and arrested them and survivors over to the military. As one report puts it, CJTF was successful in driving "many insurgents out of Maiduguri and largely stopping Boko Haram killings and bombings in the city."[43] Although the joint operations by CJTF and the army proved effective in halting violence within Maiduguri, the initiative nonetheless had some shortcomings, especially cases of human rights violations through extra-judicial killings and unnecessary search of innocent civilian homes. Such practices infuriated some residents on the grounds that it violated Islamic norms of privacy. When President Buhari came to power in 2015, he intensified the war against Boko Haram by directing the Defense headquarters to relocate its field operational headquarters to Maiduguri. Between 2015 and 2017, the intensification of the counter-insurgency decimated Boko Haram's so-called Caliphate and forced most of its fighters to either surrender, others were killed through bombardments of its camps in the Sambisa Forest. While a significant number of the group's fighters may have been exterminated or captured, there are a few who have dispersed into rural areas and others have sneaked back into Maiduguri and continue to hit civilian targets through suicide bombings. For example, in February 2018, a convoy of Boko Haram fighters fled the outskirts of Sambisa forest and traveled through Damboa into Yobe State. They targeted Government Girls Secondary School Dapchi (a town located within the vicinity of Kanamma, where the "Nigerian Taliban" rebellion began). About 110 girls were abducted, almost in the same pattern as the Chibok girls abduction of 2014.[44] Although the school had a contingent of soldiers deployed for security, the soldiers were withdrawn just before the attack. Such security lapses certainly constitute a major drawback in Nigeria's war against Boko Haram terrorism. Although most of the Dapchi girls have so far been released,[45] the incident shows that Boko Haram, as an organized fighting force, may have been decimated and denied a territorial base for its Caliphate, but its capacity to unleash destructive civilian casualties on innocent targets including women, children, and the elderly remains potent. By 2016, Boko Haram's targeted war against Western education had led to the closure of almost all secondary schools in northern Borno and Yobe states, thereby entrenching illiteracy, ignorance, poverty, and underdevelopment in a region that lags behind in all indicators of human development. One major security implication of the Boko Haram insurgency in Nigeria is that it has led a massive displacement of people in the northeastern states of Borno, Yobe, and Adamawa. A UNHCR Report on human displacement in the Lake Chad Basin reveals that a total of about 2.3 million civilians are refugees in IDP camps spread across Nigeria, Chad, Cameroun, and Niger.[46] The dislocation of civilians in urban and rural communities has also affected agricultural productivity and other economic activities including fishing as well as commerce in the region, thereby undermining livelihoods. With approximately 80 to 90 percent of the population in the region depending on agriculture, fisheries, and livestock for their livelihood, the insurgency has exposed about 6.9 million people to the threat of food insecurity.[47] A second implication of the insurgency for Nigeria's security is that it has exacerbated the flow of small and light weapons not only in the northeastern part of the country, but also in the Middle Belt region, as discussed elsewhere in this book. Boko Haram fighters escaping from the Sambisa Forest with their weaponry move into other communities to perpetrate violence or sell their weapons to other criminal groups that intensify conflicts, such as the cattle herders and farmers violent clashes in Benue and Plateau states. Third, the availability of small and light weapons arising from the Boko Haram insurgency may potentially exacerbate communal violence, especially during elections. In Nigerian politics, predatory elites manipulate ethno-religious identities to gain political power; hence, the flow of weapons could increase unnecessary killings of innocent civilians. Thus, the fight against terrorism in northeastern Nigeria should not just be about retaking territory from Boko Haram or curtailing their attacks against schools, villages, traditional institutions, and security agencies, but also clearing small and light weapons in the region to avert future violent conflicts. Although the Nigerian state along with its regional partners including Chad, Cameroun, and Niger as part of the Multinational Joint Task Force (MNJTF) has made significant efforts in regaining territory from Boko Haram, the internal factionalization of the Boko Haram has reframed the threats at both local and regional levels.

The Factionalization of Boko Haram

The sources of internal factionalization within Boko Haram terrorist group can be traced not only to struggles over leadership, but even more fundamentally, around the theological interpretation of *takfir* (excommunication and killing of a fellow Muslim for unbelief). Following the death of Mohammed Yusuf in 2009, Abu Shekau emerged as the dominant leader of Boko Haram and intensified violent attacks against security agencies, Christians, Muslims, beer parlors, and markets. Top leaders of Boko Haram such as Khalid al-Barnawi were critical of Shekau's *ultra-takfirism* which targeted fellow Muslims. In 2012, they broke away and established another faction known as *Ansaru* with the support of Al Qaeda in the Islamic Maghreb (AQIM). Ansaru's attacks included the abduction of foreigners and targeting Nigerian troops that were deployed in Mali. Following the declaration of loyalty to the Islamic State (ISIS) by Shekau in 2015, Mamman Nur and other top commanders of Boko Haram intensified their criticism of Shekau on the grounds that targeting fellow Muslims and innocent civilians contradicted the long-term objectives of the movement. With the support of ISIS leadership, Mamman Nur and Abu Musab al-Barnawi (the son of late Mohammed Yusuf) established the Islamic State West Africa Province (ISWAP), which openly challenged Shekau's leadership of the jihadist movement in the Lake Chad basin. Mamman Nur castigated Shekau and criticized him not only for abusing his position for personal gain, but also for twisting "scripture to justify violence against his opponents and those who stood in his way."[48] Furthermore, ISWAP asserted that Shekau's enslavement of over 700 abductees, including some of the Chibok girls, tainted the legitimacy of the jihad. Shortly thereafter, Musab al-Barnawi was declared the leader of ISWAP, which was later involved in several attacks, targeting military bases around the Chad Basin region and abduction of university lecturers.[49] In 2019, ISWAP's *Shura* Council announced Abdullah Ibn al-Barnawi (also known as Ba Idrisa) as its new leader. Under Ba Idrisa's leadership, ISWAP has expanded its campaign of terror and abductions around the Lake Chad basin region, especially in Niger and Chad. Between January and June 2019, ISWAP abducted around thirty civilians in Diffa (over half of them women) and besieged a military base at Woula, killing five gendarmes. In March 2019, ISWAP attacked four villages in Niger killing ten people; and around June 4–5, it targeted security forces base at the Diffa airport killing fifty soldiers. Also, on March 22, ISWAP attacked Chadian soldiers in Dangdallah killing twenty-three; and on June 22, ISWAP targeted and killed the sultan of Bol.[50] ISWAP has also been linked to attacks on military bases in Nigeria, especially at villages such as Marte, Dikwa, and Kirenowa leaving scores of soldiers dead. Meanwhile, internal leadership turmoil and factionalism continue within ISWAP with the purging of Mamman Nur, who was later killed on the orders of ISIS. Musab al-Barnawi has also been sidelined and placed under house arrest.[51] The incumbent Governor of Borno State, Babagana Umar Zullum, recently revealed that the challenges of fighting terrorism in the Chad Basin region are enormous and that the insurgency remains highly intractable.[52] The internal factionalization of Boko Haram and the rise of ISWAP have, indeed, made the war on terrorism in the Chad Basin region more complicated because these factions operate across rural and urban areas, thereby exacerbating insecurity as the violence deepens into the fabric of countries in the region.

Conclusion

Although several scholars have discussed the socio-economic, religious, and political factors that led to the rise of Boko Haram's insurgency in northeastern Nigeria,[53] only few studies have closely interrogated the linkage between Salafi-jihadi ideological appropriation of theological doctrines such as *al-wala wa-l-bara*, *tawhid*, and *takfir* and their weaponization for perpetrating terrorism and undermining Nigeria's national security. The claim by Salafi-jihadis such as Mohammed Yusuf and his successor Shekau to purify and reform Islam in Nigeria along the tradition of *Salaf-al-Salih* (The Pious Predecessors) leads to unnecessary discord not only within the Salafi sect but also between them and other Muslims and non-Muslim communities in northern Nigeria's religious market place. This certainly undermines the security of the Nigerian state and exacerbates identity-driven violent conflicts that threaten national cohesion and development. This chapter has demonstrated that the politicization of purity, as illustrated by the ideological polemics of Salafi-jihadis such as the Boko Haram terrorist, not only escalates sectarianism but also exacerbates communal division in a deeply divided polity like Nigeria, thereby intensifying violence and insecurity. Drawing selectively from twisted ideological interpretations of specific Islamic creeds and doctrines within broader Salafism, Shekau continues to unleash terrorist violence in northeastern Nigeria. Boko Haram and its supporters believe that the failure of the Nigerian state and governments at national and local levels to derive legitimate authority from *Shari'a* has made the rulers and their followers unbelievers who ought to be killed through jihadi struggle. By unleashing violence against the state and its security forces, Christians, and Muslims, Boko Haram engages in a collective application of *takfir* without following the prescribed internal doctrinal restraints against such generalized use of violence. Although the Nigerian government in conjunction with the regional Multinational Joint Task Force (MNJTF) has decimated Boko Haram as a fighting force, the group has nonetheless filtered back into urban centers such as Maiduguri to engage in suicide bombings forcing women and children to perpetrate its heinous crimes against humanity. IDP camps and markets continue to be soft targets for Boko Haram suicide bombers. Resolving the security challenges of Boko Haram insurgency will necessarily require some form of dialogue not only with the group, but also with Islamic clerics in northern Nigeria to mitigate extremism in the process of proselytization. It is also imperative to design a coherent program of de-radicalization, especially for those fighters who have surrendered their arms and are willing to change into productive citizens of civil society. As I have argued elsewhere,[54] the disintegration of sacred authority in northern Nigeria is an important mechanism that drives religious extremism in the form of Boko Haram terrorism. Moving forward, there are three possible trajectories for the future of Boko Haram's insurgency and its impact on Nigeria's national security. First, having lost most of its territory and core fighting cadre, Boko Haram is likely to remain a weak insurgency movement that may not be capable of engaging Nigerian troops or the MNJTF in direct military battle. A second scenario that seems to be the most likely outcome is that Boko Haram may infiltrate urban centers such as Maiduguri and Damaturu in northeastern Nigeria and continue to mount suicide bombings against soft civilian targets. A third scenario is that Boko Haram and its ardent supporters may insert themselves for now into society, begin an underground campaign of radicalization within the *Izala* movement, and re-emerge in the future to challenge the Nigerian state again through violent terrorism. This third possibility implies that Nigeria's security agencies must necessarily engage in active surveillance and collecting human intelligence to nip any future eruption of Salafi-jihadi terror movement in northern Nigeria in its early stages. To address the problem of radicalization and terrorism in Nigeria, it is imperative for governments at national, state, and local levels to ensure structured coordination in the way that clerics conduct their religious obligation toward their followers, the community, and the Nigerian state in general. It is also imperative for the federal government and local authorities to design a concerted strategy of clearing and curtailing the spread of small and light weapons arising from the Boko Haram insurgency, so that political elites and their supporters or other violent non-state actors will not access such weaponry to unleash further violence that will threaten the security and territorial integrity of the state.

Notes

1. For more details on the Nigerian civil war and the politics of the national question, see John Stremlau, *The International Politics of the Nigerian Civil War, 1967–70*.
2. Universal Primary Education was initiated by General Yakubu Gowon's military regime; but implementation was so poor that most products of the program could not succeed in securing admission into higher levels of education. One of the arguments which Boko Haram uses against the Nigerian State, namely the bankruptcy of "Western Education," gains traction amongst Muslims in Northern Nigeria because of the evident failure of this program. Government encouraged them to enroll their children in schools that failed to change their social and economic livelihood.
3. Structural Adjustment Program (SAP) was an externally driven neoliberal economic reform crafted by the International Monetary Fund and the World Bank for countries experiencing financial crisis, especially domestic budgetary deficit and low foreign exchange earnings. Its implementation in Nigeria and several African countries not only weakened the post-colonial state, but also exacerbated unemployment, collapse of social services especially in the health and educational sectors.
4. As Nigeria earned more foreign exchange revenue from oil, corruption, nepotism, patronage, and the criminalization of the state for personal profit also increased under both military and civilian regimes. For details on this unfortunate tragedy, see Richard Joseph, Young and Beckett; Bayart.
5. From the 1980s, Nigeria experienced several violent ethno-religious conflicts, including the Kafanchan riots of 1987, Zangon-Kataf riots, Jos and Kaduna riots, 1982 Maitatsine riots in Kano, Maiduguri-Bulumkutu, Gombe and Yola. Thousands of civilian lost their lives in these violent uprisings.
6. In his famous anti-Sufi polemic *al-Aqida al-Sahiha bi-Muwafaqat al Shari'a* (The True Belief in Accordance with the Shari'a), Gumi describes Sufi clerics as "Venal scholars" (*Ulama al-su*, a concept drawn from Uthman dan Fodio, the revered Islamic reformer and founder of the nineteenth-century Sokoto Caliphate). He describes Sufi followers as "idiots" who are cheated by the "*Ulama* of wickedness." Gumi goes further to declare that any Muslim who recites the Tijaniyya litany of *salat al-fatih* is an apostate and should be killed. In its criticism of Sufism and Northern Nigeria's religious establishment, Boko Haram draws on these lines of attack to discredit the *Tijaniyya* and *Qadiriyya* orders in Nigeria.
7. At its inception, *Izala*'s headquarters was established in Jos, a primarily Christian city in the Middle Belt zone of Nigeria. Not only it drew supporters from the local Muslim masses across Northern Nigeria, but most importantly *Izala* had its members in federal and state bureaucracies, military and security agencies, universities as well as the wealthy business community in Nigeria. However, in the 1980s, *Izala* split into two; and a competing branch was established in Kaduna, mainly dominated by a younger generation of clerics. The internal divisions within *Izala* were not only over issues of financial accountability, but also centered on doctrinal and ritual practices. For in depth analyses of the *Izala* internal split, see Amara, B. Ramzi. 2011. "The Izala Movement in Nigeria: Its Split, Relationship to Sufis and Perceptions of Shari'a Re-Implementation." Dissertation, University Bayreuth, June.
8. The perception of threats to Islam, as a religion, in Nigeria is one of the excuses that Boko Haram would exploit in its war against the state. For a perceptive analysis on this, see the works of Alexander Thurston, especially *Salafism in Nigeria: Islam, Preaching and Politics*. 2016. Cambridge: Cambridge University Press.

9. Thurston, A. 2018. *Boko Haram: The History of an African Jihadist Movement.* Princeton: Princeton University Press.
10. Since the 1970s, there has been heated debate between Christians and Muslims in Nigeria about the implementation of Shari'a law as part of the Criminal code at local and federal levels. During the Constituent Assembly debates of 1988–1989, in which I was privileged to participate, the controversy brought the deliberations of the Assembly to a complete stalemate. The then head of state General Ibrahim Babangida had to dispatch his deputy Admiral Augustus Aikhomu to remove the section on *Shari'a* from deliberations of the Constituent Assembly. Nonetheless, the 1989 Constitution clearly states that neither the Federal nor State governments in Nigeria can "declare any religion as a state religion." However, the decision of Zamfara state governor along with eleven other Muslim majority states in Northern Nigeria to implement Shari'a in 1999–2004 exacerbated national uncertainty and inter-religious conflicts, especially in Jos and Kaduna. Sufi clerics and some Salafis took up government appointments with the responsibility of implementing Shari'a in the states. Radical Salafis such as Mohammed Yusuf felt marginalized in the politics of Shari'a implementation. See Thurston, 2018. *Boko Haram.*
11. See International Crisis Group, 2014. "Curbing Violence in Nigeria (11): The Boko Haram Insurgency." Africa Report, No. 216.
12. The doctrinal and ideological rivalries between Sufi Orders (*Qadriyya* and *Tijaniyya*), *Izala* Movement, mainstream Salafis and Salafi-jihadis in Northern Nigeria's religious landscape are beyond the scope of this paper. Well-documented accounts can be found in Thurston, 2016. *Salafism in Nigeria;* Thurston. 2015. "Nigeria's Mainstream Salafis: Between Boko Haram and the State," *Islamic Africa* 6; Anonymous. 2012. "The Popular Discourses of Salafi Radicalism and Salafi Counter-Radicalism in Nigeria: A Case Study of Boko Haram." *Journal of Religion in Africa* 42, no. 2. On the politics of Shari'a implementation and divisions within the Muslim clerics, see Thurston, A. 2015. "Muslim Politics and Shari'a in Kano State, Northern Nigeria." *African Affairs* 114, no. January 1: 28–51, https://doi.org/10.1093/afraf/adu077.
13. For a recent work on Boko Haram and post-9/11 global war on terrorism, see Varin, Caroline. 2016. *Boko Haram and the War on Terror.* Barbara, CA: Praeger.
14. On the role of Jordanian Salafi theologian, Abu Muhammad al-Maqdisi who reconceptualized Islamic doctrines such as *al-wala-wal-bara* (Loyalty and disavowal) and *tawhid* (Oneness and sovereignty of *Allah*) into violent Salafi-jihadi ideology, see Wagemakers, Joas. 2009. "The Transformation of a Radical Concept." In *Global Salafism: Islam's New Religious Movement,* edited by Roel Meijer. New York: Columbia University Press; Wagemakers, J. 2011. "Reclaiming Scholarly Authority: Abu Muhammad al-Maqdisi's Critique of Jihadi Practices," *Studies in Conflict and Terrorism,* no. 34: 534. Abu Musabi al-Zarqawi, the founder of Al Qaeda in Iraq that would later mutate into ISIS, drew his inspiration from Maqdisi's teachings when both were imprisoned in Jordan. Mohammed Yusuf's theology also draws from al-Maqdisi.
15. Thurston, *Boko Haram.*
16. The prominent pious theologians from whom Salafi-jihadis draw their doctrinal inspiration include Ahmad Ibn Hanbal (780–855), and Taqi al-Din Ahmed Ibn Taymiyya (1263–1328) whose works inspired Mohammed Yusuf and named his Maiduguri Mosque *Marqaz* Ibn Taymiyya; Muhammad Ibn 'Abd al-Wahhab (1703–1792). Other modernist Salafi-jihadis include Hassan al-Banna (1906–1949), Sayyid Qutb (1906–1966), and Abdullah Azzam—the teacher of Osama bin Laden at the

Abd al-Aziz University in Jeddah, Saudi Arabia. Both Azzam and bin Laden fought in the Afghan war against the Soviet Union. Azzam has been the prime instigator of the "Afghan Arab" volunteers, who, after fighting in the Afghan war would return to their different countries to initiate the jihad.

17. Alshech, Eli. 2014. "The Doctrinal Crisis within the Salafi-Jihadi Ranks and the Emergence of Neo-Takfirism." *Islamic Law and Society*, September 4, no. 21: 419–452. DOI: 10.1163/15685195-00214p04.
18. See Wagemakers, J. 2016. *Salafism in Jordan: Political Islam in a Quietist Community*. New York: Cambridge University Press, 44, for detailed discussion of the notion of *al-wala wal-bara* and its usage by Salafist to propagate their agenda of Islamic purification.
19. Umar, S. Mohammad. 2015. "Salafi Narratives against Violent Extremism in Nigeria" *Centre for Democracy and Development*, 3.
20. It is pertinent to mention that in securing the land for their *hijra* to Kanamma in the early 1990s, the so-called Nigerian Taliban composed of children of wealthy businessmen and senior civil servants from Borno and Yobe states, had support from the then Governor of Yobe state, Bukar Abba Ibrahim. During the Shari'a controversy of early 2000s, Governor Bukar is noted for making a statement that Muslims are "prepared to fight another Civil war" for the entrenchment of Shari'a in Nigeria. For further details, see Marc-Antoine Perouse de Montclos. 2014. *Boko Haram: Islamism, Politics, Security and the State in Nigeria*. Los Angeles, CA: Tsehai, 35.
21. Thurston, *Boko Haram*, p. 97.
22. Ibid.
23. Ibid., 109.
24. For details, see Mustapha, R. Abdul. 2014. "Understanding Boko Haram." In *Sects and Social Disorder: Muslim Identities and Conflict in Northern Nigeria*. London: James Curry.
25. It is pertinent to note here that Shekau's evolving strategy of widening Boko Haram's terrorist campaign after the 2009 uprising was, first, to stoke the outbreak of religious and sectarian crisis in Nigeria; and by so doing, he thought, gain the support of Northern Nigerian Muslim community (*Ummah*) to join in the jihad. Demographically, Nigeria is almost evenly divided between Muslims (mainly in the North) and Christians (primarily in the South). However, that is not to say that practitioners of either faith are not found in the other region. There are several Christian minority groups in the North, just as there are significant Muslim population in the South, especially among the Yorubas and cosmopolitan Lagos city. Second, by attacking the UN office in Abuja, Shekau was trying to draw the attention of the international community toward Boko Haram's evolving terrorism; and third, to gain some Salafist ideological credibility and legitimacy within the global jihadi activists, especially Al-Qaeda and the emerging Islamic State.
26. This section draws from an incisive account on the rise of Boko Haram provided by the International Crisis Group Report, 2014. "Curbing Violence in Nigeria (11)."
27. See UNHCR, 2017. "Vulnerability Screening Report" North East Nigeria, 3.
28. Thurston, *Boko Haram*, 166.
29. Ibid., 222.
30. International Crisis Group, 2014. "Curbing Violence in Nigeria (11)"; Human Rights Watch, 2016. "They Set the Classrooms on Fire: Attacks on Education in Northeast Nigeria."
31. See Thurston, *Boko Haram*, 220.

32. Human Rights Watch, "They Set the Classrooms on Fire," 2016. This invaluable report provides detailed account of the impact of Boko Haram's attacks on education and civilian population in Northeastern Nigeria.
33. Ibid., 32.
34. Human Rights Watch, "They Set the Classrooms on Fire," 35.
35. For details on Boko Haram attacks targeting schools, see Ibid.
36. Cited in Thurston, A. 2016. "The Disease Is Unbelief: Boko Haram's Religious and Political Worldview." *Brookings*, January 22, 16.
37. See Wagemakers, "Reclaiming Scholarly Authority," 534.
38. Thurston, *Boko Haram,* 272.
39. International Crisis Group, "Curbing Violence in Nigeria (11)," 30.
40. For further details on Federal government's military response to security threat arising from Boko Haram's attacks, see Ibid.
41. Ibid., 34.
42. Thurston, *Boko Haram,* 208.
43. International Crisis Group, "Curbing Violence in Nigeria," 35.
44. Thurston, *Boko Haram,* 283.
45. There is, however, one Christian girl named Leah who still remains in captivity from the Dapchi abduction. Like most of the Chibok girls, Leah's fate remains unknown to date. Although President Buhari described the Dapchi abduction as a "national disaster," his regime has remained inept in providing a decisive panacea for addressing Nigeria's numerous instances of insecurity. These include Boko Haram's bombings, abductions and Fulani-Herder clashes in Benue and Plateau states that have left thousands dead and many displaced as refugees.
46. UNHCR, Vulnerability Report, 2017.
47. Ibid.
48. Thurston, *Boko Haram,* 278.
49. Between 2017 and 2018, ISWAP attacked Nigerian National Petroleum Company (NNPC) workers in Borno State that included University of Maiduguri Lecturers, killing four and abducting three others for ransom.
50. See Jacob Zenn, *Terrorism Monitor*, vol. 17, no. 12: 3–5. The Jamestown Foundation, 2019.
51. Ibid., 4.
52. Author, field interview, August 11, 2019.
53. For details on these competing perspectives, see Thurston, Mustapha, Varin, Kassim, Umar, and Perouse de Montclos.
54. This possibility is based on the local history of radical sectarianism in Northern Nigeria, including *Maitatsine* riots in the 1980s, Bulumkutu and Yola riots between 1982 and 1984, the Zaria-based Shi'tte movement and its intermittent altercations with the federal government as well as Izala—Sufi rivalries, and more recently intra-Salafi sectarianism and assassination of leading clerics such as Sheikh Ja'afar Adam in 2007.

Chapter 10

SECESSIONIST MOVEMENTS AND STRUCTURAL DETERMINISM IN NIGERIA

Usman A. Tar and Bashir Bala

Introduction

Nigeria's development process has been fraught with a crisis of legitimacy amidst an incessant clamor for political determinism by disparate elements in the country. These political deterministic tendencies are constructed around forces of fragmentation, in particular, ethnicity, religiosity and geography. The draining nature of political determinism has had adverse repercussions on the country's fledgling democracy. Nigeria returned to democracy in May 1999 after three decades of intermittent military rule and attendant authoritarian dictatorship. The restoration of democracy has not yielded the much-desired democratic dividends largely because of a bevy of internal contradictions that bedevil the country. One such contradiction is the rise of agitations for the devolution of national power structure and the restructuring of the country's federalist system. These agitations and protests are largely based on ethnic/enclave politics and spearheaded, recently, by the country's youth. Nigeria's crisis of democracy is symptomatic of the absurdity of building a liberal democracy in a contested federal formation. While

---

This chapter draws partly from Prof Usman Tar's "Fuel for Crises: A Critical Analysis of Political Determinism in Nigeria's Development Process," a Lead Paper presented at the *National Broadcast Summit* themed "Broadcast Content Development and Peaceful Co-existence" organized by the National Broadcasting Commission (NBC) held on July 18, 2017, at Silk Suites, Rayfield, Jos, Plateau State. However, the sections on secessionist movements and implications for Nigeria's national security are a product of additional research conducted with the co-author.

Professor of political science and defense studies, and Head of the Centre for Defence Studies and Documentation at the Nigerian Defence Academy, Kaduna. Email: uatar@nda.edu.ng

Captain in the Nigerian Army and Research Fellow at the Centre for Defence Studies and Documentation, Nigerian Defence Academy, Kaduna. Email: basheerbala@gmail.com

many post-colonial societies have achieved significant progress in democracy and development (e.g., Botswana and South Africa), Nigeria has been described as being in "an unfinished state of uncertainty."[1] In addition to popular agitations and clamors for restructuring, Nigeria is bogged down by multiple structural and institutional crises—such as corruption, terrorism, militancy, insurgency—leading to such labeling of Nigeria as "the open sore of a continent."[2]

Historical antecedents play an important role in Nigeria's current dilemma, but contemporary realities tend to exacerbate the crisis and undermine the continued existence of the state. The federating units of Nigeria seem to have lost confidence in the state, largely because of its failure to meet the basic needs of its citizens and the rampant corruption and manipulation of the political elite. Nigeria's dilemma is deeply rooted in colonial and neo-colonial legacies of the nation-state, as well as the paradox of building a "modern" nation-state on the vestiges of inherited traditions and cultural legacies. Nigeria's dilemma is a product of the simultaneous but contradictory existence of, on the one hand, fledgling capitalist structures such as a market economy, emerging classes, huge reserve of skilled and unskilled labor, and a robust civil society—all features seemingly conducive to democracy and development. On the other hand, these are foisted upon counterproductive features of a dependent neo-colonial economy formally managed by a political class beholden to the whims and exigencies of donors and foreign investors. Popular discontent with Nigeria's democratic system abound largely because of the discordant and inchoate construction of the state and the nonchalant attitude of its ruling elites who tend to unleash popular discontents that are expressed in destructive, rather than constructive, ways.[3]

Background: The State and Paradoxes of Development and Democracy in Nigeria

Nigeria demonstrates a curious paradox.[4] On the one hand, the country exhibits a plethora of factors and institutions that are potentially conducive to the construction of democracy. By African standards, Nigeria has developed some of the finest and most advanced capitalist structures that ought to facilitate the creation of a stable liberal democracy: a relatively developed industrial base; an emerging class structure; abundant natural resources, a highly skilled manpower replenished by numerous educational institutions, a huge reserve of unskilled labor, a robust market base; a vibrant civil society; and a relatively independent judiciary (this is in spite of recent controversies that engulfed some judicial officials).[5] On the other hand, however, Nigeria exhibits the typical features of a failing peripheral state: a self-centered governing class beholden to the centers of global capital, and surviving through "cuts" from state revenues and corrupt practices; an economy effectively tied to the metropolitan center[6]; and politics driven by appeal to tradition rather than modernity.[7] The foregoing paradoxes have conspired to deprive Nigeria of a functional democratic system throughout its post-colonial history, and since 1999 they have manifested in attempts by some demographic and geographic segments of the society to seek the restructuring of the state.

Nigeria operates one of the least stable federal and presidential democratic systems in the world: its diverse ethnic and cultural panorama (comprising over 500 ethnic groups) was fortuitously amalgamated by British colonialists into a single nation-state. Nigeria's federating entities (currently comprising thirty-six states and a federal center) exist as the "usual suspects," each competing for a fair share of the commonwealth. They are also divorced from any real sense of collective nationalism but rather rooted in deceptive appeal to religion, ethnicity, and regionalism as the bases for negotiating access to power and resources. There are regular clashes between a strong federal center and contending states regarding a number of issues, for example, distribution formula for federal income accrued largely from petroleum resources, the adoption of Shari'a law by some states, and localization of policing and security. There are three fundamental issues of contention enshrined in the country's constitution: first, exclusive matters, considered as "no go area" or as the guarded preserve of the federal government, including foreign policy, defense and security, and revenue allocation; second, concurrent matters, considered as a common ground for both the federal center and federating units/states, including taxation, road construction, education, election administration, and water supply; and finally, residual matters, considered as a common ground for all units of the federation, including the local government, including education, drainage, social and community service, and local government levies on local small-scale businesses. Typically, the federal center has always resisted attempts by states and local governments to negotiate greater power on issues that impinge on its exclusive domain, such as the establishment of state police forces and revenue generation from the extractive sector.[8] This has too often resulted in skirmishes between the federal government and states/local governments. The reality is that an active civil society is increasingly appropriating sections of state functions, particularly in the area of security and law and order.

Nigeria has, therefore, been variously characterized as "a mere geographic expression," "an artificial entity," "a mistake of 1914," "a product of colonial expansion," "an all-time imposition," "a forced marriage," and so on.[9] For observers, it was colonialism that brought Nigeria's diverse ethno-religious and cultural populace together under imperialist tutelage via direct rule in the South, and indirect rule in the North. After independence, Nigeria was bequeathed with a rational legal bureaucracy existing alongside a plethora of primordial institutions. Instead of rallying around the modern state or rescuing it from incipient threats, Nigerians have resorted to patrimonialism and sectarianism as the basis of political interaction. This fed into adversarial political culture and centrifugalizing the Nigerian state as "the usual suspect." Herein lies the recent struggle by some disgruntled elements to dismantle "Project Nigeria" in favor of their narrow construction of an ethnic-nation-state (Biaxit/Biafra, Yoruexit/Oduduwaland, Arexit/Arewa Republic), as unfashionable and un-normal as this seems.[10]

The contentious nature of Nigerian federalism means that development, democracy, and nation-building are difficult to achieve. In the aftermaths of independence, the Nigerian ruling class failed to achieve the ideals of self-rule and national emancipation, the rallying banners of the struggles for independence. Elected representatives became local champions, drawing support from their disparate religions/ethnicities, effectively transforming the state into a theatre of ethnic politics. Between 1960 and 1966, Nigeria's first experiment in Westminster-style liberal democracy became a "cropper" as politicians abused the state apparatus for personal aggrandizement and perpetuating power by appealing to ethnic and regional cleavages. This paved the way for a prolonged military intervention (1966–1979) as well as a civil war (1967–1970) in which over 4 million lives were lost and vital social and political infrastructures destroyed. Between 1979 and 1983, Nigeria witnessed a second democratic experiment led by Alhaji Shehu Shagari, a seasoned politician who had served as junior minister in the First Republic. The new democratic government carried forward and/or reinvented the ills of the First Republic. In particular, the ruling class resorted to prebendal politics[11] by transforming the state into an instrument of personal enrichment through client-patron relationships between the political class and those loyal to it.

On December 31, 1983, the military overthrew the Shagari administration on the grounds of the rapidly deteriorating economic situation and the turmoil that followed the rigged 1983 national elections by the ruling National Party of Nigeria. The military remained in power—largely through deceit, repression, and manipulation—for a protracted period (1983–1999), in what has been described as a period of "permanent transition."[12] In May 1999, General Abubakar who "inherited" state power from General Abacha, following the latter's death in August 1998, eventually restored democracy. Since the restoration of democracy, Nigeria seems to have broken a long-standing norm of regular military interventions. The country is now enjoying its longest stretch of uninterrupted civilian rule since independence in 1960.

In spite of achieving democracy since 1999, Nigerians have not witnessed the so-called democratic dividends: the transition to civilian rule has not delivered a democratically accountable government for Nigerians.[13] The usual chaos and rancor that characterized politics in the first and second republics are evident in the new democratic era and continue to pervade public life. Governments and elected representatives at all levels of the federation are preoccupied with self-centered "power politics," rather than social welfare. The turnover of people-oriented policies and programs has remained largely erratic and inadequate, due to the embedded tendencies amongst the political class seeking to outdo each other and negotiate policies and legislations on the basis of personal cut or gatekeepers of primordial loyalties. In the politics of ethnicity and religion, the political classes have carved a niche as incredible manipulators of the public's imagination. Most importantly, they enlist sectarian sentiments, with all the associated risk of whipping communal violence.

Following the 2015 general elections, Nigeria experienced a change of government. The All Progressive Congress (APC), a tenuous coalition of progressive opposition political parties, successfully defeated the Peoples Democratic Party (PDP) government, which had ruled the country for sixteen years, without much to show in terms of the so-called dividends of democracy. If anything, the PDP era saw the blossoming of corruption, plundering of the national treasury, and primitive accumulation by the ruling elite. The ascension of APC-led government has brought about relative change in terms of the fight against corruption, improved security, and job creation. However, the progress is nowhere near the public's level of expectation. The APC government inherited huge public debt, unpaid wages, an infrastructural crisis, and crises of security especially in the Niger Delta and northern part of the country plagued by the Boko Haram insurgency, detailed earlier in this book. Perhaps more importantly, the post-2015 era also witnessed increased clamor for the restructuring of the country's federal setup, including the revival of secessionist movement by youth elements from the southeastern part of the country.

In sum, agitations and protests for secessionist revivalism in Nigeria are a direct consequence of the contradictions embedded in Nigeria's body polity. This includes a national culture of corruption, regional struggles for power and resources, elite manipulations of ethno-regional sentiments, generational frictions between a mainly elderly self-centered governing elite and disenfranchised youths, a "youth bulge"—defined as the externality of generational shifts in which a teeming population of young people is not accommodated by the state and economy in terms of job creation, legitimate means of livelihood, and political engagement. Short of this, the youth are likely to seek existential solace in illegitimate activities such as political banditry/hooliganism, armed robbery and kidnapping to make ends meet—this is known as the "Queer Ladder" which stands in contrast with the "legitimate ladder" or "due process" of self-actualization as sanctioned by the society.[14]

A Critical Diagnosis of Secessionist Agitations and Structural Determinism in Nigeria

Within the last decade, some of the nationalist movements that emerged represented virtually all the geopolitical zones in Nigeria. The central theme anchoring their movements and deterministic resolve is the quest to separate their ethnic people from the Nigerian entity. In this regard, Ebiem notes that these movements are for the common good and development of divergent ethnic entities.[15] The modalities, which the groups adopt in their agitations, symbolize the singular most important socio-political development in Nigeria since the post-colonial era. All too often, expressions such as "Self-Determination," "Nationalist Movement," "Separatist Movement," "Civil Rights Movement," and "Indigenous Peoples' Rights Movement" have been used to qualify these agitations.[16] In the eastern part of Nigeria, the first non-violent movement to capture public attention is the Movement for the Actualization of the Sovereign State of Biafra (MASSOB). Ralph Uwazuruike, a lawyer who was trained in India, formed the group. It received little attention from the international stage, notwithstanding its several confrontations with law enforcement agencies at different times leading to the arrest of its leader.[17] In an effort to rekindle the dream of actualizing the Sovereign State of Biafra, Nnamdi Kanu, a Nigerian-British based in London, reinvigorated the methodology of MASSOB and formed the Indigenous People of Biafra (IPOB). Kanu's use of the emerging communication technology, especially social media and online radio broadcasts/podcasts to lure millions of pro-Biafra independence activists, supporters, and sympathizers to his Biafran cause, is legendary.[18] The success recorded in mobilizing youthful sympathizers through these mind games further emboldened Kanu to employ the tools of provocative expressions against the Nigerian government. Kanu's wanton use of hate speech heightened tensions across the country particularly in the East dominated by Igbos. His call for the supply of arms and ammunitions coupled with the outsourcing of logistics to wage war against the northern Hausa-Fulani people, because of their resistance to an independent Biafra, fanned the embers that threaten the existence of Nigeria. His excessive use of vituperations and hate speeches also redefined the dimension of secessionist movements in Nigeria.

O'odua People's Congress (OPC) remains a vibrant organization in the southwest of Nigeria. It was established in 1994 and campaigns to protect the interests of the Yoruba ethnic group and seek substantial independence for the Yoruba people. The OPC revolves with the tides of the changing nature of the complexities that replete Nigeria's political environment. The group attempts to end what it termed "the political marginalization and exclusion" of the Yorubas in the schemes of national affairs.[19] Another Pan Yoruba group that came lately into the limelight is the O'odua Nationalist Coalition (ONAC), which has called on Yoruba people to clamor for a sovereign nation, Oodua Republic. ONAC subsidiaries include the OPC, Oodua Liberation Movement (OLM), Oodua Republic Coalition (ORC), Yoruba Revolutionary Congress (YORC), Oodua Muslim-Christian Dialogue Group (OMDG), Yoruba Students Nationalist Front (YOSNF), Oodua Hunters Union (OHUN), and eleven other groups.[20] The activities of these groups have assumed different dimensions in their bid to promote Yoruba culture and push for Yoruba autonomy. Their activities have sometimes resulted in violent confrontations with members of other ethnic groups, particularly the Hausa-Fulani. There are equally allegations of human rights violations leveled against groups such as the OPC following their resort to ethnic militancy and vigilantism.[21]

In northern Nigeria, a coalition of socio-political groups called the Arewa Youth Forum Consultative Assembly (AYFCA) further heat up the politics of secessionism. The group in its Kaduna Declaration of June 2017 issued an ultimatum to people of Igbo ethnic nationality residing in the North to relocate to their Southeast homeland before October 1.[22] The groups that signed the declaration included Arewa Citizens Action for Change, Arewa Youth Consultative Forum, Arewa Youth Development Foundation, Arewa Students Forum, and Northern Emancipation Network.[23] The ultimatum by the northern youths was an apparent reactionary measure against the secessionist demand of some Igbo groups, including IPOB.[24] The moves and countermoves from the various groups fueled secessionist provocations, deepening ethnic mistrust with grave consequences for Nigeria's national cohesion.

Secessionist movements are not limited to the regions dominated by Nigeria's three major ethnic groups—Hausa, Igbo, and Yoruba. Nigeria's oil-rich Niger Delta is another hotspot of violent struggles that manifest mainly as ethnic militancy with a tinge of separatist undertone. The ethnic minority groups in the Delta region largely spearhead these agitations. The Niger Delta has been a hotbed of agitation since the early days of Nigerian independence: for instance, immediately after Nigeria's independence, Isaac Adaka Boro led a movement to emancipate the Delta from the tyranny of the elites and central government in Lagos. In 2004, groups like Movement for the Emancipation of the Niger Delta (MEND), Niger Delta People's Volunteer Force (NDPVF), Joint Revolutionary Council (JRC), and Niger Delta Vigilante (NDV) emerged to protest the perceived marginalization of the region by the Nigerian state (see Chapter 8). The continued escalation of violence in the area saw the emergence of newer groups such as the Niger Delta Avengers in 2016. Among these groups, the NDPVF led by Asari Dokubo and the NDV headed by Ateke Tomare were more violent and involved in pyro- acts of terrorism before the actual unveiling of the Niger Delta Avengers. MEND and Niger Delta Avengers are conducting attacks and high-profile sabotage against the Nigerian state under the guise of seeking autonomy for the Niger Deltans.[25] The existence and modus operandi of these secessionist movements have impacted on the political and social equilibrium of Nigeria.

Secessionist Movements and Implications for Nigeria's National Security

Protests and agitations for democratic expansion, environmental justices, and restructuring of Nigeria's contested federal formation have been an enduring feature of the post-colonial Nigerian state. These include the Niger Delta rebellion led by Isaac Adaka Boro (1960s), the Nigerian Civil War (1967–1970), and Niger Delta environmental movement (1990s–present): they were/are executed through resort to full-scale violence between the federal forces against rebelling elements. Other violent crises, such as the Maitatsine rebellion (1980s) and Boko Haram crisis (2009–present), that sought to challenge the authority of the state were not necessarily rooted in the struggle for democratic expansion, but their emergence has unveiled questions on the failure of the post-colonial state to provide an enabling environment for socio-economic and political opportunities that will strengthen mass loyalty to the state, and make a resort to violence undesirable. With the exception of these cases, the state has often managed protest and agitations for political determinism through peaceful means, which range from dialogue to compromise such as through the introduction of derivation formula for oil-bearing states. So far, the state has used both the "stick" (Biafra, Zaki Biam, Odi) and "carrot" (Niger Delta Amnesty Programme) to deal with agitations for political determination. Thus, the Nigerian state has devised some constructive, albeit contested, means of managing its internal contradictions.

A divisive variant of agitations that is staring the Nigerian state in the face is the recent rumbles for the abandonment of project Nigeria and its replacement with ethnic nation-states as demonstrated by the agitations of IPOB and MASSOB, among others. The IPOB agitation is rooted in earlier forms of struggles for succession[26] and Isaac Adaka Boro's independent state of Niger Delta (1960s). For over forty years, some groups in the southern part of Nigeria have agitated for the restructuring of the state with a view to achieving sovereignty for their tribal enclaves. And since 2015—following the assumption of power by the APC-led government of President Muhammadu Buhari—the secessionist elements have achieved some mileage in terms of pushing the secessionist agenda into the subnational and national platforms. The IPOB and MASSOB are the two most prominent groups in terms of their ability to raise popular consciousness in southeastern Nigeria for the revival of Biafra. The case of Nnamdi Kanu and IPOB is quite interesting. IPOB emerged with a violent strain of the Biafra movement by challenging the legitimacy of the Nigerian state, establishing a clandestine media station that openly broadcast hate message against "Hausa-Fulani owned contraption called Nigeria"[27] and calling on the peoples of southern Nigeria (South-South and South-East) to rise against the Nigerian state and emancipate Biafra from the shackles of Nigeria's "forced federalism."[28] Both Kanu and IPOB remained obscure until the present APC-government arrested and detained Kanu on grounds of treason and incitement of rebellion. The federal government detained Kanu for longer than legally permissible. His continued detention gradually shifted the discourse, especially amongst Igbo politicians and citizens and southern media from "Kanu as rebel" to "Kanu as hero."[29] Whilst in prison, Igbo politicians—including some state governors—paid nocturnal visits to Kanu and provided him with material support. When he was eventually released on bail, Kanu effectively transformed into a local hero in southeast Nigeria—akin to Colonel Chukwuemeka Odimegu Ojukwu, the leader of the Biafra secession, who bestrode popular support in the region fifty years earlier!

The secessionist revivalism in southeastern Nigeria has not only animated violent struggle in Igboland, but has also had a boomerang effect across the Niger River.[30] On December 2, 2015, there were massive shootings and exchanges of fire between the IPOB member and security forces in Nigeria. Consequently, some protesters threatened to march to the federal capital, Abuja, if Kanu was not released following his incarceration by the Nigerian government. Against popular speculation of his possible assassination by the Nigerian security agencies, Kanu resurfaced, mysteriously performing a pilgrimage in Israel in October 2018, and he later released a social media interview threatening to continue with the IPOB struggle. Moreover, there were further attacks on mosques and northern business interests in the Southeast which have triggered retaliatory violence against Ibos and their businesses in the North, particularly Jos and Kano.[31] Recently, other parts of the country, especially the North, appear to have joined the bandwagon for restructuring Nigeria. Public opinion in the North is taking a dramatic turn from cautious straddling against breaking up Nigeria, to bold calls for "let the Igbos go with their Biafra" and "let's build our own independent Arewa Republic."[32] In the Southwest too, there are calls by Yoruba secessionist elements to disengage from Nigeria and walk away with the Republic of Oduduwaland.[33]

The generational dimension of the clamor for restructuring and secession in Nigeria is equally astonishing. In June 2017, the youth of southeastern, northern, and southwestern Nigeria have issued in quick and competitive sequence "quit notices" against "alien" or "settler" tribes[34] residing in their home regions—as if Nigeria were a tribal real estate. Mainly regional and tribal youth movements issued flurries of declarations, across the country: "Biafra Declaration" (*Biaxit*),[35] "Kaduna Declaration" (*Arewaxit*),[36] and "Lagos Declaration" (*Yoruexit*).[37] This "Tripod Threats of Secession" and subsequent minority declarations have sought to challenge the corporate existence of Nigeria. Smaller ethnic enclaves, such as the Ijaws, Itsekiris, Kalabaris, and Middle Belt, have equally taken the cue and issued their own enclave declarations,[38] warning "aliens" to depart their territory within given period or risk forceful removal. These skirmishes have been appropriately termed "theatre of the absurd."[39] They create the impression that the Nigerian state has lost its bearing as the flag bearers of national sovereignty and territorial integrity by allowing ethnic nationalities (Igbos, Hausas, Yorubas, Efiks, Itsekiris, Idomas, etc.) take control of their enclaves.

Thus, in every region of Nigeria, there are disparate movements seeking to dismantle the Nigerian state and replace it with an ethnic one. This is clear contradiction as most states of the world are made up of diverse ethnic groups living together as nation-states, while Nigerian nationalities are seeking to achieve the opposite, "tribal-states." This is an anathema that needs to be understood and tamed appropriately through pragmatic steps and prescriptions. Some points are worth observing. First, popular agitations have undermined and eroded the constitutional legitimacy of the Nigerian state. In a process described by Claude Ake as "Salient Duality," Nigerians are migrating from the mainstream formal state to informal primordial platforms—defined by ethnicity, religion, culture, and territory.[40] The concept of "salient duality"[41] captures the contradiction of the Nigerian state. Ake argued that Nigerians are beholden to two contradictory tendencies: the formal state (weak loyalty) and primordial tendencies (strong loyalty). There is concurrent migration from secularism to fragmentalism/sectarianism. Second, recent popular agitations represent the voices of the major ethnic groups in Nigeria—Hausas, Igbos, and Yorubas. Other so-called minority ethnic groups—Edo, Efik, Ibibio, Idoma, Itsekiri, Kanuri, and Tiv, among others—are clearly out of the dominant picture, and are therefore constructing a parallel litany of voices each seeking to articulate a space for its own ethnic domain-cum-state. Third, there appears to be a generational contradiction that is brewing in Nigeria. Recent ethnic declarations are issued by the youths to the exclusion of elders of their respective regions: indeed, the elders in regions have since distanced themselves from the excessive determinism of their youth. There appears to be a generational friction in Nigeria's body polity. Most Nigerian leaders are elderly (sixty years and above), while quite a few have served as political appointees in most regimes since independence. Indeed, the youth leader of the opposition PDP is above forty years of age. The real youth have lost confidence in the selfish aging political class, and are eager to challenge/replace them. Fourth, and related to the youth resurgence, we are now witnessing what experts call a "youth bulge,"[42] a situation where lack of leadership, entrepreneurship, and material worth has forced the youth to resort to violence and destruction to make ends meet and thus secure political and material relevance.

To be sure, the Nigerian state has a constitutional mandate to ensure the territorial integrity, peaceful coexistence, and stability of the country. It also has the moral responsibility to guarantee rule of law and human rights—which provide the basis for groups and citizens to exercise their rights of expression, peaceful assembly, and conscience. However, the exercise of such rights by individuals or groups is not expected to compromise the rights of other individuals or the unified existence of the Nigerian state. Herein lies the challenge posed by the resurgence of secessionist or separatist agitations. The situation implicates the delicate balance between national security and democratic freedoms. Both are essential for the development of the nation, but they can be contradictory at times.

Political Determinism and National Security in Nigeria

There are numerous dimensions to the ongoing spates of political determinism in Nigeria, with serious implication for national security. First, the structural and constitutional dimension deals with the context of the faulty construction of governance systems and perception of lopsided national institution building. Years of military rule and perception of sectional marginalization have led to crisis of legitimacy of the Nigerian state. Aspects of the state's governance system have evolved rather unsteadily over the past fifty years. For instance, the basis of power-sharing and resource distribution appears to be contested as no entity is satisfied with the existing formula for political governance, fiscal federalism, and economic governance. The running of the thirty-six federal structures is seen as costly, leading to calls for the restructuring of the federal architecture to make it more effective, manageable, and less costly. Many states can no longer pay the salaries of civil servants. According to the National Union of Teachers in Nigeria (NUT), these states include Osun topping the list with 28 months followed by Nasarawa, 26; Kogi, 25; Benue, 12; and Ekiti, 9 months. Others are Bayelsa, 7.5 months; Taraba, 6 months; Abia and Kaduna, 5 months; Ondo, 4 months; Kwara and Delta, 2 months; and Oyo, 1 month.[43] These states are therefore unsustainable and past their use-by dates (shelf life).

Second, the cultural and civilization dimension emerged from the territorialization of ethnicity and material culture by different primordial groups in Nigeria. Each ethnic group looks down on the "other." In addition, there are well-known pervasive innuendoes, name-calling, and stereotyping used to despise and insult the "other" that pervade popular consciousness: the Hausas and Fulanis are seen as fool-hardy, backward, and uncivilized parasites;[44] the Igbos are seen as immature, selfish, canny, materialist, and domineering folks;[45] the Yorubas are seen as condescending, sophisticated morons, dubious, conspiratorial, domineering, and hateful.[46] This clash of civilization has only helped fuel the embers of hate and contempt between and among ethnic or sectional groups in Nigeria. Furthermore, religion, which ought to be a leveler of ethnic and sectional tensions, has not helped matters. Nigeria has been classified as the world's second most religious country, with a phenomenal rise in the number of evangelical churches.[47] However, religion has not helped to calm ethnic tensions in the country. The dual menaces of the religionization of politics and the politicization of religion have crippled Nigeria's body polity especially since the return of democratic order in 1999.[48] There is a need to find the appropriate place for religion in society. In other words, we need to tame religion to make it user-friendly and a force for good. At the moment, Nigerian religions (Christianity, Islam, and traditional religions) are largely abused, commercialized, and commodified by the ruling and governing elites—of which the theocratic class is a part—to serve their material interests. Citizens are indoctrinated with profane sentiments and hate messages, which, in the political realm at least, has further created deep-rooted division and contempt between incompatible faith groups.

Nigeria is officially a secular state as enshrined in the 1999 Constitution. However, in practice both the state and society are inundated with religious dogmatism and ritual symbolisms of religion. Beyond the current formality of constitutional provision, secularism is yet to be institutionalized in Nigeria.[49] In addition, religion has permeated from private domains (churches, mosques, families, etc.) to the public sphere. The inclusion of religion as a marker for formal documentations (application forms for jobs and admission to institutions of learning) has too often been abused to advance sectarian interests. Furthermore, the lack of a clear national policy on religion, which is backed by neither law nor institutional structure, has played into the hands of political demagogues, and conscripted religion as instruments of political struggle. The lack of national value formation, which is not addressed adequately by the lead national agencies such as the *Federal Ministry of Education, Federal Ministry of Information, National Orientation Agency,* and *National Media Agencies,* has led to sheer dearth of national patriotism. Furthermore, there are concerns about the failure of the federal Ministry of Education and National Curriculum Development Agency to properly institutionalize courses that advance national pride and patriotism: *history, civic education, national ethics, values,* etc., which ought to be embedded as core and general studies subjects at all levels of education.

Third, the generational dimension manifest in the changing demographic dynamics of the country. Nigeria's population is largely young: 68 percent of the population is classified as youth below the age of 30.[50] Depending on how this youthful population is governed, Nigeria will either be confronted with a huge reserve of human talent, or become a ticking time bomb (youth bulge). The Nigerian youth are watching the exploits and achievements of their peers across the world: France readily comes to mind with a 39-year-old newly elected President. The Nigerian youth are clearly marginalized and in need of opportunity to serve their country. But there are questions to be asked: have the Nigerian youth constituted themselves into a critical mass of a power block that is prepared to challenge the status quo and take up leadership positions and add value—not destroy the system? Have the youth acquired the discipline, maturity, focus, patriotism, tolerance, and enlightened self-interest to take over the commanding heights of the national power and economy? Have the youth come out of their ethnic umbilical cords and tribal cocoons to extend their hands of friendship and camaraderie to their other peers across River Niger? It is questionable whether the Nigerian youth have demonstrated the potential to present a formidable alternative constituency for national leadership.

The *Nigerian youth are a victim of double jeopardy*: on the one hand, they are a *victim of a prebendal system that failed to cater for its future generations*[51] and thus unleashed a trail of an emerging generation that is unemployed, regionalized, racialized, poorly cultured, and tribalized to levels far worse than those of their elders. On the other hand, many among the *Nigerian youth have placed themselves on the trajectory of self-destruction* by allowing themselves to be tribalized and ethnicized.[52] They are largely oblivious of the principles of enlightened self-interest (which suggests that people tend to engage in activities that protect their existential and material interest, even if such acts will concurrently benefit others). Nevertheless, in spite of the foregoing picture, youths all over the world have historically proved to be an agile and dynamic demography that can easily overcome their challenges and find their bearing:[53] with a creative initiative that can rescue the youth from self-destruction. The authors believe that it would not take much time to turn around the fortune of the Nigerian youth. There is need to create a *culture of patriotism* amongst our youths. With a clean start on our value orientation—as suggested above—the Nigerian youth can be mustered into a force for good. In addition to the National Youth Service Corps (NYSC), Nigeria should revamp Unity Colleges and initiate more programs of youth integration.

Fourth, the economic and material dimensions manifest in the failing economic fundamentals, which tend to affect the youth and other marginalized social groups. Clearly, the ongoing webs of political determinism are undergirded by economic motives, and this constitutes the "externality of marginalization." Research or studies have shown that a country with a large youthful population and endowed with huge natural resources, but poorly governed, stands the risk of unraveling or experiencing major internal crisis.[54] This suggests a strong correlation between susceptibility to civil conflicts and burgeoning youth populations in underdeveloped and developing countries. In societies where the productive talents of youth population are poorly harnessed, the risk of youth involvement in crime, violence, and hooliganism becomes higher.[55] If the Nigerian government invests progressively and consistently in creating real opportunities for material empowerment, the youth will be creatively and constructively influenced to engage in legitimate endeavors as well as appreciate the dignity of labor. Conversely, where the youth are denied opportunities for legitimate livelihood, some could resort to armed robbery, advance fee fraud, banditry, political hooliganism, militancy, and terrorism for ideological and economic ends. The Nigerian economy should create opportunities for the youth, so they do not have to resort to illegitimate means of survival.

Fifth, the geographical dimension is concerned with the disaggregated ecologies of agitations for self-actualization in which each geographic entity

(North, Southeast, South-South, Southwest, etc.) is concerned with getting the best bargain for its territory from the Nigerian state, including in the worst-case scenario, self-determination or independence for the specific political geography. The Nigerian youth have joined the bandwagon to entrench geographic injustice against outsider elements or non-indigenes living in their enclaves. Many Nigerians, especially the youth, harbor provincial mindset and enclave mentality in their public and transactional conducts. Tribal lords or "area fathers" have ambushed the real estate known as Nigeria and their local youth who carry a matching label of "area boys." There are allegations that in some parts of Nigeria, the so-called settlers are not allowed to acquire property, contest for elective posts, or own businesses.[56] This clearly contradicts the provisions of the Constitution (1999) and Land Tenure Act,[57] both of which allow citizens to own land and property as well as aspire for elective position in their place of permanent residency. In the realm of power relations, geography has proved to be an asset for local folks, and a burden for settlers. For instance, following Nigeria's return to democracy in 1999, in Jos Plateau, particularly local politicians of Birom extraction have utilized indigenous rights to deny "sattlers" (*Hausawa* or Jasawa) access to elective and appointive positions. With the exception of the FCT where settlers can pursue their political and commercial dreams without encumbrances, in most states of Nigeria non-indigenes are denied access to their rights.

Sixth, the behavioral or psychological dimensions of political determinism in Nigeria are concerned with the mindset and outlook of Nigerians toward one another. This is closely associated with years of poor governance, which is gradually producing a large proportion of hostile, intolerant, and insolent people from the growing Nigerian population. The culture of respect, dignity, and tolerance is in short supply in the public sphere. This is perhaps because most Nigerians are "local champions" who have not travelled out of their enclaves or "comfort zones" either out of fear or failure of national integration. Most cannot stand the "other" because of poor understanding of, and lack of interaction with, peoples from other geographic and ethnic backgrounds. Existing national policies and programs that seek to break cultural and psychological barriers amongst Nigerians—such as Federal Character Principle, NYSC, Unity Colleges, etc.—have so far not allayed mutual distrust among Nigerians. At the moment, only few segments of the Nigerian population have managed to overcome their difference and coexist in relative peace, namely: *political class* that has managed to work together for their collective class interest and political benefit; *organized civil society and professional associations* (paradoxically including some youth organizations) that have imbibed the culture working together to foster their existential interests without prejudice to identity difference; and the *religious fraternity* that has, in an exclusive sense, managed to forge a common ground in their missions.

Finally, the virtual and technological dimensions are concerned with the role of the technologies of mass media, including new social media, in forging political and associational ties amongst citizens. Virtual technologies have proved to be *enabler* of popular agitation in Nigeria and across the world. There is growing reliance on and use of ICT, especially social media platforms, by the citizens for communication and information dissemination. However, poor regulation of social media platforms has implications for security and stability in Nigeria against the backdrop of prevalence of hate speech and disinformation. There is need to regulate how individuals and groups harness virtual technologies and new social media as platforms for popular agitation and political expression. While not all social media platforms can be effectively regulated by the Nigerian state, ICTs can be subjected to better regulation in the country. For instance, the National Cyber-Security Policy (2015) provides a national framework for regulating virtual domains, internet protocols, and service providers. Where necessary, the Nigeria state should not hesitate to take necessary measures to manage violent agitations or enclave cyber-warfare as taking place in the ongoing agitations.

The foregoing reveals that there are varying but interconnected dimensions of political determinism in Nigeria, each posing a threat to the country's national security. These dimensions unveil the ambivalence and contradictions of the Nigerian state, arising principally from the failure of the political elite to build an all-embracing state. The result has been the exclusion of the youth and other minorities from the exercise of power, cries of marginalization, youth restiveness, ethnic separatism, cultural jingoism, and resurgent secessionist agitations. It appears the vanguards for political determinism in Nigeria are largely oblivious of the constitutional encumbrances associated with any attempt to dismantle the state.

Conclusion

This chapter examined the dynamics of secessionist movements and structural determinism in Nigeria, which have grown in manifestation and intensity since Nigeria's return to democracy in 1999. The analysis reveals that Nigeria is deeply divided by forces of ethnicity, religion, and demography. The popular agitations for restructuring the country's federalism, including the incipient revival of political determinism, demonstrate the crisis of legitimacy that confronts the Nigerian state. Growing youth agitation is the latest and most potent layer of historical continuity of agitations in the country. This, associated with the gulf between national loyalty and loyalty to primordial platforms, poses a significant threat to the existence and corporate integrity of the country.

Popular agitations for restructuring the state are informed largely by weak allegiance to the state and, by extension, strong affinity to geography, ethnicity, and religion. It is important to manage the discussion to restructure the Nigerian state in a controlled and moderated manner. As these discussions continue, Nigerians should think with their heads not hearts: rather than breaking up the state, the discussion should rather focus on restructuring and improving the functionality and utility of the state so that it provides the greatest amount of happiness for the greatest number of people.[58] It is also apparent that where there are limited legitimate opportunities for self-actualization, marginalized youthful elements can resort (and they appeared to have resorted) to illegitimate and destructive means of survival—kidnapping, armed robbery, vandalism, terrorism, and, of recent, active agitations to restructure the state. While the ongoing agitations to restructure the Nigerian state is gathering momentum, it should not be allowed to spiral out of control to the point of dismembering the state. There is a lot to be had in the country's "unity in diversity." Indigene-settler dichotomy should be outlawed and national integration should be further institutionalized. Nigerians in all sides of the geographic divides should be enlightened on the essence of property relations and land ownership, and the fact that all Nigerians are constitutionally guaranteed to settle, own land, or aspire for opportunities in any part of the country. Firm political and civic action is essential to ensure equal opportunity for all: in addition to mass civic awareness on the part of executive and civil society, there is need for legislative action, law enforcement, and litigation to firm up legal and juridical support for equal opportunity for all citizens. Since some states are still unable to pay monthly salaries due to low budgetary allocation from the federal government, they are therefore unsustainable and past their use-by dates (shelf life). There is a need to reduce the number of states, even if that will mean more protests and agitations. Associated with that, it is not a bad idea to consider the confederal system for Nigeria—as it is done in Switzerland and Canada—where the regions enjoy autonomy over defense, diplomacy, policing, and resource exploitation. Nevertheless, Nigeria's center should not be killed altogether contrary to the wish of some agitators. There is tremendous opportunity to be had in sustaining the core of Nigeria's (con) federal system.

Notes

1. Agbaje, Adigun. A. 2004. "Nigeria: The Prospects for the Fourth Republic." In *Democratic Reforms in Africa: The Quality of Progress*, edited by E. Gyimah-Boadi. Boulder, CO: Lynne Rienner.
2. Soyinka, Wale. 1997. *The Open Sore of a Continent: A Personal Account of the Nigerian Crisis*. Oxford: Oxford University Press.
3. Tar, U. A. 2017. "Managing Agitations and Protest in Nigeria: Appropriate Approaches." Panel Discussion Paper presented at the *National Policy Monitoring Dialogue* (3rd edition) Themed "National Unity, Integration and Devolution of Power/Restructuring" organized by the Savannah Centre for Diplomacy, Democracy and Development in Partnership with Ford Foundation, Nigeria, held on July 13–14 at Ladi Kwali Hall, Sheraton Hotel and Towers, Abuja. & Tar, U. A. 2016. "Terrorism, Violent Conflict and Democratic Governance in Nigeria." Being Lead Paper presented at the National Conference on *The Dynamics of Democratic Practice in Nigeria, 1999-2015* held at the Aminu Kano Centre for Democratic Research and Training, Mambayya House, Bayero University Kano, November 9–10.
4. Tar, "Managing Agitations and Protest in Nigeria."
5. Ibid.; Tar, U. A. 2007. "A Hollow Giant on Agile Feet? The Challenges of Democratic Consolidation in Nigeria." *African Renaissance* 4, no. 3 & 4: 29–40; Tar, U. A. 2007. "Building Democracy in a Regressive State: The Travails of Electoral Politics in Nigeria." In *State-Society Relations in Nigeria: Democratic Consolidation, Conflicts and Reform*, edited by K. Omeje. London: Adonis & Abbey.

6. Beckman, Björn. 1982. "Whose State? State and Capitalist Development in Nigeria." *Review of African Political Economy*, 23: 37–51.
7. Ake, Claude. 2000. *The Feasibility of Democracy in Africa*. Dakar: CODESRIA.
8. Adebayo, A. 1998. Revenue Allocation: A Historical Analysis of the Nigerian Experience. Lagos: Longman; Akinjide, R. 2000. "Revenue Allocation and Federalism." In *The Challenges of True Federalism and Resource Control in Nigeria*, edited by Mudiaga Odje. Lagos: Quadio Impressions and Banji Ventures; Okolo, P. O and Raymond, A. O. 2014. "Federalism and Resource Control: The Nigerian Experience." *Public Policy and Administration Research* 2: 99–107; Babalawe, T. 1998. "The Impact of the Military on Nigerian Federalism." In *Re-Inventing Federalism in Nigeria: Issues and Perspectives*, edited by Kunle Amuwo and Tunde Babalawe. Ibadan: Spectrum Books; Egwaikhide, F. 2003. "Revenue Allocation: Perspectives from the Oil Producing States." In Fiscal Federalism and Revenue Allocation in Nigeria, edited by Akpan Ekpo and Enamidem Ubokudom. Ibadan: Future Publishing Company; Onwioduokit, E. 2002. *Revenue Allocation for a Stable Democracy in Nigeria: Options and Challenges*. Achimota: African Christian Press.
9. Awa, E. 1973. *Issues on Federalism*. Lagos: Academic Press; Azaiki, S. 2003. *Inequities in Nigerian Politics*. Yenagoa, Nigeria: Treasure Communication Resource Limited; Ugwu, S. C. 1998. *Federal System the Nigeria Experience*. Enugu, Nigeria: Mary Dan Publishers.
10. Tar, "Managing Agitations and Protest in Nigeria"; Tar, U. A. 2009. *The Politics of Neoliberal Democracy in Africa: State and Civil Society in Nigeria*. London/New York: I. B. Tauris.
11. Joseph, Richard 1987. *Democracy and Prebendal Politics in Nigeria: The Rise and Fall of the Second Republic*. Cambridge: University Press.
12. Beckett, P and Young, C. 1997. *Dilemmas of Democracy in Nigeria*. Rochester: Rochester University Press.
13. Human Rights Watch, 2003. "The O'ODUA People's Congress: Fighting Violence with Violence in Nigeria." 15, no. 4 (A).
14. Agbor, Julius, Taiwo, Olumide, and Smith Jessica. 2012. "Sub-Saharan Africa's Youth Bulge: A Demographic Dividend or Disaster?" In *Africa Growth Initiative*. Washington, DC: The Brookings Institution, 9–11; Bloom, D. E. and Humair, S. 2010. "Economic Development in Nigeria: A Demographic Perspective," Committee on African Studies, Harvard Africa Seminar, April 13; Omoju, Oluwasola E. and Abraham, Terfa W. 2014. "Youth Bulge and Demographic Dividend in Nigeria." *African Population Studies*, 27, no. 2 Supp (March): 352–360; Okafor, E. E. 2011. "Youth Unemployment and Implications for Stability of Democracy in Nigeria." *Journal of Sustainable Development in Africa* 13, no. 1: 358–373.
15. Ebiem, O. 2011. "The Many Separatist Movements in Nigeria." *Modern Ghana*. Available from: https://www.modernghana.com/news/333825/1/the-many-separatist-movements-in-nigeria.html.
16. Ibid.
17. Adekson, Adedayo Oluwakayode. 2004. *The "Civil Society" Problematique: Deconstructing Civility and Southern Nigeria's Ethnic Radicalisation*. London: Routledge Publishers, 102; *Vanguard Newspaper* (Nigeria). 2017, August 1. "Uwazuruike Opens Another Radio in Germany." Available from: https://www.vanguardngr.com/2017/08/miscreants-infiltrated-ranks-ipob-2/.
18. Ugorji, B. 2017. "Indigenous People of Biafra (IPOB): A Revitalized Social Movement in Nigeria." International Center for Ethno-Religious, NewYork Mediation, Available

from https://www.icermediation.org/publications/indigenous-people-of-biafra-ipob-a-revitalized-social-movement-in-nigeria/ [accessed March 22, 2018].
19. Human Rights Watch, "The O'ODUA People's Congress."
20. Akoni, O. 2017. "Igbo Quit Notice: Pan Yoruba Group Calls for Oodua Republic." *Vanguard*. Available from: https://www.vanguardngr.com/2017/06/igbo-quit-notice-pan-yoruba-group-calls-oodua-republic/.
21. Human Rights Watch, 2003. "The O'Odua People's Congress."
22. Ezea, S. 2017. "Arewa Youths' Ultimatum and Frailty of Nigeria's Unity." *The Guardian*. Available from: https://guardian.ng/politics/arewa-youths-ultimatum-and-frailty-of-nigerias-unity/.
23. Sahara Reporters, 2017. "Northern Youths Declare War on Igbos in the North, Ask Them Tot 'Leave' within Three Months." Available from: http://saharareporters.com/2017/06/06/northern-youths-declare-war-igbos-north-ask-them-%E2%80%98leave%E2%80%99-within-three-months
24. Ezea, "Arewa Youths' Ultimatum and Frailty of Nigeria's Unity."
25. Tar, U. A and Bala, B. 2019. "Boko Haram Insurgency, Terrorism and the Challenges of Peacebuilding in the Lake Chad Basin." In *Peacebuilding in Africa*, edited by Kenneth Omeje. London: Routledge.
26. Biafra Civil War from 1967 to 1970.
27. Uwazurike, G. 2018. "Tiv, Junkun, Kanuri People Were Never Conquered by Fulani." *Punch Newspaper*, February 17. An electronic interview available from: https://punchng.com/tiv-junkun-kanuri-people-were-never-conquered-by-fulani-uwazurike/ [accessed October 2, 2018].
28. Coffey, M. 2014. "'She Is Waiting': Political Allegory and the Specter of Secession in Chimamanda Ngozi Adichie's Half of a Yellow Sun." *Research in African Literatures* 45, no. 2: 63–85. DOI: 10.2979/reseafrilite.45.2.63.
29. Obi, Paul. 2017. "Igbo Leaders Visit Nnamdi Kanu, Call for His Immediate Release." *ThisDay Live Newspaper*, March 1. Available from: https://www.thisdaylive.com/index.php/2017/03/01/igbo-leaders-visit-nnamdi-kanu-call-for-his-immediate-release/ [Accessed November 1, 2015].
30. Keazor, Emeka. 2018. "Igbo Historiography: Milestones, Triumphs and Challenges." *Premium Times*, June 2. Available from: https://opinion.premiumtimesng.com/2018/06/02/igbo-historiography-milestones-triumphs-and-challenges-by-edemeka-keazor/ [Accessed October 2, 2018].
31. Obasi, N. 2015. "Nigeria's Biafran Separatist Upsurge." *International Crisis Group*. Available from: http://blog.crisisgroup.org/africa/nigeria/2015/12/04/nigerias-biafran-separatist-upsurge/ [Accessed November 1, 2018].
32. Punch Newspaper. 2017. "Igbo Free to Form Their Own Nation, We Can Live without Them—Arewa Youths," June 11. Available from: https://punchng.com/igbo-free-to-form-their-own-nation-we-can-live-without-them-arewa-youths/ [Accessed October 30, 2018].
33. *Vanguard Newspaper*. 2017. "Breaking: Give us, Kanu Oduduwa, Biafra republics; Too Late for Restructuring—Yoruba Group," July 31. Available from: https://www.vanguardngr.com/2017/07/breaking-yoruba-group-demand-oduduwa-republic-says-late-restructuring/ [Accessed October 29, 2018].
34. *Vanguard Newspaper*. 2017. "What Arewa Youths' Quit Order Means to Other Tribes—Evah," June 10. Available from: https://www.vanguardngr.com/2017/06/arewa-youths-quit-order-means-tribes-evah/ [Accessed October 28, 2015].
35. *Vanguard Newspaper*. 2018. "I'll Take Over Enugu as President, Declare Biafra Independence, Says Released BZF President," July 20. Available from: https://

36. Simon Kolawole. 2017. "Matters Arising from 'Kaduna Declaration.'" *TheCable*, June 11. Available from: https://www.thecable.ng/matters-arising-kaduna-declaration [Accessed October 28, 2018].
37. *NewsRescue*. 2017. "Bury Biafra or Get Out of Our Land—Youths of Oduduwa Republic Lagos Declaration," June 11. Available from: https://newsrescue.com/bury-biafra-get-land-youths-oduduwa-republic-lagos-declaration/ [Accessed October 30, 2018].
38. Emuedo, C. G. O. 2015. "Oil Multinationals and Conflicts Construction in Oil-Host Communities in the Niger Delta." *African Journal of Political Science and International Relations* 9, no. 5: 170–180. DOI: 10.5897/AJPSIR2014.0736.
39. Egbo, U. Solomon. 2018. "Mr President, I Am Renouncing My Nigerian Citizenship and This Is Why." *Independent*, July 26. Available from https://www.independent.co.uk/news/long_reads/biafra-independence-movement-nigeria-war-president-buhari-nnamdi-kanu-a8452366.html [Accessed November 1, 2018].
40. Ake, Claude. 2001. *Democracy and Development in Africa*. Washington, DC: Brookings Institution Press.
41. Ake, *The Feasibility of Democracy in Africa*.
42. Lin, Y. Justin. 2012. "Youth Bulge: A Demographic Dividend or a Demographic Bomb in Developing Countries?" *World Bank*, May 1. Available from: https://blogs.worldbank.org/developmenttalk/youth-bulge-a-demographic-dividend-or-a-demographic-bomb-in-developing-countries [Accessed November 2, 2018].
43. Okeke, Chidimma C., Agbese, Andrew, Abah, Hope, Itodo, and Sule, Daniel. 2018. "Osun, Nasarawa, Kogi, Benue Top List of States Owing Teachers." *Daily Trust Newspaper*, February 2. Available from: https://www.dailytrust.com.ng/osun-nasarawa-kogi-benue-top-list-of-states-owing-teachers.html [Accessed November 2, 2018].
44. Okafor, Chido, Okere, Roseline and SulaimanSalau, hido Okafor. 2016. "Militants List Terms for Truce, Seek Action on Confab Report." *The Guardian*, May 9. Available from: https://guardian.ng/news/militants-list-terms-for-truce-seek-action-on-confab-report/ [Accessed November 2, 2018].
45. Opejobi, Seun. 2017. "Biafra: Igbos Are Selfish, Not Mature to Handle Their Affairs—Rev. Fr. Obidimma." *Dailypost Newspaper*, August 22. Available from: http://dailypost.ng/2017/08/22/biafra-igbos-selfish-not-mature-handle-affairs-rev-fr-obidimma/ [Accessed November 1, 2015].
46. Gwangwazo, M. Kabiru. 2018. "Who Are the Morons of Nigeria? Certainly Not Yorubas, Igbos, or Christians!" *Vanguard Newspaper*, June 22. Available from: https://www.vanguardngr.com/2018/06/morons-nigeria-certainly-not-yorubas-igbos-christians/ [Accessed October 30, 2018].
47. *Vanguard Newspaper*. 2016 "Nigeria Is the World's Second Most Religious Country," December 11. Available from: https://www.vanguardngr.com/2016/12/nigeria-worlds-second-religious-country/ [Accessed October 29, 2015].
48. Tar, U. A. and Shettima, A. G. 2010. "Engendered Democracy? The Struggle for Secularism and Its Implications for Politics and Democracy in Nigeria." *Nordic Institute of African Studies*. Discussion Paper #49. Uppsala, Sweden.
49. Ibid.
50. Mbachu, Dulue & Alake, Tope. 2016. "Nigeria Population at 182 Million, with Widening Youth Bulge." *Bloomberg*, November 8. Available from: https://www.

bloomberg.com/news/articles/2016-11-08/nigerian-population-hits-182-million-with-widening-youth-bulge [Accessed October 30, 2018].
51. Ojo, Fola. 2018. "Nigerian Youth: A Generation on Edge." *Punch Newspaper*, November 2. Available from: https://punchng.com/nigerian-youth-a-generation-on-edge/ [Accessed November 2, 2018].
52. Adedokun, Niran. 2018. "Dilemma of the Nigerian Youth." *Punch Newspaper*, April 26. Available from: https://punchng.com/dilemma-of-the-nigerian-youth/ [Accessed October 1, 2015].
53. World Bank, 2018. *Digital Jobs for Youth: Young Women in the Digital Economy, Solutions for Youth Employment*. 2018 International Bank for Reconstruction and Development/The World Bank.
54. Beehner, L. 2007. "The Effects of 'Youth Bulge' on Civil Conflicts." *Council on Foreign Relations*.
55. Feseha, M. 2018. "The Nexus between 'Youth Bulge' and Armed Conflict." *Africa Portal*. Available from: https://www.africaportal.org/features/nexus-between-youth-bulge-and-armed-conflict/ [Accessed October 30, 2018].
56. Akintola, E. Olusola, and Yabayanze, A. Joseph. 2017. "Settlers-Indigenes Question in Nigeria: Much Rhetoric, No Answers." *European Scientific Journal* 13, no. 10. DOI: http://dx.doi.org/10.19044/esj.2017.v13n10p%25p.
57. Chapter 202, Laws of the Federation of Nigeria, 1990.
58. Tar, U. A. 2017. "Managing Agitations and Protest in Nigeria."

Chapter 11

INTERNALLY DISPLACED PERSONS AND SECURITY IN NIGERIA

Olajumoke Yacob-Haliso and Michael Ihuoma Ogu

Introduction

As governments and several organizations, local and international, continue to make efforts in combating insecurity across many parts of Africa and West Africa in particular, more incidences appear to be arising that deepen and complicate the nature of insecurity in the region. Internal displacement, in the recent past, has been one major challenge that has not only resulted in an increased national budget on security in many of the states in West Africa generally and in Nigeria in particular, but has also become complicated by several other factors, compounded by massive human rights violations.

As early as 2009, the president of the International Committee of Red Cross, Jakob Kellenberger, in a special summit on refugees, returnees, and internally displaced persons (IDPs) in Africa, asserted:

> *It bears repeating that internal displacement poses perhaps one of the most daunting humanitarian challenges of today. The impact on many millions of displaced men, women and children, but also on countless host families and resident communities is hard, if not impossible, to measure. While figures are notoriously hard to come by, no-one would deny that Africa is the hardest hit continent in terms of numbers of IDPs.*[1]

Since this assertion, new armed conflicts have continued to break out in many parts of Africa, and Nigeria in particular, especially in the last half a decade, leading to the displacement of many men, women, and children. Elizabeth Ferris also observed that there are many more IDPs in Africa than refugees, nearly five times more IDPs than refugees, making Africa the region with the largest number of IDPs globally.[2] For example, the UNHCR reported that Sub-Saharan Africa had an estimated 4.4 million refugees and 11 million IDPs in 2016. At the end of 2016, the number of displaced and stateless persons in Africa was estimated at almost 19.6 million.[3] As of December 2017, the three countries in Africa with the highest number of IDPs were Democratic Republic of Congo (4,480,000 IDPs), South Sudan (1,899,000 IDPs), and Ethiopia (1,078,000 IDPs).[4]

Internal displacement continues to deepen, regardless of the many efforts at mitigating this growing humanitarian challenge, such as the African Union Convention for the Protection and Assistance of IDPs, humanitarian assistance, and emergency responses by various relief agencies and organizations in many parts of Africa and in Nigeria. By November 2016, the World Health Organization reported that out of 14.8 million people affected by the terrorist activities of Boko Haram in the region, and 3.7 million persons targeted for medical service, about 1.4 million Nigerians were displaced in Borno State alone. Consequences of these security challenges are far-reaching, affecting the psychology and emotions of victims, as well as the economy of affected communities as commercial activities are largely minimized, if not completely grounded, and investors find such communities unattractive and unsafe for investment of whatever kind.

How is internal displacement a cause and consequence of insecurity in Nigeria particularly and Africa in general? What are the causes of internal displacement in Nigeria, in comparison with other selected cases within the African region? What is the probable future of this humanitarian crisis in Africa? These are some of the key areas of concern addressed in this chapter.

Nature of Security in Nigeria

While it is not the intent of this chapter to explore the varied definitions of security, it may be important to our purposes to provide some historical background into the concept of security. Czeslaw Mesjasz observed that the English concept "security" originated from the Latin word "securus" ("se" meaning without and "curus" meaning "uneasiness"), hence "security" originally meant "freedom from uneasiness," or a peaceful condition devoid of risks or threats.[5] From the preceding submission, Emmanuel Musa Jatau asserted, particularly in the case of Nigeria, that security can be assigned the following meanings.[6] First, a traditional meaning of security perceives security as an attribute of the state, the absence of military conflicts or military security; security used in a broader sense to refer directly to the phenomena taking place in international relations either directly or indirectly caused by inter-state relations; security is seen as public good; and security in a universal sense includes human security, which according to Barry Buzan would include social, economic, environmental, political, food and the tradition military aspects of security.[7]

The Nigerian security challenge is one that dates back to the very origin of the state itself. Michael I. Ogu observed that West Africa, and particularly Nigeria, can be described as the conflict hotspot in the region.[8] Dr. Anthony Danladi Ali and Dr. Abdullahi Adamu added that the demands, by the various groups in the state, for true federalism and fiscal and political restructuring since independence have contributed to mostly violent reactions by aggrieved groups in the country, inhibiting the security, unity, and development of the Nigerian state.[9] Collins Friday

Obialor and Henry Ugochukwu Ozuzu towed a similar line when they observed that Nigeria's security challenges appear to emanate from its lack of national identity over the five decades after political independence.[10] They continue by observing that significant mistrust, suspicion, and bad faith amongst the Nigerian people at tribal, religious, individual, and communal levels are manifested in the communal conflicts and seeming unending nature of terrorist activities across the country. Some of the conflict incidences that amount to security challenges in Nigeria include those of Urhobo-Itsekiri-Ijaw, Adono-Ndoni, Ogoni-uprising, the Niger-Delta militancy, as well as the Birom versus Fulani in Plateau Ctate, Aguleri-Umuleri in Anambra State, the Zango-kataf in Kaduna State, Tiv-Jukun in the Benue and Taraba states, among others. Terrorism has further complicated the security situation in Nigeria; the disappearance and non-accountability of over a hundred school girls from Dapchi, Yobe State, as well as the endemic and changing nature of increasingly devastating and terrorizing attacks by herders on several farming and other communities, seem to suggest that Nigeria's war on terrorism is far from being over. Ogu, along with John Sislin and Anup Shah, among other scholars, has investigated the links between small arms and conflicts in many parts of Africa, a phenomenon that has been described as "Africa's Siamese twins."[11,12,13]

Dr. Olabanji Olukayode Ewetan and Dr. Ese Urhie identified some outcomes of insecurity on the Nigerian state and it is interesting to observe that displacement, particularly internal displacement, tops the list of consequences that insecurity has had on the Nigerian state.[14] Other implications of insecurity in Nigeria include: social dislocation and population displacement; social tensions and new patterns of settlements that encourage Muslims/Christians or members of an ethnic group moving to Muslim/Christian-dominated enclaves; heightened citizenship question that encourages hostility between "indigenes" and "settlers"; dislocation and disruption of family and communal life; a general atmosphere of mistrust, fear, anxiety, and frenzy; dehumanization of women, children, and men especially in areas where rape, child abuse, and neglect are used as instruments of war; deepening of hunger and poverty in the polity; discouraged local and foreign investment; halted business operations during periods of violence and outright closure of many enterprises in the areas or zones where incidences of insecurity are rife and occur on a daily basis; increased security spending by business organizations and governments; and the migration of people from areas or regions where there is a prevalence of insecurity, among others.

Nature and Causes of Internal Displacement

Numbers of IDPs in many parts of Africa fluctuate, with the instances of a rise overshadowing the arguably sparse cases of a fall in the phenomenon. For instance, Ferris observed that between 2010 and 2011, the number of IDPs in Sub-Saharan Africa decreased 13 percent from 11 million IDPs to an estimated 9.7 million IDPs by the end of 2011.[15] However, in the last half of the decade, the number of IDPs in Nigeria has continued to increase, defying many of the efforts and responses from the government and other agencies and assuming more complicated and devastating dimensions, including deepening human rights violations.

The International Organization for Migration (IOM), together with the National Emergency Management Agency (NEMA) in October 2016, reported in its Displacement Tracking Matrix (DTM) program that there are 2,155,618 estimated IDPs across thirteen states in Nigeria.[16] By December 2016, the DTM report estimated 1,770,444 IDPs in the northeast zone of Nigeria alone. In 2017, the UNHCR corroborated this assertion by observing that 1.7 million persons were displaced in Adamawa, Borno, and Yobe states, with more than 56 percent of this figure made up mostly of children, many of whom see government-run IDP camps as an option of last resort, rather preferring to reside in clustered "camp-like" conditions around schools, churches, and mosques.

There are numerous reasons explaining the rise in IDPs in Nigeria, including natural disasters and environmental degradation, inter-communal/inter-ethnic clashes, disputes over land, boundary conflicts between indigenous people and settlers, communal and ethno-religious clashes, electoral violence, as well as insurgency, particularly in the Northeast, leaving over 2 million persons displaced within the Nigerian state.[17]

It is evident that most of the causes and drivers of internal displacement in Nigeria are man-made, from political, social, and economic variables. While the political (civil war/Biafra, electoral violence, insurgency in the Northeast, inter-communal violence, protracted displacement, infrastructural development, Bakassi dispute) and social (urban migration, migration across borders, ethno-religious and inter communal clashes, criminality leading to rural banditry including cattle rustling) drivers of internal displacement may not sufficiently explain the explosion of challenges currently facing the Nigerian state, the economic and environmental drivers, particularly those related to conflicts between agricultural and pastoral communities over competition for scarce water and land resources, have been predominately responsible for internal displacement in the recent past.

Adamu and Ben, confirming the above argument, reported that in just two years, conflicts between farmer and herder groups had resulted in the loss of 8,100 lives in twelve local government areas (LGAs) and the destruction of 195,576 thatched and tin roof houses and 30 churches in eight LGAs, in Benue state alone.[18] The many recent endemic attacks by herdsmen across Nigeria only help to support the above argument as more Nigerians are forced to flee their homes and seek safety in camps.

The challenge of internal displacement in Nigeria has also resulted in certain outcomes that are detrimental to development at all levels of state: life, security, and peace. Some of the impacts of internal displacement documented by a 2017 United Nations High Commission on Refugees (UNHCR) report include, but are not limited to the following:[19]

First, difficult security conditions, particularly in the northeastern zone, where the many military actions in Nigeria are expected to result in the capture of more territories and secure civilian locations promoting access to humanitarian organizations and aid. However, new, targeted attacks by Boko Haram continue to severely impact the humanitarian situation and restrict humanitarian access. Reaching all people in need remains a big challenge, as the operational reach and effectiveness of humanitarian actors continue to be severely impeded by the largely endemic nature of conflict in the region.

Secondly, there are widespread protection concerns resulting from the extreme level of violence and the widespread destruction of private and public infrastructure over the past eight years, particularly in the northeastern part of the country. The growing level of violence and insecurity has resulted in fear and apprehension among the population in the region and exacerbated social divisions and distrust, especially toward members of society suspected of any association with the insurgency movement. In northeast Nigeria, many IDP camps remain under the control of the military, which has led to some protection concerns and, are in some cases, targeted by Boko Haram and infiltrated by militants. In 2017, Nigeria's Humanitarian Needs Overview (HNO) revealed that 6.7 million people were in need of protection and assistance in Adamawa, Borno, and Yobe states. Civilians in these regions faced grave human rights violations and abuse, including death, injuries, sexual and gender-based violence (SGBV), arbitrary detention, disappearances, forced displacement, and forced recruitment. The psychological needs of the displaced population are particularly significant and remain largely unmet given the magnitude of the problem and limited government infrastructure provisions for mental health. Loss and fear among the displaced are aggravated by a sense of lost dignity as many feel ashamed of their living conditions.

Third, women and children remain arguably some of the most vulnerable groups during conflict situations. The UNHCR has reported an increasing number of households headed by women, children, and older people. In 2016, for instance, 17,700 vulnerable households were profiled by the UNHCR's vulnerability screening, and in 18 percent (6,800 households) of the cases had unaccompanied or separated children, including 14 percent (5,400 households) with orphaned children; 15 percent (4,900 households) had children hawking or begging; and 3 percent (1,100 households) reported one or more of their children to be missing.[20]

SGBV is a significant outcome of internal displacement in many parts of Nigeria among women and children, and is suspected to be largely under-reported. Women continue to be targets of abduction, forced marriages, rape and used as suicide-bombers particularly by Boko Haram in recent years. Inadequate humanitarian assistance in camps and newly accessible areas has also resulted in a high level of sexual abuse and exploitation. Many women are allegedly coerced into resorting to survival sex in order to obtain food for themselves and their children or to be able to move in and out of the camps.

In addition, the lack of national ID documents and difficulties in proving nationality continue to affect access to safety, services, and justice. In 2016, UNHCR's reported that 17,700 households lacked legal documentation, a particular challenge in Niger's Diffa region where an UNHCR study revealed that over 80 percent of displaced people interviewed were without documentation on which their legal status and rights of residence, movement, employment, and property depend.[21] Although the level of illiteracy among the locals in these communities has been identified as one major factor responsible for the poor identification of IDPs in many of these states, the slow and seeming inefficiency with policy implementation cannot be excused as a significant factor resulting in such inadequate documentation.

Poor living conditions are also a significant problem, as displaced populations live in squalid conditions characterized by overcrowding and limited access to safe, sanitary, and dignified accommodation. The UNHCR regional report for February 2018 reported that forty women in Maiduguri had graduated from the Women Development Centre, after completing a livelihoods program jointly organized by the UNHCR in collaboration with the University of Nigeria. Despite such efforts by national and international agencies to bring respite to the humanitarian challenges in Nigeria, the challenge persists.[22]

IDPs in Nigeria are hosted in camps and displacement sites, and are often living in congested shelters or isolated in insecure or inhospitable areas, making them vulnerable to exploitation and abuse. The situation is most precarious in settlements such as government-owned camps, displacement sites, and unfinished buildings. The lack of shelter is, therefore, a major and persistent challenge, coupled with precarious health conditions and poor access to health services. In addition, access to food and drinking water, as well as meeting their basic needs, remains problematic for most displaced people. Numerous outbreaks of cholera and other water-borne diseases continue to be reported in displacement-affected areas, particularly in Cameroon and Nigeria. Severe malnutrition has become more prevalent among displaced communities in Nigeria as the quantity and quality of available food have dramatically decreased as a result of combined factors of growing humanitarian needs and corruption, particularly among emergency workers and administrators. Affected households have had consecutive years of restricted income levels, destruction of assets and livelihoods, and reduced food access, leading to an increase in negative coping strategies, as well as disrupting traditional cross-border trade and herding, resulting in increased market prices in neighboring countries.

The Nigerian Punch newspaper in December 2017 reported that the IDP camp in Ngala community of Borno State was the most populated government-run IDP camp in the country, with a population of over 108,698 displaced persons.[23] The camp that is located in a school compound in the community continues to battle epidemics of "cough, malaria, diarrhea and acute respiratory disorders as a result of unhygienic living conditions and the harsh weather,"[24] which have also led to the death of many individuals in the camp, particularly children. It was also reported that health workers receive about fifteen childbirths weekly, although many IDPs still give birth on their own, without the aid of health workers.[25] It has been alleged that the increased birth rate in most of the IDP camps results from the rape of female IDPs by their male counterparts and/or by the military, camp officials, and other relief officers working onsite. On May 7, 2018, the Nigerian *Vanguard* newspaper also reported health care challenges in the IDP camps, with respect to the availability of drugs to treat the common health issues highlighted above. According to the report, the IDPs complained that "the National Commission for Refugees, Migrants and Internally Displaced Persons (NCFRMI) brought drugs (medication) since March. We have not received any again (since) and the major sickness is diarrhea, malaria and stomach pain, especially in the kids."[26] The very poor living conditions in most of the IDP camps across the Nigerian state have arguably had a tremendous effect on the health, psychology, and physical development of IDPs. It has been reported that IDPs are radicalized there, which may provide an explanation for bombing incidents recorded in IDP camps.

Finally, large refugee return movements, mainly across the border between Cameroon and Nigeria, are of particular concern as some refugees find themselves in IDP or IDP-like situations. The endemic attacks and growing insecurity in Borno State created a new emergency for the UNHCR and other actors, where the population in the IDP site, located at the Banki—Bama Local Government Area, doubled from some 20,000 to more than 45,000 displaced people within a two-week period during May 2017, leaving the IDP site with no further capacity for expansion. Increased demand for space in camps, coupled with the various manifestations of corruption among camp administrator and other emergency workers, inadequate food supplies and cooking fuel, absence of free movement in and out of the IDP sites, prevalent health risks resulting from the near-total absence of water and sanitation services, among others, are some of the challenges confronting the IDPs.

While the above submissions may not exhaustively reveal the very highly devastating nature of internal displacement in Nigeria, they do help to explain and provide insight into the increasingly complex nature of the challenge and the difficulty to completely address this condition, regardless of the many efforts by government and other humanitarian agencies working in the affected areas.

Displacement and Insecurity in Africa: A Comparative Analysis

Internal displacement and insecurity in Africa are two variables that appear intrinsically linked and mutually reinforcing; insecurity reinforces internal displacement, and displacement also deepens the level of insecurity in many parts of the continent. However, the important question remains what are the drivers of these conditions; while there are several drivers of internal displacement in Africa as well as insecurity, it may be a wrong diagnosis to conclude that all forms of displacement and insecurity in Africa are driven by the same phenomenon. Again, identifying displacement drivers will help to properly direct efforts in mitigating the challenge within the region. Ellie Kemp observed that conflict, violence, and natural disasters are some of the major factors that force millions of Africans from their homes, communities, and livelihoods each year; hence, frequent analysis of displacement trends and patterns will be an important contribution by helping relief agencies and other stakeholders to understand and act on the factors that drive displacement, and thus bring the numbers down as well as assist and protect those affected.[27] Table 11.1 shows an estimate of displaced persons in Nigeria compared to other countries in the region in the first and second quarter of 2017.[28]

Table 11.1 Displacement population in some West African state as of 2017

State	Displacement population as of January 2017	Current displacement population as of June 2017
Nigeria	1,717,330	1,754,228
Cameroun	182,978	219,305
Chad	105,070	90,911
Niger	121,391	127,299
Total	**2,126,769**	**2,191,743**

Source: Culled from UNHCR (2017:11)

On a larger scale, Kemp observed that about 3.5 million people were internally displaced as a result of conflict, violence, and "rapid-onset disasters" in Africa during 2015—an average of more than 9,500 people uprooted from their homes every day. Out of this figure, 2.4 million persons were displaced by conflict and violence, and 1.1 million by natural disasters. Some of the figures of displacement in some African countries, resulting from conflict or violence and disaster in 2015, are shown in Table 11.2.

Table 11.2 Internal displacement from conflict and disaster

State	Displacement by conflict or violence	Displacement by disaster
Niger	47,000	38,000
Nigeria	737,000	100,000
Somalia	90,000	59,000
Ethiopia	56,000	104,000
Democratic Republic of Congo	621,000	106,000
Egypt	78,000	
Libya	100,000	
Sudan	144,000	
Chad	36,000	
Cameroon	71,000	
Central African Republic	210,000	
Burundi	23,000	
South Sudan	199,000	
Kenya		105,000
Madagascar		87,000
Mozambique		61,000

Culled from: Kemp, E. (2016)

Wyndham further described West Africa, in particular, as being heavily affected by displacement, occasioned by the many internal conflicts resulting from ethnic tensions and rivalries, political instability, disputes over the control of natural resources, natural disasters, poverty, and food insecurity, among others.[29] The civil wars in Liberia and Sierra Leone and the effects of these conflicts on neighboring Guinea-Bissau and Guinea, and the crises in Côte d'Ivoire, Senegal, Togo, and Nigeria have forced people to flee their homes and have resulted in massive developmental deficiencies in these states. In the very recent past, the growing endemic clashes between farming and herder groups in many parts of Nigeria, allegedly over the struggle for control of declining land and water resources and their effects on means of economic livelihood, have also become major driver of internal displacement in many states in Nigeria, particularly in the northeastern zone, with consequences for neighboring communities. The Human Rights Watch in its 2018 report on Nigeria observed that "violence between nomadic and farming communities spread beyond the north-central region to southern parts of the country in 2017," leading to the killing of hundreds and displacement of thousands of people, and the governor of Kaduna State calling on the Economic Community of West African States to intervene in what it described as "perennial violence between the two groups."[30]

Although most of these conflicts identified above have ended, especially those of civil war type, Wyndham maintained that as many as 1 million people are estimated to still be internally displaced, particularly in Côte d'Ivoire, Guinea, Nigeria, Senegal, and Togo, and there are significant risks of further large-scale displacement in these and other parts of the continent.[31]

Factors such as internal conflicts, natural disasters, poverty, food insecurity, and underdevelopment result in internal displacement and/or insecurity, which mutually reinforce each other, although this illustration does not take care of the consequences of this mutual reinforcement among these variables.

Management of Internal Displacement in Nigeria

Combating displacement in Africa and Nigeria in particular has remained a major challenge for stakeholders, and especially the government, as many of the efforts at mitigating this growing challenge appear unable to effectively control the menace, as evidenced in the upward and sparsely downward movement of figures of displaced persons, as well as the many complications of the challenge, including massive human rights abuses. This sad reality can be attributed to the perceived insincerity on the government's part to protect lives and properties, deeply entrenched levels of corruption in both government and civil service, inefficient policy implementation, among others. Regardless of the progress or the lack of it, when managing internal displacement in Nigeria, it is necessary to continue to promote policies, programs, and actions that target to lessen the burden of internal displacement in Nigeria particularly and Africa in general.

Over the years, national governments as well as international organizations, civil society, and other humanitarian groups have advanced several institutions and frameworks to help in managing internal displacement across many parts of Africa, and particularly in Nigeria, especially in the very recent past. Some of these efforts, beginning with the 1998 United Nations Guiding Principles on Internal Displacement, to regional and national dimensions, include, but are not limited to the following:

a. The African Charter on Human and Peoples' Rights, Cap. A9, Laws of the Federation of Nigeria, 2004

On August 31, 1982, Nigeria signed the African Charter on Human and Peoples' Rights, and was among the first member states of the African Union to sign this treaty. The Charter, which was ratified on June 22, 1983, and implemented as the African Charter on Human and Peoples' Rights as Cap.10 LFN 1990 or Cap. A9 LFN 2004, outlined the rights to education, housing/shelter, health, food, employment, social security, adequate standard of living, safe environment, cultural life, and development, all of which Nigeria has arguably remained committed to ensuring, as evidenced in legislations and other institutional measures, including the National Human Rights Commission (Amendment) Act, 2011. However, the reality suggests otherwise; these rights only extend as far as a legislation and have not translated into tangible improvements for displaced persons in Nigeria.

b. The African Union Convention for the Protection and Assistance of IDPs in Africa, 2009

At the first Conference of West African States on Internal Displacement, held in April 2006 in Abuja, the UN Guiding Principles on Displacement was adopted and formed the basis of the 2009 AU Convention, also known as the Kampala Convention. Forty AU member states, including Nigeria, have signed the Convention, but just twenty-seven have ratified, including Nigeria. Although a Committee on IDPs was established in the Nigerian National Assembly in October 2015, no further steps have been taken to integrate the convention into Nigerian law.

The National Human Rights Commission

In line with the UN General Assembly resolution, the National Human Rights Commission (NHRC) was established by the NHRC Act, Cap.N46 Vol.11 Laws of the Federation of Nigeria 2004, and entrusted with promoting and protecting human rights, as well as providing services to victims of human rights violations in Nigeria. Although the NHRC has been active in condemning human rights violations of displaced persons, it lacks the capacity to make binding decisions in responding to human right violations.[32]

c. **The National Commission for Refugees, Migrants, and Internally Displaced Persons (NCFRMI)**

This Commission, established by Decree 52 of 1989 now Cap. N21, Laws of the Federation of Nigeria, 2004 (NCFRMI Act), is responsible for coordinating all migration-related issues in Nigeria. The Commission's mandate was expanded in 2002 and 2009 to include issues relating to IDPs and the coordination of migration and development respectively, although the legal standing of the Commissions remains a subject of controversy as the NCFRMI act currently makes no reference to the protection of IDPs.

National Policy on Internal Displacement in Nigeria

The draft of the National Policy on Internal Displacement outlines the roles and responsibilities of the federal, state, and local governments, stakeholders in civil society, as well as national and international actors. It is also intended to educate the populace on their rights and obligations before, during, and after displacement. The policy has been revised twice in 2009 and 2012, but Mohammed argues that it has remained a "draft" policy, as it is yet to be adopted by the legislature.[33]

The National Emergency Management Agency (NEMA)

NEMA has a mandate to address disaster-related issues, coordinate responses to all emergencies, and provide relief through the establishment of concrete structures and measures. The agency, established by Act 12, and amended by Act 50 of 1999, is guided by a number of plans and frameworks, including the National Contingency Plan, Search and Rescue and Epidemic Evacuation Plan, National Disaster Management Framework (NDMF), and Emergency Response Standard Operating Procedures. NEMA operates a 24/7 situation room that monitors and provides, in collaboration with the State Emergency Management Agencies (SEMA), relevant information in the case of disasters. NEMA and SEMA are leading agencies in management and humanitarian support for IDPs as well as search and rescue missions in disaster situations in Nigeria. The NEMA and SEMA have continued to help in various relief interventions in Nigeria, particularly for IDPs. However, these agencies have been accused of some level of graft and inefficiency, particularly with respect to the distribution and monitoring of aid in the affected areas. Adam Alqali observed that these agencies were accused of diverting aid meant for IDPs in the six states of Nigeria's northeastern region. He documented the report of one of the United Nations High Commission for Refugees (UNHCR) IDP protection monitors in Geidam, Yobe State, which asserted that only very few of the IDPs benefitted from relief materials that were delivered and received by the authorities of the local council, because the NEMA officials bribed the local council officials by giving them a portion of the items while they carted away the bulk of the materials, which were later seen displayed openly for sale at the local market in Geidam.[34] Alqali further reported that NEMA and SEMA rarely carried out any kinds of needs assessment ahead of relief interventions, which was evident in the rate at which IDPs sold off the relief items given to them by these agencies.[35]

State Emergency Management Agencies (SEMA)

The Act establishing NEMA, also prescribed the establishment of state emergency management committees for each state of the Federation, which should be headed by a Chairperson, appointed and paid by the governor of the state, and collaborates with other institutions such as the State Ministry of Women and Social Welfare, Health, State environmental protection Agency, Police Force, Security and Civil Defence Corps, as well as the Nigerian Red Cross Society. Mohammed observed that out of the thirty-six states in the federation, only Borno, Adamawa, and Yobe states have established SEMAs, particularly working with IDPs,[36] arguably as a result of the high vulnerability level of security in these states, as well as the cases of humanitarian crises prevalent in these states.

Ministry of Reconstruction, Rehabilitation and Resettlement (MRRR), Borno State

The Borno State government set up a Ministry of Reconstruction, Rehabilitation, and Resettlement, in 2015, with a mandate to facilitate the return of Boko Haram-induced displaced persons to their communities, rebuild destroyed homes and public buildings, and support the restoration of livelihoods for IDPs. The Ministry actively participated in a Recovery and Peacebuilding Assessment (RPBA) by the EU, UN, and World Bank in early 2016, and is currently in the process of setting up an administrative and management structure for recovery and peace building. It has, with the support of the SEMA, been involved in the reconstruction of infrastructure in LGAs declared safe for return in the state. Borno appears to be the only state with a designated ministry responsible for managing internal displacement in the state, as other states have, at best, set up committees that fall back to the SEMA in management of crises, particularly internal displacement.

The above submissions reveal the existence of institutions and policies for managing the challenge of internal displacement in Nigeria, although it appears that, with the exception of just a few, many of these frameworks and policies are either yet to be crystallized and properly implemented, or overlap in terms of responsibilities. This reality translates to temporary, superficial, or lop-sided management of this problem, which arguably focuses more on humanitarian relief and aid, instead of on more complex concerns of human rights violations and abuses.

Conclusion

While it can be argued that internal displacement is a challenge that has plagued communities across the globe for quite a while, it is more interesting to emphasize that this challenge has assumed near, if not completely overwhelming dimensions in the very recent past in Nigeria, owing to drivers such as environmental change, struggle for declining resources, and several other causal agents of internal conflicts, rising poverty, and nature of underdevelopment, all of which continue to deepen the level of insecurity in the region. Judging from the rise and occasional fall in the statistics, it is arguable that internal displacement has defied attempts made by governments and other relevant agencies and stakeholders to nip this problem in the bud. However, it is imperative that current efforts are made more effective and concerted, coupled with the formulation and implementation of policies and institutions that seek to provide solutions or at least considerable solace to victims of this unfortunate condition. In the light of challenges documented in previous sections of this chapter, we are making the following recommendations for both government and particularly agencies involved with IDPs:

a. Officials of NEMA, SEMA, NHRC, and other agencies providing support for IDPs need to be constantly re-oriented and properly sensitized about the delicate nature of their job and how it impacts on the present and future condition of the IDPs.
b. Strict sanctions should be meted out to officers who are found guilty of any corrupt charges relating to IDPs.
c. The government should encourage whistle blowing within the IDP camps, so that IDPs themselves can whistleblow about inefficiencies and corruption perpetrated in the camps without fearing any attacks on their lives.
d. The camps should be made more accessible to civil society groups to evaluate the efforts of such relief agencies periodically.

Notes

1. Kellenberger, J. 2009. "Root Causes and Prevention of Internal Displacement: The ICRC Perspective 23-10-2009 Statement." Special Summit on Refugees, Returnees and IDPs in Africa, Kampala, Uganda, 1, October 23, 2009.
2. Ferris, E. 2012. "Internal Displacement in Africa: An Overview of Trends and Opportunities." Presentation at the *Ethiopian Community Development Council Annual Conference* themed "African Refugee and Immigrant Lives: Conflict, Consequences, and Contributions" May 2–4, 2012.
3. Update on UNHCR's operations in Africa; Executive Committee of the High Commissioner's Programme Sixty-eighth session Geneva, September 19, 2017. Available from: http://www.unhcr.org/59c284577.pdf.
4. Internal Displacement Monitoring Centre (IDMC) 2017; Global Internal Displacement Database. Available from: http://www.internal-displacement.org/database/displacement-data.

5. Mesjasz, C. 2004. "Security as an Analytical Concept." A paper presented at the 5th *Pan-European Conference on International Relations* held at Hague, September 9–11 (2004): 5.
6. Jatau, E. M. 2017. "National Security Policy in Nigeria," September 10. Available from: http://www.iacspsea.com/site/wp-content/uploads/2017/09/National-Security-in-Nigeria.pdf.
7. Buzan, B. 1991. "New Patterns of Global Security in the Twenty-First Century." *International Affairs* 67, no. 3 (July 1991): 431–451.
8. Ogu, M. I. 2017. "Farmer-Herder Conflict and Arms Proliferation in Nigera." In *Discourses on Peace and Conflict in Nigeria: An Interdisciplinary Approach*, edited by E. Chijioke Ogbonna. Lagos: Emaphine Reprographic Limited.
9. Adamu, A. 2005. "True Federalism in the 21st Century Nigeria." A Lecture Delivered at University of Jos Alumni Association, Lagos, March 24; Ali, A. D. 2013. "Security and Economic Development in Nigeria since 1960." *Arabian Journal of Business and Management Review* 2, no. 6: 1–7.
10. Obialor, C. F. and Ozuzu, H. U. 2017. "Terrorism and Counter-Insurgency in Nigeria: The Boko Haram Experience (2006–2017)." *International Journal of Innovative Research in Social Sciences & Strategic Management Techniques | IJIRSSSMT* 4, no. 2 (September).
11. Ogu, M. I. 2015. "Small Arms Proliferation and Prevalent Conflicts in Africa." In *Issues in Conflict, Peace and Governance*, edited by D. O. Also. Nigeria: Fodnab Ventures.
12. Sislin, John and Pearson, S. Frederic. 2001. *Arms and Ethnic Conflict*. London: Rowman and Littlefeild.
13. Shah, Anup. 2010. "The Arms Trade Is Big Business." *Global Issues*. http://www.globalissues.org/article/74/the-arms-trade-is-big-business
14. Ewetan, O. O. and Urhie, E. 2014. "Insecurity and Socio-Economic Development in Nigeria." *Journal of Sustainable Development Studies* ISSN 2201–4268 5, no. 1: 40–63.
15. Ferris, "Internal Displacement in Africa."
16. IOM Nigeria Situation Report 2016.
17. Mohammed, F. K. 2017. "The Causes and Consequences of Internal Displacement in Nigeria and Related Governance Challenges." Working Paper FG 8, Stiftung Wissenschaft und Politik (SWP), *German Institute for International and Security Affairs*, Berlin April 2017.
18. Adamu, A. and Ben A. 2017. "Nigeria: Benue State under the Shadow of 'Herdsmen Terrorism' (2014–2016)." *Africa Conflict and Security Analysis Network* (ACSAN) (Formerly NCSAN—Nigeria Conflict and Security Analysis Network), Working Paper No. 5, Abuja, Nigeria, November 2017. Available from: https://www.researchgate.net/publication/322759537_Nigeria_Benue_State_under_the_shadow_of_herdsmen_terrorism_2014-2016_Africa_Conflict_and_Security_Analysis_Network_ACSAN_Formerly_NCSAN-Nigeria_Conflict_and_Security_Analysis_Network [accessed June 4, 2018].
19. UNHCR, 2017. "Nigeria Situation 2017: Supplementary Appeal (January–December 2017)." Available from: http://www.unhcr.org/597704b87.pdf [accessed January 30, 2018].
20. UNHCR, 2017. "Nigeria Situation 2017: Supplementary Appeal (January–December 2017)." Available from: http://www.unhcr.org/597704b87.pdf [accessed February 2018].
21. Ibid.

22. UNHCR, 2018. "Regional Update—Nigeria Situation," February 1–28, 2018. Available from: https://data2.unhcr.org/en/documents/details/62606 [accessed May 27, 2018].
23. The Punch. 2017. "Tears from Ngala: Nigeria's Largest IDPs Camp in the Throes of Hunger, Diseases," December 3. Available from: http://punchng.com/tears-from-ngala-nigerias-largest-idps-camp-in-the-throes-of-hunger-diseases/.
24. Ibid.
25. Ibid.
26. The Vanguard, 2018. "IDPs Urge FG to Address Healthcare Challenges in Camps," May 7. Available from: https://www.vanguardngr.com/2018/05/idps-urge-fg-to-address-healthcare-challenges-in-camps/.
27. Kemp, E. 2016. "Africa Report on Internal Displacement." *The Internal Displacement Monitoring Centre (IDMC),* December.
28. UNHCR, 2017. "Nigeria Situation 2017: Supplementary Appeal (January–December 2017)." Available from: http://www.unhcr.org/597704b87.pdf [accessed January 30, 2018].
29. Wyndham, J. 2016. "The Challenges of Internal Displacement in West Africa." *Brookings Institution-University of Bern Project on Internal Displacement.* Available from: https://www.brookings.edu/wp-content/uploads/2016/06/0919westafrica_wyndham_en.pdf.
30. Human Rights Watch, 2018. "Country Summary—Nigeria," January. Available from: https://reliefweb.int/sites/reliefweb.int/files/resources/nigeria_2.pdf [accessed May 27, 2018].
31. Wyndham, "The Challenges of Internal Displacement in West Africa."
32. Dina, Y. Akintayo, J. and Ekundayo, F. 2015. "Guide to Nigerian Legal Information." *New York University School of Law.*
33. Mohammed, "The Causes and Consequences of Internal Displacement in Nigeria and Related Governance Challenges."
34. Alqali, A. 2016. "Nigeria: When Aid Goes Missing." *Partners Global and the Institute for War & Peace Reporting.* Available from: https://iwpr.nct/global-voices/nigeria-when-aid-goes-missing.
35. Ibid.
36. Mohammed, "The Causes and Consequences of Internal Displacement in Nigeria and Related Governance Challenges."

Chapter 12

INFORMAL SECURITY SECTOR AND SECURITY PROVISIONING IN NIGERIA: TRENDS, ISSUES, AND CHALLENGES

Ufiem Maurice Ogbonnaya

Introduction

Structurally, the Nigerian security sector is divided into three main segments. The first is the Armed Forces of the Federation made up of all the military establishments as enshrined in the 1999 Constitution of the Federal Republic of Nigeria (as amended). The Armed Forces include the Nigerian Army (NA), Nigerian Navy (NN), and the Nigerian Air Force (NAF), which for administrative purposes are under the Ministry of Defence. Operationally, the Armed Forces have the responsibilities of:

(i) Defending Nigeria from external aggression;
(ii) Maintaining its territorial integrity and securing its borders from violation on land, sea, or air;
(iii) Suppressing insurrection and acting in aid of civil authorities to restore order when called upon to do so by the President; and
(iv) Performing such other functions as may be prescribed by an Act of the National Assembly.[1]

The second segment of the security sector comprises the Nigeria Police Force (NPF) and other para-military agencies, namely, the Nigerian Security and Civil Defence Corps (NSCDC), the Nigerian Immigration Services (NIS), the Nigerian Customs Service (NCS), the Nigerian Prisons Service (NPS), the Federal Fire Service (FFS), the National Drug Law Enforcement Agency (NDLEA), among others, which are under the Ministry of Interior.

The third segment is the intelligence community, made up of the Department of State Security (DSS), the Defence Intelligence Agency (DIA), and the National Intelligence Agency (NIA). The Nigerian intelligence community established by the National Security Agencies Act, CAP. 273, LFN, 2004 (as amended), is a community of specialized security agencies established for the purposes of collection of intelligence from within and outside the Nigerian state. They are also responsible for the provision of security services.[2] Statutorily, the DSS collects local intelligence and provides internal security, the NIA collects external intelligence, while the DIA collects defense and security intelligence both within and outside Nigeria. Given the formality of their establishment and the legitimacy of their statutes of operations, the Armed Forces and the Police, the para-military agencies, and the intelligence community, as enumerated above, make up the traditional or formal security sector.

Because of largely increasing developments and dynamics of security sector governance around the world, the security sector in Nigeria has in recent times expanded beyond the traditional and formal security institutions to include the judiciary and human rights and civil liberties institutions. The expansion beyond the traditional and formal security institutions to include the justice system has also been occasioned by the realization that the justice system plays significant roles in guaranteeing not just security provisioning by the traditional and formal institutions but that the services are provided within the dictates of the law and with respect to human rights.[3]

Besides the justice system, the increasing participation of non-state security actors, otherwise referred to as the informal security actors, such as community vigilante, neighborhood watch groups, and Private Guard Companies (PGCs)/Private Security Organizations (PSOs) in security provisioning, especially since the beginning of the twenty-first century, has resulted in further expansion of the sector[4] (see Table 12.1).

As some scholars have noted, although the existence of community vigilantes and neighborhood watch groups, especially in the southern part of Nigeria, dates back to pre-colonial times, their proliferation and increasing participation in the security space have become part of the defining feature of Nigeria's security architecture in the twenty-first century.[5] This development has been necessitated by an increasing wave of violence and criminality, "the involvement of local groups in political conflicts and a more general framework of a possible decline of state law enforcement agencies" especially in rural communities.[6] Thus, core security-related functions that were once the exclusive preserve of formal security institutions—arrest and prosecution of suspected criminals, public safety, crime and violence prevention—now constitute key functions performed by the informal security institutions.[7] This increasing participation of the informal sector in security provisioning in Nigeria has reinforced two fundamental developments in security studies. First, it strengthens the theoretical assumptions that security, as a "public good," is no longer the exclusive preserve of the state because it has lost a significant portion of its monopoly of the use of force as well as a degree of legitimacy as a security provider to the informal actors.[8] Second, the development has significantly transformed the security sector so that it has become a very broad and complex environment comprising a wide range of actors and institutions both within and outside the realm of the state[9] that requires a clear delineation of responsibilities.

Table 12.1 Profile of non-state security providers in selected states of Nigeria

Zone	State	Name of non-state actor	Sponsors
Southeast Zone	Abia	Abia State Vigilante Group	Abia State Government
		Neighbourhood Watch	Host Communities
	Anambra	Anambra State Vigilante Services	Anambra State Government
		Neighbourhood Watch	Host Communities
	Ebonyi	Ebonyi State Neighbourhood Watch	Ebonyi State Government
		Community Vigilante	Host Communities
	Enugu	Enugu State Neighbourhood Association and Watch Groups	Enugu State Government
		Community Vigilante	Host Communities
	Imo	Imo Security Watch and Vigilante Group	Imo State Government
		Vigilante Group of Nigeria	Private Individuals
		Neighbourhood Watch	Host Communities
Southwest Zone	Ekiti	Ekiti State Vigilante Group	Ekiti State Government
		Oodua People's Congress	Private Individuals
		Vigilante Group of Nigeria	"
	Lagos	Lagos Neighborhood Safety Corps (LNSC)	Lagos State Government
		Oodua People's Congress	Private Individuals
		Vigilante Group of Nigeria	"
	Ogun	Vigilante Service of Ogun State	Ogun State Government
		Oodua People's Congress	Private individuals
		Vigilante Group of Nigeria	"
	Osun	Harmonized Vigilante Group	Osun State Government
		Oodua People's Congress	Private Individuals
		Vigilante Group of Nigeria	"
	Oyo	Yoruba K'OYA Movement	"
		Oodua People's Congress	"
		Vigilante Group of Nigeria	"

Zone	State	Group	Sponsor
South-South Zone	Akwa Ibom	Mboho Mme Ette Idung ke Akwa Ibom State	Akwa Ibom
		Vigilante Group of Nigeria	Private Individuals
		Community Vigilante Groups	Host Communities
	Bayelsa	Bayelsa State Volunteer Service	Bayelsa State Government
		Egbesu Boys of Africa	Private Individuals
		Vigilante Group of Nigeria	"
	Delta	Vigilante Group of Nigeria	Private Individuals
		Niger Delta Vigilante	
	Edo	Edo State Integrated Vigilante Service	Edo State Government
		Vigilante Group of Nigeria	Private Individuals
	Rivers	Neighbourhood Safety Agency of the Rivers State Government	Rivers State Government
		Vigilante Group of Nigeria	Self-Sponsored
North-Central Zone	Benue	Vigilante Group of Nigeria	"
		Civilian Joint Task Force (CJTF)	Benue State Government
		Neighbourhood Watch	Host Communities
	Nasarawa	Nasarawa State Youth Empowerment Scheme (NSYES)	Nasarawa State Government
		Vigilante Group of Nigeria	Self-Sponsored
		Neighbourhood Watch	Host Communities
	Kogi	Vigilante Group of Nigeria	
		Enyidudu Community	Host Communities
	Plateau	Operation Rainbow	Plateau State Government
		Vigilante Group of Nigeria	Self-Sponsored
		Neighbourhood Watch	Host Communities
		Yan Banga (Night Watch)	"
Northeast Zone	Adamawa	Vigilante Group Adamawa State	Adamawa State Government
		Civilian Joint Task Force (CJTF)	"
		Amalgamated Union of Nigerian Hunters	Self-sponsored
	Bauchi	The Sarasuka	Host Community
		The Vigilante Group of Wunti	"
	Borno	Civilian Joint Task Force (CJTF)	Self-Sponsored
		Borno Youth Empowerment Scheme (BOYES)	Borno State Government

	Gombe	Gombe Vigilante Group	Gombe State Government
		The Hunters Association	Self-Sponsored
		The Kalare Youth	"
	Taraba	The Vigilante Group of Nigeria (VGN) also known as the Taraba State Vigilante Group (TSVG)	Taraba State Government
	Yobe	Civilian Joint Taskforce (CJTF)	Gombe State Government
		The Hunters Association	Self-Sponsored
		The Youth Vigilante group	Host Local Governments
Northwest Zone	Jigawa	Jigawa State Vigilante Group of Nigeria (JVGN)	Jigawa State
	Kaduna	Kaduna Vigilante Group of Nigeria (K-VGN)	Kaduna State Government
		Civilian Joint Taskforce (JTF) also known as Kabala Concern Forum (*Jarumai da Gora*)	
	Kano	Kano State Vigilante Group of Nigeria (KVGN)	Kano State Government
		Hisbah	
	Zamfara	Zamfara State Vigilante Service	Zamfara State Government
		Hisbah	

Source: Author's compilation

Beyond the foregoing, however, the development has expectedly generated some policy and scholarly discourses that border on a number of issues: these include the factors that account for the emergence, proliferation, and sustenance of informal security institutions; the utility or otherwise of informal security actors in security provisioning; the degree of legitimacy given the informal arrangements for security provisioning by citizens and groups that exercise their demand for security through these informal sources, on the one hand, and the institutions of the state, on the other hand; the socio-cultural, political, and economic dynamics in their existence, that is, how they operate and how they are funded; the adequacy or otherwise of regulatory institutional and legal frameworks for the informal security sector; the nature of their relationship with traditional security institutions; the role and implication of the informal sector in general elections; and the possibility of a future security sector reform in Nigeria that will incorporate the informal security institutions. Among other objectives, this chapter seeks to situate these discourses in clear and critical perspectives. It also seeks to analyze the trends and examine the issues and challenges associated with the informal security sector in Nigeria.

Overview of Nigeria's Informal Security Sector

In Nigeria, the informal security sector includes groups such as community guards/ traditional police/community vigilantes/neighborhood watch groups, militia groups, PGCs/PSOs, and groups that have been co-opted by state structures.[10] Broadly, therefore, four categories of security providers can be identified in the informal sector:

Community Guards

This category of security providers includes: (1) community vigilante and neighborhood watch groups, Community Development Unions (CDUs), and age-grades and youth organizations that are most prevalent in the southern and north-central parts of Nigeria. In most communities, these groups specifically provide such services as safety and protection of lives and property, traffic control, and community development services, among others; (2) the village guards, which comprise an assortment of experienced traditional hunters, are prevalent in the northeastern and northwestern parts of Nigeria. In recent years, the village guards have transformed into what is now referred to as the "Civilian Joint Task Force" (CJTF) that has volunteered to play a significant role in complementing the military in the war against terrorism and the insurgency in the Northeast zone of the country. The role of these security providers in ensuring the security of lives and property is well acknowledged and appreciated by the people. In most communities, vigilantes and neighborhood groups have transformed from just security provisioning to performing other important roles such as resolving land disputes and domestic conflicts and the enforcement of community development projects.[11]

Militia Groups

Within the context of this chapter, "militia groups" is used in the non-violence sense to define associations that provide security based on primordial ties of kinship, language, religion, and group solidarity, rather than the popular context of ethnic militias with pre-determined interests and agendas for separatism, secessionist agitations, self-determinism, and insurgency—although the conceptual line between the two may be blurred given the fluidity in the metamorphosis of non-violent militia groups to violent separatist, secessionist, and insurgent movements. Within this context, groups such as Bakassi Vigilante Group (Bakassi Boys) in Aba, Abia State; Egbesu Boys of Africa, in the Ijaw and Itshekiri communities of the Niger Delta region; and the O'odu Peoples' Congress (OPC) in the southwestern part of Nigeria operate as militias. Others include the Hisbah group, an Islamic vigilante group, in the predominantly Muslim states of Bauchi, Borno, Gombe, Jigawa, Kaduna, Kano, Katsina, Kebbi, Niger, Sokoto, Yobe, and Zamfara, that has adopted the Sharia legal system. As Ernest Ogbozor has noted, "Hisba enforces the Sharia legal system and serves as a mechanism for safeguarding the welfare and laws of the community. It operates alongside other informal security actors, such as the Kano State chapter of the Vigilante Group of Nigeria (VGN), the Kano State Security Guard, and the Kano Road and Transport Authority (KAROTA)."[12]

These militia groups are essentially youth-based groups formed with the purpose of promoting community and group security and protection based on parochial interests and primordial ties of kinship, language, religion, and group solidarity. For instance, the formation of the Bakassi Vigilante Group in Aba by the Aba Main Market Traders Association (AMMATA) in 1997 was a response to the security challenges occasioned by the activities of criminal elements in the society that threatened their businesses and economic activities.[13] In some cases, however, the militia groups identified here have their origin in political or militant organizations designed to ensure that the interests of specific ethnic groups in different parts of the country prevail. Such is the case of OPC, created to promote the interests of the Yoruba ethnic group in the Southwest zone and the Egbesu Boys, based in the oil-producing region of the Niger Delta, to protect the rights of the Ijaw ethnic group.[14]

Private Guard Companies/Private Security Organizations

The promulgation of the Private Guard Companies Act of 2004, which regulates the licensing, operations, control, and administration of PGCs/PSOs and stipulates the limits of their activities and penalties for breach of regulations, has liberalized the establishment of PGCs/PSOs across Nigeria. As noted in a study, the industry has experienced phenomenal growth since its founding.[15] From three companies in the early 1970s, Nigeria now has approximately 1,163 registered private security outfits with NSCDC,[16] playing major roles in the security and economic sectors with over 100,000 employees servicing major industrial organizations and some government agencies across the country. Basically, PGCs/PSOs provide services to corporate organizations and private individuals under the supervision of the NSCDC, which has oversight authority over them, including conducting periodic inspections of these firms as well as annual renewal of their licenses. PGCs/PSOs as security providers are generally accepted and have become relevant especially in the corporate world as evidenced by their robust presence in major corporate organizations and in urban and semi-urban centers across Nigeria.

Groups Co-Opted by State Structures

The crisis of confidence and legitimacy coupled with recurrent abuse of human rights that characterized the operations of many vigilante groups, especially the militia groups across several states, led to the intervention of some state governments, which were geared toward refocusing and repositioning the groups. Thus, as Amnesty International has noted that "armed vigilante groups carry out law enforcement activities in an ever-growing number of states with the tacit, and sometimes explicit, endorsement from the state governments."[17] This is because, in some states such as Abia, Adamawa, Anambra, Ebonyi, Enugu, Imo, Lagos, Kaduna, Kano, Plateau, and Taraba, among others, state governments have co-opted extant vigilante groups, defined their organizational and operational structures, supported them with funds, and provided regulatory and supervisory frameworks.

In Abia State, for example, the Bakassi Vigilante Group was taken over by the state government and renamed Abia State Vigilante Group (ABSVG). In Enugu State, although non-state security outfits had been part of the security framework right from the old Anambra State, their spread, occasioned by an escalation in insecurity, resulted in some challenges such as human rights violations, among other illegalities, which informed the efforts by the state government to restructure the community vigilante system by ensuring their control and regulation through the enactment of the Enugu State Neighbourhood Association and Watch Groups Law 2006 that gave rise to the emergence of the state-controlled security outfit called Enugu State Neighbourhood Association and Watch Group. In Plateau State for instance, one of the most notable decisions made by the Plateau State government in response to rising threats of insecurity was the establishment of Operation Rainbow (OR) and Neighbourhood Watch and the enactment of the Plateau State Rainbow and Neighbourhood Watch Law 2012 that came into effect on March 20, 2013.[18]

The co-optation of extant but errant community vigilantes and neighborhood watch groups by state governments is on the ascendancy as evident by experiences across the states. This development has been informed by two fundamental policy and constitutional lacunas in security sector governance in Nigeria. First is the escalating security challenge across Nigeria coupled with the increasing inability of the formal security institutions, especially the police, to respond adequately to these challenges. Policy-wise, this has had a negative impact on the ability of state governments to achieve human and physical developments in their various states with attendant implications for the legitimacy and stability of political regimes. This played out in Anambra State in 2017, where Governor Willie Obiano was elected for a second term because of the revolutionary nature of his security policies in the state.[19] The second is that constitutionally, security in Nigeria is in the exclusive legislative list. This means that only the federal government is constitutionally empowered to control formal security institutions. Thus, despite serving as chief security officers of their states, governors do not have control over state security agencies and institutions. Depending on the political party in power at both the state and federal levels, the instrumentality of state security can pose a threat to the political future of any state governor as was the case of Dr. Chris Ngige of Anambra State in 2003, who was abducted from office and forced to resign his position as governor by officials of the NPF "following orders from above."[20] Implicitly, therefore, the co-optation of extant vigilante groups or the establishment of state-controlled security outfits by state governors serves policy and political purposes, at least at the state level.

Theoretical Perspectives and Considerations

Beyond the arguments and submissions of the pre-colonial theories of security governance that vigilantism was part of communal efforts at securing lives and property in that era,[21] extant literature in modern scholarship on security studies in Nigeria and around the world has generated a substantial body of theoretical contributions. These new theories seek to explain the emergence, proliferation, and increasing participation of the informal sector in security provision. With particular focus on Nigeria, some of the theories include, among others, the failed state hypothesis that focuses on the inadequacies of traditional or formal security institutions. Principally, the theory argues that the proliferation and increasing participation of actors in security provisioning outside the formal sector in Nigeria is occasioned by the obvious failure of state security actors and institutions to provide the much-needed security and protection of lives and property for the people, especially for citizens in rural communities. For instance, with a current workforce of about 370,000 personnel to about 180 million Nigerians, which does not meet the United Nations recommendation of 222 police officers per 100,000 citizens or 1 police officer for 400 citizens, it is argued that the Nigerian state is highly under-policed.[22] The implication of this is that police stations and outposts are remotely located only in urban and semi-urban centers at the exclusion and detriment of the rural centers. Thus, in rural communities, accessing state security assistance in emergency and crisis situations is often difficult. This situation coupled with the increasing wave of violence and criminality, due largely to the decreasing internalization of traditional norms and increasing lack of voluntary compliance with the law, has created a security vacuum resulting in the privatization of security and the proliferation of informal security providers in both urban and rural areas across the country.[23]

There is also the prebendal politics theory that locates its arguments within the nature and character of the Nigerian state and the conduct of its ruling class elite. The basic assumption of the theory is that, in most cases, informal security organizations have their origins in political or militant organizations designed to ensure that the interests of specific class elite or ethnic groups in different parts of the country prevail in an attempt at self-preservation or self-perpetuation, either of the class or of the groups, especially in conflict situations.[24] Finally, there is the theory of globalization that locates local happenings in Nigeria within the context of global transformations, especially in international politics and security. Basically, this theory argues that the emergence of the informal sector, and specifically PSOs, is part of the outcomes of the transformation that the international system has undergone since the end of the Cold War in the late 1990s. The submission here is that the post-Cold War era has witnessed a shift in the nature of armed conflicts from inter-state to intra-state dimensions so that it has now become imperative to address security matters outside the realm of the state, taking into consideration issues of human security and the security of the ethnic nationalities in which citizens participate directly in security provisioning through community vigilante organizations and neighborhood watch groups.[25]

Most fundamentally, however, a clear and adequate understanding of the emergence and participation of the informal security sector in security provisioning in Nigeria cannot be attained without an in-depth knowledge of the political history and economy of the contemporary Nigerian state, nor can the workings of the informal security institutions that are created and sustained be understood without a good knowledge of the personal preferences and ideological inclinations and proclivities of those who operate both the formal and informal systems. As Yolamu Barongo has indicated, in a very real sense, the nature of political life in a particular society, the type of institutions that are created and sustained, and the peculiar patterns of political processes that emerge are a function of the interplay among three main factors, namely, the condition of the base of the society; the history and the experiences of the society; and the actors' perception, interpretation, and response to environmental stimuli.[26] These theoretical assumptions may well explain the emergence, proliferation, sustenance, and increasing participation of the informal sector in security provisioning in Nigeria.

Legal and Regulatory Framework

Security provisioning by actors in the informal sector in Nigeria is characterized by a number of operational, institutional, policy, and legal issues, among others. These are discussed in detail below:

A fundamental challenge to the operations of informal security providers in Nigeria is the absence of a national legal and regulatory framework. At the state level, however, some states such as Adamawa, Anambra, Enugu, Kaduna, Kano, Lagos, Plateau, and Taraba, among others, have legalized the activities of vigilante groups through state laws, while others, namely, Abia, Ebonyi, among others, are working toward developing a legal framework that will regulate the operations and activities of vigilante and neighborhood groups. In Enugu State, for instance, the Enugu State Neighbourhood Association and Watch Groups Law 2006 controls and regulates the recruitment, operations, funding, and logistics of the Enugu State Neighbourhood Watch Groups. In Plateau State, the Operation Rainbow and Neighbourhood Watch Law 2012 performs a similar function. In Kaduna State, the Kaduna State House of Assembly ratified the State Vigilante Service Law on June 6, 2013, which legalized the operation of vigilante groups that have been in existence since 1982. According to the law, the "Vigilante Service is a registered service of people in a community that have agreed to render assistance on crime detection, prevention, and promotion of security consciousness in the community."[27] In Kano State, the Kano State Gazette of March 8, 2012, established the KVGN as a Neighbourhood Watch Group.[28] Similarly, Lagos State House of Assembly in 2016 passed a law to establish the LNSC, which is a uniformed security agency established to assist the police and other security agencies to maintain law and order in the state. The legalization of and support for vigilante activities enable the vigilantes in these states to act as local police.[29]

At national level, however, vigilante and neighborhood watch groups generally do not have any form of overarching national legislation that regulates and controls the nature of their existence and operations, logistics, and funding apart from the Private Guard Companies Act of 2004, which regulates the licensing, operations, control, and administration of PGCs/PSOs. Amnesty International had in 2002 alluded to this challenge when it observed that

> the increasing incidence of crime since the end of the military regime has favoured the proliferation of heavily armed vigilante groups of various conditions and interests in nearly every corner of Nigeria. There is no pattern to define who creates them, and what they fight for or the methods they employ, *and most importantly, there is not a clear code of conduct binding them, nor an official register of legal vigilante groups*.[30] (emphasis added)

Recruitment and Operational Modalities

The absence of a national legislation for vigilante and neighborhood watch groups has occasioned a number of issues. First, it has created operational difficulties for security actors in the sector arising from the lack of logistics and funding supports from the federal government. Second, vigilante and neighborhood watch groups suffer from a crisis of legitimacy, especially at the federal level.[31] As Amnesty International has noted, "the position of the Federal Government towards armed vigilante groups remains unclear, since they are often regarded as an internal matter of the states and not as a federal issue."[32] Third, even in states with extant legal and regulatory frameworks, the mode of recruitment, operational modalities, and organizational structures for the sector differ. This absence of uniformity has implications for the efficiency and effectiveness in security provisioning in the informal sector. For instance, most informal security providers have weak internal and external accountability systems. Internally, group leaders or village heads provide oversight of a group's activities. External monitoring by official security agencies exists in some cases but are not formalized and so cannot be enforced.

There is, however, the Vigilante Group of Nigeria (VGN), which is a voluntary security outfit that assists in the maintenance of law and order, reduces criminal acts, protects lives and properties, assists in accident or any other occurrence of natural disasters, arrests and hands over suspected criminals to the police, provides intelligence information to the police, and seeks to serve as a national institutional framework and umbrella body that regulates the operations and activities of all community vigilante groups across the country.[33] The challenge is that the VGN is unknown to law as its existence is not statutorily guaranteed. While the Bill seeking to legalize the existence of the VGN may have been passed by the National Assembly as of October 2017, the NPF has continued to treat vigilante groups as illegal entities.[34]

Funding and Logistics

Across Nigeria, the informal security sector, just like the formal sector, is faced with the challenges of logistics, funding, and sustainability. Although some states have co-opted informal security structures by providing logistics and funding, the laws do not clearly define their funding modalities. Even in states with extant legal frameworks for the informal security operators, funding for the sector is not clearly defined by the law. The consequence of this is that the responsibility of funding groups in the informal sector, especially vigilante and neighborhood watch groups, lies with host communities through community development unions, which impose security levies on residents. In some cases, the imposition of security levies has caused conflicts between residents and members of community vigilante groups.

In Abia State, for example, the challenge of funding the operations of the Bakassi vigilante group resulted in its co-optation by the state government as the Abia State Vigilante Group (ABSVG). Despite this co-optation, funding and logistics for the ABSVG remain a major challenge as subventions from the government have remained inadequate. Thus, the Group has resorted to imposing Community Security on members of the public to fund its activities. In Ebonyi State, funding of the state-owned neighborhood watch is not clearly defined. In some cases, the Local Government Area Councils have been largely responsible for the funding of the group as is the case in Ivo, Afikpo North, Afikpo South, and Ezza North local government areas (LGAs). In Enugu, the law does not provide any form of state funding for the neighborhood watch groups. However, subventions from state and local governments, donations from corporate bodies and spirited individuals, as well as security levies imposed on the public are sources of funding for the groups. In Plateau State, the government provides funding and logistics for Operation Rainbow. However, this is not statutory, which makes it subject to potential abandonment by successive administrations. In Kano State, the main sources of funding for the KVGN include contributions from the government, donations from wealthy individuals and philanthropists, endowment funds, grants from LGAs, and house-to-house fund raising initiatives.[35]

The absence of statutory, regular, and sustainable funding streams for actors and security providers in the informal sector remains a major feature of the sector. This has occasioned a number of challenges. First, it threatens the sustainability of the actors in the sector and makes a prediction of their future trajectory very difficult. Second, it threatens the efficiency and effectiveness of security providers in terms of service delivery, especially in remote and rural places, during an emergency and crisis situations. Third, politicians who extend financial and logistics support to vigilante and neighborhood watch groups have been found to use such groups in the pursuit of their own political ends. In the southeast and northeast regions, for instance, vigilante groups have been hijacked by highly placed politicians and other public office holders for their personal interests. The consequence of this has been the factionalization of groups, resulting in inter-group rivalries and clashes that have negatively impacted on the peace and security of the affected communities.

On March 6, 2016, seven persons were killed and about nineteen others fatally injured when two factions of a vigilante group clashed during the "coronation of two officials of amalgamated union of Nigerian hunters" in Gombi, Adamawa State.[36] On September 8, 2017, one person was killed and several others injured when two factions of the O'odua Peoples Congress clashed when a meeting of Yoruba leaders titled "Yoruba Standpoint on Restructuring" was held at the Lekan Salami Stadium, Adamasingba Ibadan, Oyo State.[37] The OPC is a predominant vigilante group in the southwest region of Nigeria. In the build-up to Nigeria's transition from military to democratic governance, OPC was factionalized. One faction loyal to Frederick Fasheun supported the Alliance for Democracy (AD) and helped to ensure its electoral victory in the Southwest; the other faction loyal to Ganiyu Adams opposed OPC's involvement in the transition.[38] The crisis has lingered till this day.

Human Rights Abuses and Violations

Another fundamental challenge that is associated with actors in the informal security sector is recurrent human rights abuses and violations, especially by vigilante and neighborhood watch groups. According to the Amnesty International, "armed vigilante groups in Nigeria are reported to carry out extrajudicial executions and killings of suspected criminals and perpetrate acts of torture, cruel, inhuman and degrading treatment, unlawful detention and 'disappearances'. Allegations of extortion, harassment, arson, destruction of public property or armed robbery are often made against members of these groups."[39] Recurrent human rights abuses and violations by vigilante and neighborhood watch groups arise basically from their total lack of or limited knowledge or training on human rights issues. This has implications for their relationships with the civilian population. Human Rights Watch and CLEEN Foundation vividly captured the case of the then Bakassi Boys as being responsible for scores of extrajudicial executions and hundreds of cases of torture and arbitrary detentions, resulting in the call for the government to disband vigilante groups.[40]

Besides human rights violations and abuses, there are no established cases of corresponding punishment meted out to members of the groups. Although members found culpable during investigations and enquiries are usually suspended or dismissed from the groups, Ernest Ogbozor has noted that "dismissal or suspension is sometimes the most severe punishment vigilantes face, for they often escape any punishment from the formal legal system for even severe crimes, such as rape and murder."[41] Thus, virtually in all situations, members of state vigilante groups are not formally held accountable for their actions. According to Carina Tertsakian and Brown Manby, underlying the vigilante groups' ability to operate freely and without accountability is the fundamental inability of the national police force to perform its law enforcement functions effectively, and the consequent lack of public confidence in the police.[42] On the one hand, the lack of public confidence in the NPF stems from institutional corruption, lack of accountability, and poor relationship between the police and the public that characterize the organization. In 2017, the United Nations Office for Drug and Crimes (UNODC) reported that police officers, judges, and prosecutors are the most corrupt public officials in Nigeria with about N400 billion spent annually by Nigerians on bribes to public officials.[43] This was corroborated by Nigerian Bureau of Statistics (NBS) 2017 National Corruption Survey report that 46.4 percent of Nigerian citizens have had "bribery contact" with police officers.[44] On the other hand, inefficiency by the Nigerian police is occasioned by institutional inadequacy, low budgetary allocation, poor remuneration, and demeaning working conditions for officers and men of the NPF. For instance, between 2010 and 2015, budgetary allocation to the police service was the lowest within the formal security sector and the trend has not changed for the better (see Table 12.2)

This has resulted in the perception, from members of the public, that it is futile to report crimes to the police or expect any remedial action from them.[45] Similarly, Amnesty International has noted that the police have been accused of inaction and neglecting to investigate, and when required, arrest and prosecute members of armed vigilante groups. Although the police have arrested several members of armed vigilante groups, the suspects are often released after a few months through the intervention of authorities of the state and their charges dropped before going to trial.[46] In July 1999, when two men were killed by Bakassi Boys in the Safari restaurant in Umuahia, Abia State, the police received instructions from higher authorities to release the Bakassi Boys they had arrested. In another case, the chairman of the Bakassi Boys in Anambra, who was culpable of the killing of one Chief Okonkwo, was released after three months despite evidence of his personal involvement in several other cases of human rights abuses due to political interferences. In most cases, members of vigilante groups against whom there have been serious and credible allegations of complicity in abuse have not had to answer for these allegations before the judicial authorities.[47]

Increasing human rights abuses and violations perpetrated by actors in the informal sector may be informed by two factors. The first factor is that some security actors in the informal sector bear arms illegally but openly. In Abia, Anambra, Enugu, Lagos, Plateau, and other states in the northeast region, members of community vigilante groups and the CJTF bear arms openly. Yet, the Firearms Act, F28 LFN 2004 prohibits illicit possession, transfer, manufacturing, dealing in, and housing of fire arms, small arms, and light weapons, except as may be approved by the president or by the inspector general of police.[48] Equally worrisome was the hiring of foreign private military companies from South Africa, by the Goodluck Jonathan Administration, for the campaign against Boko Haram.[49] This is because the control of the territoriality and security of any nation are a function of the sovereign and for the state to allow the existence of autonomous armed groups in its territory is a partial abdication and abandonment of its sovereignty. This calls for the rebuilding of the capacity of state security agencies. This situation is made worse by the fact that members of community vigilante and neighborhood

Table 12.2 Security sector budgetary allocations: 2010–2017

MDAs	2010 (₦ billion)	2011 (₦ billion)	2012 (₦ billion)	2013 (₦ billion)	2014 (₦ billion)	2015 (₦ billion)	2016 (₦ billion)	2017 (₦ billion)	Total (₦ billion)
Defence	291.719	348.037	359.736	397.756	340.332	358.466	443.077	469.838	**3009.817**
Police Affairs	82.552	13.279	5.979	8.506	7.268	4.318	NA*	NA*	**121.902**
Police Service Commission	3.865	2.611	2.238	2.229	1.796	0.784	0.947	1.465	**15.935**
Office of the National Security Adviser	107.148	109.855	123.488	116.459	110.725	84.130	88.875	123.490	**864.170**

Source: Author's compilation for various Appropriation Acts as passed by the National Assembly
* In the 2016 restructuring of MDAs, Police Affairs was brought under Police Formations and Command Headquarters

watch groups who bear arms do not in any way receive any form of training on arms and weapons handling from relevant security institutions. Thus, as a fundamental issue in security provisioning in Nigeria, proliferation of illicit arms among actors in the informal security sector raises a number of issues. First, as some scholars have argued, not only illicit possession of arms by actors in the informal sector threatens human security, it also constitutes a threat to national security.[50] Second, it negates the traditional concept of vigilante in Nigeria, which exclusively refers to unarmed voluntary citizen groups created in local communities to help the security forces confront common criminality and social violence, by arresting suspected delinquents and handing them over to the police.[51] This lawfulness of vigilante groups arresting suspected criminals provided they are unarmed and that the suspect is immediately handed over to the police is recognized by law.[52] Third, it raises a serious security dilemma of what groups like the CJTF could become in the future after the counter-terrorism campaign in Nigeria's northeast region or what role the political class may create for them in future elections in Nigeria. Past experiences with the Bakassi Boys in Aba, OPC in Lagos, among others, have shown that vigilante groups that bear arms illegally become laws unto themselves and can be security threats to the community, especially in the absence of institutional mechanisms to conduct what analysts have described as "a reasoned disarmament."[53] In these experiences, vigilante groups have been found to play partisan politics in favor of certain groups. The second factor that explains the perpetration of human rights abuses and violations by actors in the informal sector is that members of community vigilante and neighborhood watch groups do not receive training on state laws and rules of engagement or on how to operate as a security outfits in the country. As this author has argued elsewhere, vigilante and neighborhood watch groups in Nigeria have very limited knowledge or training on human rights issues. The implication of this is that there are cases of human rights violations associated with the groups.[54]

Relationship with Formal Security Institutions

The nature and character of the relationship with formal security establishments, especially the armed forces and the police, are another fundamental issue for the informal security sector. While there is no statutorily defined relationship between the two sectors, in some states, informal security groups maintain robust and cordial relationships with formal security actors. In the southeast region generally, community vigilante and neighborhood watch groups receive training and logistics from the police, facilitated by state governments. This is also the case in places such as Lagos, Plateau, Kaduna, and Kano states.[55] Another evidence of the relationship with the formal sector is that in some cases, the formal security agencies use members of community vigilante groups to generate intelligence from their communities, while in other cases they conduct joint operations as is the case in the northeast region, where members of the CJTF have collaborated significantly with the military in counter-terrorism operations against Boko Haram in what the International Crisis Group has describes as the "watchmen of the Lake Chad."[56] This is due largely to the fact that members of the informal sector, especially vigilante groups, are recruited from within the community and are well acquainted with the environment.

However, in states where community vigilante groups operate without law or state recognition, the relationship with the formal sector has been crisis-ridden. This rancorous relationship is most common with NSCDC. In some states, for instance, officials of NSCDC do not work closely with community vigilante and neighborhood watch groups for two reasons. First, it is not within the mandate of the NSCDC, statutorily, to supervise, monitor, or work with community vigilante and neighborhood watch groups. Second, in some cases, community vigilante groups have become "breeding grounds or provide cover for cultists and criminals" who disguise as members of vigilante groups. The NSCDC would prefer to "crush vigilante groups if given the opportunity."[57] Generally, the cordiality or otherwise of the relationship with the formal sector has significant impacts on the efficiency and effectiveness of the actors in the informal sector, in terms of service delivery.

Although these identified issues and challenges, especially, alleged and established cases of human rights violations, may have continued to undermine the legitimacy and image of informal security actors in Nigeria, it is evident as some analysts have argued that self-help vigilante groups are positively reshaping Nigeria's security landscape, especially in crisis-ridden communities as is the case in the northeast region.[58] For instance, on December 23, 2015, interventions by members of the Civilian JTF prevented attacks by Boko Haram members on a mosque in Borno State during the Maulud celebration.[59] In Ebonyi State, intelligence provided by vigilante groups assisted the police in tracking and arresting a murder suspect in Ezza North LGA in June 2016 and in foiling a kidnap attempt in Akaeze in December 2016. Similarly, between January and June 2017, the Special Anti-Track Team of the Anambra State Vigilante Services in Okija, Ihiala LGA, rescued no fewer than ten kidnapped persons.[60]

There are three plausible reasons for why actors in the informal security sector are positively reshaping the security landscape. First is the obvious failure of state security agencies, especially in the rural areas to quickly respond to emergency security situations. The second reason is that membership of community vigilante and neighborhood watch groups, which are the major actors in the informal sector, is composed of indigenes of the communities, with good knowledge of the people, terrain, and sensitivity of their various communities, thereby building confidence among community members. Third, informal security outfits serve as a means of employment creation, particularly for the youth. For instance, while PGCs/PSOs provide full-time employment, membership in vigilante groups, especially at state and local government levels, is also considered full-time employment, with names of members in state payroll as is the case in some states like Abia, Anambra, Enugu, Lagos, and Plateau, among others.

Conclusion: Future Trajectory and Policy Recommendations

The forgoing clearly points to the fact that security actors in the informal sector have both positive and negative impacts on the communities in which they operate. While their relevance and utility are widely accepted, there are also cases of their abuses and misuse in many communities, which result in the identified issues and challenges. Addressing these challenges becomes very much an imperative in order to enthrone an inclusive security sector governance that is characterized by robust and cordial relationships between formal and informal security actors, especially in joint patrol and intelligence sharing. The utility and acceptability of community vigilante and neighborhood watch groups, especially in the rural areas due to the inability of the formal sector to effectively and adequately respond to emergency crisis and security situations, have become apparent. Thus, it has become imperative to develop a policy framework for security sector reform in Nigeria, by the federal government, through the Ministry of Interior, with a view to incorporating security actors in the informal sector into the national security architecture. This reform will achieve two purposes. First, it will help in bridging the gap occasioned by the failure of state security agencies, especially in the rural areas, to quickly respond to emergency security situations. Most importantly, it will help the state, at all levels, to rebuild and reinforce its law enforcement and security provisioning capacity in order to diminish the role played by the informal security sector.

Second, like the PGCs Act of 2004, which regulates the formation and operations of PGCs/PSOs in the country, the federal government, through the Office of the Attorney General and Ministry of Justice, should collaborate with the National Assembly to set in motion a process for the enactment of a federal legislation to regulate the formation and activities of vigilante and neighborhood watch groups across the country. The Act should recognize and legalize the extant Vigilante Group of Nigeria (VGN) and confer it with the power and mandate to coordinate the operations and activities of all vigilante groups across the country. Third, the proposed law should establish a statutory and independent source of funding for the informal sector, especially at the state level. Thus, state governments may take advantage of this to make provisions for adequate funding for state-owned vigilante groups. Adequate funding by federal, state, and local governments will help in the provision of necessary logistics that will boost the capacities and competences of actors in the sector in providing prompt and effective security services.

The federal and state governments should make provisions for extensive capacity building and regular trainings for actors in the informal sector on human rights, rule of engagement, and weapons handling in order to enhance quality service delivery and reduce the rate of human rights abuses and violations. Among other things, the proposed federal legislation should provide, for members of vigilante and neighborhood watch groups, provisions for them to be charged for violations of the disparate vigilance service laws, and justice should be sought for victims of human rights abuses and violations. While it is necessary that these abuses should be addressed, it has to be in such a way that the role of vigilante groups, as protectors of their communities, is preserved and their effectiveness enhanced.[61]

Particularly, state government can encourage cordial and robust relationships between actors in the informal sector and the police in order to expand, deepen, and sustain collaboration within the security sector. This can be done through the formation of statewide platforms for meetings, dialogue, and collaborative trainings, especially for actors in the informal sector. Part of the proposed statewide platforms for meetings and dialogue should include training of group members on human rights observation and the sensitization of community members and the general public on the functions and roles of vigilante groups and need for a harmonious relationship between and among them.

Notes

1. See Section 217(1) of the 1999 Constitution of the Federal Republic of Nigeria (as amended).
2. Dokubo, Charles. 2011. "Structure of Decision-Making for Defence in Nigeria." In *Defence Policy of Nigeria: Capability and Context*, edited by Celestine Bassey and Charles Dokubo, 60–75. Indiana: Author House.
3. Kwaja, Chris, Ogbonnaya, Ufiem Maurice, and Udoh, Ubon. 2017. *Structural and Institutional Mechanisms for Security Sector Oversight in Nigeria: Issues and Challenges*. Abuja: For Policy and Legal Advocacy Centre (PLAC) and Geneva Centre for Democratic Control of Armed Forces (DCAF).
4. DCAF and ECOWAS Parliament. 2011. "Parliamentary Oversight of the Security Sector: ECOWAS Parliament-DCAF Guide for West African Parliamentarians." A Publication of the Geneva Centre for the Democratic Control of Armed Forces (DCAF) and the Parliament of the Economic Community of West African States (ECOWAS Parliament).
5. See Okeke, Ogadimma. 2013. "Community Policing, Vigilante Security Apparatus and Security Challenges in Nigeria: A Lesson from Britain and Igbo Traditional Society of Nigeria." *British Journal of Arts and Social Sciences* 14, no. 11: 306–323; Ogbonnaya, Ufiem Maurice. 2017. "Non-State Security Actors in the South-East Zone of Nigeria." In *Non-State Security Actors and Security Provisioning in Nigeria*, edited by Chirs Kwaja, Kemi Okenyodo, and Val Ahmadu-Haruna, 49–66. Abuja: Cephas and Clems Nig. Ltd for Partners West Africa-Nigeria (PWAN).
6. Fourchard, Laurent. 2008. "A New Name for an Old Practice: Vigilante in South-Western Nigeria." *Africa, Cambridge University Press*, 78, no. 1: 16–40.
7. Kwaja, Chris. 2014. "Vigilantes, Public Safety, Crime and Violence Prevention in Nigeria." *Jos Journal of Social*, Issues 7, no. 1: 22–56.
8. Engerer, Hella. 2011. "Security as a Public, Private or Club Good: Some Fundamental Considerations." *Journal of Defence and Peace Economics* 22, no. 2: 135–145; Abrahamasen, Rita and Williams, Michael C. 2010. *Security beyond the State: Private Security in International Politics*. Cambridge: Cambridge University Press.
9. Ogbozor, Ernest. 2016. "Understanding the Informal Security Sector in Nigeria." United States Institute of Peace Special Report 391, September; Atelhe, George, Adams, John Anyabe, and Abunimye, Sunday B. 2016. "Overview of Security Sector Reforms and the Transformation of the Nigerian's Security Agencies." *American International Journal of Social Science* 5, no. 3 (June): 151–158.

10. Alemika, Etannib and Chukwuma, Innocent. 2004. The Poor and Informal Policing in Nigeria: Report on Poor Peoples' Perceptions and Priorities on Safety, Security and Informal Policing in A2J Focal States in Nigeria. Lagos: Center for Law Enforcement Education (CLEEN) Foundation; Ogbozor, "Understanding the Informal Security Sector in Nigeria."
11. Ogbonnaya, Ufiem Maurice. 2017. "Informality in the Security Sector: Vigilantes and Neighbourhood Watch Groups in South East Nigeria." Paper presented at the 60th Annual Meeting of African Studies Association (ASA) on the theme "Institutions: Creativity and Resilience in Africa," at the Chicago Marriott Downtown Magnificent Mile, Chicago, IL, USA, November 16–18.
12. Ogbozor, "Understanding the Informal Security Sector in Nigeria," 8.
13. Ukiwo, Ukoha. 2002. "Deus Ex Machina or Frankenstein Monster? The Changing Roles of Bakassi Boys in Eastern Nigeria." *Democracy and Development: Journal of West African Affairs* 3, no. 1 (September): 39–51; See also Harnischfeger, Johannes. 2003. "The Bakassi Boys: Fighting Crime in Nigeria." *The Journal of Modern African Studies* 41, no. 1 (March): 23–49.
14. Amnesty International, 2002. "Nigeria: Vigilante Violence in the South and South-East." AFR 44/014/2002.
15. Bamidele, Afolabi Muyiwa, Akinbolade, Olurunke O., and Nuhu, Adi I. 2016. "Private Security Outfits and Internal Security in Nigeria: An X-Ray of Kings Guards Nigeria Limited, Abuja." *Kuwait Chapter of Arabian Journal of Business and Management Review* 6, no. 2 (October): 13–31.
16. This figure, confirmed from the Department of PGCs, NSCDC Headquarters, Abuja, was correct as at February 12, 2018.
17. Amnesty International, 2002. Nigeria: Vigilante Violence in the South and South-East, 1.
18. Kwaja, Chris. 2017. "Non-State Security Actors in the North-Central Zone of Nigeria." In *Non-State Security Actors and Security Provisioning in Nigeria*, edited by Chris Kwaja, Kemi Okenyodo, and Val Ahmadu-Haruna, 9–21. Abuja: Cephas and Clems Nig. Ltd for Partners West Africa-Nigeria (PWAN).
19. Chindo, Angelina. 2017. "Obiano's Security Revolution Resonates in Anambra." *Daily Sun*, October 25. Available from: http://sunnewsonline.com/obianos-security-revolution-resonates-in-anambra/ [accessed February 10, 2018]; Ameh, Comrade Godwin. 2017. "Anambra Election: Why We Are Backing Obiano for Second Term—Ezeife." *Daily Post*, November 15. Available from: http://dailypost.ng/2017/11/15/anambra-election-backing-obiano-second-term-ezeife/ [accessed February 10, 2018].
20. Thisday, 2013. "Anambra: Any End to Ngige, Uba Saga?" November 24. Available from https://allafrica.com/stories/200311240529.html [accessed July 17, 2018].
21. Human Rights Watch, 2005. "Rest in Pieces: Police Torture and Deaths in Custody in Nigeria." 17, no. 11(A), July, 9.
22. News Agency of Nigeria. 2017. "Nigeria Requires Additional 155,000 Police Personnel—IG." *Premium Times*, May 11. Available from: https://www.premiumtimesng.com/news/top-news/230966-nigeria-requires-additional-155000-police-personnel-i-g.html [accessed February 10, 2018].
23. Atelhe, Adams, and Abunimye, "Overview of Security Sector Reforms and the Transformation of the Nigerian's Security Agencies," 151–158; Ogbonnaya, "Informality in the Security Sector."
24. Egwu, Samuel. 2011. "Ethno-Religious Conflicts and National Security in Nigeria: Illustrations from the Middle Belt." In *State, Economy, and Society in Post-Military Nigeria*, edited by Said Adejumobi, 49–83. New York: Palgrave Macmillan.

25. See Nnoli, Okwudiba. 2006. *National Security in Africa: A Radical New Perspective*. Enugu: Pan African Centre for Research on Peace and Conflict Resolution (PACREP).
26. Barongo, Yolamu, ed. 1983. *Political Science in Africa: A Critical Review*. London: Zed Publishers.
27. See the Kaduna State Vigilante Law, Kaduna State of Nigeria Gazette 9 (47), June 13, 2013.
28. See Neighbourhood Watch (Vigilante Security) Groups Law 2012 (1433.H), Kano.
29. Ogbozor, "Understanding the Informal Security Sector in Nigeria."
30. Amnesty International, 2002. *Nigeria: Vigilante Violence in the South and South-East*, 4.
31. See Obi, Paul. 2018. "IG Orders Police CPs to Disband Militia, Vigilante Groups." *This Day*, February 2. Available from: https://www.thisdaylive.com/index.php/2018/02/02/ig-orders-police-cps-to-disband-militia-vigilante-groups/ [accessed February 17, 2018].
32. Amnesty International, 2002. *Nigeria: Vigilante Violence in the South and South-East*, 4.
33. Vigilante Group of Nigeria, 2012. "Welcome to Vigilante Group of Nigeria." December 5. Available from: http://vigilantegroupnig.com/blog/2012/12/05/hello-world/#more-1 [accessed July 17, 2018].
34. Abuh, Adamu. 2017. "Representatives Pass VGN Bill." *The Guardian*, October 13. Available from: https://guardian.ng/news/representatives-pass-vgn-bill/ [accessed February 17, 2018]; Obi, "IG Orders Police CPs to Disband Militia, Vigilante Groups."
35. Kura, Suleiman. 2017. "Non-State Security Actors in the North-West Zone of Nigeria." In *Non-State Security Actors and Security Provisioning in Nigeria*, edited by Chris Kwaja, Kemi Okenyodo, and Val Ahmadu-Haruna, 37–48. Abuja: Cephas and Clems Nig. Ltd for Partners West Africa-Nigeria (PWAN).
36. Fulani, Iro Dan. 2016. "Seven Killed as Rival Vigilante Factions Clash in Adamawa." *Premium Times*, March 13. Available from: https://www.premiumtimesng.com/news/top-news/200102-seven-killed-rival-vigilante-factions-clash-adamawa.html [accessed May 18, 2018].
37. Adebayo, Daramola. 2017. "1 Killed, Several Injured as Two OPC Factions Clash in Ibadan." *Daily Post*, September. Available from: http://dailypost.ng/2017/09/08/1-killed-several-injured-two-opc-factions-clash-ibadan%E2%80%8E/ [accessed May 18, 2018].
38. Nolte, Insa. 2007. "Ethnic Vigilantes and the State: The Oodua People's Congress in South-Western Nigeria." *International Relations* 21, no. 2 (June): 217–235.
39. Amnesty International, 2002. *Nigeria: Vigilante Violence in the South and South-East*, 4.
40. Human Rights Watch and CLEEN Foundation, 2002. "Nigeria: Government Must Disband Vigilante Groups." Available from: https://www.hrw.org/news/2002/05/20/nigeria-government-must-disband-vigilante-groups [accessed February 14, 2018].
41. Ogbozor, "Understanding the Informal Security Sector in Nigeria," 11.
42. Tertsakian, Carina and Brown, Manby. 2003. *Nigeria, the O'Odua People's Congress: Fighting Violence with Violence*. Washington, DC: Human Rights Watch.
43. United Nations Office for Drug and Crimes (UNODC), 2017. *Corruption in Nigeria Bribery: Public Experience and Response*. Vienna: UNODC.
44. Nubuisi, Francis. 2017. "NBS: Roughly N400bn in Bribes Given to Public Officials Annually." *ThisDay*, August 17. Available from: https://www.thisdaylive.com/index.

php/2017/08/17/nbs-roughly-n400bn-in-bribes-given-to-public-officials-annually/ [accessed July 2, 2018].
45. Tertsakian, Carina and Brown, Manby. 2003. *Nigeria, the O'Odua People's Congress: Fighting Violence with Violence*. Washington, DC: Human Rights Watch.
46. Amnesty International, 2002. *Nigeria: Vigilante Violence in the South and South-East*.
47. Human Rights Watch and CLEEN Foundation, 2002. "The Bakassi Boys: The Legitimization of Murder and Torture." 14, no. 5 (A) May, 36.
48. See Sections 3 and 4 of the Firearms Act, F28, F28 LFN 2004.
49. See Freeman, Colin. 2015. "South African Mercenaries' Secret War on Boko Haram." *The Telegraph*, May 15. Available from: https://www.telegraph.co.uk/news/worldnews/africaandindianocean/nigeria/11596210/South-African-mercenaries-secret-war-on-Boko-Haram.html [accessed May 18, 2018]; Malik, Samuel. 2016. "How Nigeria Engaged South African Mercenaries to Fight Boko Haram." *International Centre for Investigative Reporting* (ICiR). April 5. Available from: https://www.icirnigeria.org/how-nigeria-engaged-south-african-mercenaries-to-fight-boko-haram/ [accessed May 18, 2018].
50. See Onuoha, Freedom Chuwkudi. 2011. "Small Arms and Light Weapons Proliferation and Human Security in Nigeria." *Conflict Trends*, no. 1, 50–56; Okeke, Ogadimma and Raymond O. Oji. 2014. "The Nigerian State and the Proliferation of Small Arms and Light Weapons in the Northern Part of Nigeria." *Journal of Educational and Social Research* 4, no. 1 (January): 415–428.
51. Amnesty International, 2002. *Nigeria: Vigilante Violence in the South and South-East*.
52. See Section 14(1) of the Nigerian Criminal Procedure Act.
53. International Crisis Group, 2017. "Watchmen of Lake Chad: Vigilante Groups Fighting Boko Haram." Africa Report N°244, February 23. Brussels, Belgium: International Crisis Group, 22.
54. Ogbonnaya, "Non-State Security Actors in the South-East Zone of Nigeria."
55. Ogbozor, "Understanding the Informal Security Sector in Nigeria"; Ogbonnaya, "Non-State Security Actors in the South-East Zone of Nigeria."
56. International Crisis Group, 2017. "Watchmen of Lake Chad," 1.
57. Interview with the Head, Department of Private Guard Companies, Abia State Command of NSCDC, Umuahia, on December 30, 2016.
58. See Okoli, Chukwuma Al. 2017. "Self-Help Vigilante Groups Are Reshaping Security against Boko Haram." *The Conversation*. Available from: https://theconversation.com/self-help-vigilante-groups-are-reshaping-security-against-boko-haram-81139 [accessed February 14, 2018].
59. International Centre for Investigative Reporting (ICiR), 2015. "Civilian JTF Foils Terrorist Attack in Borno State." *ICiR*, December 24. Available from: https://www.icirnigeria.org/civilian-jtf-foils-terrorist-attack-in-borno-state/ [accessed February 21, 2018].
60. Nweke, Nweke. 2017. "Anambra: Vigilante Group Rescues 10 Kidnapped Persons; Red Cards Criminals." *247ureport*. Available from: http://247ureports.com/anambra-vigilante-group-rescues-10-kidnapped-persons-red-cards-criminals/ [accessed February 21, 2018].
61. Ogbozor, Ernest. 2016. "Understanding the Informal Security Sector in Nigeria," 15.

CONCLUSION: THE NIGERIAN SECURITY DILEMMA

Caroline Varin and Freedom Chukwudi Onuoha

The Colonial Legacy

Many decades after Nigeria attained formal independence in 1960, colonial legacies and contradictions continue to underpin Nigeria's political and security fragility. Some of these legacies included but are not limited to forced governance, divide and rule system, and the seeding of false consciousness that incubated ethnic politics in Nigeria. In particular, the impact of colonialism on contemporary Nigeria's security environment is intrinsically linked to the faulty foundation of the Nigerian state established through the amalgamation of southern and northern protectorates into a unified colony on January 1, 1914, without due consultation of the various constitutive ethnic nationalities. This experience precariously lumped together different ethnic and tribal groups, some of whom have grown to distrust each other since the amalgamation, leading to accusation of marginalization and even a struggle for independence from the post-colonial Nigerian state.

The colonial contradiction has been partly blamed for the problem of lack of inclusiveness, both in the administration of the country and in the governance of its security architecture. For instance, indirect rule executed by colonial masters reinforced rivalries between ethnicities and prevented the development of a national consciousness. The adoption of the "divide and rule policy" completely ignored the reality of ethnic diversity, underpinning the issue of rivalry and sectionalism that are implicated in contemporary conflicts in Nigeria. Hence, identity crisis has continually confronted Nigeria as most of her citizens are attached to their ethnic identity rather than their national (Nigerian) identity. From a security perspective, resurgent separatist agitation in Nigeria's Southeast, evidenced by pro-Biafra movements, represents an organized protest against the character of the post-colonial Nigerian state. The negative impacts of colonialism may as well continue to shape Nigeria's security environment until such time that fundamental restructuring of the post-colonial Nigerian state is effected.

Sixty years of British rule has had an oversized impact on the country's psyche and political system. The last sixty years of independence have been an experiment in governance, democracy, military rule, and institution-building, with a mixed bag of results. In Chapter 1, Michael Ugwueze argues that "colonial patterns of administration that thrived on *forced governance* laid the foundation for military rule through military intervention in politics, poor governance through elite rivalry and corruption, as well as violent political culture through electoral malpractice." The ensuing ping-pong of military coups and intermittent elections is explained by the British colonial experience, where the mandate of the colonial armies was clearly to protect the national boundaries and suppress domestic unrest. The army was used by the colonial powers as an instrument of control and coercion. In the years following independence from colonial rule, the African continent has seen no less than eighty-five successful military coups and nineteen presidential assassinations.[1] Civilian governments have used the army "to defend (their) authority, and not society; it almost always came to the support of the state in suppressing political dissidents, democrats, socialists and others."[2]

As is evident throughout this volume, there has been a growing *policefication* of the armed forces in Nigeria—the political deployment and (mis)use of the military in the performance of routine law and order duties reserved for the police. This growing trend in the domestic deployment of the military to act as a police force has resulted in the suppression of legitimate civilian protests and gross human rights violations, undermining any hope for a balanced social contract between the population, the government, and the security forces. Furthermore, perceived electoral corruption and the slow and distorted pace of policies have led to the widespread belief after independence that elected leaders are illegitimate and incompetent, and therefore unfit to rule. Ethno-tribal competition within the armed forces has also exacerbated existing distrust between democratically elected governments and the military institution, prompting various wings of the army to rise against their rulers and attempt to govern in their place. Liberian politician George Klay Kieh argues that "military intervention in African politics was rationalised by the soldiers as a patriotic and selfless exercise to rid the continent of corrupt, inefficient, incompetent and decadent politicians."[3] With civilian institutions in Nigeria perceived as inept and corrupt, the apparent discipline and superior organizational capability of the army offer the hope of improved governance.[4] This is a doomed experiment, according to military theoretician Samuel Finer, as the military is technically unable to "administer any but the most primitive community" and "lack legitimacy: that is to say, their lack of a moral title to rule."[5] The colonial adventure and its consequential legacy on the character of the Nigerian state and emergent institutions, particularly the armed forces, invariably laid down the foundations for the deep insecurities that Nigeria faces and its inability to successfully address many of the threats it faces today.

Old and New Threats

Too many of Nigeria's current security threats have been recurrent or ongoing events over the last three to four decades. Secessionist movements in Biafra have rumbled on since the 1960s (Chapter 10). Militancy in the Niger Delta can be traced back to the 1990s (Chapter 7). And while the origins of Boko Haram are "only" twenty years old, religious uprisings in the country were already manifest in the 1980s, with the Maitatsine riots causing several thousand deaths in northern Nigeria (Chapter 9). The dynamics of SALWs proliferation (Chapter 4) are further evidence of the country's flailing security infrastructure, underpinning exponential rise in criminality and the increase in piracy attacks (Chapters 5 and 6). This is the result of decades of disinvestment and poor training of the police and military. Allegations of corruption (Chapter 2) transcend both institutions with reports of billions of dollars worth of stolen equipment, graft, and kickbacks, resulting in the military (and police) "insufficiently trained, low in morale and under resourced."[6] As a consequence, incidents of police brutality and military failings have exacerbated the security environment; the civilian population is distrustful and uncooperative, leading them to organize parallel security outfits ranging from gangs and vigilantes to private security corporations (Chapter 12). And violent non-state actors have taken advantage of this vacuum of power to challenge the state, as evidenced by Boko Haram's seizure and administration of several towns and communities in 2015. Furthermore, there is literally no deterrent for violent operatives who act with relative impunity due to a weak judicial system accused of a lack of transparency, accountability, and integrity. Bribes are rampant among lawyers and judges, political influence on the judiciary is common, and prisons are congested with inmates awaiting trial—one report identified 50,000 pre-trial prisoners to 17,000 convicts.[7]

New security threats have recently emerged in Nigeria, exacerbating existing threats and further straining the country's political resilience. The authors of this volume have repeatedly identified climate change as a force-multiplier that has been driving violent competition for resources (Chapter 3). The Delta militants are mobilized by shrinking resources and the pollution of their land and water sources. Boko Haram has been recruiting among the disaffected youths of a shrivelled Lake Chad. And herders and farmers are finding that a change in rainfall has endangered an already precarious lifestyle. It is undeniable that climate change is one of the great new security challenges facing Nigeria today, but one that will require a political rather than a military response.

Likewise, climate change and recurrent violence have caused a huge displacement of Nigerians across the country (Chapter 11). Over 2 million people—equivalent to roughly 1 percent of the Nigerian population—have been uprooted from their homes due to conflict and environmental emergencies and are living in temporary camps or shelters. These IDPs are particularly vulnerable to food insecurity, malnutrition, and epidemics as a result of the terrible living conditions and lack of access to basic services and infrastructure. The government's inability or failure to address this crisis has created a situation that is potentially explosive. From a security standpoint, IDP camps have allegedly become breeding grounds for extremism and social unrest. From an economic perspective, the largely farmer communities that have been displaced have led to a food crisis as shortages are reported around the country. And in terms of human security, this population is unable to return to their homes or rebuild their lives, leaving them in an hopeless state of poverty and uncertainty.

The Way Forward

It is nearly impossible to suggest a starting point to address Nigeria's security dilemma. Several authors in this volume have recommended a consultation to assess whether the country should be broken up into several political entities that reflect the different ethnic identities of the people. Such an initiative would take time and be politically contentious on many levels. Secessionist groups around the world have typically been met with violence, and the countries that (rarely) emerge struggle with the same problems that they faced before independence: poor governance, corruption, poverty, minority identities, and unfriendly neighbors. The situation in Sudan and newly formed South Sudan and the ongoing tinder box of the Balkans are evidence of the complications that persist when breaking up a political entity.

The security forces in Nigeria clearly need to improve their relationship with the people. Both the military and the police force have both received training from foreign countries, including the United States and the United Kingdom, that include civil-military relations, humanitarian and human rights law, and counter-terrorism methods that work in partnership with the civilian population. However, these training programs need to go beyond the leadership and access every soldier and policeman as each individual incident of police/military brutality is counter-productive. The Nigerian non-profit Cleen Foundation has also made strides in this direction, hosting a program on civil-military relations that integrates a "need for positive civil military relations" and recognizing the urgency of "changing the narrative that makes civilian perceive the military as their enemy."[8] In addition to rigorous training of state security forces to instill discipline and commitment toward respecting human rights, a comprehensive communications campaign is also needed to reframe the perception of the military and integrate the security forces into the lives of ordinary citizens.

Police and military brutality, however, is not solely the result of poor training and colonial legacy. The weak and corrupt judicial system has frustrated the efforts of security forces to bring suspected criminals and terrorists to justice, prompting them to bypass the rule of law and take matters into their own hands—as evidenced in the 2009 crackdown and extrajudicial killing of Boko Haram leader, the preacher Mohammad Yusuf. In conjunction with reforming the security forces, a thorough cleaning-up of the judicial branch is a requisite for any meaningful change. This means holding judges and lawyers accountable for their actions, pursuing individuals in positions of power who accept bribes, accelerating the process for those awaiting trial, and improving transparency through access to information for the press and public, which will help restore faith in the system. These changes are possible but require political will, strong leadership, and professional consultation. Professor Attahiru Jega's appointment to the Independent National Electoral Commission in 2010 and the ensuing peaceful and successful presidential elections—the first of its kind in Nigeria—

under his stewardship show how one person with integrity, leadership skills, and a vision can have a transformative effect on the institutions. Such a person at the helm of judicial reform in Nigeria can help change the prevailing corrupt environment and the public and military's perception of the legal branch. There are already steps in place to make this happen, as evidenced by an EU-funded United Nations Office on Drugs and Crime (UNODC) program in partnership with the main Nigerian judicial branches to help further train lawyers and judges on the rule of law and human rights, improve the collection of information and coordination between various institutions, give access to justice for disadvantaged and vulnerable groups, and bolster the capacity to decrease pre-trial detention and prison congestion.[9] However, these changes take time and once more require leadership within Nigeria's judiciary.

Furthermore, political leaders and candidates need to be held accountable for encouraging violence and manipulating public sentiment around ethno-religious lines as these accentuate the breakdown in the social contract with the people. Hate speeches by politicians, religious leaders, and members of the press must be prohibited and those who arm gangs to influence the outcome of elections have to be held accountable. Once more, this depends on the competence of the judicial branch and the cooperation of the security forces.

The social contract between Nigeria's leadership, the population, and the security forces has been eroded by the colonial legacy and pervasive corruption, political greed, and military and police brutality. There are immediate steps that the government can take to invest in the relationship with its people, which will help restore faith in the system and reduce the propensity for violence around the country. Investing in the capacity of the National Emergency Management Agency with a focus on addressing the needs of IDPs will improve the lives of hundreds of thousands with immediate effect, reduce the opportunity for social unrest, and demonstrate the government's interest in its role as guardian of the nation. The usual advice of investing in the education of the country's youth is evident; it needs to be urgently prioritized to prevent a bad security situation from getting even worse as it is through education that norms can be changed and the social contract forged anew. It is also the most valuable tool for addressing not only the twin problems of poverty and unemployment, but also corruption, violence, and political divide—the example of the French turning "Peasants into Frenchmen" in the nineteenth century comes to mind.[10]

Finally, the authors of this volume on Security in Nigeria have offered a plethora of in-depth analysis and suggestions to address the Nigerian security dilemma. While there are many obstacles on the way, it is clear that there is a large community of interested parties with expertise and ideas who are ready to contribute to the nation's future. The manpower, capacity, and experience already exist in Nigeria. What remains are political will and leadership, successful implementation of key policies, and time.

Notes

1. Kieh, G. and Agbese, P. 2004. *The Military and Politics in Africa*. Aldershot: Ashgate, 45.
2. Perlmutter, A. 1981. *Political Roles and Military Rulers*. London; Totowa, NJ: F. Cass, 255.
3. Kieh, G.1992. *Dependency and the Foreign Policy of a Small Power: The Liberian Case*. San Francisco: Mellen Research University Press, 5.
4. Finer, S. 2002. *The Man on Horseback: The Role of the Military in Politics*. Abingdon: Routledge, 6.
5. Ibid., 14.
6. Kavakeb, D. 2017. "International Community Must Join Fight against Defence Corruption in Nigeria—Transparency International Defence & Security." *Transparency International Defence & Security*. Available from: http://ti-defence.org/international-community-must-join-fight-defence-corruption-nigeria/#more-936.
7. Emmanuel, C. 2018. "Nigeria: Decongesting Nigerian Prisons to Recongest Them Afresh." *AllAfrica*. Available from: https://allafrica.com/stories/201806220064.html.
8. The Cleen Foundation. *Civil-Military Relations Project*. Cmr.cleen.org.
9. UNODC, 2016. "Justice Sector Reform." Available from: https://www.unodc.org/nigeria/en/judicial-reform.html.
10. Weber, E. 1976. *From Peasants into Frenchman. The Modernization of Rural France 1870–1914*. Stanford, CA: Stanford University Press.

BIBLIOGRAPHY

Introduction

Abdulraheem, S., and A. R. Oladipo. "Trafficking in Women and Children: A Hidden Health and Social Problem in Nigeria." *International Journal of Sociology and Anthropology* 2, no. 3 (2010): 34.

Adenubi, Tola, Austin Ebipade, Micheal Ovat, A. Callistus Agwaza, Tunde Ogunesan, and Ishola Michael. "21 Million Guns, Ammo Smuggled into Nigeria—Investigation," *Nigerian Tribune*, January 21, 2018. Available online: http://www.tribuneonlineng.com/21-million-guns-ammo-smuggled-nigeria-investigation/.

Ayoob, Mohammed. "The Security Problematic of the Third World." *World Politics* 43, no. 2 (1991): 257–283.

Ayoob, Mohammed. *The Third World Security Predicament*. Boulder, CO: Lynne Rienner Publishers, 2005.

Azar, Edward E., and Chung-in Moon. *National Security in the Third World*. Aldershot: Edward Elgar [Centre for International Development and Conflict Management], 1988.

Ball, Nicole in Ayoob, Mohammed. "The Security Problematic of the Third World." *World Politics* 43, no. 2 (1991): 257–283.

BBC News. "Migration to Europe in Charts," September 11, 2018. Available online: https://www.bbc.co.uk/news/world-europe-44660699.

Campbell, John. "Nigerian Minister Warns against Nigerian Citizens Seeking Asylum in Germany," *Council on Foreign Relations*, June 8, 2018. Available online: https://www.cfr.org/blog/nigerian-minister-warns-against-nigerian-citizens-seeking-asylum-germany.

Collier, Paul, and Anke Hoeffler. "Greed and Grievance in Civil War." *Oxford Economic Papers* 56, no. 4 (2004): 563–595.

Elbadawi, Ibrahim, and Nicholas Sambanis. "How Much War Will We See? Estimating the Incidence of Civil War in 161 Countries." *Policy Research Working Paper*, no. 2533 (2001).

IMB. "Pirate Attacks Worsen in Gulf of Guinea," *ICC Commercial Crime Services*, April 10, 2018. Available online: https://www.icc-ccs.org/index.php/1244-pirate-attacks-worsen-in-gulf-of-guinea.

Internal Displacement Monitoring Centre. "Fragmented Response to Internal Displacement Amid Boko Haram Attacks and Flood Season," July 23, 2018. Available online: http://www.internal-displacement.org/sites/default/files/publications/documents/201307-af-nigeria-overview-en.pdf.

IOM Nigeria Situation Report 2016. Available online: https://nigeria.iom.int/media/news/situation-report-%EF%82%9F-16-30-september-2016.

Kaldor, Mary. *New & Old Wars*. Stanford, CA: Stanford University Press, 2007.

Klare, Michael T. "The Arms Trade: Changing Patterns in the 1980s." *Third World Quarterly* 9, no. 4 (1987): 1257–1281.

Nafziger, E. Wayne, and Juha Auvinen. *Economic Development, Inequality and War: Humanitarian Emergencies in Developing Countries*. Hampshire: Palgrave Macmillan UK, 2003.

Nasong'o, Wanjala S. *The Roots of Ethnic Conflict in Africa*. New York: Palgrave Macmillan, 2015.

Osumah, O., and I. Aghedo. "Who Wants to Be a Millionaire? Nigerian Youths and the Commodification of Kidnapping." *Review of African Political Economy* 38, no. 128 (2011): 277–287.

Premium Times. "Nigeria Accounts for over 70% of 500 Million Illicit Weapons in West Africa," August 2, 2016. Available online: https://www.premiumtimesng.com/news/more-news/207969-nigeria-accounts-for-over-70-of-500-million-illicit-weapons-in-west-africa.html.

Rothschild, Emily. "What Is Security?" *Daedalus* 124, no. 3 (1995): 53–98.

Thomas, Caroline. *In Search of Security*. Boulder, CO: Rienner, 1987.

UNHCR. "Nigeria Emergency," 2018. Available online: http://www.unhcr.org/uk/nigeria-emergency.html.

UNICEF Nigeria. "Child Trafficking Information Sheet," April 2007. Available online: https://www.unicef.org/wcaro/WCARO_Nigeria_Factsheets_ChildTrafficking.pdf.

United Nations System in Nigeria. "Nigeria: United Nations Sustainable Development Partnership Frameworks (UNSDPF) 2018–2022," 2017. Available online: http://www.undp.org/content/dam/undp/library/corporate/Executive%20Board/2017/Second-regular-session/DPDCPNGA3_Master%20Consolidated%20UNSDPF%202018-2022%2023-May-2017.doc.

United Nations Trust Fund for Human Security. *Human Security Handbook*. Human Security Unit, January 2016. Available online: https://www.un.org/humansecurity/wp-content/uploads/2017/10/h2.pdf.

Chapter 1

Achebe, Chinua. *There Was a Country: A Personal History of Biafra*. New York: Penguin Books Ltd, 2012.

Adekoya, Preye. "The Succession Dispute to the Throne of Lagos and the British Conquest and Occupation of Lagos." *African Research Review* 10, no. 3 (2016): 207–226.

Adigwe, Francis. *Essentials of Government for West Africa*. Ibadan: Ibadan University Press Limited, 1974.

Ajayi, J. F. A. *Christian Missions in Nigeria 1841–1891*. Hong Kong: Commonwealth Printing Press, 1965.

Awolowo, Obafemi. *Path to Nigerian Freedom*. London: Faber & Faber, 1947.

Ayers, A. J. "Sudan's Uncivil War: The Global-Historical Constitution of Political Violence." *Review of African Political Economy* 37, no. 124 (2010): 153–171.

Bello, Ahmadu. *My Life*. Cambridge: Cambridge University Press, 1962.

Colonial Reports. *Nigeria: Annual General Report for 1923, No 1197*. London: His Majesty's Stationery office, 1923.

Duru, A. "Dangerous Memory: The Nigerian Civil War, the Postwar Generation, and a Legacy of Frustration." In *The Nigeria-Biafra War*, edited by C. J. Korieh, 233–260. Amherst, NY: Cambria Press, 2012.

Duruji, Moses M. "Ethnic Militias in Post-Military Rule Nigeria." In *The State in Contemporary Nigeria: Issues, Perspectives and Challenges*, edited by J. S. Omotola and I. M. Alumona, 269–292. Ibadan: John Arches Publishers Ltd, 2016.

Duruji, Moses M., and Dominic E. Azu. "The Challenges of Combating Corruption in Nigeria." In *The State in Contemporary Nigeria: Issues, Perspectives and Challenges*, edited by J. S. Omotola and I. M. Alumona, 166–186. Ibadan: John Arches Publishers Ltd, 2016.

Ezirim, Gerry, and Peter Mbah. "Electoral Process and Political Violence in Africa: Preview of 2011 General Elections in Nigeria." In *Social Dynamics of African States*, edited by O. U, 1–23. Nnadozie. Nsukka: REK Books, 2011.

Heerten, L., and D. Moses. "The Nigeria–Biafra War: Postcolonial Conflict and the Question of Genocide." *Journal of Genocide Research* 16, no. 2–3 (2014): 169–203.

Huffington Post. "Obama Ghana Speech: FULL TEXT," July 11, 2009. Available online: https://www.huffingtonpost.com/2009/07/11/obama-ghana-speech-full-t_n_230009.html.

Ibeanu, Okey, and Luckham Robin. *Niger-Delta: Political Violence, Governance and Corporate Responsibility in a Petro-State*. Abuja: Centre for Democracy and Development, 2006.

Igwe, Obasi. *Politics and Globe Dictionary*. Aba: Eagle Publishers, 2005.

Joseph, Richard. "Prebendalism and Dysfunctionality in Nigeria," *Africaplus*, July 26, 2013. Available online: https://africaplus.wordpress.com/2013/07/26/prebendalism-and-dysfunctionality-in-nigeria/.

Joseph, Richard A. *Democracy and Prebendal Politics in Nigeria: The Rise and Fall of the Second Republic*. Ibadan: Spectrum Books Limited, 1987.

Kurfi, Amadu. *Election Context: Candidate's Companion*. Ibadan: Spectrum Books Limited, 1989.

Little, Daniel. "False Consciousness," n.d. Available online: http://www-personal.umd.umich.edu/~delittle/iess%20false%20consciousness%20V2.htm.

Mustapha, M. "The 2015 General Elections in Nigeria: New Media, Party Politics and the Political Economy of Voting." *Review of African Political Economy* 44, no. 152 (2017): 312–321.

Nnoli, Okwudiba. *Ethnic Politics in Nigeria*. Enugu: Fourth Dimension Publishers, 1978.

Nze, Chris. "Nigeria's Unity and the Conquest Mentality," *The Guardian*, October 6, 2017. Available online: https://guardian.ng/opinion/nigerias-unity-and-the-conquest-mentality/.

Ochonu, Moses. "1914 and Nigeria's Existential Crisis: A Historical Perspective" (parts 1 & 2). An *NVS Essay on Nigeria's Centenary Celebration*, May 29 and June 6, 2004.

Ochonu, Moses. "The Roots of Nigeria's Religious and Ethnic Conflict," *Global Post*, March 10, 2014. Available online: https://www.pri.org/stories/2014-03-10/roots-nigerias-religious-and-ethnic-conflict.

Ogbeidi, Michael M. "Political Leadership and Corruption in Nigeria since 1960: A Socio-Economic Analysis." *Journal of Nigeria Studies* 1, no. 2 (2012): 1–25.

Onuoha, Freedom. "The Audacity of the Boko Haram: Background, Analysis and Emerging Trend." *Security Journal* 25, no. 2 (2012): 134–151.

Onuoha, Jonah, and Michael I. Ugwueze. "United States Security Strategy and the Management of Boko Haram Crisis in Nigeria." *Global Journal of Arts Humanities and Social Sciences* 2, no. 2 (2014): 22–43.

Panter-Brick, S. K. *Nigerian Politics and Military Rule: Prelude to the Civil War*. London: The Athlone Press, 1970.

Shaw, Flora. "Letter." *The Times of London*, January 8, 1897: 6.

Suberu, Rotimi T. *Ethnic Minority Conflicts and Governance in Nigeria*. Ibadan: Spetrum Books Limited, 1996.

Tharoor, Shashi. "The Partition: The British Game of 'Divide and Rule,'" *Al Jazeera*, August 10, 2017. Available online: http://www.aljazeera.com/indepth/opinion/2017/08/partition-british-game-divide-rule-170808101655163.html (accessed 10/10/2017).

Transition Monitoring Group. *An Election Programmed to Fail: Final Report of the April 2007 General Elections in Nigeria*. Nigeria: Transition Monitoring Group, 2007.
Ugwu, Tagbo C. O. *Corruption in Nigeria: Critical Perspectives*. Nsukka: Chuka Educational Publishers, 2002.
Ugwueze, Michael I. "Ethno-Religious Conflicts and Nigeria's National Security." In *The State in Contemporary Nigeria: Issues, Perspectives and Challenges*, edited by J. S. Omotola and I. M. Alumona, 253–268. Ibadan: John Arches Publishers Ltd, 2016.
Ugwueze, Michael I., Jonah Onuoha, and Ejikeme J. Nwagwu. "Electronic Governance and National Security in Nigeria." *Mediterranean Journal of Social Sciences* 7, no. 6 (2016): 363–374.
Ukiwo, Ukoha. "The Study of Ethnicity in Nigeria." *Oxford Development Studies* 33, no. 1 (2005): 7–23.
Ukiwo, Ukoha, and I. Chukwuma. *Governance and Insecurity in South-East Nigeria*. Lagos: Cleen Foundation, 2012.
Uwechue, Raph. "Ndigbo: Nigeria's Nation Builders." A speech delivered at the *Igbo Day 2009 Celebration*, held at Dan Anyaiam Stadium, Owerri, Imo state on September 29, 2009.
Weber, Eugen. *Peasants into Frenchmen: The Modernization of Rural France, 1870–1914*. Stanford: Stanford University Press, 1976.
Xypolia, Ilia. "Divide et impera: Vertical and Horizontal Dimensions of British Imperialism." *Critique: Journal of Socialist Theory* 44, no. 3 (2016): 221–231.

Chapter 2

Abubakar, Ahmed. "Elite's Brinkmanship and the Politicization of Anti-Corruption Project in Nigeria: An Overview of the Anti-Corruption War under the Buhari Administration," 2018. Available online: http://www.hrpub.org/download/20171230/SA7-19610545.pdf.
Agha, Eugene. "NIMASA Takes over 20 Vessels from Tompolo's Firm," *Daily Trust*, March 16, 2016. Available online: https://www.dailytrust.com.ng/news/general/nimasa-takes-over-20-vessels-from-tompolo-s-firm/138104.html.
Allen, Dave, Will Cafferky, Abdallah Hendawy, Jordache Horn, Karolina Maclachlan, Stefanie Nijssen, and Eleonore Vidal de la Blache. "The Big Spin: Corruption and the Growth of Violent Extremism," *Transparency International Defense & Security*, February 2017. Available online: http://ti-defence.org/wp-content/uploads/2017/02/The_Big_Spin_Web-1.pdf.
Amundsen, Inge. "Good Governance in Nigeria: A Study in Political Economy and Donor Support," *Norad Report 17/2010 Discussion*, August 24, 2010. Available online: https://www.researchgate.net/profile/Inge_Amundsen/publication/256952861_Good_Governance_in_Nigeria/links/0c960524177e5c1d4b000000/Good-Governance-in-Nigeria.pdf.
Anderson, Eva, and Matthew Page. "Weaponising Transparency: Defence Procurement Reform as a Counterterrorism Strategy in Nigeria," *Transparency International*, May 2017. Available online: http://ti-defence.org/wp-content/uploads/2017/05/Weaponising_Transparency_Web.pdf.
Anti-Corruption Evidence (ACE). "Anti-Corruption in Nigeria: Accepting the Constraints, and Moving Forward," Briefing Paper 002, October 2017. Available online:

https://ace.soas.ac.uk/wp-content/uploads/2017/07/ACE-BriefingPaper002-NG-AntiCorruption-171027-LowRes.pdf.

Ayodeji, Dr Gafar. "The Role of Corruption in Festering Boko Haram Insurgency and Terrorism under Jonathan Administration (2016)," *SSRN*, December 6, 2016. Available online: https://ssrn.com/abstract=2881193 or http://dx.doi.org/10.2139/ssrn.2881193.

Baffour, Katherine. "Boko Haram's Source of Weapons Revealed," *Naij*, 2014. Available online: https://www.naija.ng/66368.html#59827.

Baker, Aryn. "Nigeria's Military Quails When Faced with Boko Haram," *Time*, February 10, 2015. Available online: http://time.com/3702849/nigerias-army-boko-haram/ (accessed July 2018).

BBC News. "Nigeria's Sambo Dasuki Charged '$68m Fraud'," December 14, 2015. Available online: https://www.bbc.co.uk/news/world-africa-35093785.

Chayes, Sarah. "Corruption and Extremism: From Recognition to Response," Interview in *World Policy Journal*, February 12, 2016. Available online: https://carnegieendowment.org/2016/02/12/corruption-and-extremism-from-recognition-to-response-pub-62760 (accessed 20/07/2018).

The Eagle Online. "Army Inaugurates E-NAPS for Payment of Salaries," April 19, 2018. Available online: https://theeagleonline.com.ng/army-inaugurates-e-naps-for-payment-of-salaries/.

Economic and Financial Crimes Commission. "Government Ekpemupolo (AKA Tompolo)," 2019. Available online: https://efccnigeria.org/efcc/wanted/1723-government-ekpemupolo-a-k-a-tompolo (accessed 3/07/2018).

Gibbs, Margot. "Dereliction of Duty: How Weak Arms Export License Controls in the UK Facilitated Corruption and Exacerbated Instability in the Niger Delta," *Corruption Watch UK*, 2017: 36. Available online: https://docs.wixstatic.com/ugd/54261c_3f990fe3175c48c5b90ed65a41192d59.pdf.

Global Witness. *International Thief Thief*, October 11, 2010. Available online: https://www.globalwitness.org/en/campaigns/corruption-and-money-laundering/banks/international-thief-thief/.

Godwin, Comrade Ameh. "Court Affirms Forefeiture of Tompolo's Assets to Nigerian Government," *Daily Post*, October 28, 2017. Available online: http://dailypost.ng/2017/10/28/court-affirms-forfeiture-tompolos-assets-nigerian-government/.

Mo Ibrahim Foundation. "Ibrahim Index of African Governance: Index Report," 2017. Available online: http://s.mo.ibrahim.foundation/u/2017/11/21165610/2017-IIAG-Report.pdf.

Institute of Economics and Peace. "Peace and Corruption 2015: Lowering Corruption—A Transformative Factor for Peace," 2015. Available online: https://reliefweb.int/sites/reliefweb.int/files/resources/Peace%20and%20Corruption.pdf.

Isah, Ahuraka. "Nigeria: UN Raises the Alarm over 350 Million Illicit Weapons in Nigeria," *All Africa*, December 13, 2017. Available online: http://allafrica.com/stories/201712130072.html.

Junghae, Waithera. "Okokrim Secures Conviction as UK CAS-Global Probe Continues," *Global Investigations Review*, May 16, 2017. Available online: https://globalinvestigationsreview.com/article/1141762/%C3%98kokrim-secures-conviction-as-uk-cas-global-probe-continues.

MacLachlan, Karolina. "The Fifth Column: Understanding the Relationship between Corruption and Conflict," *Transparency International*, July 2017: 17. Available online: http://ti-defence.org/wp-content/uploads/2017/09/The_Fifth_Column_Web.pdf.

Martini, Maira. "U4 Expert Answer: Nigeria: Evidence of Corruption and the Influence of Social Norms," *Transparency International*, September 26, 2014. Available online: https://www.transparency.org/files/content/corruptionqas/Nigeria_overview_of_corruption_and_influence_of_social_norms_2014.pdf.

Naija Per Minute. "Buhari's Act of Politicizing His Anti-Corruption War: A Reinforcement of Hostility among Southerners—Tom Marino," September 2016. Available online: http://www.naijaperminute.com.ng/2016/09/04/buharis-act-politicizing-anti-corruption-war-reinforcement-hostility-among-southerners-tom-marino/.

NRGI Reader. "The Resource Curse: The Political and Economic Challenges of Natural Resource Wealth," *Natural Resource Governance Institute*, March 2015. Available online: https://resourcegovernance.org/sites/default/files/nrgi_Resource-Curse.pdf.

Odunlami, Temitayo. "Tompolo: The Billionare Militant—TheNEWS Africa," *Sahara Reporters*, August 16, 2012. Available online: http://saharareporters.com/2012/08/16/tompolo-billionaire-militant-thenews-africa.

Okeowo, Alexis. "Missing," *The New Yorker*, May 19, 2014. Available online: https://www.newyorker.com/magazine/2014/05/26/missing-4.

Onuoha, Freedom C. "Why Do Youth Join Boko Haram?," *United States Institute of Peace (USIP) Special Report*, June 2014. Available online: https://www.usip.org/sites/default/files/SR348-Why_do_Youth_Join_Boko_Haram.pdf.

Ososanya, Tunde. "Dasukigate: Witness Testifies against Dasuki, Says Ex-NSA Transferred N280.4m to Individuals' Accounts," *Naij*, 2018. Available online: https://www.premiumtimesng.com/news/top-news/267090-corruption-two-naval-officers-forfeit-lekki-houses-n11-million-to-nigerian-govt.html; https://www.naija.ng/1178249-dasukigate-witness-testifies-dasuki-nsa-transferred-n2804m-individuals-accounts.html#1178249.

Page, Matthew. "Camouflaged Cash: How 'Security Votes' Fuel Corruption in Nigeria," *Transparency International Defence and Security*, May 2018. Available online: http://ti-defence.org/wp-content/uploads/2018/05/DSP_Nigeria_Camouflage_Cash_Web2.pdf.

PM News. "ACN Queries Plans to Privatize Nigeria's Maritime Security," July 3, 2018. Available online: https://www.pmnewsnigeria.com/2012/01/22/acn-queries-plans-to-privatize-nigerias-maritime-security/.

Premium Times. "Corruption: Two Naval Officers Forfeit Lekki Houses, N11 Million to Nigerian Government," May 3, 2018. Available online: https://www.premiumtimesng.com/news/top-news/267090-corruption-two-naval-officers-forfeit-lekki-houses-n11-million-to-nigerian-govt.html.

Roberts, Sam. "Diepreye Alamieyeseigha, Nigerian Notorious for Corruption, Dies at 62," *The New York Times*, October 14, 2015. Available online: https://www.nytimes.com/2015/10/15/world/diepreye-alamieyeseigha-nigerian-ex-governor-dies-at-62.html.

Robertson, Nic. "Nigerian Soldiers Discuss Boko Haram Fight," *CNN*, January 2015. Available online: http://edition.cnn.com/videos/world/2015/01/15/ctw.

Torbjornsson, Daniel, and Michael Jonsson. "Boko Haram: On the Verge of Defeat or a Long Term Threat? FOI-R–4488—SE," November 2017. Available online: https://www.academia.edu/35419972/Boko_Haram_-_on_the_Verge_of_Defeat_or_a_Long-term_Threat.

Transparency International. "Global Corruption Barometer 2015/16/17, Supplementary Data, Global Results," 2015. Available online: https://www.transparency.org/news/feature/global_corruption_barometer_citizens_voices_from_around_the_world (accessed 20/07/2018).

Transparency International. "Corruption Perceptions Index 2017," 2017. Available online: https://www.transparency.org/news/feature/corruption_perceptions_index_2017 (accessed 20/07/2018).

Transparency International Defence and Security. "Government Defence Anti-Corruption Index 2015, Nigeria Assessment," 2015. Available online: http://government.defenceindex.org/countries/nigeria/.

UK Department for Business, Innovation & Skills. "Guidance on Consolidated EU and National Arms Export Licensing Criteria," November 21, 2012. Available online: https://www.gov.uk/government/publications/consolidated-eu-and-national-arms-export-licensing-criteria.

Chapter 3

Adelekan, I. O., and B. O. Adegebo. "Variation in Onset and Cessation of the Rainy Season in Ibadan, Nigeria." *Journal of Science Research* 13 (2014): 13–21.

Agbu, O. "Global Warming: An Overview and Implications for Nigeria." In *Climate Change and Human Security in Nigeria*, edited by O. Eze and O. Oche, 47–66. Lagos: Nigerian Institute of International Affairs, 2010.

Akingbade, T. "Climate Change Effects in Nigeria: Heat, Dust, Weather Raise Health Concerns," *The Guardian Newspaper*, October 3, 2010.

Annan, K. "Secretary-General Salutes International Workshop on Human Security in Mongolia." Two-Day Session in Ulaanbaatar, May 8–10, 2000. Press Release SG/SM/7382. Available online: http://www.org/News/Press/docs/20000508.sgsm7382.html (accessed 27/12/2018).

Atake, C. E. "Sea Level Rise in Coastal Areas of Nigeria?," *Voices of Youth*, 2016. Available online: http://m.voicesofyouth.org/en/posts/sea-level-rise-in-coastal-areas-of-nigeria- (accessed 23/11/2018).

Audu, E. B., H. O. Audu, N. L. Binbol, and J. N. Gana. "Climate Change and Its Implication on Agriculture in Nigeria." *Abuja Journal of Geography and Development* 3, no. 2 (2013): https://pdfs.semanticscholar.org/edbf/7ea74362b2922dd8c753c35c1d1e02673306.pdf?_ga=2.158771327.45262751.1576527757-1012230644.1576527757. (accessed 16/10/2019).

Audu, H. O., R. B. Balogun, R. C. Nwoga, R. B. Kalejaiye-Matti, G. Amadi, and E. B. Audu. "Climate Change: Causes, Implications and Mitigation Strategies." In National Conference Proceedings on Climate Change Impact and Adaptation: Is Nigeria Ready? Published by the *Nigerian Meteorological Society*, 2010.

Ayodele, I. "Confronting Climate Change Doom in Lagos," *The Guardian*, February 4, 2016. Available online: https://guardian.ng/features/science/confronting-climate-change-doom-in-lagos/ (accessed 9/07/2018).

"Buhari Decries Negative Effects of Climate Change," *Nigerian Tribune*, October 19, 2018. Available online: https://www.tribuneonlineng.com/169698/ (accessed 14/12/2018).

Department of Climate Change. "Climate Smart Agriculture," December 3, 2015. Available online: http://climatechange.gov.ng/climate-smart-agriculture/ (accessed 11/07/2018).

Emodi, N. V. "Climate Change in the Nigerian Context." Presentation at the APEC Climate Center, 12, Centum 7-ro, Haeundae-gu Busan 48058, Republic of Korea, June 2015. Available online: http://www.researchgate.net/profile/Nnaemeka_Emodi/publication/280774425_CLIMATE_CHANGE_IN_THE_NIGERIAN_CONTEXT/

links/55c5b41908aeca747d6190fd/CLIMATE-CHANGE-IN-THE-NIGERIAN-CONTEXT (accessed 6/11/2018).

Ezirim, G. E. "Petropolitics and Environmental Criminality in the Niger Delta: Advocacy for Enforcement of Global Convention." *University of Nigeria Journal of Political Economy* 2, no. 1 & 2 (2008): 215–230.

Ezirim, G. E., and F. C. Onuoha. "Climate Change and National Security: Exploring the Theoretical and Empirical Connections in Nigeria." *Journal of International Politics and Development Studies* 4, no. 1 & 2 (2008): 89–108.

Federal Government of Nigeria. "NIGERIA Post-disaster Needs Assessment 2012 Floods." A report by The Federal Government of Nigeria with Technical Support from the World Bank, EU, UN, and Other Partners, 2013.

Federal Ministry of Environment (Special Climate Change Unit). "National Environmental, Economic and Development Study (Needs) for Climate Change in Nigeria," September 2010: 24–25. Available online: http://unfccc.int/files/adaptation/application/pdf/nigerianeeds.pdf.

Federal Ministry of Environment Abuja, Nigeria (Special Climate Change Unit). "National Environmental, Economic and Development Study (Needs) for Climate Change in Nigeria" (Final Draft), September 2010. Available online: http://unfccc.int/files/adaptation/application/pdf/nigerianeeds.pdf (accessed 13/08/2018).

Festus Owete, Evelyn Okakwu, Lois Ugbede, and Quenn Esther Iroanusi. "Nigeria: Buhari's Ministers' Scorecard after Two Years (Concluding Part)," *Premium Times*, January 5, 2018. Available online: https://www.premiumtimesng.com/news/headlines/254503-analysis-buharis-ministers-scorecard-two-years-concluding-part.html (accessed 15/08/2018).

Gómez, Oscar A., and Des Gasper. "Human Security: A Thematic Guidance Note for Regional and National Human Development Report Teams, p2," *UNDP*, n.d. Available online: http://hdr.undp.org/sites/default/files/human_security_guidance_note_r-nhdrs.pdf (accessed 7/12/2018).

Hodson, M., and S. Marvin. *World Cities and Climate Change: Producing Urban Ecological Security* 44. Berkshire: Open University Press/McGraw-Hill House, 2010.

Hubert, D. "Human Security: Safety for People in a Changing World." Presented at a Regional Conference on The Management of African Security in the 21st Century. Lagos: Nigerian Institute of International Affairs, June 23–24, 1999.

Muhammad, Rakiya A. "Nigeria: Stemming the Impact of Climate Change," July 21, 2008. Available online: https://allafrica.com/stories/200807211032.html (accessed 15/08/2018).

NASA. "What's in a Name? Weather, Global Warming and Climate Change," 2018. Available online: https://climate.nasa.gov/resources/global-warming/ (accessed 21/05/2018).

National Agency for the Great Green Wall (NAGGW). "Combating Desertification in Nigeria," October 15, 2016. Available online: http://ggwnigeria.gov.ng/tag/frontline-states/ (accessed 23/07/2018).

National Research Council. "Climate Change, Evidence, Impacts and Choices: Answers to Common Questions about the Science of Climate Change," 2012. Available online: http://nas-sites.org/americasclimatechoices/files/2012/06/19014_cvtx_R1.pdf (accessed 21/05/2018).

National Research Council of the National Academies. *Advancing the Science of Climate Change*. Washington, DC: The National Academies Press, 2010.

NEMA Nigeria. "The National Disaster Response Plan [NDRP]," November 7, 2013: 15. Available online: http://nema.gov.ng/the-national-disaster-response-plan/ (accessed 24/11/2018).

Niyi. "7 Million Nigerians Displaced by Flood—NEMA," *Information Nigeria*, September 4, 2013. Available online: http://www.informationng.com/2013/09/7-million-nigerians-displaced-by-flood-nema.html (accessed 30/07/2018).

Nnodim O. "Nigeria Highly Vulnerable to Climate Change—NIMET," *Punch*, December 12, 2016. Available online: http://punchng.com/nigeria-highly-vulnerable-climate-change-nimet/ (accessed 9/11/2017).

Obi, N. I., and C. J. Okekeogbu. "Erosion Problems and Their Impacts in Anambra State of Nigeria: A Case of Nanka Community." *International Journal of Environment and Pollution Research* 5, no. 1 (2017): 24–37.

Oche, O. "Security, Globalization and Climate Change: A Conceptual Analysis." In *Climate Change and Human Security in Nigeria*, edited by O. C. Eze and O. Oche, 35–45. Lagos: Nigeria Institute of International Affairs, 2010.

Odogwu, G. "Nimet's 2016 Seasonal Rainfall Prediction," *Punch*, March 10, 2016. Available online: https://punchng.com/nimets-2016-seasonal-rainfall-prediction/ (accessed 9/11/2017).

Ogata & Sen. "Women Environment and Development Programme, Gender, Climate Change and Human Security: Lessons from Bangladesh, Ghana and Senegal" (2003). www.gdnonline.org/resources/WEDO_Gender_CC_Human_Security.pdf.

Oguamanam, C. "Nigeria Faces New Security Threat Fuelled by Climate Change and Ethnicity," *The Conversation*, May 12, 2016. Available online: http://theconversation.com/nigeria-faces-new-security-threat-fuelled-by-climate-change-and-ethnicity-58807 (accessed 09/10/2018).

Ojetunde, D. "How Climate Change Is Fueling Conflicts in Nigeria," *International Centre for Investigative Reporting*, November 2, 2017. Available online: https://www.icirnigeria.org/how-climate-change-is-fueling-conflicts-in-nigeria/ (accessed 11/12/2018).

Okeke, C. "Issues as Desert Encroachment Takes Toll on Nigerian landmass," *Latest Nigerian News*, October 30, 2016. Available online: https://www.latestnigeriannews.com/news/3652017/issues-as-desert-encroachment-takes-toll-on-nigerian-landmass.html (accessed 15/08/2018).

Okeke, C. "Frontline States: Concern over Deepening Desertification Despite Relocation," *Leadership Newspaper*, October 31, 2017. Available online: https://leadership.ng/2017/10/31/frontline-states-concern-deepening-desertification-despite-relocation/ (accessed 7/08/2018).

Okoye, Anthony C. "Political Economy of Climate Change and Human Security in Nigeria," PhD diss., University of Nigeria Nsukka, Department of Political Science, August 2017.

Okoye, Anthony C. *Victims, Not Perpetrators: Boko Haram Insurgency and the Juvenisation of Suicide Bombing in Nigeria*. Paper presented at the 31th annual conference of the Nigeria Political Science Association (NPSA), held at the Ebonyi State University, Abakaliki, March 26–29, 2018.

Oladipo, Emmanuel. "Towards Enhancing the Adaptive Capacity of Nigeria: A Review of the Country's State of Preparedness for Climate Change Adaptation." Report submitted to Heinrich Böll Foundation Nigeria, 2010.

Omoyemen, O. E. "Climate Change and Human Security: A Gender Perspective." In *Climate Change and Human Security in Nigeria*, edited by O. C. Eze and O. Oche, 285–298. Lagos: Nigeria Institute of International Affairs, 2010.

Premium Times. "Over 2,800 Active Erosion Sites in South-east Nigeria—Group," July 4, 2018. Available online: https://www.premiumtimesng.com/regional/ssouth-east/274938-over-2800-active-erosion-sites-in-south-east-nigeria-group.html (accessed 8/12/2018).

Raimi, L., and Jackson T. C. B. Jack. "How Does Climate Change Pose Human Security Threats in the Niger Delta? Implications for Policy Makers." *Maiduguri Journal of Arts and Social Sciences* 14 (2017): 80–90.

Rakiya, A. M. "Nigeria: Stemming the Impacts of Climate Change," *Daily Trust* distributed by all Africa Global Media, 2008. Available online: http://allafrica.com (accessed 12/12/2018).

Reliefweb. "Nigeria Flood. Acaps, Briefing Note," September 21, 2018. Available online: https://reliefweb.int/sites/reliefweb.int/files/resources/20180921_acaps_briefing_note_floods_in_nigeria_0.pdf (accessed 11/12/2018).

Sawa, B. A., A. A. Adebayo, and A. A. Bwala. "Dynamics of Hydrological Growing Season at Kano as Evidence of Climate Change." *Asian Journal of Agricultural Sciences* 6, no. 2 (2014): 75–78.

Solomon, S., D. Qin, M. Manning, Z. Chen, M. Marquis, K. B. Averyt, M. Tingor, and H. L. Miller. "The Physical Science Basis." Contribution of Working Group I to the Fourth Assessment Report of the Intergovernmental Panel on Climate Change. Cambridge: Cambridge University Press (IPCC Report), 2007.

Thakur, Ramesh. "From National to Human Security." In *Asia-Pacific Security: The Economics-Politics Nexus*, edited by Stuart Harris and Andrew Mack, 52–80. Sydney: Allen & Unwin, 1997.

UNDP. "Climate Change in Least Developed Countries," 2011. Available online: http://www.undp.org/content/dam/undp/library/corporate/fast-facts/english/FF-Climate-Change-in-Least-Developed-Countries.pdf (accessed 9/04/2018).

United Nations. *Human Security Handbook: An Integrated Approach for the Realization of the Sustainable Development Goals and the Priority Areas of the International Community and the United Nations System*, January 2016. Available online: https://www.un.org/humansecurity/wp-content/uploads/2017/10/h2.pdf (accessed 7/12/2018).

United Nations Development Programme (UNDP). *Human Development Report 1994*. New York: Oxford University Press, 1994: 23.

United States Environmental Protection Agency. "International Climate Impacts," January 19, 2017. Available online: https://19january2017snapshot.epa.gov/climate-impacts/international-climate-impacts_.html (accessed 5/06/2018).

USAID. "Nigeria Climate Vulnerability Profile," 2013. Available online: https://www.climatelinks.org/sites/default/files/asset/document/nigeria_climate_vulnerability_profile_jan2013.pdf (accessed 17/10/2018).

Usman, Y. D., and B. I. Dije. "Potential Challenges of Climate Change to the Nigeria Economy." *Journal of Environmental Science, Toxicology and Food Technology* 6, no. 2 (2013): 7–12.

WIRED. "What Is Climate Change? The Definition, Causes and Effects," May 15, 2018. Available online: http://www.wired.co.uk/article/what-is-climate-change-definition-causes-effects.

World Bank. "Combating Erosion in Nigeria: New Project Spells Hope in Seven States," November 26, 2013. Available online: http://www.worldbank.org/en/news/feature/2013/11/26/combating-erosion-in-nigeria-new-project-spells-hope-in-seven-states (accessed 20/03/2015).

The World Bank. "Development and Climate Change: World Development Report 2010," 2010. Available online: http://documents.worldbank.org/curated/en/201001468159913657/pdf/530770WDR02010101Official0Use0Only1.pdf (accessed 13/08/2018).

The World Bank. "Climate Change Knowledge Portal for Development Practitioners and Policy Makers: Nigeria Dashboard Natural Hazards," n.d. Available online: http://sdwebx.worldbank.org/climateportal/countryprofile/home.cfm?page=country_profile&CCode=NGA&ThisTab=NaturalHazards (accessed 8/12/2018).

Worland, Justin. "How Climate Change Unfairly Burdens Poorer Countries," *Times*, February 5, 2016. Available online: http://time.com/4209510/climate-change-poor-countries/ (accessed 11/12/2017).

Chapter 4

Abubakar, Aminu. "Banned Weapons Stoke Deadly Violence in Nigeria," *AFP*, 2018. Available online: http://www.digitaljournal.com/news/world/banned-weapons-stoke-deadly-violence-in-nigeria/article/52423.

Adebayo, Moshood. "2007: It's Do or Die—Obasanjo," *The Sun*, February 1, 2007.

Adenubi, Tola, Austin Ebipade, Micheal Ovat, A. Callistus Agwaza, Tunde Ogunesan, and Ishola Michael. "21 Million Guns, Ammo Smuggled into Nigeria—Investigation," *Tribune*, January 21, 2018. Available online: http://www.tribuneonlineng.com/21-million-guns-ammo-smuggled-nigeria-investigation/.

Agbese, Dan. "Fulani Herdsmen? Here Are the Grim Statistics," *The Guardian*, November 3, 2017. Available online: https://guardian.ng/opinion/fulani-herdsmen-here-are-the-grim-statistics/.

Agha, Eugene. "How Illegal Arms Find Their Way into the Country," *Daily Trust*, April 23, 2017. Available online: https://www.dailytrust.com.ng/how-illegal-arms-find-their-way-into-the-country.html.

Al Jazeera. "Fact and Figures: Global Trade in Small Arms," March 18, 2013. Available online: https://www.aljazeera.com/news/americas/2013/03/201331885519413442.html.

Anaba, Innocent, and Onozure Dania. "I Paid DSS Men, Others N1m to Bring in 661 Rifles," *Vanguard*, February 20, 2018. Available online: https://www.vanguardngr.com/2018/02/paid-dss-men-others-n1m-bring-661-rifles/.

Anza, Philips. "Jos Crisis Is More Than Religious," *Newswatch*, 2010.

Bah, Alhaji. "Micro-Disarmament in West Africa: The ECOWAS Moratorium on Small Arms and Light Weapons." *African Security Review* 13, no. 3 (2004): 33–46.

Bello, Emmanuel. "Nigeria: Politicians Fault Obasanjo over Utterances," *Daily Trust*, February 12, 2007. Available online: http://allafrica.com/stories/200702121248.html.

Chelule, Esther. "Proliferation of Small Arms and Light Weapons: Challenge to Development, Peace and Security in Africa." *Journal of Humanities and Social Science* 19, no. 5 (2014): 81.

ECOWAS. "ECOWAS Promotes Peaceful Cross-Border Transhumance," *ECOWAS Press Release*, April 26, 2018. Available online: http://www.west-africa-brief.org/content/en/ecowas-promotes-peaceful-cross-border-transhumance.

Ekemenah, Alex. "National Security and the Menace of Weapon Proliferation in Nigeria," *Business World*, 2013: 25. Available online: http://businessworldng.com/web/articles/2847/1/National-Security-and-the-Menace-of-Weapon-Proliferation-in-Nigeria/Page1.htm.

Eze, Chinedu. "Nigeria Risks Influx of Illegal Arms through Airstrips," *This Day*, 2012. Available online: http://www.thisdaylive.com/articles/nigeria-risks-influx-of-illegal-arms-through-airstrips/130767/.

Hubert, Don. "Human Security: Safety for People in a Changing World." In *Beyond Conflict Resolution: Managing African Security in the 21st Century*, edited by Richard A. Akindele and Bassey E. Ate, 87–102. Ibadan: Vantage Publishers, 2001.

Ibuku, Yinka. "Nigeria's Boko Haram Caused $9 Billion in Damage since 2011," *Bloomberg*, April 4, 2016. Available online: https://www.bloomberg.com/news/articles/2016-04-04/nigeria-s-boko-haram-caused-9-billion-in-damage-since-2011.

Ifijeh, Godwin. "SSS Raises Alarm over Arms Proliferation," *This Day*, 28 May 2006.

Ikelegbe, Augustine. "Special Report: Proliferation of Illegal Weapons Blamed on Our Porous Borders," *Frontier News*, 2013. Available online: http://frontiersnews.com/index.php/news/5726-special-report-proliferation-of-illegal-weapons-blamed-on-our-porous-borders-.

Internal Displacement Monitoring Centre. "Fragmented Response to Internal Displacement Amid Boko Haram Attacks and Flood Season," July 23, 2018.

Jekada, Kabirat Emmanuel. "Proliferation of Small Arms and Ethnic Conflicts in Nigeria: Implication for National Security," MA diss., Clement University, September 2005. Available online: http://www.stclements.edu/grad/gradjeka.pdf.

Mercy Corps. "The Economic Costs of Conflict and the Benefits of Peace: Effects of Farmer-Pastoralist Conflict in Nigeria's Middle Belt on State, Sector, and National Economies." Portland; USA: Mercy Corps, 2016.

Moulaye, Zeine. *Democratic Governance of Security in Mali: A Sustainable Development Challenge*. Nigeria: ADPROMO Ltd, 2006.

Muanya, Chukwuma. "Nigeria, 36 Others Need Help on Food Security, Says FAO," *The Guardian*, March 8, 2018. Available online: https://guardian.ng/news/nigeria-36-others-need-help-on-food-security-says-fao/.

NAN. "Abuja Police Uncover Illegal Firearm Factory, Arrest Three Suspects," *Premium Times*, September 22, 2017. Available online: https://www.premiumtimesng.com/news/top-news/243919-abuja-police-uncover-illegal-firearm-factory-arrest-three-suspects.html.

Office of the National Security Adviser, *National Security Strategy*. Abuja: ONSA, 2014.

Ohia, Paul. "Gambia Cuts Ties with Iran over Nigeria's Arm Seizure," *This Day*, November 23, 2010.

Ojeme, Victoria, and Ruth Odiniya. "Nigeria Has over 1,499 Illegal Entry Routes—Interior Minister," *Vanguard*, June 19, 2013. Available online: http://www.vanguardngr.com/2013/06/nigeria-has-over-1499-illegal-entry-routes-interior-minister/.

Ojo, Jide. "Arming Jobless Youths to Win Elections," *Punch*, May 15, 2013.

Okeke, Vincent, and O. Richard Oji. "The Nigerian State and the Proliferation Small Arms and Light Weapons in the Northern Part of Nigeria." *Journal of Educational and Social Research* 4, no. 1 (2014): 415–428.

Okeke-Uzodike, Ufo, and Victor Ojakorotu. "Oil, Arms Proliferation and Conflict in the Niger Delta of Nigeria." *African Journal of Conflict Resolution* 6, no. 2 (2006): 85–106.

Olayiwola, S. S. "Proliferation of Arms and Security Challenges in Nigeria." *International Journal of History and Cultural Studies* 3, no. 3 (2017): 33–38.

Omonobi, Kingsley, and Henry Umoru. "Killings: Senate Summons Security, Service Chiefs, Customs Boss, Others," *Vanguard*, 2018.

Omotola, S. J. "Engendering the Legislature in Nigeria: Faltering Prospects and New Hopes." In *Nigeria beyond 2007: Issues, Perspectives and Challenges*, edited by Hassan

A. Saliu, I. O. Taiwo, R. A. Seniyi, B. Salawu, and A. Usman, 209–244. Ilorin: Faculty of Business and Social Sciences, University of Ilorin, 2008.
Onuoha, Freedom Chukwudi. "Corruption and National Security: The Three Gap-Thesis and the Nigerian Experience." *Nigerian Journal of Economic & Financial Crimes* 1, no. 2 (2009): 1–13.
Onuoha, Freedom Chukwudi. "Youth Unemployment and Poverty: Connections and Concerns for National Development in Nigeria." *International Journal of Modern Political Economy* 1, no. 1 (2010): 115–136.
Onuoha, Freedom Chukwudi. "Small Arms and Light Weapons Proliferation and Human Security in Nigeria." *Conflict Trends* 2011, no. 1 (2011): 50–56.
Onuoha, Freedom Chukwudi. "Porous Borders and Boko Haram's Arms Smuggling Operations in Nigeria," *Report*. Doha: Al Jazeera Centre for Studies, 2013.
Pettinger, Tejvan. "Containerisation," *Economics Help*, June 26, 2013. Available online: https://www.economicshelp.org/blog/7637/trade/containerisation/.
Premium Times. "Nigeria Accounts for over 70% of 500 Million Illicit Weapons in West Africa," August 2, 2016.
Small Arms Survey. *Profiling the Problem*. Oxford: Oxford University Press, 2001.
Small Arms Survey. *Guns in the City*. Cambridge: Cambridge University Press, 2007.
Thomas, Caroline. "Introduction." In *Globalisation, Human Security and the African Experience*, edited by Caroline Thomas and Peter Wilkin, 1–22. London: Lynne Rienner, 1999.
Ujumadu, Vincent. "Anambra and Defiant Abductors: 200 Kidnappings and the N1 Billion Ransom," *Vanguard*, July 27, 2014.
United Nations. "Report of the Panel of Governmental Experts on Small Arms," August 27, 1997. Available online: https://www.sipri.org/sites/default/files/research/disarmament/dualuse/pdf-archive-att/pdfs/un-report-of-the-panel-of-governmental-experts-on-small-arms.pdf.
United Nations Development Programme. *Human Development Report*. New York: Oxford University Press, 1994.
Wellington, Bestman. "Weapons of War in the Niger Delta." *Terrorism Monitor* 5, no. 10 (2007): 8–10.
Xinhua. "Nigeria Worried about Cost of Lingering Ethno-Religious Crisis," *Xinhua News Agency*, 2004. Available online: http://www.encyclopedia.com/doc/1P2-16579278.html.

Chapter 5

Abdulmalik, Jibril, Olayinka Omigbodun, Omeiza Beida, and Babatunde Adedokun. "Psychoactive Substance Use among Children in Informal Religious Schools (Almajiris) in Northern Nigeria." *Mental Health, Religion and Culture* 12, no. 6 (2009): 527–542.
Abdulraheem, S., and A. R. Oladipo. "Trafficking in Women and Children: A Hidden Health and Social Problem in Nigeria." *International Journal of Sociology and Anthropology* 2, no. 3 (2010): 34.
Abubakar, Shehu, Vincent Egunyanga, and Monday Osayande. "In Edo, Delta, Women Trafficking to Europe for Sex Is a Pride," *Daily Trust*, July 16, 2010. Available online: https://www.dailytrust.com.ng/news/others/in-edo-delta-women-trafficking-to-europe-for-sex-is-a-pride/4505.html.

Abubakr, Aminu, and Steve Almasy. "Girl, 13: Boko Haram Tried to Force Me to Become a Suicide Bomber—CNN.Com," *CNN*, January 4, 2015. Available online: http://edition.cnn.com/2014/12/26/world/africa/nigeria-teenage-girl-suicide-bombing/index.html.

Adekoye, Vincent. "NAPTIP Arrests 11 Child Traffickers in Anambra State ... Rescues 3 Children—NAPTIP," March 1, 2018. Available online: https://www.naptip.gov.ng/?p=1679.

Aghedo, Iro, and Surulola James Eke. "From Alms to Arms: The Almajiri Phenomenon and Internal Security in Northern Nigeria." *The Korean Journal of Policy Studies* 28, no. 3 (2013): 97–123.

Aibangbe, Mary O. "Child Trafficking: A Hindrance to the Girl-Child Education." *Planning and Changing; Normal* 46, no. 3–4 (2015): 311–323.

Akpan, Eno-Obong. "Early Marriage in Eastern Nigeria and the Health Consequences of Vesicovaginal Fistulae (VVF) among Young Mothers." *Gender & Development* 11, no. 2 (July 1, 2003): 70–76.

Akpan, Nseabasi S. "Kidnapping in Nigeria's Niger Delta: An Exploratory Study." *Journal of Social Sciences* 24, no. 1 (2010): 33–42.

Arogundade, Fatiu Abiola. "Kidney Transplantation in a Low-Resource Setting: Nigeria Experience." Kidney International Supplements, Disparities in Renal Disease-moving towards Solutions: Proceedings from the *WCN 2011 Satellite Symposium* 3, no. 2 (May 1, 2013): 241–245. Available online: https://doi.org/10.1038/kisup.2013.23.

Beyrer, Chris. "Global Child Trafficking." *The Lancet* 364, no. 16–17 (2004): 16–17.

Braimah, Tim S. "Child Marriage in Northern Nigeria: Section 61 of Part I of the 1999 Constitution and the Protection of Children against Child Marriage." *African Human Rights Law Journal* 14, no. 2 (2014): 474–488.

Budiani-Saberi, D. A., and F. L. Delmonico. "Organ Trafficking and Transplant Tourism: A Commentary on the Global Realities." *American Journal of Transplantation* 8, no. 5 (2008): 925–929. Available online: https://doi.org/10.1111/j.1600-6143.2008.02200.x.

Bukoye, Roseline Olufunke. "Case Study: Prevalence and Consequences of Streets Begging among Adults and Children in Nigeria, Suleja Metropolis." *Procedia—Social and Behavioral Sciences*, 5th ICEEPSY International Conference on Education & Educational Psychology 171 (January 16, 2015): 323–333. Available online: https://doi.org/10.1016/j.sbspro.2015.01.129.

Capron, Alexander M., and Francis L. Delmonico. "Preventing Trafficking in Organs for Transplantation: An Important Facet of the Fight against Human Trafficking." *Journal of Human Trafficking* 1, no. 1 (2 January 2015): 56–64. Available online: https://doi.org/10.1080/23322705.2015.1011491.

Chiaramonte, Perry. "Girls Held by Boko Haram Face Auction, Life as Sex Slaves if Rescue Fails," *Fox News*, 8 May 2014. Available online: http://www.foxnews.com/world/2014/05/08/girls-held-by-boko-haram-face-auction-life-as-sex-slaves-if-rescue-fails/.

Cristiansson, Terese. "Expressen Reveals Baby Factories," *Expressen*, 15 December 2013. Available online: http://www.expressen.se/nyheter/exclusive-expressen-reveals-baby-factories/.

Dessy, Sylvain E., Flaubert Mbiekop, and Stéphane Pallage. "The Economics of Child Trafficking (Part II)." *Cahier de Recherche/Working Paper* 5 (2005): 9.

Elbagir, Nima, Raja Razek, Alex Platt, and Bryony Jones. "People for Sale: Where Lives Are Auctioned for $400," *CNN*, 2018. Available online: https://www.cnn.com/2017/11/14/africa/libya-migrant-auctions/index.html (accessed 11/03/2018).

Fawole, Olufunmilayo I., Ademola J. Ajuwon, Kayode O. Osungbade, and Olufemi C. Faweya. "Prevalence and Nature of Violence among Young Female Hawkers in Motor-Parks in South-Western Nigeria." *Health Education* 102, no. 5 (2002): 230–238.

Fayokun, Kayode Olatunbosun. "Legality of Child Marriage in Nigeria and Inhibitions against Realisation of Education Rights," *US-China L. Rev.* 12 (2015): 812.

Federal Government of Nigeria. "An Act to Provide and Protect the Right of the Nigerian Child and Other Related Matters, 2003," *UNICEF*, 2003. Available online: http://www.unicef.org/nigeria/ng_publications_Childs_Right_Act_2003.pdf.

Fitzgibbon, Kathleen. "Modern-Day Slavery? The Scope of Trafficking in Persons in Africa." *African Security Studies* 12, no. 1 (2003): 81–89.

Heinrich, Kelly Hyland. "Ten Years after the Palermo Protocol: Where Are Protections for Human Trafficking Victims?" *Human Rights Brief* 18 (2010): 2–5.

Hoechner, Hannah. "Striving for Knowledge and Dignity: How Qur'anic Students in Kano, Nigeria, Learn to Live with Rejection and Educational Disadvantage." *The European Journal of Development Research* 23, no. 5 (2011): 712–728.

Huntley, Svetlana. "The Phenomenon of Baby Factory in Nigeria as a New Trend of Human Trafficking," October 2013. Available online: http://www.internationalcrimesdatabase.org/upload/documents/20131030T045906-ICD%20Brief%203%20-%20Huntley.pdf.

Hyland, Kelly E. "The Impact of the Protocol to Prevent, Suppress and Punish Trafficking in Persons, Especially Women and Children." *Human Rights Brief* 8, no. 2 (2001): 12.

Igbanoi, Jude. "Maimuma the Child Bride in Katsina Finally Released from Death Row," *PressReader*, September 13, 2016. Available online: https://www.pressreader.com/nigeria/thisday/20160913/281981787045628.

Igbinovia, Patrick Edobor. "Begging in Nigeria." *International Journal of Offender Therapy and Comparative Criminology* 35, no. 1 (March 1, 1991): 21–33. Available online: https://doi.org/10.1177/0306624X9103500103.

Ikọtun, Reuben, and Temitọpẹ Balogun. "Alms-Begging and Human Rights in Yorùbá Land." *Ihafa: A Journal of African Studies* 8, no. 1 (2016): 176–198.

Jedy-Agba, Elima E., Emmanuel A. Oga, Michael Odutola, Yusuf M. Abdullahi, Abiodun Popoola, Peter Achara, Enoch Afolayan, et al. "Developing National Cancer Registration in Developing Countries—Case Study of the Nigerian National System of Cancer Registries," *Epidemiology*, July 30, 2015: 186. Available online: https://doi.org/10.3389/fpubh.2015.00186.

Makinde, Olusesan Ayodeji. "Infant Trafficking and Baby Factories: A New Tale of Child Abuse in Nigeria." *Child Abuse Review* 25, no. 6 (November 1, 2016): 433–443. Available online: https://doi.org/10.1002/car.2420.

Makinde, Olusesan Ayodeji, Olufunmbi Olukemi Makinde, Olalekan Olaleye, Brandon Brown, and Clifford O. Odimegwu. "Baby Factories Taint Surrogacy in Nigeria." *Reproductive Biomedicine Online* 32, no. 1 (2016): 6–8.

Makinde, Clifford Obby Odimegwu, and Stella O. Babalola. "Reasons for Infertile Couples Not to Patronize Baby Factories." *Health & Social Work* 42, no. 1 (February 1, 2017): 57–59. Available online: https://doi.org/10.1093/hsw/hlw054.

Makinde, Olalekan Olaleye, Olufunmbi Olukemi Makinde, Svetlana S. Huntley, and Brandon Brown. "Baby Factories in Nigeria: Starting the Discussion toward a National Prevention Policy." *Trauma, Violence & Abuse* 18, no. 1 (January 2017): 98–105. Available online: https://doi.org/10.1177/1524838015591588.

Makinde, Cheluchi Onyemelukwe, Abimbola Onigbanjo-Williams, Kolawole Azeez Oyediran, and Clifford Obby Odimegwu. "Rejection of the Gender and Equal

Opportunities Bill in Nigeria: A Setback for Sustainable Development Goal Five." *Gender in Management: An International Journal* 32, no. 3 (May 2, 2017): 234–240. Available online: https://doi.org/10.1108/GM-02-2017-0023.

Mancuso, Marina. "Not All Madams Have a Central Role: Analysis of a Nigerian Sex Trafficking Network." *Trends in Organized Crime* 17, no. 1–2 (2014): 66–88.

Martin, Michel. "In Dapchi, Mourning after Mass Kidnapping of Schoolgirls: NPR," *National Public Radio*, March 11, 2018. Available online: https://www.npr.org/templates/transcript/transcript.php?storyId=592766452.

Murray, Christopher J. L., Theo Vos, Rafael Lozano, Mohsen Naghavi, Abraham D. Flaxman, Catherine Michaud, Majid Ezzati, et al. "Disability-Adjusted Life Years (DALYs) for 291 Diseases and Injuries in 21 Regions, 1990–2010: A Systematic Analysis for the Global Burden of Disease Study 2010." *The Lancet* 380, no. 9859 (December 2012): 2197–2223. Available online: https://doi.org/10.1016/S0140-6736(12)61689-4.

National Population Commission, Federal Republic of Nigeria, and ICF International, Maryland USA. *Nigeria Demographic and Health Survey 2013*. Abuja, Nigeria & Rockville, Maryland, USA: National Population Commission, June 2014.

Obokata, Tom. "Trafficking of Human Beings as a Crime against Humanity: Some Implications for the International Legal System." *International and Comparative Law Quarterly* 54, no. 2 (2005): 445–458.

Ogunkan, David V., and Olufemi A. Fawole. "Incidence and Socio-Economic Dimensions of Begging in Nigerian Cities: The Case of Ogbomoso." *International NGO Journal* 4, no. 12 (2009): 498–503.

Okafor, U. H. "Transplant Tourism among Kidney Transplant Patients in Eastern Nigeria." *BMC Nephrology* 18 (July 5, 2017): 215. Available online: https://doi.org/10.1186/s12882-017-0635-1.

Okonofua, F. E., S. M. Ogbomwan, A. N. Alutu, Okop Kufre, and Aghahowa Eghosa. "Knowledge, Attitudes and Experiences of Sex Trafficking by Young Women in Benin City, South-South Nigeria." *Social Science & Medicine* 59, no. 6 (2004): 1315–1327.

Ollus, Natalia. "The United Nations Protocol to Prevent, Suppress and Punish Trafficking in Persons, Especially Women and Children: A Tool for Criminal Justice Personnel." *Resource Material Series*, no. 62 (2002). Available online: http://www.ungift.org/docs/ungift/pdf/knowledge/unafei_analysis.pdf.

Olowoopejo, Monsuru. "Lagos Seals Three Baby Factory, Rescues 162 Abandon Babies," *Vanguard News*, April 25, 2018. Available online: https://www.vanguardngr.com/2018/04/lagos-seals-three-baby-factory-rescues-162-abandon-babies/.

Omorodion, Francisca Isi. "Vulnerability of Nigerian Secondary School to Human Sex Trafficking in Nigeria." *African Journal of Reproductive Health* 13, no. 2 (2009): 33–48.

Onuoha, Browne. "The State Human Trafficking and Human Rights Issues in Africa." *Contemporary Justice Review* 14, no. 2 (June 1, 2011): 149–166. Available online: https://doi.org/10.1080/10282580.2011.565973.

Onuoha, Freedom C. "The Evolving Menace of Baby Factories and Trafficking in Nigeria." *African Security Review* 23, no. 4 (September 4, 2014): 405–411. Available online: https://doi.org/10.1080/10246029.2014.941886.

Osumah, Oarhe. "Boko Haram Insurgency in Northern Nigeria and the Vicious Cycle of Internal Insecurity." *Small Wars & Insurgencies* 24, no. 3 (July 1, 2013): 536–560. Available online: https://doi.org/10.1080/09592318.2013.802605.

Osumah, Oarhe, and Iro Aghedo. "Who Wants to Be a Millionaire? Nigerian Youths and the Commodification of Kidnapping." *Review of African Political Economy* 38,

no. 128 (June 1, 2011): 277–287. Available online: https://doi.org/10.1080/03056244
.2011.582769.

Para-Mallam, Funmi Josephine. "Gender Equality in Nigeria." In *Gender Equality in a Global Perspective, First*, 23–53. *Routledge Advances in Management and Business Studies* 68. New York: Routledge, 2017. Available online: https://www.routledge.com/Gender-Equality-in-a-Global-Perspective/Ortenblad-Marling-Vasiljevic/p/book/9781138193246.

Peters, Michael A. "'Western Education Is Sinful': Boko Haram and the Abduction of Chibok Schoolgirls." *Policy Futures in Education* 12, no. 2 (2014). Available online: https://doi.org/dx.doi.org/10.2304/pfie.2014.12.2.186.

Premium Times. "Nigerian Civic Groups Reject Gender Equality Bill," April 3, 2016. Available online: http://www.premiumtimesng.com/news/top-news/201201-nigerian-civic-groups-reject-gender-equality-bill.html.

Rahman, Sophia. "Child Bride Poisons Husband," *The Mirror*, December 23, 2014. Available online: https://www.mirror.co.uk/news/world-news/child-bride-aged-14-killed-4867292.

Rao, Smriti, and Christina Presenti. "Understanding Human Trafficking Origin: A Cross-Country Empirical Analysis." *Feminist Economics* 18, no. 2 (April 1, 2012): 231–263. Available online: https://doi.org/10.1080/13545701.2012.680978.

Sahara Reporters. "Nigeria Army Busts Baby Factory in Enugu," August 26, 2015. Available online: http://saharareporters.com/2015/08/26/nigeria-army-busts-baby-factory-enugu.

Silverman, Jay G., Michele R. Decker, Jhumka Gupta, Ayonija Maheshwari, Brian M. Willis, and Anita Raj. "HIV Prevalence and Predictors of Infection in Sex-Trafficked Nepalese Girls and Women." *Jama* 298, no. 5 (2007): 536–542.

Todres, Jonathan. "Taking Prevention Seriously: Developing a Comprehensive Response to Child Trafficking and Sexual Exploitation." *Vanderbilt Journal of Transnational Law* 43, no. 1 (January 2010). Available online: http://heinonlinebackup.com/hol-cgi-bin/get_pdf.cgi?handle=hein.journals/vantl43&section=4.

Togunde, Dimeji, and Arielle Carter. "Socioeconomic Causes of Child Labor in Urban Nigeria." *Journal of Children and Poverty* 12, no. 1 (March 1, 2006): 73–89. Available online: https://doi.org/10.1080/10796120500502201.

Togunde, Dimeji, and Arielle Carter. "In Their Own Words: Consequences of Child Labor in Urban Nigeria." *Journal of Social Sciences* 16, no. 2 (2008): 173–181.

"Trafficking in Persons (Prohibition) Law Enforcement and Administration Act 2003." Nigeria, 2003.

UN General Assembly. "United Nations Convention against Transnational Organized Crime and the Protocols Thereto." New York, 2000.

UN General Assembly. "Protocol to Prevent, Suppress and Punish Trafficking in Persons, Especially Women and Children, Supplementing the United Nations Convention against Transnational Organized Crime," 2002.

UNESCO. "Human Trafficking in Nigeria: Root Causes and Recommendations," *Policy Paper Series*. Paris: UNESCO, 2006. Available online: http://unesdoc.unesco.org/images/0014/001478/147844e.pdf.

UNICEF. "Convention on the Rights of the Child," *Cornell University ILR School*, November 1989. Available online: http://digitalcommons.ilr.cornell.edu/cgi/viewcontent.cgi?article=1007&context=child.

UNICEF Nigeria. "Child Labour," 2007. Available online: https://www.unicef.org/children_1935.html.

UNICEF. "25 Years of the Convention on the Rights of the Child: Is the World a Better Place for Children?," November 2014. Available online: http://www.unicef.org/publications/index_76027.html.
UNODC. "Transnational Trafficking and Rule of Law in West Africa: A Threat Assessment." Vienna, Austria, 2009.
UNODC. "Human Trafficking," *Transnational Organized Crime*, n.d. Available online: http://www.unodc.org/toc/en/crimes/human-trafficking.html (accessed 13/03/2015).
UNODC. *Global Report on Trafficking in Persons 2016*. Vienna, Austria: United Nations, December 2016.
US Department of State. "Trafficking in Persons Report 2017." USA, 2017. Available online: https://www.state.gov/j/tip/rls/tiprpt/2017/.
The World Bank. "Nigeria Data," 2016. Available online: http://data.worldbank.org/country/nigeria.

Chapter 6

Abiodun, Eromosele. "Nigeria Strategic to Tackling Maritime Crimes in GoG, Says NIMASA," *This Day*, February 2, 2018. Available online: https://www.thisdaylive.com/index.php/2018/02/02/nigeria-strategic-to-tackling-maritime-crimes-in-gog-says-nimasa/.
Adamu, Ladi S. "The Media's Role in Quelling Violent Conflict Involving Youths as Foot Soldiers: A Content Analysis of News Report on Boko Haram Suicide Bombers and Civilian Joint Task Force-CJTF." *International Journal of Innovative Research & Development* 5, no. 9 (2016): 257–266.
Adongoi, Toakodi, Aniekan Brown, and Lawrence Udensi. "The Impact of Sea Robbery on Artisanal Fishing in Rural Settlements in Niger Delta Region of Nigeria." *International Journal of Innovation and Sustainability* 1 (2017): 32–43.
Agbinibo, Murdoch. "Happy Doomed Year Nigeria; Get Ready for Operation Bringing Down FPSO," *Niger Delta Avengers*, January 17, 2018. Available online: http://www.nigerdeltaavengers.org/2018/01/happy-doomed-year-nigeria-get-ready-for.html.
Aghedo, Iro. "Sowing Peace, Reaping Violence: Understanding the Resurgence of Kidnapping in Post-Amnesty Niger Delta, Nigeria." *Insight on Africa* 7, no. 2 (2015): 137–153.
Amaize, Emma. "Underground for 2 Yrs, Tompolo Still Looms Large in Ijaw Nation," *Vanguard*, December 16, 2017. Available online: https://www.vanguardngr.com/2017/12/underground-2-yrs-tompolo-still-looms-large-ijaw-nation/.
Anyimadu, Adjoa. *Maritime Security in the Gulf of Guinea: Lessons Learned from the Indian Ocean*. London: Chatham House, 2013.
Bamidele, Oluwaseun. "Civilian Joint Task Force (CJTF)—A Community Security Option: A Comprehensive and Proactive Approach of Reducing Terrorism." *Journal for Deradicalization*, no. 7 (Summer 2016): 124–144.
Barua, Akrur, and Anshu Mittal. "Shipping: Sailing in Troubled Waters," *Deloitte Insights*, February 14, 2017. Available online: https://www2.deloitte.com/insights/us/en/economy/global-economic-outlook/2017/shipping-industry-crisis.html.
Ben-Ari, Nirit. "Piracy in West Africa," *Africa Renewal*, 2013. Available online: http://www.un.org/africarenewal/magazine/december-2013/piracy-west-africa.

Brume-Eruagbere, Omovigho Cynthia. "Maritime Law Enforcement in Nigeria: The Challenges of Combating Piracy and Armed Robbery at Sea," MSc diss., World Maritime University. Malmö, 2017.

Busari, Stephanie. "Nigerian Navy Recovers Hijacked Oil Tanker after Gun Battle," *CNN*, February 23, 2016. Available online: https://edition.cnn.com/2016/02/23/africa/nigeria-navy-rescues-oil-tanker/index.html.

Cropley, Ed, and David Lewis. "Nigeria Drafts in Foreign Mercenaries to Take on Boko Haram," *Reuters*, March 12, 2015. Available online: https://uk.reuters.com/article/uk-nigeria-violence-mercenaries/nigeria-drafts-in-foreign-mercenaries-to-take-on-boko-haram-idUKKBN0M80VT20150312.

Dauda, Oluwakemi. "NIMASA Raises the Alarm over 'False Pirates' Reports,'" *The Nation*, December 2, 2014. Available online: http://thenationonlineng.net/nimasa-raises-alarm-false-pirates-reports/.

Ejoh, Ediri. "Nigeria Navy Seeks Collaboration to Fight Piracy," *Vanguard*, December 27, 2012. Available online: https://www.vanguardngr.com/2012/12/nigeria-navy-seeks-collaboration-to-fight-piracy.

Forster, Bruce. "Modern Maritime Piracy: An Overview of Somali Piracy, Gulf of Guinea Piracy and South East Asian Piracy." *British Journal of Economics, Management & Trade* 4, no. 8 (January 2014): 1251–1272.

Freeman, Colin. "'South African Mercenaries' Secret War on Boko Haram," *The Telegraph*, 10 May 2015. Available online: https://www.telegraph.co.uk/news/worldnews/africaandindianocean/nigeria/11596210/South-African-mercenaries-secret-war-on-Boko-Haram.html.

Gibbs, Margot, Paul Holden, and Susan Hawley. "Dereliction of Duty: How Weak Arms Export Licence Controls in the UK Facilitated Corruption and Exacerbated Instability in the Niger Delta," *Corruption Watch*, May 2017. Available online: https://docs.wixstatic.com/ugd/54261c_3f990fe3175c48c5b90ed65a41192d59.pdf.

Harper, Mary. "Danger Zone: Chasing West Africa's Pirates," *BBC News*, November 13, 2014. Available online: http://www.bbc.co.uk/news/world-africa-30024009.

Hoffmann, Leena Koni, and Paul Melly. *Nigeria's Booming Borders: The Drivers and Consequences of Unrecorded Trade*. London: Chatham House, 2015.

Human Rights Watch. *The Price of Oil: Corporate Responsibility and Human Rights Violations in Nigeria's Oil Producing Communities*. New York: Human Rights Watch, 1999.

IMB. "Maritime Piracy and Armed Robbery Reaches 22-Year Low," *ICC Commercial Crime Services*, January 10, 2018. Available online: https://www.icc-ccs.org/index.php/1240-maritime-piracy-and-armed-robbery-reaches-22-year-low-says-imb-report.

IMB. "Pirate Attacks Worsen in Gulf of Guinea," *ICC Commercial Crime Se*rvices, April 10, 2018. Available online: https://www.icc-ccs.org/index.php/1244-pirate-attacks-worsen-in-gulf-of-guinea.

International Maritime Organization. *Circular 367: Piracy and Armed Robbery (incl. Add. 1 and Add. 2)*. London: IMO, 1983.

Matfess, Hilary. "Nigeria Wakes Up to Its Growing Vigilante Problem," *The New Humanitarian*, May 9, 2017. Available online: https://www.irinnews.org/analysis/2017/05/09/nigeria-wakes-its-growing-vigilante-problem.

Mungai, Christine. "Another Twist from the Oil Price Crash—Pirates Off West Africa Don't Want to Steal It, and They Are More Violent than Somalia's," *Mail & Guardian Africa*, 2016. Available online: http://mgafrica.com/article/2016-05-03-trends-in-piracy-2015-report.

Nincic, Donna. "Maritime Piracy in Africa: The Humanitarian Dimension." *African Security Review* 18, no. 3 (2009): 2–16.

Oceans beyond Piracy. *The State of Maritime Piracy Report 2014*. Denver, CO: One Earth Future Foundation, 2015.

Oceans beyond Piracy. *The State of Maritime Piracy Report 2016*. Denver, CO: One Earth Future Foundation, 2016. Available online: http://oceansbeyondpiracy.org/reports/sop/east-africa.

Ogbuokiri, Paul. "NIMASA's Satellite Surveillance System Down in 2017-Sources," *New Telegraph*, 2018. Available online: https://newtelegraphonline.com/2018/01/nimasas-satellite-surveillance-system-2017-sources/.

Olawoyin, Oladeinde. "Buhari Pledges to Rid Nigerian Waters of Pirates," *Premium Times*, April 25, 2017. Available online: https://www.premiumtimesng.com/news/more-news/229534-%E2%80%8Ebuhari-pledges-rid-nigerian-waters-pirates.html.

Onuoha, Freedom. "Piracy and Maritime Security in the Gulf of Guinea: Trends, Concerns, and Propositions." *The Journal of Middle East and Africa* 4, no. 3 (2013): 267–293.

Onuoha, Freedom. *The Resurgence of Militancy in Nigeria's Oil-Rich Niger Delta and the Dangers of Militarisation*. Doha: Al Jazeera Centre for Studies, 2016.

Otto, Lisa. "Maritime Crime in Nigeria and Waters beyond Analysing the Period 2009 to 2013." *Africa Insight* 45, no. 1 (2015): 15–29.

Sahara Reporters. "Jonathan Gives 'Tompolo' Contract to Supply 20 Marine Patrol Vessels to Navy," July 24, 2012. Available online: http://saharareporters.com/2012/07/24/jonathan-gives-'tompolo'-contract-supply-20-marine-patrol-vessels-navy.

Siebels, Dirk. "International Standards for the Private Security Industry." *The RUSI Journal* 159, no. 5 (2014): 76–83.

Starr, Stephen. "Maritime Piracy on the Rise in West Africa." *CTC Sentinel* 7, no. 4 (2014): 23–25.

Steffen, Dirk. "Troubled Waters? The Use of the Nigerian Navy and Police in Private Maritime Security Roles," *CIMSEC*, July 1, 2014. Available online: http://cimsec.org/troubled-waters-use-nigerian-navy-police-private-maritime-security-roles/11918.

Steffen, Dirk. "Essay: Quantifying Piracy Trends in the Gulf of Guinea—Who's Right and Who's Wrong?," *USNI News*, 19 June 2015.

Tattersall, Nick. "Nigeria Attack Stops Shell's Bonga Offshore Oil," *Reuters*, June 20, 2008. Available online: https://uk.reuters.com/article/uk-nigeria-shell-attack/nigeria-attack-stops-shells-bonga-offshore-oil-idUKL1961289220080620.

Thompson, Andrew. "West African Pirates Taking Hostages for Ransom as Oil Prices Tank," *ABC News*, February 19, 2018. Available online: http://www.abc.net.au/news/2018-02-20/struggling-west-african-pirates-taking-hostages-to-survive/9462082.

Uche, Usim. "Nigeria: Sea Pirates Killing Nigeria's Fishing Industry. Fishery Committee for the West Central Gulf of Guinea," *FCWC*, February 3, 2016. Available online: https://fcwc-fish.org/publications/news-from-the-region/780-nigeria-sea-pirates-killing-nigeria's-fishing-industry.

Una, Emma. "Navy Assures on Sustained Fight against Piracy, Others," *Vanguard*, June 3, 2014. Available online: https://www.vanguardngr.com/2014/06/navy-assures-sustained-fight-piracy-others/.

United Nations Economic Commission for Africa. *Africa's Blue Economy: A Policy Handbook*. Addis Ababa: Economic Commission for Africa, 2016.

Visal, John. "Shell Oil Paid Nigerian Military to Put Down Protests, Court Documents Show," *The Guardian*, October 3, 2011. Available online: https://www.theguardian.com/world/2011/oct/03/shell-oil-paid-nigerian-military.

Wackett, Mike. "NYK Quits as Asia-West Africa Trade Goes 'from Bad to Worse' with Rates and Volumes Falling," *The Loadstar*, December 8, 2015. Available online: https://theloadstar.co.uk/nyk-quits-asia-west-africa-trade-goes-bad-worse-rates-volumes-plunging/.

Chapter 7

Adetayo, Olalekan, and Theophilus Onejeghen. "Tompolo, Militants Clash over Avengers' Threats to Attack Oil Facilities," *Punch*, November 7, 2017. Available online: http://punchng.com/tompolo-militants-clash-over-avengers-threats-to-attack-oil-facilities/.

Adeyeri, Olusegun. "Nigerian State and the Management of Oil Minority Conflicts in the Niger Delta: A Retrospective View." *African Journal of Political Science and International Relations* 6, no. 5 (2012): 97–103.

Aduloju, Ayodeji, and Omowunmi Pratt. "Oil and Adolescents in the Contemporary Niger Delta, Nigeria." *Journal of Child and Adolescent Behaviour*, no. 3 (2015): 3.

Akinosho, Tosin. "The North Does Not Control Nigerials Oli Blocs," *Premium Times*, March 7, 2013. Available online: https://www.premiumtimesng.com/opinion/123588-the-north-does-not-control-nigerias-oil-blocks-by-toyin-akinosho.html.

Akukwe, Obinna. "20 Owners of Richest Oil Blocks in Nigeria—Their Names Will Shock You," *Faces International Magazine*, 2015. Available online: http://facesinternationalmagazine.org.ng/?p=2533.

Banjo, Temi. "Revealed: Check Out the Full List of Owners of Nigerian Oil Blocks," *Nigerian Monitor*, 2015. Available online: http://www.nigerianmonitor.com/revealed-check-out-the-full-list-of-owners-of-nigerian-oil-blocks/.

Bassey, Ben. "The Niger Delta Avengers: Heroes or Terrorists?," *Pulse News*, June 5, 2016. Available online: http://www.pulse.ng/news/local/the-niger-delta-avengers-heroes-or-terrorists-id5114167.html.

Bassey, Celestine O. "Oil and Conflict in the Niger Delta: A Reflection on the Politics of State Responses to Armed Militancy in Nigeria." *Mediterranean Journal of Social Sciences* 3, no. 11 (2012): 77–90.

Collier, Paul. *The Bottom Billion*. Oxford: Oxford University Press, 2007.

Ejibunu, Hassan Tai. "Nigeria's Niger Delta Crisis: Root Causes of Peacelessness." *European University Centre for Peace Studies (EPU) Research Papers*, no. 07/07 (2007).

Frynas, Jędrzej George. "Corporate and State Responses to Anti-Oil Protests in the Niger Delta." *African Affairs* 100 (2001): 27–54.

Human Rights Watch. "Protest and Repression in the Niger Delta," 1999. Available online: https://www.hrw.org/reports/1999/nigeria/Nigew991-08.htm.

Ibaba, S. Ibaba. "Violent Conflicts and Sustainable Development in Bayelsa State." *Review of Political Economy* 36, no. 122 (2009): 555–573.

Ibaba, S. Ibaba, and Augustine Ikelegbe. "Militias, Pirates and Oil in the Niger Delta." In *Militias, Rebels and Islamist Militants: Human Insecurity and State Crises in Africa*, edited by Wafula Okumu and Augustine Ikelegbe, 219–254. Pretoria, South Africa: Institute for Security Studies, 2010.

Idowu, Sylvester, and Emmanuel Addeh. "Again, Soldiers Invade Tompolo's Community, in Search of Militants," *This Day*, November 13, 2016. Available online: https://www.thisdaylive.com/index.php/2016/11/13/again-soldiers-invade-tompolos-community-in-search-of-militants/.

Ikeke, Nkem. "List of 17 Oil Blocs Owned by Atiku, Danjuma and Other Northerners and South-Westerners," *Naij*, 2016. Available online: https://www.naija.ng/827931-list-17-oil-blocs-owned-by-atiku-danjuma-northerners-south-westerners.html#827931.

Interview with Kurobo, Don Jacob, Ex-militant MEND. In Yenagoa, Bayelsa State, Nigeria on October 15, 2017.

Interview with Jonathan, Goodluck, former president of Nigeria. February 8 2017, at Baybridge Road, Yenagoa, Bayelsa State, Nigeria.

Kpae, Gbenemene. "Cultism and Violent Crime: An Appraisal of the Security Challenges in the Niger Delta of Nigeria." *International Research Journal of Social Sciences* 5, no. 12 (December 2016): 37–41.

The News. "Niger Delta Avengers 10 Point Demand for Peace," May 10, 2016. Available online: http://thenewsnigeria.com.ng/2016/05/niger-delta-avengers-10-point-demand-for-peace/.

The News. "Niger Delta Avengers: Why We Are Crippling the Oil Sector," May 27, 2016. Available online: http://thenewsnigeria.com.ng/2016/05/niger-delta-avengers-why-we-are-crippling-oil-sector/.

Nwogwugwu, Ngozi, et al. "Militancy and Insecurity in the Niger Delta: Impact on the Inflow of Foreign Direct Investment to Nigeria." *Kuwait Chapter of Arabian Journal of Business and Management Review* 2, no. 1 (2012): 23–37.

Odunsi, Wale. "Niger Delta Warlords List Demands, Vow to Declare Republic September 1," July 17, 2017. Available online: http://dailypost.ng/2017/07/17/niger-delta-warlords-list-demands-vow-declare-republic-september-1/.

Oluwaniyi, Oluwatoyin. "Women's Protests in the Niger Delta Region." In *Oil and Insurgency in the Niger Delta: Managing the Complex Politics of Petro-Violence*, edited by Cyril Obi and Siri Aas Rustad, 150–163. New York: Zed Books, 2011.

Oriola, Temitope. *Criminal Resistance? The Politics of Kidnapping Oil Workers*. Surrey, England: Ashgate, 2013.

Powell, Jim. "Militant Nonviolence: A Biography of Martin Luther King, Jr.," *Libertarianism*, July 4, 2000. Available online: https://www.libertarianism.org/publications/essays/militant-nonviolence-biography-martin-luther-king-jr.

Sayne, Aaron. "What's Next for Security in the Niger Delta? United States Institute for Peace, Special Report 333," May 2013: 4. Available online: www.usip.org.

Simkins, Chris. "Non-Violence Was Key to Civil Rights Movement," *VOA News*, January 20, 2014. Available online: https://www.voanews.com/a/nonviolencekey-to-civil-rights-movement/1737280.html.

This Day. "Niger Delta: Osibanjo and the Unresolved Etche Question," February 26, 2017. Available online: https://www.thisdaylive.com/index.php/2017/02/26/niger-delta-osinbajo-and-the-unresolved-etche-question/.

Vanguard. "Tompolo: Niger-Delta Students Fume, Ask FG to Drop Charges against Ex-Militant," December 29, 2017. Available online: https://www.vanguardngr.com/2017/12/tompolo-niger-delta-students-fume-ask-fg-drop-charges-ex-militant/.

Watts, Michael. "Petro-Insurgency or Criminal Syndicate? Conflict and Violence in the Niger Delta." *Review of African Political Economy* 34, no. 114 (2008): 637–660.

Wellington, Bestman. "Nigeria's Cults and Their Role in Niger Delta Insurgency." *Terrorism Monitor* 5, no. 3 (July 6, 2007). Available online: https://jamestown.org/program/nigerias-cults-and-their-role-in-the-niger-delta-insurgency/.

Chapter 8

Alemika, Etanibi. "Crime and Public Safety in Nigeria." Abuja: CLEEN Foundation, 2014.

Alusala, Nelson. "Lessons from Small Arms and Weapons Control Initiatives in Africa." Bonn International Centre for Conversion (BICC) Working Paper, 2016.

Bagu, Chom, and Katie Smith. *Past Is Prologue: Criminality and Reprisal Attacks in Nigeria's Middle Belt*. Washington, DC: Search for Common Ground, 2017.

Ibrahim, Jibrin. "Pastoralist Transhumance and Rural Banditry," *Premium Times*, 2014. Available online: https://www.premiumtimesng.com/opinion/157305-pastoralist-transhumance-rural-banditry-jibrin-ibrahim.html.

International Crisis Group. "Herders against Farmers: Nigeria's Expanding Deadly Conflict." Report no. 252, September 2017.

Kwaja, Chris. "Blood, Cattle, and Cash: Cattle Rustling and Nigeria's Bourgeoning Underground Economy." *West African Insight* 4, no. 3 (2014): 1–4.

Kwaja, Chris. "Towards Re-Energising the Nigerian Military and Other Security Agencies to Meet Urgent National Demand." Presentation at the House of Representatives Hearing of the House Committee on Army, House of Representatives, National Assembly, Abuja, Nigeria, November 22, 2017.

Kwaja, Chris. "Understanding Farmer-Herder Relations: A Driver of Conflict?" Presentation at the ECOWAS Secretariat, 2018.

Kwaja, Chris, and Abdu Hussaini. "Rural Banditry and Social Conflicts in Plateau State." In *Rural Banditry and Conflicts in Northern Nigeria*, edited by Kuna Mohammed and Ibrahim Jibrin, 319–353. Abuja: Centre for Democracy and Development, 2015.

Kwaja, Chris, and Adelehin Bukola. "Responses to Conflicts between Farmers and Herders in the Middle Belt Region of Nigeria: Mapping Past Efforts and Opportunities for Violence Prevention." Search for Common Ground (SFCG), Policy Brief, January 2018.

Lamptey, Afua. "Rethinking Border Management Strategies in West Africa: Experiences from the Sahel," Kofi Annan International Peacekeeping Training Centre, Policy Brief 12, 2013.

Mohammed, Kyari, and Alimba Chinyere. *Social Impact of Rural Banditry, in Rural Banditry and Conflicts in Northern Nigeria*, edited by Kuna Mohammed and Ibrahim Jibrin. Abuja: Centre for Democracy and Development, 2015.

Olabode, Abiodun, and L. T. Ajibade. "Environment Induced Conflict and Sustainable Development: A Case of Fulani-farmers' Conflict in Oke-Ero LGAs, Kwara State, Nigeria." *Journal of Sustainable Development in Africa* 12, no. 5 (2010): 259–2743.

Olaniyan, A., and A. Yahaya. "Cows, Bandits and Violent Conflicts: Understanding Cattle Rustling in Northern Nigeria." *Africa Spectrum* 51, no. 3 (2016): 93–105.

Onuoha, Freedom. "Porous Borders and Boko Haram's Arms Smuggling Operation in Nigeria," Aljazeera Centre for Studies, Report, September 2013.

Rexson, Eval. "Between Manslaughter and Cattle Rustling: The Tale of Fulani Herdsmen and Rural Banditry in Nigeria," *Calabarre Reporters*, January 13, 2018. Available online: https://www.calabarreporters.com/31436/manslaugtering-cattle-rustling.

Sow, Mariama. "Figure of the Week: The Shrinking Lake Chad, Brooking," *Brookings*, 2017. Available online: https://www.brookings.edu/blog/africa-in-focus/2017/02/09/figure-of-the-week-the-shrinking-lake-chad/.

Chapter 9

Alshech, Eli. "The Doctrinal Crisis within the Salafi-Jihadi Ranks and the Emergence of Neo-Takfirism: A Historical and Doctrinal Analysis." *Islamic Law and Society*, no. 21 (2014): 419–452.

Amara, Ramzi Ben. "The Izala Movement in Nigeria: Its Split, Relationship to Sufis and Perceptions of Shari'a Re-Implementation," A dissertation submitted for the degree of Doctor of Philosophy at Bayreauth International Graduate School of African Studies, BIGSAS, University of Bayreuth, Germany. Diss, 2011.

Anonymous. "The Popular Discourses of Salafi Radicalism and Salafi Counter-Radicalism in Nigeria: A Case Study of Boko Haram." *Journal of Religion in Africa*, no. 42 (2012): 118–144.

Hansen, William. "Boko Haram: Religious Radicalism and Insurrection in Northern Nigeria." *Journal of Asian and African Studies* 52, no. 4 (2015): 1–19.

Human Rights Watch. "They Set the Classroom on Fire: Attacks on Education in Northeast Nigeria." New York, 2016.

International Crisis Group. *Curbing Violence in Nigeria 11: The Boko Haram Insurgency*, Africa Report, no. 216 (2014).

Kassim, Abdulbasit. "Defining and Understanding the Religious Philosophy of Jihadi-Salafism and the Ideology of Boko Haram." *Politics, Religion and Ideology* 16, no. 2–3 (2015): 173–200.

Kassim, Abdulbasit. "Boko Haram beyond the Headlines: Analyses of Africa's Enduring Insurgency." *Combating Terrorism Center (CTC)*, West Point. (May 2018): 1–32.

Lauziere, Henri. "The Construction of Salafiyya: Reconsidering Salafism from the Perspective of Conceptual History." *International Journal of Middle East Studies*, no. 42 (2010): 369–389.

Mustapha, Abdul Raufu. *Sects and Social Disorder: Muslim Identities and Conflict in Northern Nigeria*. London: James Curry, 2014.

Ostebo, Terje. "African Salafism: Religious Purity and the Politicization of Purity." *Islamic Africa*, no. 6 (2015): 1–29.

Perouse de Montclos, Marc-Antoine. *Boko Haram: Islamism, Politics, Security and the State in Nigeria*. Los Angeles, CA: African Academic Press, 2015.

Thurstan, Alexander. "Muslim Politics and Shari'a in Kano State, Northern Nigeria." *African Affairs* 114, no. 454 (2014): 28–51.

Thurstan, Alexander. "Nigerian Mainstream Salafis between Boko Haram and the State." *Islamic Africa*, no. 6 (2015): 109–134.

Thurstan, Alexander. *Salafism in Nigeria: Islam, Preaching and Politics*. Cambridge: Cambridge University Press, 2016.

Thurstan, Alexander. *The Disease Is Unbelief: Boko Haram's Religious and Political World View*. Washington, DC: The Brookings Institution Analysis Paper, 2016.

Thurstan, Alexander. *Boko Haram: The History of an African Jihadist Movement*. Princeton, NJ: Princeton University Press, 2018.

Umar, Muhammad Sani. "*Salafi Narratives against Violent Extremism in Nigeria*. Abuja, Nigeria: Center for Democracy and Development Monograph, 2015: 1–14.
Varin, Caroline. *Boko Haram and the War on Terror*. Santa Barbara, CA: Praeger, 2016.
Varin, Caroline, and Dauda Abubakar. *Violent Non-State Actors in Africa: Terrorists, Rebels and Warlords*. New York: Palgrave Macmillan, 2017.
Wagemakers, Joas. "A Purist Jihadi-Salafi: The Ideology of Abu Muhammad al Maqdisi." *British Journal of Middle Easter Studies* 36, no. 2 (2009): 281–297.
Wagemakers, Joas. "The Transformation of a Radical Concept: *al-wala wa-l-bara* in the Ideology of Abu Muhammad al Maqdisi." In *Global Salafism: Islam's New Religious Movement*, edited by Roel Meijer, 81–106. New York: Columbia University Press, 2011.
Wagemakers, Joas. "The Enduring Legacy of the Second Saudi State: Quietist and Radical Wahhabi Contestation of Al-Wala Wa-l-Bara." *International Journal of Middle East Studies*, no. 44 (2012): 93–110.
Wagemakers, Joas. *Salafism in Jordan: Political Islam in a Quietist Community*. Cambridge: Cambridge University Press, 2016.
Wiktorowicz, Quintan. "Anatomy of the Salafi Movement." *Studies in Conflict and Terrorism*, no. 29 (2006): 207–239.
Yusuf, Muhammad. *Hadhihi 'Aqidatuna wa-Manhaj Da'watina* (This Is Our Creed and the Method of Our Preaching). Maiduguri, 2008.

Chapter 10

Agbaje, Adigun A. "Party System and Civil Society." In *Dilemmas of Democracy in Nigeria*, edited by P. A. Beckett and C. Young. Rochester, NY, and Suffolk: University of Rochester Press, 1997.
Agbaje, Adigun A. "Nigeria: The Prospects for the Fourth Republic." In *Democratic Reforms in Africa: The Quality of Progress*, edited by E. Gyimah-Boadi. Boulder, 201–234. CO: Lynne Rienner, 2004.
Agozino, Biko, and Unyierie Idem. "Nigeria: Democratising a Militarised Civil Society." *Occassional Paper Series*, no. 5. London: Centre for Democracy and Development, 2001.
Ake, Claude. *The Feasibility of Democracy in Africa*. Dakar: CODESRIA, 2000.
Akinola, A. A. "Issues in Nigerian Democracy." *West Africa*, June 9–15, 2003.
Akoni, O. "Igbo Quit Notice: Pan Yoruba Group Calls for Oodua Republic," *Vanguard Nigerian Newspaper*, 2017. Electronic Article. Available online: https://www.vanguardngr.com/2017/06/igbo-quit-notice-pan-yoruba-group-calls-oodua-republic/ (accessed 22/03/2018).
Albin-Lackey, C., and B. Rawlence. "What's Next for Nigeria? The Whole Concept of African Democracy Is at Risk," *Guardian Unlimited*, 2007. Available online: http://commentisfree.guardian.co.uk/chris_albinlackey_and_ben_rawlence/2007/05/whats_next_for_nigeria.html (accessed 25/10/2016).
Beckett, P., and C. Young, eds. *Dilemmas of Democracy in Nigeria*. Rochester: University of Rochester Press, 1997.
Beckman, Björn. "Whose State? State and Capitalist Development in Nigeria," *Review of African Political Economy*, no. 23 (1982): 37–51.

Callaghy, T. "The State as Lame Leviathan: The Patrimonial Administrative State in Africa." In *The African State in Transition*, edited by Z. Ergas, 87–116. London: Macmillan, 1987.

Coser, Lewis A. *The Functions of Social Conflict*. Glencoe, IL: The Free Press, 1956.

Diamond, L. "Nigeria: Pluralism, Statism and the Struggle for Democracy." In *Democracy in Developing Countries, Volume 2: Africa*, edited by L. Diamond, J. J. Linz, and S. M. Lipset, 33–91. Boulder, CO: Lynne Rienner, 1988.

Ebiem, O. "The Many Separatist Movements in Nigeria," *Modern Ghana*, June 11, 2011. Available online: https://www.modernghana.com/news/333825/1/the-many-separatist-movements-in-nigeria.html (accessed 21/03/2018).

Egwu, Sam. "Contending Positions and Issues in Debating the Future of Federalism in Nigeria." In *Contentious Issues in the Review of the 1999 Constitution*, edited by O. Igbuzor and O. Bamidele. Lagos: Citizens Forum for Constitutional Reform, 2002.

Ezea, S. "Arewa Youths' Ultimatum and Frailty of Nigeria's Unity," *The Guardian Nigerian Newspaper*, June 13, 2017. Available online: https://guardian.ng/politics/arewa-youths-ultimatum-and-frailty-of-nigerias-unity/ (accessed 21/03/2018).

Forrest, Jashua B. "Asynchronic Comparisons: Weak States in Post-Colonial Africa and Medieval Europe." In *Comparing Nations: Concepts, Strategies and Substance*, edited by M. Dogan and A. Kazancigil, 260–297. Cambridge, MA: Blackwell, 1998.

Forrest, Tom. *Politics and Economic Development in Nigeria*. Boulder, CO: Westview Press, 1995.

FRN (Federal Republic of Nigeria). *The 1999 Constitution of the Federal Republic of Nigeria*. Abuja: Federal Republic of Nigeria, 2000.

Helman, Gerald B., and Steven R. Ratner. "Saving Failed States." *Foreign Policy* 89 (1993): 3–20.

Human Rights Watch. "The O'ODUA People's Congress: Fighting Violence with Violence in Nigeria." 15, no. 4a (2003).

Ibrahim, Jibrin. "Obstacles to Democratisation in Nigeria." In *Dilemmas of Democracy in Nigeria*, edited by P. A. Beckett and C. Young. Rochester: University of Rochester Press, 1997.

Igbuzor, O. "Introduction." In *Contentious Issues in the Review of the 1999 Constitution*, edited by O. Igbuzor and O. Bamidele, 9–15. Lagos: Citizens Forum for Constitutional Reform, 2002.

Ikelegbe, Augustine. "Civil Society, Oil and Conflict in the Niger Delta Region of Nigeria: Ramifications of Civil Society for a Regional Resource Struggle." *Journal of Modern African Studies* 39, no. 3 (2001): 1–24.

International Crisis Group. *Curbing Violence in Nigeria (II): The Boko Haram Insurgency*-Africa Report, no. 216 (April 2014).

International IDEA (Institute for Democracy and Electoral Assistance). *Democracy in Nigeria: Continuing Dialogue(s) for Nation-Building*. Stockholm: International IDEA, 2000.

Joseph, Richard. *Democracy and Prebendal Politics in Nigeria: The Rise and Fall of the Second Republic*. Cambridge: University Press, 1987.

Joseph, Richard. "Autocracy, Violence and Ethnomilitary Rule in Nigeria." In *State, Conflict and Democracy in Africa*, edited by R. Joseph, 359–376. Boulder, CO: Lynne Rienner, 1999.

Kasfir, Nelson. "Class, Political Domination and the African State." In *The African State in Transition*, edited by Z. Ergas, 45–60. London: Macmillan Press, 1987.

Kawonise, S. "Normative Impediments to Democratic Transition in Africa." In *Democratic Transition in Africa*, edited by B. Caron, A. Gboyega, and E. Osaghae. Ibadan, Nigeria: CREDU, 1992.

Luckham, R., and G. White. "Introduction: Democratising the South." In *Democratisation in the South: The Jagged Wave*, edited by R. Luckham and G. White. Manchester: Manchester University Press, 1996.

Mamdani, M. "The Social Basis of Constitutionalism in Africa." *Journal of Modern African Studies* 28, no. 3 (1990): 359-374.

Monga, C. *The Anthropology of Anger: Civil Society and Democracy in Africa*. Boulder, CO: Lynne Rienner, 1996.

Naanen, Ben. "Oil Producing Minorities and the Restructuring of Nigerian Federalism: The Case of Ogoni People." *Journal of Commonwealth and Comparative Politics* 33, no. 1 (1995): 46-78.

Obi, Cyril. "Nigeria: Democracy on Trial." *Occasional Electronic Paper 1*. Uppsala: Nordic Africa Institute, 2004.

Ojo, Oluwaseyi. "Military Language and Democratisation in Nigeria." In *Governance and Democratisation in West Africa*, edited by D. Olowu, A. Williams, and K. Soremekun. Dakar: CODESRIA, 1999.

Omeje, Kenneth. "The State, Conflict and Evolving Politics in the Niger Delta, Nigeria." *Review of African Political Economy*, no. 101 (2004): 425-440.

Premium Times Newspaper. "Igbo Quit Notice: Northern Elders Forum Backs Arewa Youth Group," June 9, 2017. Available online: https://www.premiumtimesng.com/news/top-news/233527-breaking-igbo-quit-notice-northern-elders-forum-backs-arewa-youth-group.html (accessed 21/03/2018).

Prezeworski, A. *Democracy and the Market: Political and Economic Reform in Europe and Latin America*. New York: Cambridge University Press, 1991.

Rimmer, D. "A Hollow Giant?" *West Africa*, June 23-29, 2003.

Sahara Reporters. "Northern Youths Declare War on Igbos in the North, Ask Them to 'Leave' within Three Months," June 6, 2017. Available online: http://saharareporters.com/2017/06/06/northern-youths-declare-war-igbos-north-ask-them-%E2%80%98leave%E2%80%99-within-three-months (accessed 22/03/2018).

Soyinka, Wale. *The Open Sore of a Continent: A Personal Account of the Nigerian Crisis*. Oxford: Oxford University Press, 1997.

Tar, U. A. "A Hollow Giant on Agile Feet? The Challenges of Democratic Consolidation in Nigeria." *African Renaissance* 4, no. 3-4 (2007): 29-40.

Tar, U. A. "Building Democracy in a Regressive State: The Travails of Electoral Politics in Nigeria." In *State-Society Relations in Nigeria: Democratic Consolidation, Conflicts and Reform*, edited by K. C. Omeje. London: Adonis & Abbey, 2007.

Tar, U. A. *The Politics of Neoliberal Democracy in Africa: State and Civil Society in Nigeria*, London/New York: I.B. Tauris, 2009.

Tar, U. A. "Terrorism, Violent Conflict and Democratic Governance in Nigeria" Being Lead Paper presented at the National Conference on *The Dynamics of Democratic Practice in Nigeria, 1999-2015* held at the Aminu Kano Centre for Democratic Research and Training, Mambayya House, Bayero University Kano, November 9-10, 2016.

Tar, U. A. "Managing Agitations and Protest in Nigeria: Appropriate Approaches," a Panel Discussion Paper presented at the National Policy Monitoring Dialogue (3rd Edition) Themed *National Unity, Integration and Devolution of Power/Restructuring* organized by the Savannah Centre for Diplomacy, Democracy and Development in Partnership with Ford Foundation, Nigeria, at Ladi Kwali Hall, Sheraton Hotel and Towers, Abuja, held on July 13–14, 2017.

Tar, U. A., and Alfred Zack-Williams. "Nigeria: Contested Elections and an Unstable Democracy." *Review of African Political Economy*, no. 113 (2007): 540–548.

Tar, U. A., and A. G. Shettima. "Engendered Democracy? The Struggle for Secularism and Its Implications for Politics and Democracy in Nigeria," Discussion Paper no. 49. Uppsala Sweden: Nordic Institute of African Studies, 2010.

Tar, U. A., and A. P. Innocent. "Elections and the Challenges of Democratic Consolidation in Nigeria: An Appraisal of 2011 General Elections." In *Democratic Governance and Political Participation in Nigeria, 1999–2013*, edited by F. Omotosho and M. I. Kehinde. Denver, CO: Spears Media Ltd., 2015.

Tar, U. A., and B. Bala. "Lake Chad Basin: Emerging Regional Architecture for Counter-Terrorism and Counter-Insurgency." In *Routlegde Handbook on Counter-Terrorism and Counter-Insurgency in Africa*, edited by U. A. Tar. London: Routledge, Forthcoming.

Udogu, E. Ike. *Nigeria and the Politics of Survival as a Nation State*. Lampeter: Edwin Mellen Press, 1997.

Ugorji, B. "Indigenous People of Biafra (IPOB): A Revitalized Social Movement in Nigeria," *International Center for Ethno-Religious, New York Mediation*, 2017. Available online: https://www.icermediation.org/publications/indigenous-people-of-biafra-ipob-a-revitalized-social-movement-in-nigeria/ (assessed 22/03/2018).

Wright, S. *Nigeria: Struggle for Stability and Status*. Boulder, CO: Westview, 1998.

Chapter 11

Adamu, A. "True Federalism in the 21st Century Nigeria." A Lecture Delivered at University of Jos Alumni Association, Lagos, 24 March 2005.

Adamu, A., and A. Ben. "Nigeria: Benue State under the Shadow of Herdsmen Terrorism (2014–2016)," *Africa Conflict and Security Analysis Network (ACSAN) (Formerly NCSAN—Nigeria Conflict and Security Analysis Network)*, Working Paper No. 5. Abuja, Nigeria, November 2017. Available online: https://www.researchgate.net/publication/322759537_Nigeria_Benue_State_under_the_shadow_of_herdsmen_terrorism_2014-2016_Africa_Conflict_and_Security_Analysis_Network_ACSAN_Formerly_NCSAN-Nigeria_Conflict_and_Security_Analysis_Network (accessed 27/05/2018).

Ali, A. D. "Security and Economic Development in Nigeria since 1960." Kuwait Chapter of *Arabian Journal of Business and Management Review* 2, no. 6 (2013): 1–7.

Alqali, A. "Nigeria: When Aid Goes Missing, PartnersGlobal and the Institute for War & Peace Reporting," Institute for War and Peace Reporting, September 5, 2016. Available online: https://iwpr.net/global-voices/nigeria-when-aid-goes-missing.

Buzan, B. "New Patterns of Global Security in the Twenty-First Century." *International Affairs* 67, no. 3 (July 1991): 431–451.

Chijioke, Ogbonna, ed. *Discourses on Peace and Conflict in Nigeria: An Interdisplinary Approach*. Lagos: Emaphine Reprographic Limited, 2017.

Dina, Y., J. Akintayo, and F. Ekundayo. *Guide to Nigerian Legal Information*. New York: New York University School of Law, 2015.

Ewetan, O. O., and E. Urhie. "Insecurity and Socio-Economic Development in Nigeria." *Journal of Sustainable Development Studies ISSN 2201-4268* 5, no. 1 (2014): 40–63.

Executive Committee of the High Commissioner's Programme, Update on UNHCR's Operations in Africa, Sixty-eighth session Geneva, September 19, 2017. Available online: http://www.unhcr.org/59c284577.pdf.

Ferris, E. "Internal Displacement in Africa: An Overview of Trends and Opportunities." Presentation at the Ethiopian Community Development Council Annual Conference: *African Refugee and Immigrant Lives: Conflict, Consequences, and Contributions*, May 2–4, 2012.

Human Rights Watch. "Country Summary Nigeria," January 2018. Available online: https://reliefweb.int/sites/reliefweb.int/files/resources/nigeria_2.pdf (accessed 27/05/2018).

Internal Displacement Monitoring Centre (IDMC). "Global Internal Displacement Database," 2017. Available online: http://www.internal-displacement.org/database/displacement-data.

International Organization for Migration. "IOM. Nigeria Situation Report," November 1–15, 2016. Available online: https://www.iom.int/sites/default/files/situation_reports/file/IOM-Nigeria-Situation-Report%20-1-15-Nov-2016.pdf.

Jatau, E. M. "National Security Policy in Nigeria," September 10, 2017. Available online: http://www.iacspsea.com/site/wp-content/uploads/2017/09/National-Security-in-Nigeria.pdf.

Kellenberger, J. "Root Causes and Prevention of Internal Displacement: The ICRC Perspective 23–10–2009 Statement." *Special Summit on Refugees, Returnees and IDPs in Africa*. Kampala Uganda, 23 October 2009.

Kemp, E. "Africa Report on Internal Displacement," *The Internal Displacement Monitoring Centre (IDMC)*, December 2016.

Mesjasz, C. "Security as an Analytical Concept." A Paper Presented at the *5th Pan-European Conference on International Relations* held at Hague, September 9–11, 2004: 5.

Mohammed, F. K. "The Causes and Consequences of Internal Displacement in Nigeria and Related Governance Challenges." Working Paper FG 8, Stiftung Wissenschaft und Politik (SWP), *German Institute for International and Security Affairs*, Berlin, April 2017.

Obialor, C. F., and H. U. Ozuzu. "Terrorism and Counter-Insurgency in Nigeria: The Boko Haram Experience (2006–2017)." *International Journal of Innovative Research in Social Sciences & Strategic Management Techniques | IJIRSSSMT* 4, no. 2 (September 2017): 126–137.

Ogu, M. I. "Small Arms Proliferation and Prevalent Conflicts in Africa." In *Issues in Conflict, Peace and Governance*, edited by D. O. Alao. Nigeria: Fodnab Ventures, 2015.

Ogu, M. I. "Farmer-Herder Conflict and Arms Proliferation in Nigeria." In E. Chijioke, *Discourses on Peace and Conflict in Nigeria: An Interdisciplinary Approach, Volume 1*. Lagos: Emaphine Reprographic Limited, 2017.

Shah, A. "Conflicts in Africa—Introduction, Global Issues Social, Political, Economic and Environmental Issues That Affects Us All," *Global Issues*, May 12, 2010. Available online: http://www.globalissues.org/article/84/conflicts-in-africa-introduction.

Sislin, J. "Arms as Influence: The Determinants of Successful Influence." *Journal of Conflict Resolution* 38, no. 4 (1999): 665–689.

The Punch. "Tears from Ngala: Nigeria's Largest IDPs Camp in the Throes of Hunger Diseases," December 3, 2017. Available online: http://punchng.com/tears-from-ngala-nigerias-largest-idps-camp-in-the-throes-of-hunger-diseases/.

The Vanguard. "IDPs Urge FG to Address Healthcare Challenges in Camps," May 7, 2018. Available online: https://www.vanguardngr.com/2018/05/idps-urge-fg-to-address-healthcare-challenges-in-camps/.

UNHCR. "Regional Update—Nigeria Situation 1–28 February 2018," February 28, 2018. Available online: https://data2.unhcr.org/en/documents/details/62606 (accessed 27/05/2018).

UNHCR. "Nigeria Situation 2017: Supplementary Appeal (January–December 2017)," 2017. Available online: http://reporting.unhcr.org/sites/default/files/Revised%20 2017%20SB%20Nigeria%20Situation_FINAL.pdf (assessed 30/01/2018).

WHO. "Operations in North Eastern Nigeria," November 2016. Available online: http://www.who.int/hac/crises/nga/appeals/nigeria-overview-november2016.pdf?ua=1 (accessed 29/01/2018).

Wyndham, J. "The Challenges of Internal Displacement in West Africa. Brookings Institution-University of Bern Project on Internal Displacement," *Brookings*, 2016. Available online: https://www.brookings.edu/wp-content/uploads/2016/06/0919westafrica_wyndham_en.pdf.

Chapter 12

Abuh, Adamu. "Representatives Pass VGN Bill," *The Guardian*, October 13, 2017. Available online: https://guardian.ng/news/representatives-pass-vgn-bill/ (accessed 17/02/2018).

Abrahamasen, Rita, and Michael C. Williams. *Security beyond the State: Private Security in International Politics*. Cambridge: Cambridge University Press, 2010.

Alemika, Etannib, and Innocent Chukwuma. *The Poor and Informal Policing in Nigeria: Report on Poor Peoples' Perceptions and Priorities on Safety, Security and Informal Policing in A2J Focal States in Nigeria*. Lagos: Center for Law Enforcement Education (CLEEN) Foundation, 2004.

Ameh, Comrade Godwin. "Anambra Election: Why We Are Backing Obiano for Second Term—Ezeife," *Daily Post*, November 15, 2017. Available online: http://dailypost.ng/2017/11/15/anambra-election-backing-obiano-second-term-ezeife/ (accessed 10/02/2018).

Amnesty International. "Nigeria: Vigilante Violence in the South and South-East," *AFR*, 2002.

Atelhe, George Atelhe, John Anyabe Adams, Sunday Abunimye. "Overview of Security Sector Reforms and the Transformation of the Nigerian's Security Agencies." *American International Journal of Social Science* 5, no. 3 (June 2016): 151–158.

Bamidele, Afolabi Muyiwa, Olurunke O. Akinbolade, and Adi I. Nuhu. "Private Security Outfits and Internal Security in Nigeria: An X-Ray of Kings Guards Nigeria Limited, Abuja." *Kuwait Chapter of Arabian Journal of Business and Management Review* 6, no. 2 (October 2016): 13–31.

Barongo, Yolamu, ed. *Political Science in Africa: A Critical Review*. London: Zed Publishers, 1983.

Chindo, Angelina. "Obiano's Security Revolution Resonates in Anambra," *Daily Sun*, October 25, 2017. Available online: http://sunnewsonline.com/obianos-security-revolution-resonates-in-anambra/ (accessed 10/02/2018).

CLEEN Foundation. "The Bakassi Boys: The Legitimization of Murder and Torture." *Nigerian Report* 14, no. 5a (May 2002). Available online: https://www.refworld.org/docid/3cea124a4.html.

DCAF and ECOWAS Parliament. *Parliamentary Oversight of the Security Sector: ECOWAS Parliament-DCAF Guide for West African Parliamentarians*. A Publication of the Geneva Centre for the Democratic Control of Armed Forces (DCAF) and the Parliament of the Economic Community of West African States (ECOWAS Parliament), 2011.

Dokubo, Charles. "Structure of Decision-Making for Defence in Nigeria." In *Defence Policy of Nigeria: Capability and Context*, edited by Celestine Bassey and Charles Dokubo, 60–75. Indiana: Author House, 2011.

Egwu, Samuel. "Ethno-Religious Conflicts and National Security in Nigeria: Illustrations from the Middle Belt." In *State, Economy, and Society in Post-Military Nigeria*, edited by Said Adejumobi, 49–83. New York: Palgrave Macmillan, 2011.

Engerer, Hella. "Security as a Public, Private or Club Good: Some Fundamental Considerations." *Journal of Defence and Peace Economics* 22, no. 2 (2011): 135–145.

Fourchard, Laurent. "A New Name for an Old Practice: Vigilante in South-Western Nigeria." *Africa, Cambridge University Press* 78, no. 1 (2008): 16–40.

Human Rights Watch. "Nigeria: Government Must Disband Vigilante Groups," 2002. Available online: https://www.hrw.org/news/2002/05/20/nigeria-government-must-disband-vigilante-groups (accessed 14/02/2018).

Human Rights Watch. "Rest in Pieces: Police Torture and Deaths in Custody in Nigeria." 17, no. 11a (July 2005). Available online: https://www.refworld.org/docid/45d2f62c2.html.

International Centre for Investigative Reporting (ICiR). "Civilian JTF Foils Terrorist Attack in Borno State," December 24, 2015. Available online: https://www.icirnigeria.org/civilian-jtf-foils-terrorist-attack-in-borno-state/ (accessed 21/02/2018).

International Crisis Group. "Watchmen of Lake Chad: Vigilante Groups Fighting Boko Haram." *Africa Report*, no. 244 (23 February 2017).

Kwaja, Chris. "Vigilantes, Public Safety, Crime and Violence Prevention in Nigeria." *Jos Journal of Social Issues* 7, no. 1 (2014): 22–56.

Kwaja, Chris. "Non-State Security Actors in the North-Central Zone of Nigeria." In *Non-State Security Actors and Security Provisioning in Nigeria*, edited by Chris Kwaja, Kemi Okenyodo, and Val Ahmadu-Haruna, 9–21. Abuja: Cephas and Clems Nig. Ltd for Partners West Africa-Nigeria (PWAN), 2017.

Kwaja, Chris, Ufiem Maurice Ogbonnaya, and Ubon Udoh. *Structural and Institutional Mechanisms for Security Sector Oversight in Nigeria: Issues and Challenges*. Abuja: For Policy and Legal Advocacy Centre (PLAC) and Geneva Centre for Democratic Control of Armed Forces (DCAF), 2017.

Kura, Suleiman. "Non-State Security Actors in the North-West Zone of Nigeria." In *Non-State Security Actors and Security Provisioning in Nigeria*, edited by Chris Kwaja, Kemi Okenyodo, and Val Ahmadu-Haruna, 37–48. Abuja: Cephas and Clems Nig. Ltd for Partners West Africa-Nigeria (PWAN), 2017.

News Agency of Nigeria. "Nigeria Requires Additional 155,000 Police Personnel—IG," *Premium Times*, May 11, 2017. Available online: https://www.premiumtimesng.com/news/top-news/230966-nigeria-requires-additional-155000-police-personnel-i-g.html (accessed 10/02/2018).

Nnoli, Okwudiba. *National Security in Africa: A Radical New Perspective*. Enugu: Pan African Centre for Research on Peace and Conflict Resolution (PACREP), 2006.

Nweke, Nweke. "Anambra: Vigilante Group Rescues 10 Kidnapped Persons; Red Cards Criminals," *247 Ureports*, June 9, 2015. Available online: http://247ureports.com/anambra-vigilante-group-rescues-10-kidnapped-persons-red-cards-criminals/ (accessed 21/02/2018).

Obi, Paul. "IG Orders Police CPs to Disband Militia, Vigilante Groups," *This Day*, February 2, 2018. Available online: https://www.thisdaylive.com/index.php/2018/02/02/ig-orders-police-cps-to-disband-militia-vigilante-groups/ (accessed 17/02/2018).

Ogbonnaya, Ufiem. "Informality in the Security Sector: Vigilantes and Neighbourhood Watch Groups in South East Nigeria." Paper presented at the *60th Annual Meeting of African Studies Association (ASA)* on the theme "Institutions: Creativity and Resilience in Africa," at the Chicago Marriott Downtown Magnificent Mile, Chicago, IL, USA, November 16–18, 2017.

Ogbonnaya, Ufiem Maurice. "Non-State Security Actors in the South-East Zone of Nigeria." In *Non-State Security Actors and Security Provisioning in Nigeria*, edited by Chirs Kwaja, Kemi Okenyodo, and Val Ahmadu-Haruna, 49–66. Abuja: Cephas and Clems Nig. Ltd for Partners West Africa-Nigeria (PWAN), 2017.

Ogbozor, Ernest. "Understanding the Informal Security Sector in Nigeria." United States Institute of Peace Special Report 391, September 2016.

Okeke, Ogadimma. "Community Policing, Vigilante Security Apparatus and Security Challenges in Nigeria: A Lesson from Britain and Igbo Traditional Society of Nigeria." *British Journal of Arts and Social Sciences* 14, no. 11 (2013): 306–323.

Okeke, O., and Raymond O. Oji. "The Nigerian State and the Proliferation of Small Arms and Light Weapons in the Northern Part of Nigeria." *Journal of Educational and Social Research* 4, no. 1 (January 2014): 415–428.

Okoli, Chukwuma Al. "Self-Help Vigilante Groups Are Reshaping Security against Boko Haram," *The Conversation*, July 24, 2017. Available online: https://theconversation.com/self-help-vigilante-groups-are-reshaping-security-against-boko-haram-81139 (accessed 14/02/2018).

Onuoha, Freedom Chuwkudi. "Small Arms and Light Weapons Proliferation and Human Security in Nigeria." *Conflict Trends*, no. 1 (2011): 50–56.

Tertsakian, Carina and Brown Manby. *Nigeria, the O'Odua People's Congress: Fighting Violence with Violence*. Washington, DC: Human Rights Watch, 2003.

Conclusion

The Cleen Foundation. *Civil-Military Relations Project*, 2019. Available online: cmr.cleen.org.

Emmanuel, C. "Nigeria: Decongesting Nigerian Prisons to Recongest Them Afresh," *AllAfrica*, 2018. Available online: https://allafrica.com/stories/201806220064.html.

Finer, S. *The Man on Horseback; the Role of the Military in Politics*. Abingdon: Routledge, 2002: 6.

Kavakeb, D. "International Community Must Join Fight against Defence Corruption in Nigeria—Transparency International Defence & Security," *Transparency International Defence & Security*, 2017. Available online: http://ti-defence.org/international-community-must-join-fight-defence-corruption-nigeria/#more-936.

Kieh, G. *Dependency and the Foreign Policy of a Small Power: The Liberian Case*. San Francisco: Mellen Research University Press, 1992: 5.
Kieh, G., and P. Agbese. *The Military and Politics in Africa*. Aldershot: Ashgate, 2004: 45.
Perlmutter, A. *Political Roles and Military Rulers*. London and Totowa, NJ: F. Cass, 1981: 255.
UNODC. "Justice Sector Reform," 2016. Available online: https://www.unodc.org/nigeria/en/judicial-reform.html.
Weber, E. *From Peasants into Frenchman. The Modernization of Rural France 1870–1914*. Stanford: Stanford University Press, 1976.

INDEX

1999 transition to civil rule 71, 143, 148, 167–170
2012 flood disaster 44, 49, 53, 56

Aba See Aba Main Market Traders Association
Aba Main Market Traders Association 209
Abba Moro 75
Abeokuta 87
Abia 205, 210, 212, 214, 216, 219
Abia State 205, 210, 214
Abia State Vigilante Group 205, 210, 214
Abu Shekau 150, 154–161
Abubakar Tafawa Balewa 23
Abuja 53, 73, 147, 155, 157, 174, 196
Action Congress of Nigeria 37
Actualization of the Sovereign State of Biafra 7, 171–174
Adamawa 34, 48, 56, 148, 150, 156, 190–191, 198, 206, 210, 212, 215
ADSB 75
Agip 128
Agulu community 52
Ahmadu Bello 17–18
airstrips 75
Ajakurama 129
Akaeze 219
Alhaji Baba Fugu 154
Alhaji Buji Foi 149, 153–154
Alhaji Malla Kachalla 148–149
Alhaji Shehu Shagari 170
al-wala-wa-l-bara 150–152, 154, 156, 160
Ambassador John Campbell 34
ammunition 65–77, 108, 112, 141, 172
amnesty 68, 119, 122, 124–127, 129–131
Amnesty International 209, 213, 216
Anambra 35, 52–53, 56
anthropogenic factors 44–45
Apapa port 72, 75
Apoi 128
AQIM – Al-Qaida in the Land of Islamic Maghreb 75, 159

Arewa Citizens Action for Change 172
Arewa Students Forum 172
Arewa Youth Consultative Forum 172
Arewa Youth Development Foundation 172
arms fabrication 69, 74
arms trafficking 2, 66, 69, 74–75, 79
Arochukwu 12
Asari Dokubo 173
Ayakromo 129

baby factories 5, 86, 89–90, 93–95
Bakassi Boys 35, 208, 215–216, 218
Bauchi 48, 56, 141, 154, 208
Bayelsa 35, 37, 53, 56, 124, 176, 206
Bayelsa State Waterways Security Patrol Task Force 35
Benin 12–13, 69, 75, 85–86, 109
Benue 14, 53, 56, 58, 74, 77, 135–136, 140, 159, 176, 189–190, 206
Biafra 13, 22, 107, 169, 171–172, 174–175, 190, 225–226
Biafra Declaration 175
Bjorn Stavrum 36
blue economy 107, 112
Boko Haram 2, 4, 5, 7–8, 31–34, 38, 44, 65, 71, 73–76, 91–94, 103, 107, 110–111, 136, 147–161, 173, 188, 191, 199, 216, 219, 226–227
Bonga 107–08
Borno 12, 34, 48–49, 56, 72, 91, 148–150, 153–160, 188, 190–193, 198, 206, 208, 219
Botswana 168
Bukola Saraki 37

Calabar 12
Cameroon 2, 13, 69, 75, 192–194
CAS Global 35–37
Chad 2, 69, 75, 154, 157–160, 194
change in precipitation 46, 50, 54
Chevron 122
Chibok girls 92, 156, 160

China 70, 72
Chris Ngige 210
civil militancy 6, 120–123
Civil Rights Movement 171
civil society groups 199
civil society organizations 59
Civilian Joint Task Force 111, 158, 206–208, 216, 218
CLEEN Foundation 32, 215
coastal erosion in Niger Delta region 52–54, 58
Cold War 67, 211
colonial legacies 11–12, 15–16, 23–24, 168, 225–226
Community Development Unions 208
concurrent matters 170
containerization 70
corruption 2, 11–12, 16, 20, 22–23, 29–39, 74, 84, 95, 111, 125–126, 138, 140, 149, 153, 168, 171, 193, 199, 215–216, 226–229
Corruption Watch UK 36
Cotonou 109
Cross River State 56, 124, 141
cultists 65, 70, 77, 120, 130–131

Dapchi school abduction 92, 158
Delta 171, 173–176, 189, 206, 209, 227
Delta state *See* Delta
Deltans 119, 127
depletion of Ozone layer 45
desert encroachment 46, 48–50
desert frontline 48–50
Diepreye Alamieyeseigha 37–38
disaster management in Nigeria 54–57, 197
displacement 2, 8, 47, 51–57, 76–77, 158, 187–199, 227
divide and rule 3, 12, 15–17, 20–25, 225
domestic trafficking 69–70
Dorayi quarters 148

early cessation of rain 49–50
Ebonyi 52–53, 56, 74, 205, 210, 214, 219
ecomigration 18, 48, 50–51
ECOMOG 149
Edo *See* Edo State
Edo State 56, 86, 88, 92, 129, 206
Efiks 175
Egbesu Boys of Africa 206, 208–209

Ekiti 12, 56, 176, 205
Ekpan 121
Ekwulobia community 52
electoral violence 12, 73, 190
emergency 4, 34, 53–59, 150, 188, 190, 193, 197–198, 211, 214, 219–220
Enugu 52–56, 90, 205, 210, 212, 214, 216, 219
Enugu State Neighbourhood Association and Watch Group 205, 210, 212
Equatorial Guinea 69
Exclusive Economic Zone 109, 110
exclusive matters 169
explosives 66, 75

false consciousness 12, 15–16, 18–24, 225
farmers 4–6, 47–49, 51–53, 57–58, 76–77, 86, 103, 135–144, 159, 227
flood disaster 49, 53, 56
food security 2, 4, 46–50, 57, 67, 77
food shortage 7, 19, 49
forced governance 12, 15–24, 225
Frederick Fasheun 215
Frustration-Aggression Theory 119

Gabon 69, 87
gangs 4–6, 70, 73–74, 77–78, 84, 86, 88, 93–94, 130, 227, 229
Ganiyu Adams 215
Gbaramatu Kingdom 121, 127–129
General Abacha, Sani 170
General Abubakar, Abdulsalami 170
ghost soldiers 34
Global West 35–37
globalization 71, 75, 83–84, 211
Gombe 141, 154, 207–208
Goodluck Jonathan 34–38, 110, 130, 150, 215
governance failure 73
Government Ekpemupolo/Tompolo 29, 35, 127–128, 130
Governor Sheriff thugs 149
Greece 69
Gulf of Guinea 5, 54, 104–106

Hausa-Fulani 18–20, 23, 89, 172, 174
Hausas 19–20, 24, 150, 173, 175–176, 179
heat wave 50

herdsmen 2, 4, 44, 51, 77, 103, 107, 136, 138, 190
Hisbah 207–208
Human Needs Theory 119
human security 3, 44, 46–48, 57–58, 65–68, 73, 76–78, 188, 211, 218, 227
human trafficking 4–5, 83–95

Ibibio 175
Ibn Taymiyya 154
Idomas 175
Igala 12
Igbo 13, 18–24, 52, 72, 90, 172–176
Igbo-Ukwu 12
Ihiala 52, 219
Ijaw 23, 121, 175, 189, 209
IMB 104–107
Imo 52, 56, 205, 210
India 1, 22, 69, 91, 108–109, 171
Indigenous Peoples' Rights Movement 171
Indimi mosque 148
indirect rule 15, 20, 169, 225
insurgency 2, 4–7, 12, 16, 20, 32, 51, 65, 74, 76–77, 87, 91, 94, 103, 107–108, 111, 120–126, 128, 131, 136, 142, 149–151, 155, 157–161, 168, 171, 190–191, 208
international trafficking 69, 83
Iran 69, 75
Isaac Adaka Boro 120, 173–174
Itshekiri 208
Izala movement 147–148, 154, 161

Jigawa 48–49, 56, 141, 207–208
Joint Revolutionary Council 173
Joint Task Force 107, 111, 141, 150, 158–159, 161, 206, 208
Jos 18–20, 167, 174, 179
Joshua Dariye 37

Kaduna 56, 74, 77, 136, 140–142, 167, 172, 175–176, 189, 195, 207–208, 210, 212, 218
Kaduna Declaration 172, 175
Kaiama Declaration 121
Kalabaris 175
Kampala Convention 196
Kanamma uprising 152–153, 158
Kanem Borno 12
Kano 20, 32, 48, 56, 87, 124, 141, 148, 154–156, 174, 207–214, 218
Kanuri 175

Kashim Shettima 34
Katsina 48, 56, 141, 154, 208
Kebbi 48, 53, 56, 141, 208
Ken Saro-Wiwa 121–122, 131
Kenyagbene 121
Kogi 53, 56, 176, 206

Lagos 13–14, 18, 21, 53, 56, 69, 72, 75, 89, 112, 173, 175, 205, 210, 212, 216, 218–219
Lagos Declaration 175
Lagos Neighborhood Safety Corps 205
Lake Chad Area 50–51, 138, 149, 154, 158–160, 219, 227
late onset of rain 49
Lekan Salami Stadium, Adamasingba Ibadan 215
Leke Oyewole 37
Liberia 1, 67, 195, 226
Libya 69, 71, 75, 86, 136, 139, 194
Libyan uprising 71
Lord Lugard 15

macro-level trafficking 70
Mahatma Ghandi 122
Maiduguri x, 32, 56, 59, 71, 148, 149, 150, 152, 154, 155, 157, 158, 161, 162, 165, 192, 240, 255
Mali 69, 80, 136, 159, 242
Mamudu Hassan 74
maritime security xi, xiii, 29, 36, 37, 41, 103, 104, 105, 106, 107, 108, 110, 111, 112, 113, 114, 115, 116, 117, 236, 248, 250
Maritime Security Agency (MASECA) 29, 37
Markaz Ibn Taymiyya 154, 163
Martin Luther King Jr. King 120, 132, 252
MEND xvii, 5, 6, 29, 32, 107, 108, 124, 126, 127, 130, 131, 133, 173, 252
meso trafficking 70
micro trafficking 70
Middle Belt 4, 5, 6, 22, 44, 81, 138, 144, 159, 162, 175, 222, 242, 253, 261
militant commanders 126, 127
militants vii, 5, 6, 7, 8, 32, 34, 67, 68, 69, 74, 111, 119, 120, 121, 123, 124, 125, 126, 127, 128, 129, 130, 131, 133, 184, 191, 227, 251, 252
Miyetti Allah Cattle Breeders Association xvii, 136
Mohammad Yusuf 228

MoU xvii, 57, 109, 112, 128
Movement for the Emancipation of the Niger Delta xvii, 5, 29, 107, 124, 131, 173
Muhammad Ibn Abd al-Wahhab 151, 163
Muhammad Ibn Saud 151
Multinational Joint Task Force xvii, 159, 161

Nana of Itsekiri 21
Nanka community 62
Nasarawa 56, 74, 77, 135, 145, 176, 184, 206
NatCom – National Commission on the Control of Small Arms and Light Weapons 78
Nationalist Movement 171
natural processes 44
Neo-Takfirism 150, 164, 254
Niger x, xvii, xix, 2, 14, 26, 50, 53, 56, 58, 69, 74, 75, 136, 145, 152, 157, 158, 159, 160, 174, 178, 194, 208
Niger Delta vii, x, xii, xvii, xviii, 4, 5, 6, 7, 14, 25, 29, 32, 34, 35, 37, 39, 44, 47, 51, 52, 53, 59, 62, 65, 68, 74, 75, 81, 91, 100, 103, 105, 106, 107, 108, 113, 114, 115, 117, 119, 120, 121, 122, 123, 124, 125, 126, 127, 128, 129, 130, 131, 132, 133, 134, 171, 173, 174, 184, 189, 206, 208, 209, 226, 233, 235, 238, 240, 242, 243, 244, 248, 249, 250, 251, 252, 253, 256, 257
Niger Delta Amnesty Programme 173
Niger Delta Avengers (NDA) xvii, 5, 6, 44, 108, 115, 125, 126, 132, 133, 134, 173, 248, 251, 252
Niger Delta People's Volunteer Force xviii, 173
Niger Delta Vigilante xviii, 173, 206
Nigerian Armed Forces 128
Nigerian Army x, xvii, 34, 38, 74, 144, 167, 203
Nigerian Navy xviii, 103, 106, 107, 108, 109, 110, 111, 112, 114, 116, 117, 203, 249, 250
Nigerian security forces 108, 115
Nigerian Taliban 152, 153, 158, 164
NIMASA xviii, 36, 37, 41, 103, 106, 111, 112, 113, 114, 117, 130, 235, 248, 249
Nnamdi Azikiwe 15, 19, 20
Nnamdi Kanu 172, 174, 183, 184
Northern Emancipation Network 172
northern oligarchs 123
Norwegian Defence Logistics Organisation ("FLO") 35, 36

Nri 12
Nsukka xi, xii, xiii, xiv, 12, 25, 26, 59, 60, 233, 234, 239

O'odua People's Congress xviii, 7, 172, 182, 183, 208, 209, 215, 218, 223, 224, 256, 262
Oba Akintoye 13, 21
Oba Kosoko 13, 21
Obafemi Awolowo 17, 20, 91
Ogharefe 121
Ogoni xvi, xvii, 121, 122, 189, 257
Ogun 56, 72, 87, 205
Oil Rivers xviii, 13, 14
Okerenkoko 128
Okija 219
Økokrim, the Norwegian anti-corruption organization 41, 235
Oliver Lyttleton 15
Oloibiri 129
Olusegun Obasanjo 73
OMS 112
Onitsha 12, 52
Oodua Hunters Union xviii, 172
Oodua Liberation Movement xviii, 172
Oodua Muslim-Christian Dialogue Group xviii, 172
Oodua Republic Coalition xviii, 172
Opobo 12, 21
organ trafficking 90, 91, 100, 244
organized crime xi, xiii, 2, 4, 6, 34, 36, 75, 83, 85, 95, 96, 136, 138, 246, 247, 248
Osun 53, 56, 176, 184, 205
Othuman Dan Fodio 18
Oyo 12, 53, 56, 176, 205, 215

Pakistan 22, 69
pastoralists 76, 137, 138, 141, 145
permanent transition 170
piracy vii, ix, xiii, 4, 5, 6, 65, 70, 77, 103, 104, 105, 107, 108, 111, 113, 114, 115, 117, 120, 123, 227, 248, 249, 250
Plateau xviii, 6, 18, 20, 37, 53, 56, 74, 77, 135, 136, 140, 141, 142, 144, 146, 159, 165, 167, 179, 189, 206, 210, 212, 214, 216, 218, 219, 253
political thugs 35, 78
porous borders 80, 145, 157, 242, 243, 253
Port Harcourt, Rivers State 56, 106, 121, 124
poverty trap 130
Pre-Amnesty Violent Insurgency 119, 122

prostitution 86, 88, 92, 93
Protectorate of Northern Nigeria 14, 15
Protectorate of Southern Nigeria 14, 15

Queer Ladder 171

Ralph Uwazuruike 171
refugees 2, 5, 9, 48, 155, 158, 165, 187, 190, 193, 197, 199, 259
residual matters 169
Rilwan Akiolu 18
Rivers 13, 14, 26
rocket launchers 75
Russia 69

Sabon Gari 19, 21
salaf-al-salih (The Pious Predecessors) 150, 151, 160
Salafism 151, 152, 161, 162, 163, 164, 254, 255
SALWs – Small Arms and Light Weapons ix, xi, xix, 2, 65, 67, 68, 69, 71, 72, 76, 78, 79, 80, 144, 216, 224, 241, 242, 243, 262
Sambisa forest 136, 150, 158, 159
Sambo Dasuki 33, 38, 40, 235
sand dunes 49
Saudi Arabia 148, 151, 153, 164
sea level rise 44, 52, 53, 54, 63, 237
security dilemma viii, 2, 3, 74, 139, 143, 218, 225, 229
security votes 34, 35, 41, 236
Self-Determination 171, 179
Senator Ali Modu Sheriff xix, 148
separatist movements 22, 171, 182, 256
sexual exploitation 77, 88, 97, 191, 247
sexual violence xix, 89, 191
Shari'a law 89
Shehu Sani 73
Sheikh Abubakar Gumi 147
Shell xix, 115, 121, 250, 251
shrinking of Lake Chad 51
small arms and light weapons ix, xix, 2, 65, 66, 68, 69, 70, 71, 72, 76, 79, 80, 144, 224, 241, 243, 262
smuggling 68, 70, 75, 86, 88, 105, 107, 112, 113, 145, 243, 253

soil erosion across communities in south eastern region 52
Sokoto 12, 17, 32, 49, 141, 150, 162, 155
Sokoto Caliphate 12, 150, 162
South Africa 1, 110, 117, 168, 216, 224
Sultan Attahiru XII 21

takfir 150, 151, 159, 160, 161
Taraba 56, 135, 145, 176, 189, 207, 210, 212
terrorism 117, 134, 157, 158, 159, 160, 161, 163, 164, 165, 168, 173, 178, 181, 183, 189, 200, 208, 218, 219, 228, 235
Tompolo 29, 36, 37, 39, 41, 111, 117, 128, 133, 134, 235, 236, 248, 250, 251, 252
transnational trafficking 70, 98, 100
Tudun Wada 21, 27

Umuechelem 121
Umuechelem massacre 121
unity in diversity 16, 22, 23, 24, 181
Urhobo 121, 189
Uthman dan Fodio 152, 162

vigilante groups xvi, xvii, xix, 8, 35, 73, 111, 158, 205, 206, 207, 208, 209, 210, 212, 213, 214, 215, 216, 218, 219, 220, 221, 223, 224, 261, 262
violent conflicts 65, 73, 76, 77, 78, 132, 136, 145, 159, 160, 251, 253

Wahhabism 151, 163, 255
Walled City 19, 21
Warri 127
water stress 50
Willie Obiano 210
Willinks Commission 121

Yobe 34, 48, 49, 56, 92, 149, 150, 152, 153, 154, 156, 158, 164, 189, 190, 191, 198
Yoruba xix, 172, 173, 174, 175, 176, 183, 184, 205, 209, 215, 255
Yoruba Revolutionary Congress xix, 172
Yoruba Students Nationalist Front xix, 172

Zamfara 48, 56, 136, 141, 148, 163, 207, 208
Zuba 74

www.ingramcontent.com/pod-product-compliance
Lightning Source LLC
Chambersburg PA
CBHW050340230426
43663CB00010B/1937